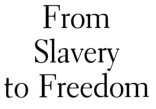

From Slavery to Freedom

A History of African Americans

Volume One: From the Beginnings through Reconstruction

From Slavery to Freedom

A History of African Americans
Volume One: From the Beginnings
through Reconstruction

SEVENTH EDITION

John Hope Franklin

Alfred A. Moss, Jr.

McGraw-Hill, Inc.
New York   St. Louis   San Francisco   Auckland   Bogota   Caracas
Lisbon   London   Madrid   Mexico City   Milan   Montreal
New Delhi   San Juan   Singapore
Sydney   Tokyo   Toronto

From
Slavery
to Freedom

A History of African Americans

Acknowledgments appear on page 293 and on this page by reference.

This book is printed on acid-free paper.

1 2 3 4 5 6 7 8 9 0 DOC DOC 9 0 9 8 7

Volume One ISBN 0-07-021989-3

This book was set in Palatino by ComCom, Inc.
The editors were Lyn Uhl and Monica Freedman;
the designer was Jo Jones;
the project manager was Susan Trentacosti;
the production supervisor was Lori Koetters.
The cover was designed by John Hite.
The photo editor was Fran Antman.
R. R. Donnelley & Sons Company was printer and binder.

Cover Painting

"Family," by Romare Bearden.
Courtesy National Museum of American Art,
Washington, DC/Art Resource, NY.

Back cover photograph of authors: Marvin T. Jones

The Library of Congress has catalogued the one-volume edition as follows:

Franklin, John Hope, (date).
    From slavery to freedom: a history of African Americans / John
Hope Franklin, Alfred A. Moss, Jr.—7th ed.
      p. cm.
    Includes bibliographical references (p.) and index.
    ISBN 0-07-021907-9
    1. Afro-Americans—History.   2. Slavery—United States—History.
I. Moss, Alfred A., (date).   II. Title.
E185.F825   1994
973'.0496073—dc20   93-44726

Published September 22, 1947
Second Edition 1956
Third Edition 1967
Fourth Edition 1974
Fifth Edition 1980
Sixth Edition 1988
Seventh Edition 1994

About
the Authors

John Hope Franklin is the James B. Duke Professor Emeritus at Duke University and, for seven years, was Professor of Legal History at Duke University Law School. Born in Oklahoma in 1915, he graduated in 1935 from Fisk University. Harvard University awarded him the master's degree in 1936 and the doctorate in 1941. Professor Franklin has taught at Fisk, St. Augustine's College, North Carolina Central University at Durham, and Howard University. He was Chairman of the Department of History at Brooklyn College and at the University of Chicago, where he remains the John Matthews Manly Distinguished Service Professor Emeritus of History. He was a Fulbright Professor in Australia and Pitt Professor of American History and Institutions at Cambridge University in England.

Dr. Franklin is a former President of the Southern Historical Association, the Organization of American Historians, the American Studies Association, the American Historical Association, and the Society of Phi Beta Kappa. Among Dr. Franklin's awards are the Jefferson Medal of the Council for Advancement and Support of Education, the Clarence Holte Literary Prize, The Jefferson Medal of the American Philosophical Society, and the National Endowment for the Humanities Charles Frankel Award, presented by President Clinton in 1993. He holds one-hundred honorary degrees. Dr. Franklin recently received the National Medal of Freedom from President Clinton and the Spingard Award.

Among his many published works are *The Free Negro in North Carolina, 1790–1860* (1943), *The Militant South 1800–1860* (1956), *Reconstruction after the Civil War* (1961), *The Emancipation Proclamation* (1963), *Racial Equality in America* (1976), *A Southern Odyssey* (1976) *George Washington Williams: A Biography* (1985), *Race and History* (1989), and *The Color Line: Legacy for the Twenty-First Century* (1993).

Alfred A. Moss, Jr. is Associate Professor of History at the University of Maryland, College Park. After completing his undergraduate work at Lake Forest College, Dr. Moss received his master's degree from the University of Chicago in 1972. He was then awarded his doctorate in 1977, also from the University of Chicago. A graduate of the Episcopal Divinity School, he is also an Episcopal priest. Dr. Moss is the author of *The American Negro Academy: Voice of the Talented Tenth* (1981) and numerous articles; co-author of *Looking at History* (1986); and co-editor of *The Facts of Reconstruction: Essays in Honor of John Hope Franklin* (1991).

■

To Aurelia

Contents

Photographs

Illustrations

■

Boxes

Maps

Tables

Preface
to the
Seventh Edition

In the nearly half-century since this work first appeared, interest in the subject it covers has quickened considerably. This is evident in the spate of works dealing with various aspects of the subject, in the increase in the number of course offerings in the field at both the secondary and higher-education levels, and in the use of materials related to it in the discussion and formulation of public policy. These developments have in turn had their effect on the several revisions through which this work has gone, and we are ever mindful of the importance of maintaining the integrity and reliability of this work as a contributor to the ongoing discussion of the problems inherent in forging a society characterized by equality, justice, and mutual respect.

In designating the group under discussion as African Americans, we are recognizing the changes that have characterized such designations in previous years. Even during the lifetime of this book, there have been three distinct names by which the group has been called: Negro, black, and African American. (Afro-American and person of color were in use before the end of the nineteenth century.) While African American is increasing in current usage, there is no reason to believe that this is a final designation; for the political and cultural winds that produced it continue to blow, perhaps sweeping before them earlier designations and bringing forth at some later time a designation as yet unknown.

It would be improper as well as awkward to use African American to describe the group before the end of the Civil War. Neither the group nor any others, in law or in practice, conceived of any designation other than black, person of color, or Negro. In recognizing the changes that have come in recent years, we must take care not to impose recent designations on persons of an earlier period. Thus, we have made every attempt to use terms that seem consonant with the period under consideration, recognizing that the search for stylistic felicity invites variation in terminology as long as it is accurate for its own time.

We have made every effort to keep abreast of the wide-ranging and significant scholarship in the field. It has affected our thinking, our approach, even our perspective. At times its effect is quite obvious in the correction of statements of "facts" in earlier editions and in new interpretations gained from new research. Most often its effect is in the way it informs our view of the problem with which we deal and the sense of security it provides in helping us sort out the complexities and meanings of those problems. These effects are at times so subtle as not to be discernable, but this does not diminish their importance. We have also sought to make even more significant, some of the features that we introduced in the sixth edition. An example is a marked increase in the number of "box" quotations that provide primary sources that add flavor as well as authority to much of the discussion. Another example is the increased attention given to popular cultures and the role of women. New features in which we, along with the publisher, take particular pride, are the color photographs of early African artifacts and a gallery, in full color, of twentieth-century African-American art. To the many scholars and laypersons who have written on the subject or who have been generous enough to write us and make suggestions, we are grateful for their assistance.

Several scholars, distinguished in the field, have reviewed the Sixth Edition of this work and have given us the benefit of their searching examinations. They are John L. Dabney, San Bernadino Valley College; Joseph Harris, Howard University; Earl Lewis, University of Michigan; Freddie L. Parker, North Carolina Central University; Marshall F. Stevenson, Ohio State University; and Walter B. Weare, University of Wisconsin, Milwaukee. In addition, several friends and colleagues have read portions of the manuscript, made suggestions in the area of their specialty, and assisted in other ways to improve the work. Among them are Eric Anderson, Marie Perinbam, Janet Ewald, Robert E. Steele, John Whittington Franklin, Christaud Geary, Genna Rae McNeil, Robyn Muncy, Winthrop R. Wright, George C. Wright, Paul Huebner, Jehu Hunter, Major Clark, Paul Finkelman, and S. O. Y. Keita.

Our families continue to give us their support in every possible way, for which we are most grateful. Margaret Fitzsimmons, beginning in 1964, has served as personal assistant and secretary-editor for five editions of this work. In her various capacities in seeing the book through to completion, she has become indispensable. In expressing our gratitude for all that she has done, we accept all responsibility for errors of fact and judgment.

John Hope Franklin
Alfred A. Moss, Jr.

January 1, 1994

Preface
to the
Sixth Edition

Forty years ago, one author, with the assistance and encouragement of many others, wrote the first edition of this work. In succeeding years, with the passage of time and the quickening of events, he prepared four succeeding editions, each of which went through numerous printings. Two considerations have led to some major changes in the preparation of the Sixth Edition, which will mark the fortieth anniversary of the book's initial appearance. One has been the growing diversity of interests as well as the increasing complexity of the problems facing Negro Americans, brought on by numerous shifts in strategies initiated by their adversaries as well as by themselves. This has required the constant monitoring and evaluation of virtually everything that occurs. The very magnitude of the task beckons more than one mind and one set of hands. The other is that with the passage of time, the original author has recognized the need for the collaboration of a younger person whose different perspectives and ample energies would assist in giving the new edition the freshness that it requires and deserves.

In this new collaboration we have learned much from each other, and it is our fond hope that our readers will benefit greatly from this joint effort. We have broadened our coverage, expanded our interests, and strengthened our grasp of the basic historical problems with which we have had to deal. We have reexamined every word of the Fifth Edition, reorganized much of the material, rewritten portions, and added a great deal that is entirely new. With the remarkable increase of excellent works in African, Caribbean, and Latin American history, we have not been inclined to repeat or summarize the findings of the scholars in those fields. Rather, we have confined our treatment of those areas to matters of obvious and immediate relevance to the history of Negroes in the United States. Meanwhile, we have brought our treatment of the subject as close to the present as we dared, remembering the wise adage that "current history is not really history, but current events."

As we have reexamined many aspects of the history of black Americans, we have become indebted to many authors for the remarkably rich outpouring of writings on the subject in recent years. Some are mentioned in the text, some in the bibliographical notes, and others remain nameless. We are grateful to them for their contributions to our own knowledge as well as to the field. Several of our colleagues have been especially helpful, among them Marie Perinbam, Eric Anderson, Winthrop R. Wright, Robert Steele, Milton Morris, Janet Ewald, and Evelyn Brooks. In addition, numerous teachers, students, and others who have used earlier editions of this book have been generous in offering corrections, criticisms, and helpful suggestions for its improvement. We also gratefully acknowledge the comments from the following reviewers: Hayward Farrar, Leon F. Litwack, Alan Schaffer, Donald Spivey, and George C. Wright. The libraries, such as the Library of Congress, the Moorland-Spingarn Research Center of Howard University, the Library of the University of Maryland at College Park, North Carolina Central University Library, the Duke University Library, and the Durham County Library, especially its Stanford Warren Branch, have been indispensable. We are deeply grateful to all of these individuals and institutions.

Our families have been generous with their patience and assistance. Serving as personal assistant and secretary-editor, Margaret Fitzsimmons has presided over the preparation of various editions of this work over the past twenty-three years. She has again performed these various functions for this edition, and with greater efficiency, resourcefulness, and wisdom than ever before. We are most grateful to her. Over her protests, we assume responsibility for errors of fact and judgment.

John Hope Franklin
Alfred A. Moss, Jr.

July 4, 1987

Preface
to the
Fifth Edition

It has been more than thirty years since the first edition of this work appeared. These have been momentous years in the history of the world, and Negro Americans, like all others, have been deeply affected by what has transpired. The emergence of the atomic age as well as the space age, either event of sufficient significance to change the course of human history, occurred in this brief period. In like fashion the Black Revolution, with its far-reaching impact on virtually every aspect of life among black Americans, has affected their position in American society as well as the manner in which other Americans view them. The recency of these events, and the consequent lack of adequate perspective, make it difficult to evaluate them with any measure of confidence, and the danger of distortion or exaggeration is very real. I have made every effort to avoid such difficulties. At the same time I have recognized the fact that all events are not of equal importance.

Since the publication of the fourth edition, many works in the general field of Afro-American history have appeared. Some of them have been highly significant and have compelled students of the field to reconsider earlier findings and conclusions. This present edition takes into account these recent developments in historical scholarship, and I am grateful to the many scholars whose works have proved so valuable. I am also grateful to the colleagues, students, and teachers who have been kind enough to offer suggestions or call my attention to errors in previous editions. It would not be possible to revise this work without the continuing assistance of such persons. My research assistants, Michael Lanza and Patrick Thompson, assisted me in more ways than I can acknowledge, and I am grateful to them.

My secretary and administrative assistant, Margaret Fitzsimmons, has not only typed and checked the manuscript but has, as usual, assumed numerous responsibilities beyond the call of duty. She would even be willing to assume some responsibility for textual and other errors, but I can only thank her deeply and assume those myself.

John Hope Franklin

Chicago, Illinois
May 30, 1979

Preface
to the
Fourth Edition

The comments I made in the preface to the third edition regarding the quickened pace of events are even more true for the period since 1966 than before that date. The growing interest in the history of Negro Americans and their greater involvement in the current struggle for equality are part of the far-reaching changes that have occurred in the status of blacks that may be regarded as revolutionary. These developments have made the revision of this work extremely difficult. The study and evaluation of vast quantities of new material, while shedding much light on many aspects of the history of Negro Americans, have also increased the difficulties of revision.

Many readers have been most generous in their observations and criticisms, which I have been most pleased to take into account. My research assistant, Rodney Ross, brought to his task a thorough knowledge of the subject and a high quality of scholarship that greatly eased my own task. My secretary, Margaret Fitzsimmons, not only has typed the manuscript but has greatly assisted with stylistic improvements and in eliminating errors and inconsistencies. To these and to many others I am grateful for their help.

John Hope Franklin

Chicago, Illinois
September 3, 1973

Preface
to the
Third Edition

Almost twenty years ago the first edition of this work appeared. Ten years ago I revised it and brought it up to date. Since that time the very pace at which events have moved has discouraged any effort to prepare a revision that would inevitably be out of date at the time of its publication. It seems fitting, nevertheless, to present a rather extensively revised edition on the occasion of the twentieth anniversary of the first edition.

I feel constrained to add that even the revolutionary developments of the last decade should not obscure the fact that this is essentially a history and not a contemporary tract. Therefore, these developments have been valuable for the historian not only in themselves but also in the new perspectives they provide as one looks at past, even remote, events. These new perspectives are reflected in some of the revisions of the earlier parts of the book.

The revisions have been greatly facilitated by the generous and helpful criticisms and suggestions of my students, colleagues, and friends. Arthur Spingarn and August Meier have assisted me in correcting several serious errors; and Richard Fuke, my research assistant, has been a virtual collaborator in his critical reading of the text and in his valuable updating of much of the material. To these and all the others who have helped in countless ways I am deeply grateful.

John Hope Franklin

Chicago, Illinois
July 4, 1966

Preface
to the
Second Edition

The nine years that have elapsed since this work first appeared have been among the most momentous in the history of the American Negro. The postwar years witnessed vigorous efforts, not always successful, on the part of Negroes and many white Americans to elevate substantially the position of the Negro in American life. The 1954 decision of the Supreme Court in the school desegregation cases was the most dramatic and significant of the frontal attacks on segregation and discrimination, but by no means was it the only one. World attention, moreover, has been focused on the issue of race as never before, and the status of the Negro in the United States has been scrutinized with extreme care by peoples in many other parts of the world. This very scrutiny has had a most salutary effect. The task of the historian in tracing and properly evaluating the numerous developments that have taken place abounds in difficulties, but it nevertheless seems worthwhile at this point to take cognizance of some of the more significant trends.

If this edition is an improvement over the first edition, it is due largely to the able assistance of many persons. The reviewers of the first edition, letters from readers, and my own colleagues and students were not only generous in praise but helpful in pointing out errors and oversights. I am grateful to these careful readers for their thoughtful generosity, and I have taken into consideration their suggestions. The increased interest in the problems of the Negro has stimulated much research and writing in the field; the numerous books and articles on almost every aspect and period of Negro life and history have greatly increased my understanding of the matters with which this book deals. At many points the influence of these works is reflected. I can only hope that I have done violence neither to the diligent work of others nor to the dramatic events that have transpired.

John Hope Franklin

Washington, D.C.
June 15, 1956

Preface
to the
First Edition

In the present work I have undertaken to bring together the essential facts in the history of the American Negro from his ancient African beginnings down to the present time. In doing so it was deemed unnecessary to relate the development of Negro life and history in other parts of the world except where there was a discernible connection with the history of the Negro in the United States. Thus only so much of African history was considered here as evolved in the area from which the vast majority of American Negroes came, and as much more as helped to shape Afro-American institutions in the Old World and the New. On the other hand, it was necessary to consider briefly the Negroes of the Caribbean and of Latin America, because their history belongs to the larger pattern of development of the Negro in the New World. For a similar reason, it was deemed desirable to give some attention to the Negroes of Canada, for they are in a large measure erstwhile citizens or residents of the United States.

I have made a conscious effort to write the history of the Negro in America with due regard for the forces at work which have affected his development. This has involved a continuous recognition of the mainstream of American history and the relationship of the Negro to it. It has been necessary, therefore, to a considerable extent, to retell the story of the evolution of the people of the United States in order to place the Negro in his proper relationship and perspective. To have proceeded otherwise would have been to ignore the indisputable fact that historical forces are all-pervasive and cut through the most rigid barriers of race and caste. It would have been impossible to trace the history of the Negro in America without remaining sensitive to the main currents in the emergence of American civilization.

While I have sought to interpret critically the forces and personalities that have shaped the history of the Negro in the United States, I have attempted to avoid a subjective and unscientific treatment of the subject. This procedure has involved the maintenance of a discreet balance between recognizing the deeds of outstanding persons and depicting the fortunes of the great mass of Negroes. To be sure there were times when dominant personalities forged to the front and assumed roles of responsibility and leadership; these individuals have been recognized. But the history of the Negro in America is essentially the story of the strivings of the nameless millions who have sought adjustment in a new and sometimes hostile world. This work is, therefore, a history of the Negro people, with a proper consideration for anonymous as well as outstanding people.

I have given considerable attention to the task of tracing the interaction of the Negro and the American environment. It can hardly be denied that the course of American history has been vitally affected by his presence. At the same time it must be admitted that the effect of acculturation on the Negro in the United States has been so marked that today he is as truly American as any member of other ethnic groups that make up the American population. That is not to say that the story of the Negro is one solely of achievement or of success. Too frequently the Negro's survival in America has depended on his capacity to adjust—indeed, to accommodate—himself to the dominant culture, and the obstacles have at times been too great to permit him to make significant achievements in the usual sense of the word. The task here has been not to recite his achievements—though naturally some have been so outstanding as to warrant consideration—but to tell the story of the process by which the Negro has sought to cast his lot with an evolving American civilization.

The obligations which I am under for direct and indirect aid received in writing this book are numerous, and it is not possible for me to indicate every instance of assistance which cooperative persons have rendered. Without the research of Carter G. Woodson, Charles H. Wesley, W. E. B. Du Bois, Luther P. Jackson, and many other scholars who have contributed significant writings to the field, it would not have been possible for me to write this book. I am grateful to all these patient, careful scholars for the indispensable services they have performed for all students of American history. I am under special obligation to the Library of Congress, which generously placed its many facilities at my disposal, and to the North Carolina College Library, the Stanford L. Warren Library, the Duke University Library, the New York Public Library, and the American Museum of Natural History for their kind assistance.

I am under obligation to the following publishers for their kind permission to make brief quotations from works published by them: The Columbia University Press: Lorenzo J. Greene, *The Negro in Colonial New England* and

Sterling Spero and Abram L. Harris, *The Black Worker;* Harcourt, Brace and Company: Claude McKay, *Harlem Shadows;* The Macmillan Company: C. Vann Woodward, *Tom Watson, Agrarian Rebel;* The University of Michigan Press: Dwight L. Dumond, *The Antislavery Origins of the Civil War;* The Yale University Press: Bell I. Wiley, *Southern Negroes, 1861–1865;* and Doubleday and Company: R. R. Moton, *Finding a Way Out.*

To Abram L. Harris, C. Vann Woodward, Mrs. Arthur P. Chippey, Howard K. Beale, L. D. Reddick, Rayford W. Logan, Clement Eaton, Mrs. Dorothy Porter, and Arthur S. Link, I am grateful for helpful suggestions and numerous criticisms. Among my colleagues who have assisted me in this effort I am especially grateful to Joseph H. Taylor, Joseph S. Himes, W. Edward Farrison, Albert L. Turner, Charles A. Ray, Albert Manley, and Miss Helen G. Edmonds. President James E. Shepard kindly relieved me of my teaching duties so that I could complete the manuscript, and I am sincerely appreciative of his generosity. The dedication of the work to my wife expresses inadequately my deep gratitude to her for her sacrifices, cooperation, and enthusiastic support of my efforts in historical writing.

John Hope Franklin

Durham, North Carolina
April 4, 1947

African-American Population of the United States, 1860 and 1990

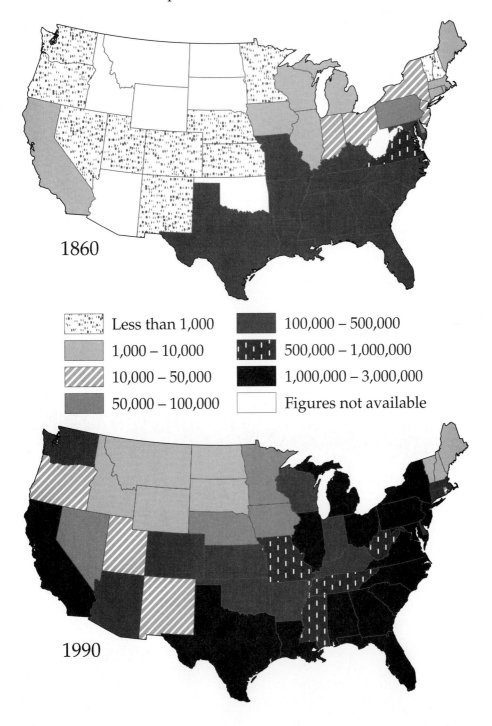

1860

Less than 1,000
1,000 – 10,000
10,000 – 50,000
50,000 – 100,000
100,000 – 500,000
500,000 – 1,000,000
1,000,000 – 3,000,000
Figures not available

1990

From
Slavery
to Freedom

A History of African Americans

Volume One: From the Beginnings through Reconstruction

CHAPTER 1

Land of Their Ancestors

In the last third of the twentieth century, it became commonplace for African Americans to speak and write sensitively of the land of their ancestors. While some of them could refer to the vast continent of Africa in only the vaguest terms, others could focus quite precisely on the specific areas from which most of their ancestors had come. The emergence of such modern independent states as Ghana, Mali, Chad, Niger, Nigeria, The Gambia, and Upper Volta evoked a deep sense of identification, even though these new countries of the twentieth century have only a slight connection with those nation-states of many centuries ago that bore similar names. The connection is there, nevertheless; and the African who left, say, Whydah, for the New World in 1800 may well have had roots in one of the African states of the Middle Ages. Those states were the land of the ancestors of New World slaves, as indeed they were the land of the forebears of their twentieth-century descendants.

When the Arabs first learned of West Africa, its civilization was already centuries old. Although the land from the Atlantic to the Nile had enjoyed limited contact with other civilized portions of the world, much of the culture that the Arabs found was indigenous to the area. It must be added that the sources of information about the history, as well as the very existence, of these states are increasing but still quite limited. One has to depend primarily on observations of travelers, reports based on information from people two or three times removed from events, and oral tradition.

1

For centuries some indigenous peoples had no interest in organizing themselves into states, perhaps seeing no need or advantage in erecting political institutions. Others, however, had different attitudes or needs and therefore set out to build governments to meet those needs. Indeed, many well-developed political states had risen and fallen before any lasting contact was established between West Africa and the Near East. These states sprang up in more or less the same general region, from the Mediterranean southward to the Gulf of Guinea and from the Atlantic eastward almost to the Nile. Successively, there arose in the region the states of Ghana, Mali, and Songhay, along with many lesser states.

■ Ghana

The first West African state of which there is any record is Ghana, which lay about 500 miles northwest of its modern namesake. It was also known by its capital, Kumbi Saleh. Although its accurately recorded history does not antedate the seventh century, there is evidence that Ghana's political and cultural history extends back perhaps into the very early Christian era. The earliest observations of Ghana were made when it was a confederacy of settlements extending along the grasslands of the Senegal and the upper Niger. Its boundaries were not well defined, and doubtless they changed with the fortunes of the kingdom. Most of the public offices were hereditary, and the tendency was for the stratified social order to become solidified.

The people of Ghana enjoyed some prosperity as farmers until continuous droughts extended the desert to their lands. As long as they were able to carry on their farming, gardens and date groves dotted the countryside, and there was an abundance of sheep and cattle in the outlying areas. They were also a trading people, and their chief town, Kumbi Saleh, was an important commercial center during the Middle Ages. By the beginning of the tenth century the Muslim influence from the East was present. Kumbi Saleh had a native and an Arab section, and the people were gradually adopting the religion of Islam. The prosperity that came in the wake of Arabian infiltration increased the power of Ghana, and its influence was extended in all directions. In the eleventh century, when the king had become a Muslim, Ghana could boast of a large army and a lucrative trade across the desert. From the Muslim countries came wheat, fruit, and sugar. From across the desert came caravans laden with textiles, brass, pearls, and salt. Ghana exchanged ivory, slaves, and gold from Bambuhu for these commodities. The king, recognizing the value of this commercial intercourse, imposed a tax on imports and exports and appointed a collector to look after his interests.

Under the rulers of the Sisse dynasty, Ghana reached the height of its power. Tribes as far north as Tichit in present Mauritania paid tribute to the king of Ghana, while in the south its influence extended to the gold mines of the Falémé and of the Bambuk. It was the yield from these mines that supplied the coffers of the Sisse with the gold used in trade with Moroccan caravans. In faraway Cairo and Baghdad, Ghana was a subject of discussion among commercial and religious groups.

The reign of Tenkamenin in the eleventh century is an appropriate point at which to observe the kingdom of Ghana. Beginning in 1062 Tenkamenin reigned over a vast empire which, through the taxes and tributes collected by provincial rulers, made him immensely wealthy. Arab writers say that he lived in a fortified castle made beautiful by sculpture, pictures, and windows decorated by royal artists. The grounds also contained temples in which native gods were worshipped, a prison in which political enemies were incarcerated, and the tombs of preceding kings. The king, highly esteemed by his subjects, held court in magnificent splendor.

During Tenkamenin's reign the people of Ghana adhered to a religion based on the belief that every earthly object contained good or evil spirits that had to be satisfied if the people were to prosper. The king, naturally, was at the head of the religion. In 1076, however, a band of Muslims called Almoravids invaded Ghana and brought the area under the influence of their religion and trade. They seized the capital and established the religion of Islam. The strife that ensued was enough to undermine the kingdom of Ghana. By the end of the eleventh century, Ghana entered a period of economic decline brought on by a series of droughts that dried up the important Wagadu and Bagana districts. Under such trying circumstances it fell easy prey to the waves of conquerors who swept in to destroy the kingdom during the twelfth and thirteenth centuries.

■ Mali

As Ghana began to decline, another kingdom in the west arose to supplant it and to exceed the heights that Ghana had reached. Mali, also called Melle, began as an organized kingdom about 1235, but the nucleus of its political organization dates back to the beginning of the seventh century. Until the eleventh century it was relatively insignificant and its mansas, or kings, had no prestige or influence.

The credit for consolidating and strengthening the kingdom of Mali goes to the legendary figure Sundiata Keita. In 1240 he overran the Soso people and leveled the former capital of Ghana. It was a later successor, however, who carried the Malians to new heights. Variously called Gonga-Musa and Mansa-Musa, this remarkable member of the Keita dynasty ruled from 1312 to 1337. With an empire comprising much of what is now francophone Africa, he could devote his attention to encouraging the industry of his people and displaying the wealth of his kingdom. The people of Mali were predominantly agricultural, but a substantial number were engaged in various crafts and

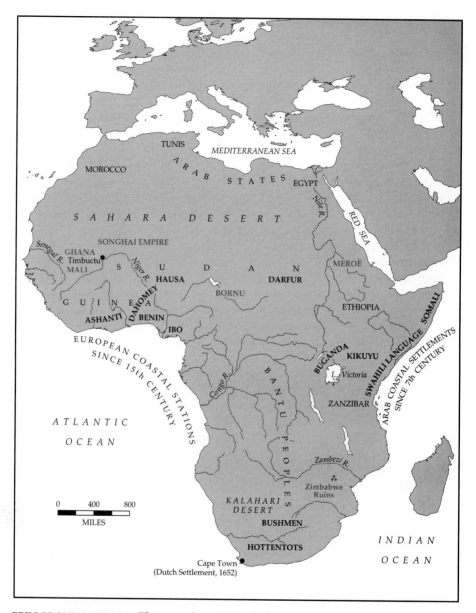

PRECOLONIAL AFRICA. This map shows Africa before European penetration in the nine-teenth century. It is difficult to indicate boundaries, for even the most extensive African kingdoms had shifting and indefinite borders. Names in gray designate ancient or medieval centers which no longer exist in modern times.

mining. The fabulously rich mines of Bure were now at their disposal and served to enrich the royal coffers.

The best information that the period affords on the level of attainment of these native kingdoms comes from the accounts of royal pilgrimages to Mecca. The kings, newly converted to the religion, were as ardent and pious as any Arabs of their day. As good Muslims, they looked forward to making the traditional pilgrimage to Mecca. Such a pilgrimage, moreover, was an excellent opportunity to display the wealth of the kingdom and to attract trade. The historic pilgrimage of Mansa-Musa in 1324 exceeded all visits to Mecca by previous royal personages from the West. Cairo's El Omari said that the entourage was composed of thousands of people, a large portion of which constituted a military escort. Gifts were lavished on the populace, and mosques were built where they were needed. As the camels approached Mecca, their burden was considerably lighter than it had been when they departed for the East.

Since any such pilgrimage was a display of wealth and power as well as a holy journey to kiss the black stone of Kaaba, there was no need to proceed directly to and from Mecca. Mansa-Musa first visited various parts of his kingdom to show his subjects and vassals his tremendous wealth and to demonstrate his benevolence. He then proceeded to Tuat, in the land of the Berbers, and after making a deep impression there he crossed the desert, visited Cairo, and finally went to the holy places of Mecca and Medina. He returned by way of Ghadames, in Tripoli, where he received many honors and from which point he was accompanied to his kingdom by El-Momar, a descendant of the founder of the dynasty of the Almohads. A more significant visitor to return with Mansa-Musa was Ibrahim Es Saheli, or Abu Ishak, a distinguished Arabian poet and architect from a Granada family, whom Mansa-Musa engaged to supervise the building of elaborate mosques at Timbuktu, Jenne, Gao, and elsewhere. These structures added further splendor to the already well-developed kingdom of Mali.

When Mansa-Musa died in 1337, Mali could boast of a political state as powerful and as well organized as any of that period. Traveling in the area a few years later, Ibn Batuta, the celebrated Arabian geographer, reported that he was greatly impressed by "the discipline of its officials and provincial governors, the excellent condition of public finance, and the luxury and the rigorous and complicated ceremonial of the royal receptions, and the respect accorded to the decisions of justice and to the authority of the sovereign." In the middle of the fourteenth century Europe was just beginning to feel the effects of its commercial revolution and European states had not yet achieved anything resembling national unity; but Mali under Mansa-Musa and his successor, Suleiman, enjoyed a flourishing economy with good international trade relations and could point with pride to a stable government extending several hundred miles from the Atlantic to Lake Chad. The people adhered to a state religion that had international connections, and learning flourished in the many schools that had been established. It was not until the fifteenth century that the kingdom showed definite signs of decline and disintegration. The powerful blows of the Songhay and the attacks of the Mossi combined to reduce the power of Mali. The decline did not go on indefinitely, however, and Mali continued to exist for many years as a small, semi-independent state.

■ Songhay

The kingdom that was in a position to dispute the power of Mali by the fifteenth century was Songhay. The latter had experienced a long and checkered career as a kingdom. Beginning in the early eighth century at Gao, near the bend of the Niger, it had remained a small, relatively inconsequential state for many years. In fact, it fell under the powerful influence of Mali, and for a time its rulers were vassals of Mansa-Musa and his successors. Undaunted, the Songhay waited for the first opportunity to throw off the yoke of Mali and to assert their own sovereignty. This they had succeeded in doing by 1355, with Sonni Ali (1464–1492) later taking Songhay, as Philip Curtin has said, "from a small riverain state to a great empire."

When Sonni Ali began his rule of the Songhay, most of West Africa was ripe for conquest. Mali was declining, and the lesser states, though ambitious, had neither the leadership nor the resources necessary to achieve dominance. The hour of the Songhay had arrived. Sonni Ali conceived of a plan to conquer the entire Niger region by building a river navy that would seize control of both banks. By 1469 he had conquered the important town of Timbuktu and then proceeded to capture Jenne and other cities. Finally he attacked the kingdom of Mali, and with its conquest the Songhay kingdom was catapulted into a position of primacy in West Africa. Because of his lack of enthusiasm for the religion of Islam, there was considerable opposition to the rise of Sonni Ali, but he was undaunted. Consequently, his years were filled with fighting, but when he died in 1492 the kingdom of Songhay was firmly established as the dominant power of West Africa.

The day of Sonni Ali and his dynasty was over, however, and in 1493 the dynasty was overthrown by a powerful general, Askia Mohammed, who became Songhay's most brilliant ruler. From 1493 to 1529 he devoted his energies to strengthening his empire, making his people prosperous, and encouraging learning. He recruited a professional army of slaves and prisoners of war and left his subjects to engage in farming and commerce. Local rulers, four viceroys, and Askia's brother Omar, as chief lieutenant, maintained peace and administered the empire. In 1494 Omar and the army conquered all of Massina, while in subsequent years most of Mali, the Hausa states, and many other West African kingdoms fell before the power of the Songhay. Finally, the empire of the Songhay was extended from the Atlantic to Bornu and from the Berber country in the north to the Mossi and Benin states in the south. It was easily the largest and most powerful state in the history of West Africa.

To be sure, Askia Mohammed was an orthodox Muslim, but one does not get the impression that his pilgrimage to Mecca in 1497 was either for ostentatious display or merely to pay homage to Allah. This shrewd ruler wanted to improve his empire, and he knew that such a journey would prove profitable from many points of view. His retinue was composed primarily of scholars and officers of state, with a military escort numbering only 1,500 men. He and his followers conversed with doctors, mathematicians, scientists, and scholars, and they doubtless benefited from these contacts. They learned much about how to improve the administration of the government, how to codify the laws of Songhay, how to foster industry and trade, and how to raise the intellectual level of the country. Even Askia Mohammed's investiture as caliph of the Sudan can be interpreted as a move to strengthen his country.

Upon his return from the East, Askia Mohammed and his advisers instituted many of the reforms they had studied. He assigned carefully chosen governors, called *fari,* to rule over subdivisions of the empire. He appointed chiefs, or *noi,* to administer provinces and large cities. He reorganized the army on a more efficient basis. The laws of Mohammed and the Koran were the bases for administering justice. In the area of economic life, banking and credit were improved. A uniform system of weights and measures was established, and scales were inspected. Arabians and the people of Songhay were encouraged to trade with other countries. Traders from Europe and Asia visited the markets of Timbuktu and Gao regularly. With government cooperation all of Songhay became prosperous. Alexander Chamberlain has observed: "In personal character, in administrative ability, in devotion to the welfare of his subjects, in open-mindedness towards foreign influences, . . . King Askia . . . was certainly the equal of the average European monarchs of the time and superior to many of them."

It was in the area of education that Askia made his most significant reforms. He established and encouraged schools everywhere. Gao, Walata, Timbuktu, and Jenne became intellectual centers where the most learned scholars of West Africa were concentrated and where scholars from Asia and Europe came for consultation and study. Scholars like El-Akit and Bagayogo, both jurisconsults, were educated at Timbuktu. By the sixteenth and seventeenth centuries a distinctly Sudanese literature was emerging. At the University of Sankore black and white youths studied grammer, geography, law, literature, and surgery, while in the mosques Askia and his subjects studied the religion of Islam in order to practice and promote it more effectively.

Civil wars, massacres, and unsuccessful military expeditions followed the reign of Askia, who was dethroned by his oldest son. Although there were brief periods of revival, the empire was definitely declining. The Moors viewed the Sudan covetously and began to push down across the desert. With Spanish renegades as their allies, Moroccans overthrew the Songhay state and began their own brief rule in Timbuktu.

■ Other States

Among the other states of West Africa was the empire of Wagadugu, commonly known as the Mossi states. It was founded near the middle of the eleventh century by an adventurer named Ubri. Never a large state, it occupied the area south of the bend of the Niger; but its population was always dense, and its people had a fiercely independent spirit. For a time there were actually five states comprising the loose confederation. Cohesion was greatest in time of emergency, and they managed to repel the attacks of Mali and Songhay and remained more or less independent up until the nineteenth century when France incorporated them into its African empire. The governors of the five states constituted the council of state and served as the chief ministers in the imperial organization. Working with them were eleven ministers overseeing such departments as the army and finance. Beneath them was a hierarchy of officials, which extended to the most insignificant local functionary.

The strength of the Mossi lay in their efficient political and military system. The emperor was absolute. His subordinates operated with carefully worked out and rigidly defined duties. Each morning the emperor received his ministers of state, who reported on the affairs of the realm. In the evening the ruler dealt with matters concerning public order and criminal justice. The procedures of hearings and decisions bore a striking resemblance to the practice of trial by jury. There was no standing army, but the political and social system was so organized as to make possible the calling up for military service of every able-bodied man on the briefest notice. The survival of the Mossi states in an area dominated by powerful empires such as Mali and Songhay is a testimonial to their efficiency and wise leadership.

The Afno, or Hausa, people are said to have had seven original states, the best known of which were Kano, Zaria, and Katsina. The Hausa states occupied roughly the area that today is northern Nigeria. Each kingdom retained its identity, with Kano emerging into the limelight for a while, then yielding to Katsina, and so on. There was commerce with the other African states and across the Sahara. Katsina became a center of learning where law and theology were studied and where the language of the people was refined. It was not until the beginning of the nineteenth century, when Islam made noticeable inroads, that the Hausa states began to yield to outside influences.

To the east and west of Lake Chad resided the people of Kanem and Bornu, respectively. These people were made up of a large number of tribes that had early been attracted to the region by the oases and the lake. Some were Berber, while others were Negroid. As an organized state, Bornu-Kanem dates from about 1220, but instability characterized the government for the next two centuries. The copper mines around the lake brought prosperity to the people, and by the sixteenth century there was a semblance of order under Idris Alooma (1573–1603). In the seventeenth and eighteenth centuries Muslims attempted to subdue these people and convert them, but

Olaudah Equiano (Gustavus Vassa)
Describes His Homeland

That part of Africa known by the name of Guinea to which the trade for slaves is carried on extends along the coast above 3,400 miles, from the Senegal to Angola, and includes a variety of kingdoms. Of these the most considerable is the kingdom of Benin, both as to extent and wealth, the richness and cultivation, the power of its king, and the number and warlike disposition of the inhabitants. . . . This kingdom is divided into many provinces or districts, in one of the most remote and fertile of which, called Eboe, I was born in the year 1745, situated in a charming fruitful vale named Essaka. The distance of this province from the capital of Benin and the seacoast must be very considerable, for I had never heard of white men or Europeans, nor of the sea, and our subjection to the king of Benin was little more than nominal; for every transaction of the government . . . was conducted by the chiefs or elders of the place. . . . My father was one of those elders . . . and was styled Embrenche, a term as I remember importing the highest distinction, and signifying in our language a *mark* of grandeur. This mark is conferred on the person entitled to it by cutting the skin across the top of the forehead and drawing it down to the eyebrows, and while it is in this situation applying a warm hand and rubbing it until it shrinks up into a thick *weal* across the lower part of the forehead. . . . My father had long borne it.

We are almost a nation of dancers, musicians and poets. Thus every great event such as a triumphant return from battle or other cause of public rejoicing is celebrated in public dances, which are accompanied with songs and music suited to the occasion. . . . We have many musical instruments, particularly drums of different kinds, a piece of music which resembles a guitar, and another much like a stickado. . . . I was named Olaudah, which in our language signifies vicissitude or fortunate; also, one favoured, and having a loud voice and well spoken. . . .

The Interesting Narrative of the Life of Olaudah Equiano or Gustavus Vassa the African, ed. Paul Edwards (New York, 1966), pp. 1–4.

with only slight success. Complete subjugation by outsiders was not achieved until 1900, when one portion of Bornu became a protectorate of Britain and another came under the influence of France.

The absence of substantial physical barriers in some areas south of the equator made possible the continuous infiltration of migratory tribes, which hampered political stability. The lands of the Bantu, San, Khoikhoi, and Pygmies certainly had some political organizations, and there is considerable anthropological and archaeological evidence to sustain the view that in some areas there existed rather advanced cultures. But it is clear that none of them reached the size or influence of West African states such as Mali and Songhay.

From the mouth of the Niger around to the Cape of Good Hope, there were a number of states that flourished for a time before the sixteenth century. For example, there was the kingdom of the Brama, which lay between Cape Lopez and the mouth of the Congo River and about which practically nothing is known. The so-called Empire of the Congo, founded in the fourteenth century, dominated the area between Setté Cama in the north and Benguella to the south. Inland it reached as far as the upper Zambezi. With its capital at Banya, modern São Salvador, its kings experienced difficulty in maintaining control over the tribes of the Congo Valley, and its boundaries shrank steadily in the seventeenth century because of the chaotic situation resulting from the arrival of Portuguese slavers.

South of the Empire of the Congo was a state near the present city of Mossamedes. Khoikhoi, Damara, and other tribes in the region constituted the population of the kingdom, whose ruler was called the Mataman. In what is modern South Africa there was a large, homogeneous state inhabited by the Bechuana, Basuto, Zulu, and Khoikhoi peoples. On the east coast the Matebelle and Makalaka peoples were incorporated in an ancient state that dated from the tenth century. Its instability was caused by frequent incursions by the Wazimba, a ferocious people living to the west. The remainder of the eastern coast fell early under the influence of the Muslims and became dependencies of various sultanates founded by the Arabs and Persians who gained control of East Africa. In the interior were the kingdoms of the Barotse, the Katanga, and Balubo, extending from the Zambezi to Lake Tanganyika.

The 1591 Moroccan conquest of Songhay had not ended the trans-Saharan trade; the southern terminals had merely shifted eastward to the Hausa states and the Bornu empire. By the early twentieth century, however, when Great Britain, France, and Germany were completing their conquests of West African states, the locus of power in West Africa had long since passed from the savannah kingdoms to forest-belt states located along the Gulf of Guinea to the south. When the Portuguese first sailed down the West African coast in the fifteenth century, they discovered two substantial states: Benin, located to the west of the Niger Delta, and the Kongo kingdom, near the mouth of the Congo River. At Benin, Portuguese sailors bought slaves, beads, and cloth, which they exchanged with Africans further west, along the coast of present-day Ghana, for gold dust. The abundance of certain West African goods so impressed European traders that they named sections of the Guinea coast after these "products"—pepper, ivory, gold, and slaves.

The slave trade, which became the area's dominant form of commerce, played a crucial role as an economic basis for emerging forest-belt kingdoms. The Yoruba people to the west of Benin organized themselves into a series of states, the most powerful of which was Oyo. It was the breakup of this empire in the early nineteenth century that created the unsettling conditions of war and disorder that led in turn to the delivery of large numbers of Yoruba into the transatlantic slave trade. As Oyo declined, Dahomey, a kingdom located within the boundaries of present-day Dahomey, threw off the yoke of its former overlord. Ironically, Dahomey, which owed its seventeenth-century origins to a determination to abstain from the Atlantic slave trade, had by the late eighteenth century become a key West African center for exporting slaves. In the nineteenth century this highly centralized state was transformed from one specializing in the slave trade to one dealing largely in palm oil products. Nonetheless, Europeans used the image of a cruel, barbaric, slaveholding nation as partial justification for the French invasion and conquest in the 1890s.

Another region to share a similar fate was that of the city-states of the Niger River delta. Ibo traders had made the transition from slaves to palm oil only to be thwarted by British commercial attempts to open up Africa to European commerce. Between 1807 and 1901 Britain and the mighty Ashanti nation of present-day Ghana fought ten wars, culminating in a British conquest of that land.

The states described in this chapter are in no way a complete listing of West African political units. Furthermore, there were other African areas that witnessed the development of impressive states. Some like Egypt, Kush, and Carthage flourished during the pre-Christian era. Others came later. Some areas, like Zimbabwe and the savannah lands south of the Congo basin, witnessed different civilizations rising on the sites of their predecessors. Muslim Swahili-speaking city-states located along the Indian Ocean traded with Arabia, India, and Indonesia at a time when European powers were fighting in the Crusades. Ethiopians have a recorded history almost 2,000 years old. Other kingdoms are of more recent origin: the Zulu people, for instance, did not become a powerful nation until the nineteenth century. To a greater or lesser degree, however, all of them had some connection with the inhabiting of the New World with black peoples.

CHAPTER 2

The African Way
of Life

It is obviously impossible to make very many generalizations concerning
the way of life in a continent as large as Africa, with so many variations
in climate, physiography, and population. As in any other area, at any other
time, Africa presents variations in degrees of civilization that run the entire
gamut from the most simple to remarkably advanced ones. At this point
little more can be done than to observe various aspects of the African way
of life with a view to understanding more adequately the cultural heritage
of these people who have come to claim the concern of Europeans and
Americans in recent centuries. If the emphasis here appears to be placed
on the way of life in West Africa, it is because there seems to be merit in
trying to secure as intimate an understanding as possible of the area in
which the bulk of the people lived who later became the black workers of
the Americas.

■ Political Institutions

Wherever we observe the peoples of Africa, we find some form of political
organization, even among the so-called stateless. They were not all highly
organized kingdoms—to be sure, some were simple, isolated family states—
but they all seem to indicate the normal capability and desire of establishing

governments to solve the problems that every community encounters. The family state prevailed in areas where the territory was divided among a number of distinct families and where there was no inclination or desire to merge resources to organize a stronger state. In such situations the chief of state was extremely powerful because his political strength was supplemented by the strength that was his by virtue of being head of the family. In some instances, several such states, the constituents of which enjoyed a common ancestry, came together to form a more powerful state known as a clan state. If it was possible to surmount the obstacles of tradition and clannishness, several groups could come together and form what came to be known as a village state or tribe seat.

Village states flourished throughout West Africa. The growth and prosperity of some prompted them to merge, voluntarily or by force, to form small kingdoms, the most popular form of government in Africa. These kingdoms, if they met with a favorable set of circumstances—able leadership, adequate resources, and strong military organization—could grow into federations or even empires, such as those of Mali and Songhay. These various degrees of political organization were attained by Africans in their successive stages of development. Despite the fact that the states existed at different times and at different places, it is remarkable that the same essential characteristics seem to have prevailed in all of them.

The power to govern a state usually resided in a given family and was transmitted by it. Two other families, however, performed important functions in establishing a royal personage on the throne, the electing family and the enthroning family. The electing family could exercise a choice within the royal family. In this way Africans recognized the stabilizing effect that a royal family might have on the political fortunes of the people. At the same time, they were practical enough to recognize the fact that the eldest son was not necessarily the ablest or most desirable and felt free to choose their ruler from among any of the male members of the royal family. The new king could exercise no authority until he had been properly invested in office by those so designated by the enthroning family. These practices had the effect of ensuring the people a more satisfactory monarch than automatic descent of authority might give them.

Each African king of any real importance had a group of ministers and advisers. Indeed, in some states custom imposed on the king the obligation of appointing a given number of advisers and delegating real authority to them. Custom generally conferred each ministerial charge on a certain family. These ministers, together with other advisers and members of the nobility, functioned as a kind of parliament, which in some instances exercised substantial authority. It is interesting to observe that a peculiar African custom served to limit the authority of many kings. If the king did not belong to the family of the first person occupying the ground in his kingdom, he had no rights over the land. Any questions involving the land were settled by the descendants of the first occupants, who could conceivably be insignificant subjects of the king or even prisoners of war. It seems that most kings were willing to conform to this ancient custom.

It is possible, however, to overemphasize the importance of the central political organization among Africans. To be sure, the power of the kings, ministers, and subchiefs was considerable, but beneath this semblance of national unity was the individual's strong attachment to local authority and local loyalties. Each locality had its own "king," and in many matters of a purely local nature this royal personage exercised power that was indisputable. It was this concept of the division of authority—a kind of dichotomy of sovereignty—that kept the great kings sensitive to the possibility of conflict within their realms. Few powerful kings of great empires and kingdoms ever achieved so much authority as to destroy completely the feeling of local rulers that they enjoyed a degree of sovereignty themselves. Stability could be achieved only through extensive military organization and a carefully organized central government. That this stability was frequently achieved is a testimonial to the wisdom, strength, and not infrequent ruthlessness of the various kingdoms.

■ Economic Life

It would be erroneous to assume that Africans were either primarily nomadic or simply agricultural. There exists in Africa such a diversity of physical environments that it would be impossible for people to evolve identical ways of life in different parts of the continent. Essentially agricultural, the peoples of Africa displayed a remarkable degree of specialization within this ancient economic pursuit. The African concept of landownership stemmed from the importance of agriculture in the peoples' way of life. The land was considered so important to the entire community that it belonged not to individuals but to the collective community, which was comprised of the first occupants of the soil. One of the most important local dignitaries was the "master of the ground," who was at the same time the grand priest of the local religion and the administrator of the soil. The importance of this official can be clearly seen, it may be recalled, in the fact that not even the political ruler could make any disposition of land without the consent of the master of the ground. Individuals or groups of people could obtain the right to use a given parcel of land, but such permission did not carry with it the right of alienation or any other form of disposition. When the land was not used productively, it reverted to the collective domain.

Whether land was held individually or collectively—and it seems that both practices were in use—the tillers of the soil devoted all their energies to the cultivation of their crops. Soil was cleared by felling trees and burning the underbrush. The ashes were used to fertilize the ground, which was in turn prepared for planting with the use of large spades with short handles. Seeds or sprouts were planted in mounds or embankments that had been carefully prepared. Frequent weeding was necessary, especially in new ground, in order to prevent the young plants from being choked. Millet, wheat, rice, cassava, cotton, fruits, and vegetables were commonly grown. Dotting the countryside were towers from which watchmen drove away birds and grain-eating animals. Harvest time was a particularly busy period during which grain was reaped, threshed, milled, and stored, while other fruits and grains were made into fermented drinks, and cotton was manufactured into thread and cloth.

Domestic animals were a part of almost every farm, but in some areas the rural people devoted most of their attention to the grazing of sheep and cattle and the raising of chickens and other fowl. In northeastern Africa some tribes were known for their great skill in the breeding and care of cattle. In the east many villages ascribed so much importance to the raising of cattle that wealth was measured in terms of heads of cattle. The Bantu and Khoikhoi engaged in farming as well as large-scale cattle raising.

Artisanry was a significant area of economic activity. Even among the so-called backward tribes, there were those who were skilled along various lines. Among many people, there was a remarkable knowledge of basketry, textile weaving, pottery, woodwork, and metallurgy. The Pygmies manufactured bark cloth and fiber baskets. The Khoikhoi devoted much time and attention to making clothing from textiles, skins, and furs. The Ashantis of the Gold Coast wove rugs and carpets and turned and glazed pottery with considerable skill. In many parts of the Sudan there was extensive manufacturing of woodenware, tools, and implements.

The use of iron was developed very early in the economy of Africa. From Ethiopia to the Atlantic, there is much evidence of adroitness in the manufacture and use of iron. Indeed, many careful students of primitive civilizations credit indigenous Africans with the discovery of iron. The anthropologist Franz Boas insisted that Africans were using iron when European peoples were still in the Stone Age. The simple processes that Africans were found to have used and the early date at which they began to make iron suggest that it was the natives of Africa, and not the Hittites, who first discovered its use. Africa exported iron for many years, and blacksmiths and other iron workers were found in many parts of Africa. With simple bellows and a charcoal fire, the native blacksmith smelted his ore and forged implements such as knives, saws, and axes. Africans also worked in silver, gold, copper, and bronze. In Benin, bronze and copper implements and art objects testified to the great skill of the smiths, while many artisans, including those of the Yoruba lands and Mali, devoted their attention to the making of ornamental objects from silver and gold.

The interest of early Africa in the outside world can best be seen in the great attention given to commerce. The tendency of tribes to specialize in some phase of economic activity made it necessary that they maintain commercial contact with other tribes and with other countries in order to secure the things that they did not produce. Some villages, for example, specialized in fishing; others concentrated on metallurgy, while others made weapons, utensils, and so on. In tribes where such specialization was practiced, traders traveled from place to place to barter and to purchase. Upon returning they were laden with goods which they sold to their fellows. Some traders from the west coast went as far north as the Mediterranean and as far east as Egypt, where they exchanged their goods for the wares of traders from other parts of the world. It is to be recalled that the travels of kings and emperors did much to stimulate this international commerce. Africa was, therefore, never a series of isolated, self-sufficient communities, but an area that had far-flung interests based on agriculture, industry, and commerce. The effect of such contacts on the culture was immeasurable. It can only be said here that these routes of commerce were the highways over which civilization as well as goods traveled and that Africa gave much of its own civilization to others and received a good deal in return.

■ Social Organization

As among other peoples, the family was the basis of social organization in early Africa. The foundation of even economic and political life in Africa was the family, with its inestimable influence over individual members. Although the eldest male was usually the head of the family, there was a widespread practice of tracing relationships through the mother instead of the father. In areas where this matrilineal practice was followed, children belonged solely to the family of the mother, whose eldest brother exercised the paternal rights and assumed all responsibility for the children's lives and actions. In tribes that admitted only female relationship, the chief of the family was the brother of the mother on her mother's side. In tribes that were, on the other hand, patrilineal, the chief was the real father. With either group, those forming the family comprised all the living descendants of the same ancestor, female in the matriarchal system and male in the patriarchal system.

In general, a wife was not considered a member of her husband's family. After marriage she continued to be a part of her own family. Since her family continued to manifest a real interest in her welfare, the bride's husband was expected to guarantee good treatment and to pay her family an indemnity, a compensation for taking away a member of the family. This indemnity was not a purchase price, as has frequently been believed. The woman did not legally belong to her husband but to her own family. Naturally, the amount of the indemnity varied both with tribal practice and with the position of the bridegroom. Indeed, in some tribes the tradition was maintained by a mere token payment out of respect for an ancient practice that had once had real significance in intertribal relationships.

Although polygamy existed in virtually every region, it was not universally practiced. The chief of the family would defray the expenses involved in the first marriage of a male member of the family, but if the husband

> ## Salih Bilali Remembers Massina—1844
> ## [as reported in a letter of James
> ## Hamilton Couper]
>
> ---
>
> His native town is Kianah, in the district of Temourah and in the Kingdom of Massina. . . . I infer from his conversation, that the town of Kianah . . . is a Foulah or Fellatah colony, established among the older nations of the Soudan, and differing from them in language. . . . The houses consist of two kinds. Those occupied by the richer classes are built of cylindrical bricks, made of clay mixed with rice chaff and dried in the sun. They contain two rooms only; one of which is used as a storeroom, and the other as an eating and sleeping apartment, for the whole family. . . . The poor classes live in small conical huts, made of poles, connected at the tops and covered with straw.
>
> The natives cultivate the soil, and keep large droves of horses, cows, sheep, goats, and some asses. The great grain crop is rice. . . . Besides rice, they cultivate a species of red maize, millet, and Guinea corn. They also grow beans, pumpkins, okra, tomatoes, cucumbers and cotton. . . . The usual food is rice, milk, butter, fish, beef and mutton. The domesticated animals are horses, used for riding, asses and camels for carrying loads; cattle, the bulls of which have lumps on their shoulders, for milk and meat—sheep with very long wool . . . goats and poultry, and dogs for guards. They have no hogs. . . .
>
> His father and mother were persons of considerable property. When about twelve years old, as he was returning from Jenne to Kianah, on horseback, he was seized by a predatory party and carried to Segu, and was transferred from master to master, until he reached the coast, at Anomabu. . . . After leaving Bambara, to use his own expression, the people had no religion, until he came to this country [the Gold Coast].
>
> William B. Hodgson, *Notes on Northern Africa, the Sahara, and the Soudan* (New York, 1844), in Philip D. Curtin, ed., *Africa Remembered* (Madison, 1967), pp. 147–151.

wanted to take a second wife, he would have to meet all the expenses himself. Religion played a part in determining the number of wives a man could have. Local religions did not limit the number. When the Muslims made inroads into the tribes of Africa, they forbade adherents to take more than four wives. Wherever the Christians established a foothold, they insisted on monogamy altogether. Where polygamy was practiced, it does not appear to have produced many evils. As a matter of fact, the division of household duties in a polygamous family had the effect of reducing the duties and responsibilities of each wife, a highly desirable condition from the point of view of the wives if the husband was without servants or slaves.

The clan, the enlarged family, was composed of all families that claimed a common ancestor. The clan would develop in the same community or area, but as it became larger and as some families found more attractive opportunities elsewhere, the clan would separate, and one or more families would go to some other area to live. Unless the separation resulted from a violent quarrel or fight, the departing families regarded themselves as still being attached to the clan. Once the unity was broken by separation, however, the clan tended to disintegrate because cooperation in war, economic activities, and religious life was no longer practicable. Under the strain imposed by separation over the course of time, the traditions and practices of the clan tended to become obscure and unimportant. Consequently, little more than a common name bound members of the same clan together, and new environments and new linguistic influences had the effect of causing clan names to be changed or modified. In such instances, members of the same clan living in different places had no way of recognizing each other.

Early in its development, Africa showed signs of social stratification in its many tribes. At the top was the nobility, "the good men," who could prove that they had descended from free men. Since they could claim the name of a respected clan, they had a right to places and positions of respect in the social order. Next was the great mass of workers, who found it difficult or impossible to raise a genealogical tree that would bear careful scrutiny. Although they might carry a perfectly good clan name, they could not prove their right to it and therefore were not able to qualify for a position in the upper class. At the bottom of the social structure were those who enjoyed no political or social rights. They were slaves, war captives, disgraced or degraded people and those living beyond the pale of the law. It must be added that the social structure had an economic base, and wealth tended to be concentrated in the upper class. Families, moreover, rather than individuals, constituted the several classes. Since families wielded economic power, through their politically important positions or through the domination of certain crafts and other economic pursuits, they had a way of influencing the nature of the social order. Work in itself did not elevate or debase a family, but the particular kind of work did. There was a definite respectability attached to certain types of work, and the gradation toward debasement was equally definite. The working of the soil was the most noble of all pursuits. Following in close order were cattle raising, hunting, fishing, construction, navigation, commerce, gold mining, and the processing of commodities such as soap, oil, and beer. There were variations from tribe to tribe, but everywhere there was the tendency to dignify or to degrade families on the basis of the types of work in which they were engaged.

It must not be assumed that people at the lower levels of the social order enjoyed no privileges or respect. All were regarded as necessary to society and were respected for what they contributed. They were accorded numerous privileges because their acknowledged skills earned for them the right to move from one place to another and entrance into groups that otherwise would have been closed to them. Nor is it to be assumed that there was

Olaudah Equiano (Gustavus Vassa, the African) Is Sold into Slavery—1756

The first object which saluted my eyes when I arrived on the coast was the sea, and a slave ship which was then riding at anchor and waiting for its cargo. . . . When I looked round the ship . . . and saw a large furnace or copper boiling and a multitude of black people of every description chained together, every one of their countenances expressing dejection and sorrow, I no longer doubted my fate; and quite overpowered with horror and anguish, I fell motionless on the deck and fainted. . . . I now saw myself deprived of all chance of returning to my native country [Nigeria] or even the least glimpse of hope of gaining the shore. . . . I was not long suffered to indulge my grief; I was soon put down under the decks, and there I received such a salutation in my nostrils as I had never experienced in my life: so that with the loathsomeness of the stench and crying together, I became so sick and low that I was not able to eat . . . but soon, to my grief, two of the white men offered me eatables, and on my refusing to eat, one of them held me fast . . . and laid me across I think the windlass, and tied my feet while the other flogged me severely. . . . One day, when we had a smooth sea and a moderate wind, two of my wearied countrymen who were chained together . . . preferring death to such a life of misery, somehow made through the nettings and jumped into the sea, immediately another quite dejected fellow . . . also followed; and I believe many more would very soon have done the same if they had not been prevented by the ship's crew. . . .

The Interesting Narrative of the Life of Olaudah Equiano or Gustavus Vassa the African, ed. Paul Edwards (New York, 1966), pp. 25–32.

absolute rigidity in the social structure of tribal Africa. As among other peoples, tact, special knowledge, wealth, or good fortune tended to create a fluidity in African society. By taste, a member of a mining family might choose to farm; although his new occupation did not of itself elevate him from the lower social position of his family, in due time he could gain so much respect and admiration as a farmer that he would be regarded as a legitimate member of the class of noble tillers of the soil. As in almost every society in the world, power and wealth could in many instances be substituted for nobility of origin.

Slavery was an important feature of African social and economic life. The institution was widespread and was perhaps as old as African society itself. Slaves were predominantly people captured in war and could be sold or kept by those who captured them. Slaves were usually regarded as the property of the chief of the tribe or the head of the family. In law, slaves were chattel property, but in practice they often became trusted associates of their owners and enjoyed virtual freedom. Some, however, were sold and exported from the country, while others were sacrificed by kings in the worship of their royal ancestors. The children of slaves could not be sold and thus constituted an integral and inalienable part of the family property. Enjoying such security, it was not uncommon for the children of slaves to be favored with manumission at the hands of their owners.

■ Religion

Certainly up to the period of the many European incursions into Africa the vast majority of the people engaged in religious practices that were indigenous to the continent. These practices were only outward manifestations of certain religious beliefs and, like symbols in other religions, they did not indicate the specific character of the religion. The religion of early Africans can most accurately be described as ancestor worship. Africans believed that the spirits of their ancestors had unlimited power over their lives. In this, as in almost every aspect of African life, the kinship group was important. It was devoutly believed that the spirit that dwelled in a relative was deified upon death and that it continued to live and take an active interest in the family. The spirits of early ancestors had been free to wield an influence for such a long time that they were much more powerful than the spirits of the more recently deceased, hence, the devout worship and the complete deification of early ancestors. Not only were the spirits of deceased members of the family worshipped, but a similar high regard was held for the spirits that dwelt on the family land, in the trees and rocks in the community of the kinship group, and in the sky above the community.

Because of the family character of African religions, the priests of the religions were the patriarchs of the families. They were the oldest living members of the descendants of the initial ancestor and had therefore inherited the earthly prerogatives of their predecessors. Thus, they had dominion over the family grounds, waters, and atmosphere. It was the family patriarch who entered into communication with the souls of his ancestors and the natural forces in his immediate vicinity. He was therefore authorized to conduct ceremonies of worship. The temples of worship could be any structures set aside for that purpose. They contained holy objects, such as the bones of the dead, consecrated pieces of wood, rock, or metal, and statuettes representing objects to be worshipped. Bells or rattles were used to invoke the spirits and the worshippers. The blood of victims—chickens, sheep, goats, or human beings—was offered as a sacrifice to appease the gods. There was never a universal practice of sacrificing human beings in Africa, but in some areas prisoners and captives were sacrificed in worship of the various deities. Libations of palm wine, beer, or some other fermented drink were offered in various forms of worship. Prayers and songs were other expressions of adoration.

It was only natural that in a society such as that found in Africa there would be considerable reliance on the magical power of amulets, talismans, and the like. Anything that helped to explain and answer the imponderables was a welcome addition to tribal practices. Magic was, therefore, practiced on a great scale. By resorting to ill-defined powers, known only to him, the magician invented techniques and created rites designed to secure for individuals the specific ends that they desired. Where religion was a collective attempt to secure satisfaction for the kinship group, magic was an individual attempt to achieve certain satisfactions on the part of a particular person. Even in areas where animistic worship prevailed, belief in magic was widespread. Many had great confidence in the efficacy of magical practices, and it may be that this reliance on the divination of sorcerers was responsible in part for the course that the civilization of Africa took.

The elaborateness of funeral rites all over the continent attests to the regard that Africans had for the idea that the spirits of the dead played an important part in the life of the kinship group. The funeral was the climax of life, and costly and extensive rituals were sacred obligations of the survivors. The dead were generally buried in the ground either beneath the huts in which they had lived or in cemeteries. Burial often took place within a few days after death, but at times the family delayed interment for several weeks or longer. The grave was not completely closed until every member of the family had had an opportunity to present offerings and to participate in some rite incident to interment. Nothing more clearly demonstrates the cohesiveness of the African family than the ceremonies and customs it practiced on the occasion of the death and burial of a member.

In all probability the early influence of the religion of Islam on the African way of life has been greatly exaggerated. This is certainly true for the period before the fourteenth century. Muslims crossed from Arabia over into Egypt in the seventh century. In the following century they swept across North Africa where they met with notable success, but religious conversion was slow below the Sahara in the land of the blacks. It will be recalled that the kingdoms of Ghana, Mali, and Songhay accepted Islam quite reluctantly, while other groups rejected it altogether. Some African kings accepted Islam for what seemed to be economic and political reasons, but their subjects frequently held tenaciously to their tribal religious practices. Muslims were never able, for example, to win over the peoples of Mali, Hausaland, and Yorubaland. The commercial opportunities offered by the Muslims were especially attractive. It must also be added that the followers of the Prophet accepted Africans as social equals and gave them an opportunity to enjoy the advantages of education and of cultural advancement that the religion offered. Even as a slave, the black Muslim was considered a brother. To many black Africans these features were doubtless as important as the purely ritualistic aspects of the new religion. Even so, numberless Africans summarily rejected Islam in preference for the cults and rituals that were historically a part of their way of life.

Christianity became entrenched in North Africa early. It was there when

Islam made its appearance in the seventh century, and these two great faiths engaged in a life-and-death struggle for the control of that area. In West Africa, where the population was especially dense and from which the great bulk of slaves was secured, Christianity was practically unknown until the Portuguese began to establish missions in the area in the sixteenth century. It was a strange religion, this Christianity, which taught equality and brotherhood and at the same time introduced on a large scale the practice of tearing people from their homes and transporting them to a distant land to become slaves. If the Africans south of the Sahara were slow to accept Christianity, it was not only because they were attached to their particular forms of tribal worship but also because they did not have the superhuman capacity to reconcile in their own minds the contradictory character of the new religion.

■ The Arts

In some areas of art Africans attained a high degree of expression. In carvings and sculptures of wood, stone, and ivory, their work displayed an originality both in technique and subject matter that marked them clearly as a people with an abundant capacity for aesthetic expression. There was, of course, a great degree of variation from place to place in the level of expression attained, but hardly any tribe failed to show some inclination toward the use of certain art forms. Benin bronze and brass works of rosettes, doorplates, and metal vases reflect great skill in the use of this difficult medium. Among the Yoruba the delicacy of form seen in the terra-cotta pieces is a testimonial to the rare artistry that these people possessed. The statuettes of people and animals widely used by African tribes in religious rites serve as a reminder that almost everywhere some Africans concerned themselves with artistic activities. From Timbuktu to the Congo there was considerable work in wood, gold, silver, ivory, clay, and the like, and it cannot be denied that many of these pieces bear witness to the fact that African art was not only indigenous but also worthy of the name.

To enhance the beauty and value of the items that they made to be sold or used, Africans decorated them in various ways. Ornamented and glazed pottery, delicately carved spoons and knives, golden jewels of filigree, and elegantly woven mats, cloth, and tapestries are outstanding examples of the application of art in industry. In the construction of houses, royal palaces, and temples, this same proclivity toward ornamentation is apparent. When Muslim architects and scientists came to the region south of the desert, there was a marked improvement in the symmetry and beauty of West African architecture. It must be added, however, that there is abundant evidence to support the view that many basic elements of beauty in African architecture were evident before the incursion of the Muslims.

An important medium of aesthetic expression in Africa is music. Among the principal musical instruments developed in Africa were the xylophone, drum, guitar, zither, harp, and flute. The most frequently used musical form was, of course, the song, with or without instrumental accompaniment. Songs were usually antiphonal and were characterized by highly developed rhythms. Some were quite complex with respect to scale, rhythm, and general organization. There was also great variation in the types of African musical forms, ranging from lullabies and dance songs to work songs and sacred melodies. Likewise, there were many forms of the African dance. Some were for recreational or social purposes, while others served ritualistic or religious functions. Africans regarded both music forms and dance as integral parts of their culture.

The numerous spoken languages found in Africa always constituted a barrier to the development of literary forms. From the Atlantic to Ethiopia, through the heart of the continent, the languages of the Sudanic group are spoken. In the southern half of Africa, Bantu is spoken. There are at least ten Semitic dialects, ranging from the Arabic in North Africa to the Berber dialects heard in the Great Desert. Besides, there are many tribal dialects and languages that have no apparent relationship with the principal language groups. Among these are the languages of Suto, Ruanda, and Banda. Thus, where there is so much heterogeneity in the spoken language, even within a relatively small area, the almost insurmountable difficulties involved in the evolution of adequate means of extensive communication become readily apparent.

In early Africa few of the languages were reduced to writing. The literature was, therefore, predominantly oral, and there was an abundance of it. Handed down principally through the kinship group, the oral literature was composed of supernatural tales, moral tales, proverbs, epic poems, satires, love songs, funeral pieces, and comic tales. Some individuals, griots, made a specialty of collecting these bits of oral literature and purveying them before kings as well as ordinary families. They sang, told stories, and recited poetry. They kept in their memories the history, law, and traditions of their people and were themselves living dictionaries who occasionally performed invaluable services to their communities. The use of Arabic by educated Muslim Africans after the fourteenth century was rather extensive and made possible the reduction of some of the oral literature to permanent form. Examples of this are *Tarikh-es-Soudan,* a history of the Sudan written by Es-Sadi, and *Tarikh-El-Fettach,* written by Kati, a Sudanese. Some African scholars even sought to adapt the Arabic alphabet to the writing of one of the African languages by adding diacritical marks to represent sounds that do not exist in Arabic. This extremely difficult feat made possible the more extensive use of Arabic in developing a written literature among Africans.

Such was the way of life in Africa up until the end of the sixteenth century. It was at this stage of development that Europeans began to make incursions for the purpose of engaging in the trade in humans. It was by no means a simple way of life that the whites found. The basic problems of existence had been solved; political, economic, and social institutions were, on the whole, stable. Whether the states were great empires or modest political entities, they were well organized with limited monarchies and a myriad of public officials. Well-defined concepts of law and order prevailed, and even if there was considerable rivalry and strife among states, there was a remarkable degree of order within the several governments. Citizens seemed to take their responsibilities and loyalties seriously. The peoples of Africa were on the whole well disciplined, and records of rebellions and revolutions are not common. This does not mean that all rulers were benevolent or that all their subjects were completely free from oppression. What it does mean is that a relatively satisfactory balance had been achieved between the people and their government. Usurpers and pretenders did emerge, to be sure, and at times they created considerable chaos, but these situations were perhaps no worse than the strife and chaos that erupted in the states of Europe during the late medieval and the early modern periods.

There was usually enough stability within African states and among them to make possible healthy economic development. The division of labor and the practice of specialization in occupations display a remarkable versatility and variety of talents and tastes. The interest in commerce and the understanding of the economic importance of contact with the European and Asian worlds show a realism similar to that of contemporary states in other parts of the world.

Nothing is more impressive in viewing the social institutions of Africa than the cohesive influence of the family. The immediate family, the clan, and the tribe undergirded every aspect of life. The rule of discipline enforced in the family was responsible in large measure for the stability that has been observed in various aspects of life. The influence and hold that the patriarch had over the members of the family was largely responsible for the stability that was characteristic of the area. The deep loyalty and attachment of the individual to the family approached reverence and indeed was the basis for most of the religious practices, in which ancestor worship played such an important part. The religions of Africa were a product of an environment in which the population lived close to nature. These sacred rites were manifestations of a people who were in a desperate search for answers to the imponderables. Their gods functioned intimately in their daily lives, and the adherents demanded effective, practical demonstrations of their deistical power in terms of better crops and victory over warring enemies. If Africans displayed a measure of religious skepticism in their willingness to accept new tribal gods or even new religions from the outside world, it was because they failed to see why additional gods would give them greater opportunities for success in their undertakings.

These people who of necessity had to devote most of their energies and attention to the important problems of existence did not neglect the aesthetic aspects of life. Evidence can be found everywhere of pronounced proclivities to artistic expression. Whether in painting, sculpture, or carving there is a delicate sensitivity and an appreciation of the beautiful that reflects a basic regard for the finer things of life. Even in the industrial arts and crafts Africans took the time to beautify their products by applying to them the best of their artistic talents and knowledge. Song and dance played an important part in their social life. With stringed and rhythm instruments they made merry with their friends, worshipped their gods, and buried their dead. Nor is their aesthetic proclivity absent from the area of literary achievement. As in every other endeavor, the literary activities of Africans were tied up closely with their everyday life. Their oral literature, made up of tales, proverbs, epics, histories, and laws, served as an educational device, a source of amusement, and a guide for the administration of government and the conduct of religious ceremonies. If their written literature was limited, it was certainly not for a want of literary interests but rather because of the technical obstacles in the way of developing written languages. The extant treatises, largely in Arabic, show that when a written language was mastered, the resulting works were worthy of serious comparison with their contemporaries in other parts of the world. Most important of all, however, is that they were worthy of esteem on their own terms and by their own standards.

■ The Transplantation of African Culture

Students of Africa and America have discussed for many years the question of the extent to which African culture was transplanted and preserved in the New World. Of course, a considerable number of students formerly contended that nothing existed in Africa that approached civilization and that there was, therefore, nothing for Africans to bring with them. As evidence to the contrary began to pile up, that position was no longer tenable. Questions still remained as to whether Africans continued to be African in ways other than color and whether any substantial elements of Africa became part of the general acculturative process taking place in America. Sociologists like E. Franklin Frazier and Robert E. Park have failed to see anything in contemporary African-American life that can be traced to the African background. On the other hand, scholars like Carter G. Woodson, Melville J. Herskovits, Lorenzo Turner, John Blassingame, and Albert Raboteau have insisted that the African cultural heritage can still be seen in many aspects of American life today. In the 1960s and 1970s the debate was revived when many blacks and some whites began to insist that a substantial portion of African culture not only survived the Atlantic crossing but has persisted to the present day. Although the controversy continues unresolved, it nevertheless seems possible to make a tentative statement about this important problem.

African slaves came from a complex social and economic life, and they were not overwhelmed or overawed by their New World experiences. Despite the heterogeneity characteristic of many aspects of African life,

African peoples still had sufficient common experiences to enable them to cooperate in the New World in fashioning new customs and traditions which reflected their African background. To be sure, there were at least two acculturative processes going on side by side in the New World. As Africans of different experiences lived together, there was an interaction of the various African cultures. This produced a somewhat different set of customs and practices, but these were still manifestly rooted deep in the African experience. This was especially true where large numbers of Africans resided in the same place, as in the Sea Islands, where they could preserve certain religious practices and even language patterns. At the same time, there was the interaction of African and Western cultures, which doubtless changed the cultural patterns of both groups. It is to be remembered that European institutions did not exist everywhere with the same degree of fixity, and where European practices were relatively weak the opportunities for African survivals were correspondingly strengthened.

In the cultural conflict that took place in the New World following the introduction of Africans, the acculturative process varied in different places and under different circumstances. In some places it was all but stymied where there was a sufficient consensus of experience among Africans to take the Western culture and reinterpret it almost wholly in terms of their own experiences. In other places, mainly Brazil and some Caribbean islands, successful revolts made possible the transplantation of an African way of life to a considerable degree. Elsewhere, the normal or gradual development of the process can be observed, but always at least some survival of African culture is obvious. When it comes to measuring or evaluating the persistence of African culture in the New World—and especially in the United States— the problem becomes much more difficult. It can be seen in the language in such words as "yam," "goober," "canoe," and "banjo." In literature the persistence of African culture can be seen in the folk tales that have been recorded in recent years by American writers. In religion there are divinations and various cult practices, some of which can be traced to the African background. In work, in play, in social organizations, and in various aesthetic manifestations there are some evidences of African culture.

The survival of varying degrees of African culture in America does not suggest that there has been only a limited adjustment of Africans to the New World situation. On the contrary, it merely points up the fact that they came out of an experience that was sufficiently entrenched to make possible the persistence of some customs and traditions. There is a certain amount of validity in the view that in the conflict of cultures only those practices will survive whose value and superiority give them the strength and tenacity to do so. African survivals in America also suggest a pronounced resiliency in African institutions. There had been sufficient intertribal and interstate intercourse to give Africans the important experience of adopting many of the practices of those with whom they came in contact while at the same time retaining much of their earlier way of life.

■

CHAPTER 3

The Slave Trade and the New World

■ European and Asian Interests

When the Christians of Western Europe began to turn their attention to the slave trade in the fifteenth and sixteenth centuries, they were not introducing a new practice. Although they displayed much originality in approach and technique, they were engaging in a pursuit that had been a concern for countless centuries. As a matter of fact, slavery was widespread during the earliest known history of Africa as well as of other continents. Doubtless there was cruelty and oppression in African slavery as there was anywhere that the institution developed. At least in some portions of Africa there was no racial basis of slavery. The Egyptians enslaved whatever peoples they captured. At times they were Semitic, at times Mediterranean, and at other times blacks from Nubia. Slavery in the Greek and Roman empires is well known. In both periods the traffic in human beings from western Asia and North Africa brought a continuous stream of slaves to perform personal services and to till the fields for the ruling class. Neither in Greece nor Rome was menial service regarded as degrading. The opportunities for education and cultural advancement were, therefore, opened up to slaves. It was not unusual to find in this class people possessing a degree of intelligence and training not usually associated with slaves.

When the Muslims invaded Africa, they contributed greatly to the development of the institution of slavery by seizing women for their harems and men for military and menial service. By purchase as well as by conquest, the Muslims recruited African slaves and shipped them off to Arabia, Persia, or some other Islamic land. As kings and princes embraced Islam, they cooperated with the Arabians in the exportation of human cargo. Long before the extensive development of the slave trade by Europeans, many of the basic practices of the international slave trade had already been established. It is to be noted, however, that slavery among the Muslims was not an institution utilized primarily for the production of goods from which wealth could be derived. There were no extensive cotton, tobacco, and sugarcane fields in Arabia, Persia, and Egypt. Slaves in these lands were essentially servants, and the extent of the demand for them depended in a large measure on the wealth of the potential masters. Slavery was, therefore, a manifestation of wealth, and the institution showed little of the harshness and severity that it possessed in areas where it was itself the foundation on which wealth was built. Although becoming Muslims did not release slaves from their duties, it did have the effect of elevating their standing and enhancing their dignity among others. While in the face of continued enslavement this was of doubtful value, it could have been viewed by slaves of a later and a more ruthless system as a straw to which to clutch.

It was the forces let loose by the Renaissance and the Commercial Revolution that created the modern institution of slavery and the slave trade. The Renaissance provided a new kind of freedom—the freedom to pursue those ends that would be most beneficial to the soul and the body. It developed into such a passionate search that it resulted in the destruction of long-established practices and beliefs and even in the destruction of the rights of others to pursue the same ends for their own benefit. As W. E. B. Du Bois has pointed out, it was the freedom to destroy freedom, the freedom of some to exploit the rights of others. If, then, people were determined to be free, who was there to tell them that they were not entitled to enslave others?

Coupled with this new concept of freedom was the revitalized economic life of Europe that was brought forth by the Commercial Revolution. The breakdown of feudalism, the rise of towns, the heightened interest in commercial activities, and the new recognition of the strength and power of capital, all of which were essential elements of the Commercial Revolution, brought about a type of competition characterized by ruthless exploitation of any commodities that could be viewed as economic goods. The rise of powerful national states in Western Europe—Spain, France, Portugal, Britain, and, later, Holland—provided the political instrumentalities through which these new forces could be channeled. While the state acted as referee for competitors within its borders, it also served to stimulate competition between its own merchants and traders and those of other countries. The spirit of the Renaissance, with its sanction of ruthless freedom, and the practices of the Commercial Revolution, with its new techniques of exploitation, conspired to bring forth new approaches to the acquisition of wealth and power. Among these was establishment of the institution of modern slavery and the concomitant practice of importing and exporting slaves.

Doubtless, some Africans who were sold to the east and north during the period of Muslim domination found their way into the markets of Western Europe. It was not until the end of the fourteenth century, however, that Europeans themselves began to bring slaves into Europe. Both Spanish and Portuguese sailors were exploring the coast of Africa in the wake of the great wave of expansionism that had swept over Europe. They went to the Canary Islands and to innumerable ports on the mainland as far as the Gulf of Guinea. They took Africans to Europe and made servants of them, feeling justified in doing so because Africans would thereby have the opportunity to cast off their heathenism and embrace the Christian religion. By the middle of the fifteenth century, Europeans were selling in their home markets many African commodities, among them nuts, fruit, olive oil, gold, and slaves. Within a very few years, the slave trade became an accepted and profitable part of European commerce. Largely under the encouragement of Prince Henry, the sailors and merchants of Portugal early saw the economic advantages that the African slave trade afforded. By the time of his death in 1460, 700 or 800 slaves were being transported to Portugal annually.

The last half of the fifteenth century may be considered the years of preparation in the history of the slave trade. Europeans, mainly Spaniards and Portuguese, were establishing orderly trade relations with Africans and were erecting forts and trading posts from which to carry on their business. It was the period in which Europeans were becoming accustomed to having black Africans do their work and were exploring the possibilities of finding new tasks for them. Europeans were attempting to settle among themselves the question of who should and who should not engage in the traffic, and the mad scramble for monopoly even before the close of the century is indicative of the importance with which that traffic was regarded. Finally, this was the period in which Europeans developed a rationalization for their deeds based on Christianity. The Portuguese and the Spaniards led Europeans in invoking the missionary zeal of Christianity to justify their activities on the African coast. If they were chaining Africans together for the purpose of consigning them to a lifetime of enforced servitude, it was a "holy cause" in which they had the blessings of both their king and their church.

There was never any profitable future for African slavery in Europe. Although Europe was undergoing drastic economic change in the fifteenth and sixteenth centuries, its new economic institutions did not utilize Africans on a sufficiently large scale to make the trade excessively profitable. Banking houses, shipyards, mercantile establishments, and the homes of the newly rich could use only a limited number of slaves. To be sure, there were many jobs to be performed, but the large white population that was dispossessed of land by the enclosure movement in England and on the Continent was in search of employment. If there were jobs to be filled, these impecunious Europeans claimed them for themselves. But the new era in economic development ushered in some activities in which Africans could perhaps be used. It was too much to expect that these activities would be confined to Europe as international competition developed. The search for new trade routes, new lands, and new commodities provided the opportunities for the use of African slaves that Europeans had been looking for. It was the New World with its vast natural resources and its undeveloped regions that could make slavery and the slave trade profitable, if indeed it could be profitable anywhere.

■ Africans in the New World

As early as 1920, when Harvard professor Leo Wiener published *Africa and the Discovery of America,* scholars advanced the view that Africans inhabited the New World before Columbus. Wiener and several scholars who followed him (notably Ivan Van Sertima, whose *They Came Before Columbus* was published in 1976) said that numerous evidences of trade and other contacts between Africa and the New World indicate that Africans, not Europeans, were the pioneers of the transatlantic West. Using linguistic as well as archaeological and historical evidence, they vigorously argued their case. Van Sertima declares, for example, that "the case for African contacts with pre-Columbian America . . . is grounded now upon an overwhelming and growing body of reliable witnesses." Although most scholars have not yet accepted these claims, it is not so much because the arguments are not convincing as it is their refusal to deny claims that had become deeply entrenched conventional wisdom for more than four centuries. Consequently the traditional story of the coming of Africans to the New World remains essentially unchanged.

From the very beginning of European exploits in the New World, Africans came as explorers, servants, and slaves. Even if Pedro Alonso Niño of Columbus's crew was not a Negro as has been claimed, there were many blacks who accompanied other European explorers to the New World. As early as 1501, Spain relinquished her earlier ban and permitted Africans to go to Spanish lands in the New World. Thirty Africans, including Nuflo de Olano, were with Balboa when he discovered the Pacific Ocean. Cortés carried blacks with him into Mexico, and one of them planted and harvested the first wheat crop in the New World. Two accompanied Velas in 1520. When Alvarado went to Quito, he took 200 blacks with him. They were with Pizarro on his Peruvian expedition and carried him to the cathedral after he was murdered. The Africans in the expeditions of Almagro and Valdivia saved their Spanish masters from the Indians in 1525.

As Spanish and Portuguese explorers moved into the interior of North America, Africans assisted in the undertakings. They were with Alarcón and Coronado in the conquest of New Mexico. They accompanied Narváez on his expedition of 1527 and were with Cabeza de Vaca in the exploration of the southwestern part of the present United States. One of the outstanding African explorers was Estevanico, who opened up New Mexico and Arizona for the Spaniards. Little Stephen, as Estevanico was known among his fellows, proceeded into the interior and sent back wooden crosses to indicate his progress. When his crosses increased in size until they were as tall as a man, the Spaniards realized that Estevanico had experienced great success. Indians brought news of Little Stephen's approach to the fabulous seven cities about which so much had been heard. Shortly after Stephen entered the city, the Indians killed him, believing him to be an imposter when he said that he was the emissary of two white men. Although Estevanico was murdered, he had prepared the way for the conquest of the Southwest by the Spaniards.

Africans were with the French in their explorations of the New World. In Canadian expeditions, they were with the Jesuit missionaries. When the great conquest of the Mississippi Valley was undertaken by the French in the seventeenth century, Africans constituted a substantial portion of the pioneers who settled in the region. Around 1790, Jean Baptiste Point du Sable, a French-speaking black, erected the first building in a place that came to be known as Chicago. While Africans did not accompany the English on their explorations in the New World, it is not without ironic significance that they were extensively engaged in the task of opening the New World for European development. If blacks helped to raise the curtain on the drama of economic life in the New World, they were to play an even more important part in the exploitation of its resources. Once fastened to a lifetime status of slavery, they became an integral part of the economic life of both the Old World and the New.

When the countries of Europe undertook to develop the New World, they were interested primarily in the exploitation of its natural resources. Labor was obviously necessary, and the cheaper the better. It was only natural that Indians, readily available, would be the first to be used. Europeans displayed excessive inhumanity in the employment of Indian slaves in the mines of Haiti, while working in the fields of the Caribbean almost exterminated them. The great susceptibility of Indians to the diseases carried by Europeans and their simple economic background did not prepare them for the disciplined regimen of the plantation system, which all but eliminated them as workers in the economic system that the Europeans established. Nowhere was Indian slavery profitable. Even if it had been, it would have been insufficient for the robust agricultural life that the European colonies were fostering in the seventeenth century. Other sources of labor supply would have to be tapped if agricultural development in the New World was not to be retarded by an insufficiency of workers. The search for acceptable workers in large quantities became a major preoccupation of the English and Spanish colonists in the seventeenth century.

Although Africans were present in Europe in considerable numbers in the seventeenth century and had been in the New World since at least 1501, European imperialists did not at first regard them as a solution to their labor problems. To be sure, Africans were being employed, but colonists and their Old World sponsors were extremely slow in recognizing them as the best possible labor force for the tasks in the New World. Before they came to see this, they resorted to the poor whites of Europe. In the first half of the seventeenth century, they brought landless, penniless whites over to do the work of clearing the forests and cultivating the fields. When the supply of those who voluntarily indentured themselves for a period of years proved insufficient, the English resorted to more desperate means. Their desperation is clearly seen in the emergence of the wide-spread practice of kidnapping children, women, prisoners, and drunken men. Eric Williams has indicated that the horrors these people experienced on the journey to the New World equaled those experienced by any group before or after. In the English colonies many landlords sought to reduce these servants to the status of slaves. Only gradually did servants achieve a position of respectability in the colonies.

England came to realize that white servants were unsatisfactory. There was the fear that they might become more interested in industry than in agriculture to the detriment of England. Even with all the means used to recruit workers, the supply was still insufficient as the tobacco, rice, and indigo plantations had an almost insatiable appetite for laborers. The terms of service of indentured people were a source of constant irritation for all concerned. Not only did servants chafe under the requirement of remaining until their indenture expired, but many went so far as to sue masters and ship captains for illegal detention. Many of them ran away, and since others of their ilk were migrating into unsettled lands, it became increasingly difficult, as well as expensive, to apprehend them once they had fled. The English began to ask themselves why they should be concerned with white servants when blacks presented so few of the difficulties encountered with whites. Because of their color, Africans could be easily apprehended. Furthermore, they could be purchased outright and a master's labor supply would not be in a state of constant fluctuation. Blacks, from a pagan land and without exposure to the ethical ideals of Christianity, could be handled with more rigid methods of discipline and could be morally and spiritually degraded for the sake of stability on the plantation. In the long run, African slaves were actually cheaper. In a period when economic considerations were so vital, this was especially important. African slavery, then, became a fixed institution, a solution to one of the most difficult New World problems. With the supply of Africans apparently inexhaustible, there would be no more worries about labor. European countries could look back with gratitude to the first of their nationals who explored the coasts of Africa and brought this black gold to Europe. It was the key to the solution of one of America's most pressing problems. At the same time it erected for Europeans one more important economic institution, the slave trade. As perhaps the last major development in the Commercial Revolution, it was in itself a source of great wealth for those who would engage in the traffic of human souls.

■ The Big Business of Slave Trading

When in 1517 Bishop Bartolomeo de Las Casas advocated the encouragement of immigration to the New World by permitting Spaniards to import African slaves, the trading of humans in the New World formally began. Las Casas was so determined to relieve Indians of the onerous burden of slavery that he recommended the enslavement of Africans. (Later, he so deeply regretted having taken this position that he vigorously renounced it.) The ban against the use of Africans was removed, and Charles II issued licenses to several Flemish traders to take Africans to the Spanish colonies. Monopoly of the trade went to the highest bidders. Sometimes it was held by Dutch traders, at other times by Portuguese, French, or English. As West Indian plantations grew in size and importance, the slave trade became a huge, profitable undertaking employing thousands of persons and involving a capital outlay of millions of dollars. By 1540 the annual importation of African slaves into the West Indies was estimated at 10,000.

Although Portugal was the first European country to engage in the African slave trade, it did not become one of the principal countries to realize great profits. At a time when other countries were granting monopolies to powerful, government-supported trading companies, Portugal elected to leave her trade in the hands of merchants, who proved ineffective matches for their competitors from other countries. Not until 1692 did Portugal license the Portuguese Company of Cacheo. By that time several strong companies from other countries had so monopolized the slave trade that Portugal did not have an opportunity to garner more than the proverbial crumbs from the table. Spain had been excluded from Africa by the papal arbitration of 1493 and was forced to content herself with granting the privilege of carrying slaves to her colonies, the much sought after *asiento,* to various companies and individuals from other countries.

The trade in humans that developed into such a big business in the seventeenth and eighteenth centuries was largely in the hands of Dutch, French, and English companies. After Holland extricated itself from the control of Spain in the late sixteenth century, it launched a bold program of competing with other European countries for a share in the wealth of the New World. When they failed to secure Angola and Brazil, the Dutch contented themselves with relatively small territorial possessions and concentrated their energies on seizing control of the commercial routes to the New World. In 1621 the Dutch West India Company was organized with a monopoly of both the African trade and trade with the Dutch colonies in the New World. The company immediately challenged the claim of Portugal to exclusive trading privileges on the African coast, and by the middle of the century it had gained a substantial foothold there. While England was preoccupied with civil wars at home, Holland was strengthening its position both in Africa and America. Dutch slavers could be seen in the ports of almost all the American colonies in the seventeenth century. They brought the first Africans to several French islands, including Martinique and Guadeloupe. On occasion they even took Africans to the Spanish islands, much against the will of Spain, their former subjector.

Holland's wars with France and England in the late seventeenth century left it considerably weakened and never again did it achieve the dominance in the slave trade that it had formerly held. Many independent Dutch traders sought wealth in Africa, a goal that the company tried to obviate by offering licenses to such people. Because of its aggressiveness in the eighteenth century, Holland encountered new difficulties with other countries. Dutch traders pushed into sections of Africa that were under French influence, while on the Guinea coast Holland's seizure of certain possessions from Portugal caused much concern in England. In the West Indies and in South America, Holland used its holdings as centers for the distribution of slaves throughout the New World. Although the end of the century brought a noticeable decline in Dutch influence both in Africa and the New World, this did not take place until after Dutch traders had reaped a bountiful harvest from the slave trade.

Long before Sir John Hawkins inaugurated the English slave trade, merchants of that country had become interested in trade between Africa and the New World. Before the end of the reign of Henry VIII, traders from Britain were developing relationships along the Guinea coast and along the Brazilian coast. By the middle of the seventeenth century, many individuals and organizations, including the powerful East India Company, showed an interest in the African slave trade. The increased needs of the flourishing English colonies in the New World and the chaotic political conditions at home stimulated concern about as well as investments in the slave trade. The relative stability of the Restoration ushered in a period of renewed activity, which was crowned with eminent success. In 1672 the king chartered the Royal African Company, the reorganized group that had held the monopoly for a decade. For almost half a century this company dominated the English slave trade and indeed became the most important single slave-trading group in the world. It jealously guarded the monopoly that the king had granted, and at the same time it attempted to drive the French and the Dutch out of West Africa. The growing number of independent traders in England bitterly fought the company's exclusive right to enjoy the African trade. Pressures at home resulted in the company's loss of its monopoly in 1698. Though it continued to trade in humans, its margin of profit declined. In 1731 it gave up the slave trade and centered its attention on ivory and gold dust.

Greater success attended England's efforts to control the west coast than the Royal African Company experienced in its efforts at national monopoly. Decisive defeats of the Dutch by the British and the French in the late seventeenth century had the effect of enhancing England's prestige in Africa. The blow sustained by France in the War of the Spanish Succession resulted in England's securing the *asiento*—the exclusive right to take slaves to the

Spanish colonies—for thirty years. With British colonies in the Caribbean and on the mainland paying handsome dividends with their bountiful productivity, England's commerce came to dominate the entire world. With a strengthened navy and almost unlimited resources in capital for investment, England could now undertake to satisfy not only the growing demand of its own colonies for slaves but the demands of other colonies in the New World as well.

During the Seven Years' War England transported more than 10,000 slaves to Cuba and approximately 40,000 to Guadeloupe. By 1788 two-thirds of all slaves brought by England to the New World were sold in foreign colonies. Naturally the planters in the English colonies objected to their competitors in the New World being provided with slaves by British traders. What the planters did not realize, perhaps, was that the slave trade had itself become an important factor in England's economic life. If England's colonies were the foundation of the English economic system, certainly in the eighteenth century the slave trade was an important cornerstone of that system.

Since England came to dominate the slave trade, the machinery for prosecuting the traffic was to a large extent the product of English ingenuity. England certainly had no monopoly on the development of slave-trading practices, but its extensive interests and its great success marked it as the country to be emulated. It is for this reason that these practices are almost invariably associated with England. The techniques of trading in slaves were developed after years of trial and failure. Trading posts, or factories, on the coast were the indispensable bases of operation. Once they had been established, and the more the better, trading could proceed. Ships laden with European goods either brought traders out or furnished those already there with goods to be traded. Cotton textiles of all descriptions, utensils of brass, pewter, and ivory, boxes of beads of many sizes and shapes, guns and gunpowder, spirits—whiskey, brandy, and rum—and a variety of foodstuffs were some of the more important items to be exchanged for slaves. The value of the cargo varied with the size of the ship and the time of trading. A typical cargo would seem to be that of the *King Solomon* which in 1720 had an inventory of £4,250 worth of goods when it left London for Cape Castle on the west coast. At each trading post were stationed a number of factors, slave traders who maintained friendly relations with Africans in order to procure slaves. The posts, often bulging with European goods, were well fortified and guarded by soldiers.

Upon arrival at a post in Africa the trader was ready to establish contacts both with the officials at the post and with local Africans who assisted in securing the desired slaves. The usual procedure was to go to the chief of the tribe, make arrangements with him, and secure "permission" to trade in his domain. The chief, after being properly persuaded with gifts, then appointed various assistants who were at the disposal of the trader. Foremost among these was the caboceer, who assumed the responsibility of gathering up those to be sold—at prices previously agreed upon between the trader and the chief. The trading proceeded apace once the captives were brought before the trader for inspection, the entire process having been promoted by the traders themselves, as Robert Rodney has suggested. It was necessary for the trader to consult with his physician and other advisers concerning purchases. Frequently, the prospective slaves had been so cleanly shaven and soaked in palm oil that it was most difficult to ascertain their age or physical condition. The prices, of course, varied greatly depending on the age and condition of the slave, the period of the trading, and the location of the post. Many transactions were mere barter, but there are accounts that reveal that in the middle of the eighteenth century £20 sterling was a typical price to pay for a healthy young man at Cape Castle or some other important post on the Guinea coast.

It must not be supposed that trading in slaves involved the simple procedure of sailing into a port, loading up with slaves, and sailing away. In addition to the various courtesy visits and negotiations that protocol required and that the traders were inclined to follow in order to keep the local leaders in good humor, it was often difficult to find enough "likely" slaves to fill a ship of considerable size. Frequently, traders had to remain at one place for two or three weeks before enough slaves were rounded up to make the negotiations worthwhile. It was not unusual for a ship to be compelled to call at four or five places in order to purchase as many as 500 slaves. Local inhabitants frequently had to scour the interior and use much coercion to secure enough slaves to meet the demands of the traders.

Another delay came in disposing of the cargo that had been brought from Europe and in provisioning the ship with supplies needed for the voyage to America. Experience taught the traders what to take, but at times they took goods not especially desired at the places where they were able to purchase their slaves. If they could not persuade the permanent post officials to take the goods, they would then have to take them all the way back to England. At the post and from Africans traders obtained supplies for the western voyage across the Atlantic. Indian corn, kidney beans, yams, fruits, coconuts, and plantains were the principal foodstuffs secured. In addition, sundry medicines were stocked so that the physician might administer to the slaves, who were almost certain to become ill en route. The last post at which the slaver could make such transactions was Gorée, on the coast of Senegal.

Africans offered stiff resistance to their capture, sale, and transportation to the unknown New World. Fierce wars broke out between tribes when members of one sought to capture members of another to sell them to traders. Slaves brought to the post for sale were always chained, for the caboceers and slave captains very early learned that without such safeguards the slaves would make their escape. One trader remarked that the "Negroes were so wilful and loth to leave their own country, that they have often leap'd out of the canoes, boat and ship, into the sea, and kept under water till they were drowned" to avoid being taken up by their captors. At the first opportunity, if indeed it ever presented itself, many would leap off the ship into the mouths of hungry sharks to avoid enslavement in the New World.

■ One-Way Passage

The voyage to the Americas, popularly referred to as the "middle passage," was a veritable nightmare. Overcrowding was most common. There are records of ships as small as 90 tons carrying a complement of 390 slaves in addition to crew and provisions. The practice of overcrowding slaves became so common that the British Parliament felt compelled to specify that not more than five slaves could be carried for every 3 tons of the burden of a ship of 200 tons. This regulation, like so many others, was not enforced. More slaves meant greater profits, and few traders could resist the temptation to wedge in a few more. There was hardly standing, lying, or sitting room. Chained together by twos, hands and feet, slaves had no room in which to move about and no freedom to exercise their bodies even in the slightest.

It was doubtless the crowded conditions on the vessels that so greatly increased the incidence of disease and epidemics during the voyage to America. Smallpox was one of the dread diseases of the period, and one experienced observer remarked that few ships that carried slaves escaped without it. Perhaps even more deadly than smallpox was flux, a frequently fatal malady from which whites on board the slave ships were apparently spared. Hunger strikes at times aggravated unfavorable health conditions and induced illnesses where previously there had been none. The filth and stench caused by close quarters and disease brought on more illness, and the mortality rate increased accordingly. Perhaps not more than half the slaves shipped from Africa ever became effective workers in the New World. Many of those that did not die of disease or commit suicide by jumping overboard were permanently disabled by the ravages of some dread disease or by maiming, which often resulted from struggling against the chains. Small wonder that one trader who arrived at Barbados with 372 of his original 700 slaves was moved to remark: "No gold-finders can endure so much noisome slavery as they do who carry Negroes; for those have some respite and satisfaction, but we endure twice the misery; and yet by the mortality our voyages are ruin'd and we pine and fret ourselves to death, to think that we should undergo so much misery, and take so much pains to so little purpose."

It may be reasonably doubted that the situation was as unfavorable as that trader pictured it. To be sure, there were difficulties of many kinds, not the least of which was the great mortality among the whites themselves. Even with the great expenses attached to the trade and the extensive loss sustained in the mortality of slaves in transit, the slave trade was still one of the most important sources of European wealth in the seventeenth and

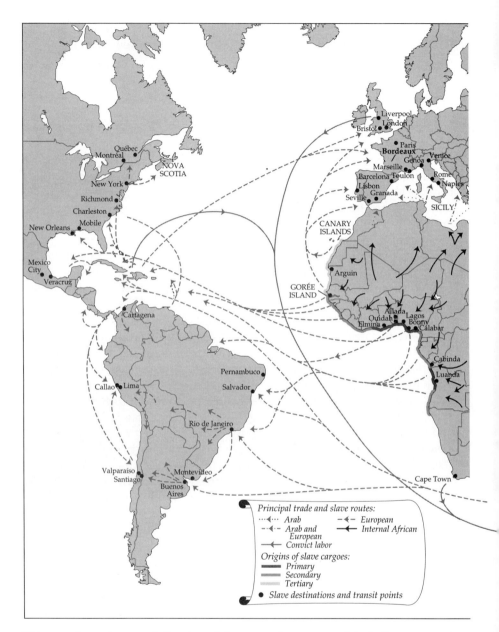

This map shows the general direction of the principal sea routes of Arab, European, and American trade in African slaves up to 1873. The selected destinations include slave debarkation and settlement areas, ports visited by African crewmen, locations of slaves taken on home leave by slaveholders and military officers, and points in England and Canada where slaves were taken following the American War for Independence in 1783.

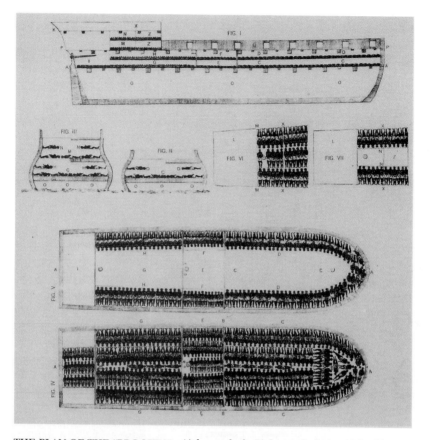

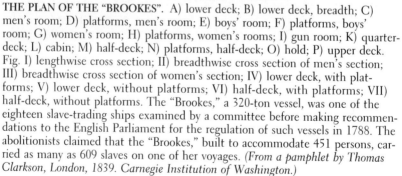

THE PLAN OF THE "BROOKES". A) lower deck; B) lower deck, breadth; C) men's room; D) platforms, men's room; E) boys' room; F) platforms, boys' room; G) women's room; H) platforms, women's rooms; I) gun room; K) quarter-deck; L) cabin; M) half-deck; N) platforms, half-deck; O) hold; P) upper deck. Fig. I) lengthwise cross section; II) breadthwise cross section of men's section; III) breadthwise cross section of women's section; IV) lower deck, with plat-forms; V) lower deck, without platforms; VI) half-deck, with platforms; VII) half-deck, without platforms. The "Brookes," a 320-ton vessel, was one of the eighteen slave-trading ships examined by a committee before making recommen-dations to the English Parliament for the regulation of such vessels in 1788. The abolitionists claimed that the "Brookes," built to accommodate 451 persons, car-ried as many as 609 slaves on one of her voyages. (*From a pamphlet by Thomas Clarkson, London, 1839. Carnegie Institution of Washington.*)

eighteenth centuries. In the late eighteenth century, it was possible for a ship captain to make a commission of £360 on the sale of 307 slaves and for the trader to earn £465 on the same sale. It was not unusual for a ship carrying 250 slaves to net as much as £7,000 on one voyage. Profits of 100 percent were not uncommon for Liverpool merchants. Perhaps those engaged in the trade did undergo much misery, but if they were seeking profits (and who among them had other motives?), it hardly seems accurate for one of them to add that they took "so much pains to so little purpose."

It is not possible to give an accurate figure of the number of slaves imported into the New World from Africa. In eleven years, from 1783 through 1793, Liverpool traders alone were responsible for the importation of 303,737, while in the following eleven years they were certainly responsible for as many more. While the closing years of the eighteenth century represented the peak in the slave trade, the preceding two centuries showed a steady increase leading to the apogee reached in the 1790s.

In 1861 Edward E. Dunbar made estimates of the number of slaves imported into the New World, and these figures were widely accepted during the following century. He estimated that 887,500 were imported in the sixteenth century, 2,750,000 in the seventeenth, 7,000,000 in the eighteenth, and 3,250,000 in the nineteenth. In 1936 R. R. Kuczynski estimated that 14,650,000 Africans had been imported into the New World. In 1969 Philip D. Curtin challenged these estimates. Basing his findings on exhaustive studies of records of slavers, records of slave importations, slave populations in the New World at various times, regional and ethnic origins of slaves imported into the New World, and other pertinent data, Curtin estimated that 241,400 slaves were imported in the sixteenth century, 1,341,100 in the seventeenth, 6,051,700 between 1701 and 1810, and 1,898,400 between 1810 and 1870. His estimate of the total number imported between 1451 and 1870 is 9,566,100. Curtin's figures were in turn challenged by J. E. Inikori, who insisted that the evidence "very strongly suggests a substantial upward revision of the estimates that Curtin made." Declining to give a total figure for the entire slave-trading period, Inikori pointed out that while Curtin's estimate for British exports between 1750 and 1807 was 1,616,100, his own research led him to conclude that the figure was at least 2,365,014. It is obvious that Inikori would place the total estimates much higher than the 9,566,100 estimated by Curtin.

In view of the great numbers that must have been killed while resisting capture, the additional numbers that died during the middle passage, and the millions that were successfully brought to the Americas, the aggregate approaches staggering proportions. The figures, whether Dunbar's, Kuczynski's, Curtin's, or Inikori's, are a testimonial to the fabulous profits realized in such a sordid business, to the ruthlessness with which the traders must have pursued it, and to the tremendous demands made by New World settlers for laborers. Perhaps poet Leopold Sedar Senghor, first president of the republic of Senegal, best summed it up when he declared that the slave trade "ravaged black Africa like a brush fire, wiping out images and values in one vast carnage."

It is more difficult to measure the effect of such an activity on African life than it is to estimate the number of persons removed. The expatriation of millions of Africans in less than four centuries constitutes one of the most far-reaching and drastic social revolutions in the annals of history. It is to be remembered that traders would have none but the best available natives. They demanded the healthiest, the largest, the youngest, the ablest, and the most culturally advanced. The vast majority of the slaving was carried on in the area of West Africa, where civilization had reached its highest point on the continent, with the possible exception of Egypt. The removal of the best of the African population deprived the continent of an invaluable resource. J. E. Inikori insists that the African population and its general well-being would have been much greater by the nineteenth century if the foreign slave trade had not existed. The encouragement that Europeans gave them to fight among themselves with European explosive weapons made it even more difficult for them to recover from the body blow that the slave trade had dealt them. Africa, which culturally was within some measurable distance of Europe at the beginning of the fifteenth century, received the worst possible influence from her Christian neighbors to the north. It was under these adverse circumstances that she entered a recession that in time would suffer the coup de grâce of the imperialistic enslavement thrust upon her in the nineteenth century.

■ Colonial Enterprise in the Caribbean

The slave trade became a tremendously important factor in European economic life primarily because of developments in the New World. The trade in men and women would have remained inconsequential had it been confined to the importation of a few servants into Europe. Its great growth came as the colonies in the New World increased and manifested a pressing need for labor to do the job of clearing the land and tilling the fields. It is, therefore, no mere accident that the seventeenth century, which witnessed the first important advances in the slave trade, also saw the growth of European interest in colonizing and developing the economic life of the New World. The Caribbean was the scene of the first serious effort to develop a lucrative agricultural economy in the New World. It was to the islands in this area that important complements of slaves were sent.

The rivalry among European countries for control of the islands in the seventeenth century presaged the more intense rivalry for hegemony on the mainland that was to develop during the following century. Spain, of course, had prior claim to the islands, thanks to the explorations of its sailors in the fifteenth century and the papal arrangement of 1493. The Spaniards took advantage of this position by channeling their energies and capital into the development of their insular possessions, the most important of which were Cuba, Puerto Rico, Hispaniola, and Jamaica. Although they were to lose some of these and other islands in various conflicts, they nevertheless made the most of them by producing staple crops, especially tobacco and sugar, with slave labor. Early in the sixteenth century large consignments of slaves went to the Spanish islands. In 1518, for example, the king of Spain granted a trader the right to ship 4,000 Africans to the Spanish islands. By 1540 the annual importation had reached approximately 10,000. It must be remembered, moreover, that there was already developing an illicit trade the size of which there was no way of determining.

The breaking of the Spanish monopoly in the Caribbean was closely connected with the slave trade. What the English first sought was an opportunity to share in the Caribbean trade which, during the early years of Elizabeth's reign, already gave promise of being decidedly profitable. When Spain rejected this bid, the English, led in both thought and action by John Hawkins, decided that the monopoly could be broken only by force. Hawkins planned to take slaves to the New World with the hope that the colonists' desire for them would be sufficient to overcome their respect for the royal ban on unlicensed trade. The pattern that he set in selling slaves and other African goods at Hispaniola in 1563 was eagerly followed by other and less discreet English imitators, who were summarily arrested and punished by Spanish officials on the island. Although for the moment Spain had checked the encroachment of Hawkins and others, it was only a matter of time before Spain would have to yield valuable ground in regard both to the commercial and the territorial monopoly it had enjoyed.

In the seventeenth century Spain lost all claim to exclusive control over the islands in the Caribbean. Denmark, Holland, France, and England acquired territory in the area. Dutch buccaneers were entrenched in Curaçao, St. Eustatius, and Tobago by 1640, and the Dutch West India Company, supported enthusiastically by its government, was promoting the slave trade. At about the same time, the French Company of the Islands of America settled Guadeloupe, Martinique, and Marie Galante. In the 1650s St. Lucia and Grenada were acquired by France. The English secured control of St. Christopher in 1623, Barbados in 1625, and Nevis, Antigua, and Montserrat in the 1630s. In 1655 they won one of the great prizes of the Caribbean by driving the Spaniards out of Jamaica. In 1671 the Danes acquired St. Thomas. The Spanish monopoly had indeed been broken, and the West Indies had become not only a pawn in European diplomacy but an important source of revenue for Europeans. African slavery proved to be invaluable in building revenue-producing institutions.

■ The Plantation System

Africans were first used on the tobacco plantations of the Caribbean islands. By 1639, however, European markets had become so glutted with the weed that the price decreased sharply and West Indian planters sustained a great loss. Some of them turned to cotton and indigo, neither of which proved to be as profitable as they had hoped. Some heeded the suggestions of Dutch merchant traders who suggested that they try sugar. It appeared to be a good opportunity, and with capital borrowed from Dutch and English merchants,

West Indian planters began to cultivate sugarcane. The results surpassed their greatest expectations, and they immediately made plans for extension of the cultivation. The problem of labor became acute, and the planters turned more and more to the use of slaves. Thus, in the middle of the seventeenth century, the importation of Africans into the Caribbean islands began in earnest.

In 1640 there were only a few hundred Africans in Barbados. By 1645, after the new sugar plantations had demonstrated their profitableness, there were 6,000, and by the middle of the century the African population had increased to 20,000. Between 4,000 and 5,000 Africans of good quality were delivered to the island in the 1660s, and they found a ready market among the sugar planters. By the end of the century Barbados had a black population of upward of 80,000. A similar growth took place in many of the other Caribbean islands in the seventeenth century. The momentum of importation was so great by the end of the century that in the next 100 years, when the demand for slaves in the islands was declining, importation continued, and in most places it even increased. By 1763, 60,000 African slaves had been imported into Cuba. In the next three decades they came in at a much more rapid rate. Through a system of granting special licenses to importers, Spain was able to bring into Cuba as many as 17,000 Africans in a single year in the 1770s. Between 1763 and 1790, about 41,000 were brought in, while between 1791 and 1825 no less than 320,000 were delivered to Havana alone. Jamaica, Nevis, Montserrat, St. Christopher, St. Vincent, and St. Lucia experienced proportionately similar increases.

The tendency to overpopulate the islands of the Caribbean arose from several important factors. Of course, many slaves who were brought to the islands were to be reexported. Furthermore, there seemed to be no substantial increase in the black population of the islands as a result of births until the emancipation in the 1830s. The death rate was so extraordinarily high that it raises the question of the treatment of slaves. In one year, for example, 2,656 Africans were born in St. Vincent, but in the same year there were 4,205 deaths. On one plantation in Jamaica more than half of the children died in infancy, while miscarriages ran high. Some authorities have attributed the high mortality rate to improper food and the ravages of disease. Doubtless these conditions were present, but the view of many masters that slaves were cheaper to purchase than to breed and the consequent imposition of undue labor on men and women of all conditions and ages apparently caused more deaths than anything else.

There were few evidences of humanitarianism on the plantations of the West Indies. Slavery was essentially an economic institution. Slaves were being extensively used for the sole purpose of producing sugar and other staple crops. Through the use of slaves to produce the rich crops the islands became the favorites of their parent countries. As one writer put it, the islands were "of immense importance to the grandeur and prosperity of England." If the importation of more slaves meant greater prosperity—and it seemed so to the island planters—they were imported with little regard for anything other than economic considerations.

It was absentee landlordism that constituted one of the most important factors in the development of practices that were manifestly destructive of health and life among slaves. Some English landlords pleaded that the climate of the sugar colonies was "so inconvenient for an English constitution that no man will chuse to live there, much less will any man chuse to settle there, without the hopes of at least supporting his family in a more handsome manner, or saving more money than he can do by any business he can expect in England, or in our plantations upon the continent of America." The islands were, therefore, regarded not as a place of residence but merely as a source of wealth. If a planter came out to the Caribbean, he regarded it as a temporary sojourn. Soon he would return to his home country, and with the wealth he had amassed buy an estate and live like a gentleman. Why, then, should he interest himself in schools, churches, and laws that would improve conditions of life for everyone?

Since black slaves were constantly being brought in from Africa, overseers found it necessary to develop a practice of "breaking in" the newcomers. In some areas they were distributed among the seasoned, or veteran, slaves whose duty it was to teach the newly arrived slaves the ways of life in the New World. In other places the newcomers were kept apart and supervised by a special staff of guardians and inspectors who were experienced in breaking in those who might offer resistance to adjusting to their new environment. The mortality rate among newly arrived slaves was exceptionally high, with estimates of deaths running to as much as 30 percent in a seasoning period of three or four years. Old and new diseases, change of climate and food, exposure incurred in running away, suicide, and excessive flogging were among the main causes of the high mortality rate.

In the West Indies slaves were sent to the farms at daybreak, and they labored all day except for a thirty-minute period for breakfast and a two-hour period in the hottest portion of the day, which was frequently the time set aside for doing lighter chores. At harvest time the workday was much longer, sometimes eighteen hours. The driver or overseer did not distinguish between men and women in work requirements or in applying the lash for dereliction of duty. Investigations made by the British Parliament in 1790–1791 brought out the fact that pregnant women were forced to work up to the time of childbirth and that a month was the maximum amount of time allowed for recovery from childbearing. Pregnant women were lashed severely when they were unable to keep pace with the other workers. Women who paused in the fields to care for their babies, whom they carried on their backs, were lashed with cart whips for idling away their time.

Food was on the whole insufficient for slaves. Planters did not often encourage any type of diversified agriculture which would have provided food for the workers. Where this was done at all, slaves were given small plots of land, sometimes far from their houses, that they could cultivate in spare moments. In Barbados, where planters had the reputation of providing for their slaves better than the planters of other islands, slaves were generally ill-fed. On one plantation each adult slave was given a pint of grain and half of a herring (not infrequently rotten) for twenty-four hours. In the famous investigation of 1790–1791 no plantation was found where a slave received more than nine pints of corn and one pound of salt meat per week. Fish of the least desirable grades were imported from the New England colonies, and where this was done the planter acquired a reputation for great benevolence.

On many islands the African population outnumbered the white population. For example, as early as 1673 there were 10,000 blacks in Jamaica and only 8,000 whites. In 1724 there were 32,000 blacks and 14,000 whites. At the end of the century the black population of St. Christopher was over 20,000, "well nigh twenty times that of the white population." It was the preponderance of blacks over whites that promoted the enactment of a slave code of excessive severity. The influence of planters in England made possible the passage, in 1667, of an "Act to regulate the Negroes on the British Plantations." It referred to the Africans in the Caribbean as "of wild, barbarous, and savage nature to be controlled only with strict severity." Slaves were not to leave the plantation without a pass, and they were not allowed to carry any weapons. If a slave struck a Christian, he was to be severely whipped, and for the second offense he was to be branded on the face with a hot iron. If an owner accidentally whipped a slave to death, he or she was not subject to fine or imprisonment. Other European countries had similar laws, but there seemed to have been considerable variation in enforcement. While the well-known French *Code Noir* was relatively humane, it became an agency of great brutality in the hands of some French colonials. When Ogé and his associates were found guilty of conspiring to revolt in the last decade of the eighteenth century, all were cruelly executed. "Their arms, thighs, legs, and backbones were broken with clubs on a scaffold. They were fastened round a wheel in such a manner that their face was turned upward to receive the full glare of the sun." The judge ordered that "Here they are to remain for so long as it shall please God to preserve them alive," after which their heads were to be cut off and exposed on tall poles.

One important ingredient in the seasoning process was the overseer's lash. A typical one was made of plaited cowhide. In the hands of a stern overseer it could draw blood through the breeches of a slave. At times the floggings were so severe as to inflict wounds so large that a finger could be inserted in them. Another favorite type of punishment was to suspend the slave from a tree by ropes and tie iron weights around his or her neck and waist. If these punishments would seem to shorten life and to reduce efficiency, it must be remembered that Africans were being brought in at an increasing rate up until the opening of the nineteenth century and that there was consequently no great inclination to preserve life.

If cruel treatment was designed to prevent uprisings and running away, it was eminently unsuccessful. On almost every island there is a record of some serious revolt against the plantation system, and everywhere there is evidence of constant running away. When the British took Jamaica in the middle of the seventeenth century, most of the slaves promptly escaped to the mountains, where they were frequently joined by other fugitives. These runaways, called Maroons, continuously harassed planters by stealing, trading with slaves, and enticing them to run away. By 1730 these ex-slaves, under Cudgo, their powerful leader, had terrorized whites to such an extent that England was compelled to send out two additional regiments to protect the planters.

Haiti also had its Maroons as early as 1620, and the outlawed colony grew to such proportions that the colonial government recognized it in 1784. It is conceded that they were largely responsible for the Haitian uprisings of 1679, 1691, and 1704. In the middle of the eighteenth century the recalcitrant Negroes of Haiti found a peerless leader in Macandal, a native-born African, who announced that he was the Black Messiah sent to drive the whites from the island. In 1758 he carefully laid his plans for a coup d'état. The water of Le Cap was to be poisoned, and when the whites were in convulsions the Negroes, under the leadership of Macandal and his Maroons, were to seize control. By accident, the plot was discovered, and the fear-stricken planters hunted down Macandal and executed him. At the time of his execution he warned his enemies and comforted his friends by telling them that one day he would return, more terrible than before. Many blacks, and perhaps some whites, were later to believe that Toussaint L'Ouverture was the reincarnation of Macandal.

Even on the small Danish islands there are records of slave resistance. The lack of sufficient food drove many slaves to steal and to refuse to work. In 1726 officials executed seventeen of the leading offenders, but this did not quiet the slaves. The situation worsened, and in 1733 the governor of St. Thomas issued a drastic decree providing for severe punishment of slave offenders by burning, whipping, and hanging. Two months later the Danish islands experienced their worst uprising, which occurred on St. John. Blacks carrying wood entered one of the forts of the Danish West India Company and murdered the guard by stabbing him. Another group of slaves attacked six soldiers and killed five of them. Having captured the garrison, they raised the flag and fired three shots from the cannon, the signal for a general uprising on all the plantations on the island. With flintlocks, pistols, and cane knives the Africans went about the bloody business of murdering all the whites they could find. Only after several days of terror was the uprising brought under control by the captain of the militia.

It was the same everywhere—conspiracies, uprisings, revolts. The seeds of cruelty reaped a bountiful harvest of murder and bloodshed. As the years passed and as slaves learned their duties, they performed them, albeit reluctantly. Time also proved that they could adjust to the climate and food of the New World. Although their terms of service on the islands were by no means satisfactory, they were regarded as seasoned within three or four years and were viewed by mainland planters as much more desirable than the "raw Negroes" fresh from the "wilds" of Africa.

Slaves were being constantly exported from the islands, especially from the British islands. In an effort to capture the slave trade with foreign islands, British traders first brought slaves to some British island and then quietly reexported them to Cuba, Puerto Rico, or some other foreign island. While it is not possible to estimate the number of Africans transported to Cuba from the British islands, it is quite clear that this was Cuba's most important source of slaves. Jamaica alone sent more than 10,000 there in 1756. Of the 90,331 Africans imported into the British West Indies between 1784 and 1787, some 19,964 were reexported; but it is not possible to determine whether they went to French, Spanish, or Portuguese markets, to other British islands, or to the mainland.

As the prosperity of the West Indies declined in the early eighteenth century and as the attention of Europe became focused on the continent of North America, more slaves were doubtless exported from the islands to the mainland. The demand for slaves in the mainland colonies was steadily increasing, and a decided preference for slaves from the islands was manifested. In 1764 several shipments of slaves were made from the West Indies to South Carolina. They came from St. Christopher, Antigua, Barbados, and even Havana. Although the islands could not satisfy the growing demand for slaves on the mainland, they sent some of their surplus yearly, as the records amply testify. Indeed, reexportation itself became a lucrative business in which many persons were engaged. On the islands of St. Christopher, Barbados, and Jamaica some firms carried on a regular business of reexporting slaves to other islands and to the mainland. In the colonies many firms did business directly with traders on the islands.

The cost of producing sugar increased as soil exhaustion manifested itself after a century of intensive cultivation. The price of slaves, moreover, was going up as the demand for them increased on the mainland. White society was so completely without resourceful and imaginative leadership that it was not able to discover areas of economic activity that would compensate for the losses it was sustaining in older activities. Desperate efforts were made both in Europe and in the island colonies to encourage whites to migrate to the Caribbean. Some islands required planters to import proportionate numbers of whites for all the slaves they brought, but many planters found it easier to pay the fines. With a surplus of slaves on their hands, the residents of the West Indies were willing to sell many of them to the mainland colonies.

The increasing exportation of slaves from the West Indies is a clear manifestation of social and economic debility. After several centuries of European occupation, religious institutions were still weak, and vice and immorality of all kinds flourished. Education was at an especially low ebb, and ignorance prevailed even among whites. The ineffectiveness of the law showed itself in its inability to prevent running away, insurrections, and widespread miscegenation. In sending many of their slaves to the mainland, the West Indies served notice to the world that they had yielded the long-held economic primacy in the New World to the mainland.

■ Slavery in Mainland Latin America

In 1501 the government in Madrid authorized the introduction of Africans to make up for the deficiency in Indian labor which the Spaniards had been using in the New World, much more than the English ever used. The condition that only such Africans should be taken as had been born under the power of Christian masters was shortly overlooked as the demand for workers increased. They were being brought into Cuba in such large numbers by 1506 that the Spanish government, for fear of a slave uprising, was moved to prohibit their future importation. For a decade the importation of Africans slowed to a trickle, and the extensive use of Indians was resumed. In 1516 Charles II issued licenses to several Flemish traders to take Africans to the Spanish colonies. In the following year the ban against the use of Africans was removed, with the stipulation that one-third of those imported should be women. By the time that Cortés launched his conquest of Mexico, Africans were in all the Spanish island colonies and were being rapidly introduced into the mainland.

In the early years of the Spanish colonies the slave trade was viewed as un-Christian and illegal. To overcome this dual disfavor, it was necessary for traders to secure special permission—the *asiento*—to bring slaves into the Spanish colonies. This made it relatively easy for the crown to subject the traffic in slaves to rigid control. Since the contracts, or permits, were monopolistic, the holders were required to pay a tax to the crown on each slave brought in. The crown reserved the right to revoke the *asiento* if the traders did not make accurate reports on the numbers of slaves imported or if they were either unhealthy or in some other way undesirable as workers. Whether the *asiento* was held by private individuals or companies, by Spaniards, or by foreigners, the crown could use its granting powers as an effective diplomatic and economic weapon to enhance its influence in both hemispheres.

It would be erroneous to assume that slave traders in Spanish America confined their activities to the insular possessions. Almost from the beginning they transported slaves to Mexico, Panama, Colombia, Peru, and Argentina, and from these points the slaves were dispersed in all directions. Only the lines of supply directly from Africa or from the Caribbean entrepôts were officially recognized, but smugglers and interlopers were not averse to bringing Africans from English, French, or Dutch colonies or from other points when it was profitable to do so. By these various routes of commerce more than 60,000 Africans entered Mexico during the first century of conquest. In the following century the number was even greater. While the islands and the adjacent continent possessed a limited capacity to absorb slaves, the Mexican market was a veritable paradise for traders. The Jesuit Father Andrés de Rivas estimated that 3,000 or 4,000 entered the country each year. Gonzalo Aguirre Beltrán, the Mexican historian, asserts that a conservative estimate for the seventeenth century would place the figure at 120,000 slaves. In the eighteenth and early nineteenth centuries importation declined sharply, with no more than 20,000 slaves entering the Viceroyalty of New Spain during that period. When Baron Alexander von Humboldt visited the country in 1793, he said that there were only 10,000 slaves. Certainly 200,000 had entered the country by that time, but the majority had become mixed with the whites and Indians so extensively that perhaps they were no longer recognizable as a distinct element in the population.

During the colonial period Central America was largely a part of the Viceroyalty of New Spain, and no separate figures are available for the importation of slaves into that region. Africans in Central America perhaps were a small but important segment of the population. They were imported into Guatemala as early as 1524, when the Spaniards occupied the land. While the number was never as large as 10,000, they were a considerable source of trouble to the Spanish authorities. Runaways would band together in the woods of Sierra de las Minas and with their bows and arrows harass the countryside for miles around. The entire military force of Guatemala City found it impossible to subdue them. Some slaves became free, developing into substantial citizens. One such freedman became an extensive landowner and herdsman. Although he made a great profit from dairy products that he sold in Guatemala City, the authorities felt that perhaps some hidden treasure was the real source of his wealth. He periodically denied this, and until his death he stood as an example of what an African was able to accomplish in Central America.

Perhaps the largest concentration of blacks in continental Spanish America was to be found in the Viceroyalty of New Granada, comprising the modern states of Panama, Colombia, Venezuela, and Ecuador. The ports along the Caribbean early became entrepôts for Negro slaves and points from which they were distributed to the interior. Panama, Caracas, and Cartagena were among the largest slave markets in the New World. By the time that accurate census figures for the area became available, Negroes were present in considerable numbers. In the Audiencia of Santa Fé—present Panama and Colombia—there were in 1810 approximately 210,000 Negroes and mulattoes, slave and free, in a total population of 1.4 million. In the Captaincy General of Caracas—present Venezuela—Negroes and mulattoes numbered 493,000 in 1810, while the total population was 900,000. About the same time, the Presidency of Quito—present Ecuador—had 50,000 Negroes and mulattoes in a total population of 600,000.

One of the most striking features of the dispersion of Negroes in Spanish America was the presence of large numbers on the Pacific coast in the colonial period. As Fernando Romero pointed out, "the slave trade in the Spanish South American colonies followed well-established lines from north to south and from south to north, the two currents converging on Peru." The Viceroyalty of Peru—roughly present Chile and Peru—was, thus, an area of concentration of Africans. Lima not only received a great share for its own exploitation but also served as a market from which Andean planters and herders could purchase black workers. Some were sent into this remote viceroyalty from Panama and Cartagena, while others were sent directly from Africa around Cape Horn. In 1622 the viceroy reported the presence of 30,000 Negroes in his domain, with 22,000 at Lima. In the middle of the following century one observer declared that there were many blacks, but that it was impossible to ascertain the exact numbers as the owners feared that the government would use the figures as the basis for a new tax.

When the first trustworthy census was taken in 1791, the population of Peru was approximately 1.25 million. Of that number, 40,000 were black and 135,000 were white. The remainder were Indians, *mestizos*—people of Indian and white ancestry—mulattoes, and various combinations of races. Blacks constituted 25 percent of the population of Lima. At about the same time the population of Chile was approximately 500,000, of which 30,000 were Negroes and mulattoes. These figures do not tell the entire story of the African population in the Viceroyalty of Peru. Accurate statistics were always difficult to secure because owners, fearing additional taxation, hid their slaves when census takers came around. The rapid absorption of Africans into the total population, moreover, made it difficult to measure their impact upon the area into which they were sent.

The absence of a considerable population of blacks in modern Uruguay and Argentina does not mean that Spain neglected to furnish these colonies with African slaves. Instead, it is suggestive of the remarkable biological and cultural fusion that occurred. Montevideo and Buenos Aires were major ports of entry for slave traders during colonial days. While there are no figures available for the total African population of the Viceroyalty of La Plata, there can be no doubt that there was a large population of blacks, especially in the area of the estuary of the Rio de la Plata. A contemporary estimated that in 1805 about 2,500 slaves were being imported annually. In 1803 the black population of Montevideo was 1,040 out of a total of 4,726. There is every indication that Buenos Aires also had a substantial black population. As late as 1827 there were seven African societies in the Argentine capital. The disappearance of Africans in the southern part of South America is an eloquent testimony of the complete absorption of a people by the tremendous migration of Europeans that occurred in the last century.

It was only natural that the Portuguese, the first to sense the importance of African slave labor, would undertake to provide their New World empire with Africans. Although they made extensive use of Indian labor throughout the sixteenth century, they introduced Africans into Brazil as early as 1538, when the first shipment from the Guinea coast reached Bahia. It was the introduction of sugar into the colony about 1540 that stimulated the importation of Africans, and after that time the slave trade continued unabated. During the period of Spanish control, 1580–1640, the slave trade to Brazil greatly accelerated. In 1585 there were 14,000 slaves in the colony out of a population of 57,000. Toward the end of the century the Spaniards brought in large numbers of slaves from Guinea, São Thomé, Mozambique, and other parts of Africa. Though there was a tendency for them to be concentrated in Pernambuco, Bahia, and Rio de Janeiro, they fanned out in various directions as sugar and coffee plantations were developed in the fertile interior valleys.

There were five centers of distribution from which slaves were sent into the various parts of Brazil. From Bahia and Sergipe they were taken to plantations and to domestic service on the coast; from Rio de Janeiro and São Paulo they were taken to cane fields and coffee plantations or were kept to work in the capital; from Minas Gerais most slaves were sent to the gold mines, such as those of Goyaz; slaves from the distribution center at Pernambuco supplied the sugar-producing provinces of the northeast, and slaves from Maranhão and Pará were sent to the cotton plantations of the north. In the seventeenth century it was estimated that more than 44,000 Africans were imported annually, while the following century witnessed an annual importation of no less than 55,000 blacks. Estimates of the number of Africans imported into Brazil vary from 5 million to 18 million. Whatever the total figures were, it is clear that between 1538 and 1828 Africans were imported in such large numbers that persons of African descent still constitute a considerable portion of the population.

In 1798 the first reliable estimate of the population listed 406,000 free blacks and 1,582,000 slaves in a total population of 3,250,000. By 1818 the total population had risen to 3,817,000, in which there were 1,930,000 slaves and 585,000 freedmen. Thus, it can be seen that in that twenty-year period Africans were largely responsible for the increase in the total population. In 1830 they constituted 28.6 percent of the population. In 1847, in a total population of 7,360,000, including 800,000 civilized Indians, there were 3,120,000 African slaves, 1,100,000 free persons of color, and 180,000 free native Africans. In 1888, the year of the emancipation of Brazil's slaves, there were 723,419 slaves.

There were three distinct groups of slaves in colonial Brazil. Urban slaves worked as servants in the town homes of planters, in shops, at the docks, and in numerous other capacities. On the whole, their lot was not difficult. Some were specially skilled in arts and crafts and performed invaluable services in helping to improve living conditions in urban areas. Others were kept in homes to render personal service. If there was insufficient work, owners sent their slaves out to find work. These freelancers, *negros de ganho,* often stood on street corners ready to assist shoppers with their packages or went from house to house offering their services to people who did not have servants. Many were able to earn fairly good wages because of their special skills and their ability to read and write. With the opportunity to hire out their own services some slaves not only made money for their masters but also eventually earned enough to purchase their own freedom.

With the discovery of gold in the seventeenth century, large numbers of slaves were employed in the mines. The simultaneous decline in the sugar economy caused many planters either to sell or hire out their slaves to prospectors and mine owners. Black Brazilians began migrating into the interior near Goyaz, Corumba, and the plateau of Matto Grosso. Some were not employed in the mines but demonstrated their aptitudes and abilities in other ways, as iron workers, shoemakers, and even architects and sculptors.

The vast majority of blacks—perhaps five-sixths—were always employed on the great sugar, coffee, cotton, and cacao plantations. These farm workers fared the worst in Brazil. They worked from sunrise to sunset and were supervised for the most part by stewards who, with whips in their hands, threatened, intimidated, and tortured them into performing their work. As in the Spanish colonies, there were laws that sought to protect slaves from cruel masters and overseers, but because such statutes were extremely difficult to enforce, they did not provide much help. The invention of instruments of torture must have taxed the ingenuity of those in command. There was the *tronco,* constructed of wood or iron, by which the slave's ankles were fastened in one place for several days; the *libambo* did the same thing to the arms. *Novenas* and *trezenas* were devices by which a slave was tied, face down, and beaten for nine or thirteen consecutive nights.

There were some mitigating features of Brazil's institution of slavery. Since there was no law against teaching slaves to read and write, many of them became proficient in the use of language. The law required that slaves be baptized within at least one year after their arrival in the country. After this rite was performed, they were expected to attend mass and confession regularly. In addition, the manumission of slaves was actually encouraged in Brazil. Faithful nurses were often set free. There was a general custom that after a slave mother had given birth to ten children she was to be set free. The clergy urged pious communicants to manumit their slaves at death if not sooner. There are perhaps no records of an owner's refusal to emancipate a slave who was able to purchase his or her freedom. Finally, there is the general view that in the colonial period Brazilians felt little, if any, race prejudice. Blacks were given many opportunities for advancement, and free blacks theoretically enjoyed the same rights and privileges before the law that whites did.

While slaves in Brazil and elsewhere were a source of profit, they were also a source of constant trouble. Living in small, crowded huts and subsisting on coarse fare, they frequently became restive and sought to break the chains of slavery. In 1550 the slaves of Santa Marta, Colombia, committed great atrocities and burned the city. Five years later an African calling himself king led a violent insurrection that was subdued only by strenuous exertions of the authorities. One of the most desperate bids for freedom in the New

World occurred in Brazil in the seventeenth century. It was the establishment of the Republic of Palmares, an African state in Alagoas in northeastern Brazil, between 1630 and 1697. Fleeing the towns and plantations between Bahia and Pernambuco, runaway slaves penetrated the heavy forests and settled rustic communities in the Rio Mundahu valley. Despite sieges laid by the Portuguese and by the Dutch, who were attempting to occupy that portion of Brazil in 1644, these Maroons held out until 1697, when the superior forces of the Portuguese soldiers entered the walled city of Palmares. Refusing to surrender, the leader and his principal assistants hurled themselves to certain death from the rocky promontory overlooking the city. Although the other insurrections and Maroon communities established in Spanish and Portuguese America perhaps never equaled Palmares, many of them were greater than any that slaves undertook in British America.

Several factors distinguished slavery in Latin America from that institution in British America. One such factor was the relatively small number of Spaniards and Portuguese in their colonies as compared to the considerable numbers of Britons in the English colonies. It was not at all unusual for slaves to outnumber by a large margin their Spanish and Portuguese owners and officials who frequently had little or no family with them and who were, all too often, infrequent visitors to their New World domains. Such a disproportionate number of blacks facilitated the many more successful insurrections and Maroon communities that arose in Latin American than arose in British America. Perhaps it also had something to do with the strict slave codes which were introduced into Latin America earlier than in British America.

Another factor was the significant role that the Catholic church played in Latin America. Priests often accompanied explorers and were usually present when settlers came. It was they who insisted that slaves be instructed in the Roman Catholic religion and baptized in the church. Owners were not permitted to work their slaves on Sundays and on the approximately thirty feast days during the year. Catholic slaves were married in the church, and the banns were published regularly. There was no law against their learning to read the catechism, and thus the whole world of reading was opened to them. Meanwhile, in the British colonies, where slaves could not enter into any kind of binding agreement, permission of the owner was the only prerequisite for marriage. Although many slaveholders in the British colonies encouraged slaves to be religious and to attend church regularly, the discipline of the Anglican church encouraged but did not require owners to tend the spiritual needs of their slaves. Far from encouraging them to learn to read and write, British colonies generally discouraged such activities, and some of them forbade them altogether. If the church in Latin America had some salutary influence on the treatment of slaves, it did not achieve complete success in eliminating cruelty altogether, as David B. Davis and others have reminded us.

A final factor was that blacks enjoyed a higher level of esteem in the Latin colonies than in the British colonies, which perhaps helps to explain why many more Spaniards and Portuguese than Britons intermarried with blacks. It should be remembered that there were relatively few Spanish and Portuguese women in the New World. Choices were therefore limited. Even so, any stigma attached to intermarrying with blacks was virtually absent, and they did so in the church. Meanwhile, if any British Americans had intimate relationships with blacks, they were generally clandestine and without benefit of clergy.

Still, it does not necessarily follow that slaves fared better in Latin America than in British America. Examples abound of inhuman cruelty in all parts of the New World, and it is well to recall that during the 1830s, long after the United States outlawed the slave trade, Brazil imported 400,000 slaves from Africa. Although converted and baptized as Christians in Latin America, slaves were appraised and sold just like any other merchandise. The point to remember is that it is virtually impossible to speak of slavery other than in terms of its inhumanity, and that few institutions, including the churches, did anything to mitigate its fundamental cruelties and the insensitivity of one person who had complete dominion over another.

■

CHAPTER 4

Colonial Slavery

■ Virginia and Maryland

The twenty Africans who were put ashore at Jamestown in 1619 by the captain of a Dutch frigate were not slaves in a legal sense. And at the time Virginians seemed not to appreciate the far-reaching significance of the introduction of Africans into the fledgling colony. These newcomers, who happened to be black, were simply more indentured servants. They were listed as servants in the census counts of 1623 and 1624, and as late as 1651 some blacks whose period of service had expired were being assigned land in much the same way that it was being assigned to whites who had completed their indenture. During its first half-century of existence Virginia had many black indentured servants, and the records reveal an increasing number of free blacks.

But as time went on Virginia steadily fell behind in satisfying the labor needs of the colony with Indians and indentured servants. It was then that the colonists began to give serious thought to the "perpetual servitude" of blacks. Virginians began to see what neighboring islands in the Caribbean had already recognized, namely, that blacks could not easily escape without being identified; that they could be disciplined, even punished, with impunity since they were not Christians; and that the supply was apparently inexhaustible. Black labor was precisely what Virginia needed in order to speed up the clearing of the forests and the cultivation of larger and better tobacco crops. All that was required was legislative approval of a practice in which many Virginians were already engaged. Indeed, by 1640, some

Africans in Virginia had become bondservants for life. The distinction between black and white servants was becoming well established. In that year, when three runaway servants, two white and one black, were recaptured, the court ordered the white servants to serve their master one additional year. The black servant, however, was ordered "to serve his said master or his assigns for the time of his natural life here or elsewhere." Thus, within the first generation of Virginia's existence, African servitude was well on the way to becoming African slavery.

The actual statutory recognition of slavery in Virginia came in 1661. The status of blacks already there was not affected if they had completed their indenture and were free. As a matter of fact, the recognition was almost casual and was first indicated in a law directed at white servants: "That in case any English servant shall run away in company with any negroes who are incapable of making satisfaction by addition of time . . . that the English so running away . . . shall serve for the time of the said negroes' absence as they are to for their owne." In the following year, 1662, Virginia took another step toward slavery by indicating in its laws that children born in the colony would be held in bond or free according to the condition of the mother. Some mitigation of slavery was intended by a 1667 law indicating that slaves could be baptized as Christians. In order to protect the institution of slavery, however, this law provided that "the conferring of baptisme doth not alter the condition of the person as to his bondage or freedome." Thus, "diverse masters, freed from this doubt, may more carefully endeavour the propagation of christianity."

At first the black population of Virginia grew quite slowly. In 1625 there were only 23 in the colony, and as late as the middle of the century scarcely 300 could be counted. With the chartering of the Royal African Company in 1672 the shipment of slaves into the colony was accelerated. By the end of the century they were being brought in at the rate of more than 1,000 per year. It was in the eighteenth century that the black population grew at what some Virginians began to view as an alarming rate. In 1708 there were 12,000 blacks and 18,000 whites. By 1756 there were 120,156 blacks and 173,316 whites, with blacks outnumbering whites in many communities.

Although Virginians greatly appreciated the importance of slave labor in the development of the colony, they soon became apprehensive about such large numbers of blacks living among whites. Already whites and blacks were mixing, and a mulatto population was emerging. There were, moreover, persistent rumors of conspiracies of rebellion, and many whites feared for their lives. Those who were apprehensive took the lead in attempting to control the importation of slaves, but commercial interests fought off these attempts with all the resources at their command. For the time being they were successful.

But the fears of insurrection were not groundless. Within two years after the first statutory recognition of slavery, the blacks of Virginia were showing clear signs of dissatisfaction and began to plot rebellion against their masters.

In 1687, while a funeral was taking place, a group of slaves in the northern neck planned an uprising, but the plot was discovered before it could be carried out. Rumors continued, and plots of varying sizes were uncovered. Where there were no plots there was general disobedience and lawlessness. By 1694 Virginia slaves had become so ungovernable that Governor Edmund Andros complained that there was insufficient enforcement of the code which, by that time, had become elaborate enough to cover most of the activities of slaves.

The Virginia slave code, borrowing heavily from practices in the Caribbean and serving as a model for other mainland codes, was comprehensive if it was anything at all. Slaves were not permitted to leave plantations without the written permission of their masters. Slaves wandering about without such permits were to be returned to their masters. Slaves found guilty of murder or rape were to be hanged. For major offenses, such as robbing a house or a store, slaves were to receive sixty lashes and be placed in the pillory, where their ears were to be cut off. For petty offenses, such as insolence and associating with whites or free blacks, they were to be whipped, branded, or maimed. The docility of slaves, about which many masters boasted, was thus achieved through the enactment of a comprehensive code containing provisions for punishment designed to break even the most irascible blacks in the colony. With the sheriffs, the courts, and even slaveless whites on their side, the masters should have experienced no difficulty in maintaining peace among their slaves.

While slavery in Maryland was not recognized by law until 1663, it came into existence shortly after the first settlements were made in 1634. As early as 1638 there was reference to slavery in some of the discussions in the legislature, and in 1641 the governor himself owned a number of slaves. Colonists had no difficulty, therefore, in turning their attention to the problem of the status of blacks and in concluding that legislation was necessary to fix their status as slaves. The law of 1663 was rather drastic. It undertook to reduce to slavery all blacks in the colony even though some were already free, and it sought to impose slave status on all blacks born in the colony regardless of the status of their mothers. It was not until 1681 that the law was brought in line with established practices by declaring that black children of white women and children born of free black women would be free.

The slave population of Maryland was slow to increase, not because of any disinclination on the part of colonists to own slaves but because they were not in ample supply during the colony's early years. This is the principal reason why, during the restoration period, laws were enacted to encourage and facilitate the importation of slaves. In 1671 the legislature declared that the conversion of slaves to Christianity would not affect their status. Masters now felt that they could import African heathens, convert them to Christianity, and thus justify the act of holding them in slavery. By the end of the century the importation of slaves was increasing steadily. In 1708 the governor reported that 600 or 700 had been imported during the preceding ten months. By 1750 there were 40,000 blacks as compared with 100,000 whites.

As in Virginia, blacks in Maryland early showed resentment against their status as slaves. In several instances white masters died at the hands of their slaves, and there was more than one case of a black cook poisoning an owner. In 1742 seven blacks were executed for the murder of their masters. Others were convicted for committing acts of sabotage such as arson, stealing of property, and the brutal treatment of livestock.

The increase in the black population and fear on the part of whites for their own safety led to the enactment of stringent laws covering their conduct and activities. In 1659 came laws relating to the return and treatment of fugitive slaves. Soon there were laws forbidding slaves to deal in stolen goods and liquor, as well as laws providing for the punishment of free blacks and slaves found guilty of murder, arson, larceny, association with whites, insolence, and going about without permission. Punishment ranged from death to branding and whipping. Enforcement was rigorous, but clemency was not rare. There are numerous examples of intervention on behalf of slaves accused by masters who, while approving of the strict enforcement of the law, wanted "on just this occasion" a bit of leniency.

There is a real possibility that the blacks in Maryland were a contributing factor to the religious strife that existed in that colony. From its very beginning in 1634, Maryland had witnessed an intense rivalry between Catholics, favored by the ruling Calverts, and Protestants, who were heartened by the Puritan ascendancy in England. In 1689 there were rumors that the Catholics were plotting against the government of Maryland. Indians were suspected of collusion with the Catholics, and the blacks of some of the southern counties were also watched with suspicious eyes. This doubtless led to the law of 1695 which prevented frequent meetings of blacks. In the eighteenth century when some Maryland colonists hoped for a Jacobite succession in England, those opposed to it continued to keep under surveillance all the Catholics, Indians, and blacks to be certain that they did not conspire to commit some devilish act. No effective rebellion ever materialized, but blacks enjoyed the distinction of being suspected of belonging to an international clique conspiring to overthrow the government of Maryland before handing it over to the French, the Indians, the English Catholics, or all three.

■ The Carolinas and Georgia

It was a foregone conclusion that slaves would be introduced into the Carolinas as soon as it was feasible. After all, four of the proprietors of the colony were members of the Royal African Company and fully appreciated the profits that could come from the slave trade. By 1680, moreover, the

DRIVING NEWLY ARRIVED BLACKS TO THE SLAVE MARKET. Prior to the American Revolution, slavery was sanctioned in all thirteen British North American colonies. As a consequence, slaves of both genders and all ages were appraised and sold just as any other merchandise. *(The Bettmann Archive.)*

examples of Virginia and Maryland led them to believe that Carolina could become prosperous, with plantation slavery as one of the important foundations of the colony's economic life. Perhaps John Locke had these things in mind when, in his *Fundamental Constitutions,* he wrote, "Every freeman of Carolina shall have absolute power and authority over his negro slaves, of what opinion or religion soever." This statement clearly sanctioned slavery and protected it against any possible destruction that might have come through the conversion of slaves to Christianity.

Blacks were present in the Carolina colony virtually from the beginning. This was undoubtedly the result of deliberate encouragement of the impor-

Gallery of African Art

Basket
Rotse peoples, Zambia
Fiber, dye
38.7 cm. (15 1/4 in.)
(Photograph by Jeffrey Ploskonka

Equestrian figure
Inland Delta Region, Mali
Terra cotta
70.5 cm. (27 3/4 in.)
(Photograph by Franko Khoury)

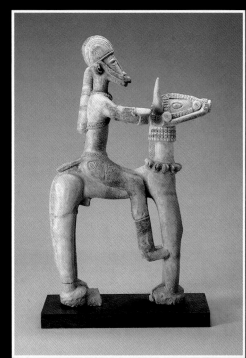

(All works of art in this insert are courtesy of
the National Museum of African Art, Eliot
Elisofon Archives, Smithsonian Institution.)

Vessel
Possibly Bamana peoples, Mali
Terra cotta
57.5 cm. (22 5/8 in.)
(Photograph by Delmar Lipp)

Chair
Sourthern Mande or Kru peoples,
Côte d'Ivoire
Wood
32.1 cm. (12 5/8 in.)
(Photograph by Franko Khoury)

Female figure and children
Yoruba peoples, Nigeria
Wood, pigment
38.5 cm. (15 1/4 in.)
(Photograph by Franko Khoury)

Plaque with multiple figures,
Mid-16th-17th century
Edo peoples, Benin Kingdom, Nigeria
Copper alloy
48.6 cm. (19 1/8 in.)

Wrapper
Asante peoples, Ghana
Cotton, silk
159.1 x 101.3 cm. (62 5/8 x 39 7/8 in.)
(Photograph by Franko Khoury)

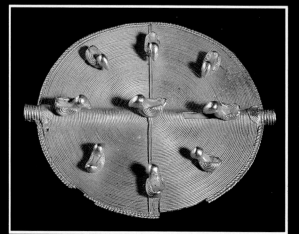

Pendant
Baule peoples, Côte d'Ivoire
Gold alloy
8 cm. (3 1/2 in.)
(Photograph by Franko Khoury)

tation of slaves by the proprietors. In 1663 they offered to the original settlers twenty acres for every black man slave and ten acres for every black woman slave brought into the colony in the first year. Somewhat smaller incentives were offered for the importation of slaves in subsequent years. Twenty years after the original settlements, the black population in the Carolinas was equal to that of the white. By 1715 blacks outnumbered whites 10,500 to 6,250. In 1724 there were three times as many blacks as whites, and the growth of the black population was to continue for decades to come.

As in the other colonies, the growth of the black population led to the enactment of legislation aimed at controlling the activities of slaves. As early as 1686 the Carolina colony forbade blacks to engage in any kind of trade, and it enjoined them from leaving their masters' plantations without written authorization. In 1722 white justices were authorized to search blacks for guns, swords, "and other offensive weapons" and to capture them unless they could produce a permit less than one month old authorizing them to carry such a weapon. Patrols were given authority to search blacks and to whip those deemed to be dangerous to peace and good order. Punishments for offenses by slaves were summary and severe.

Carolinians had not established their controls too soon, for as early as 1711 there were rumors that blacks were getting out of hand. In 1720 several slaves were burned alive and others were banished because they were implicated in a revolt near Charleston. In subsequent years there were other revolts or rumors of revolts. In 1739 the well-known Stono Rebellion twenty miles west of Charleston threw the countryside into a state of wild excitement. After slaves killed two guards in a warehouse and secured arms, they went on a full-scale drive to destroy slavery in that area. The uprising was put down, but not for several days and not before thirty whites and forty-four blacks had lost their lives. As Peter Wood has said, the black majority in South Carolina would be a continuing cause of apprehension. Later in the century there were other uprisings, and the general state of affairs led to a full-scale revision of the slave code.

Before the Revolution, South Carolina, now divided from North Carolina, had enacted one of the most stringent set of laws governing slaves to be found anywhere in the New World. The selling of liquor to slaves was prohibited. Owners were warned against undue cruelty to slaves which might incite them to revolt. Owners were prohibited from working slaves more than fifteen hours per day between March 25 and September 25 and for more than fourteen hours per day between September 25 and March 25. These last few provisions were a tacit admission that slaves could be driven to revolt. What Carolinians realized all too late was that slaves were not as tractable as they had believed and that the danger of having so large a slave population in their midst was more real than fancied.

If conditions were at all ameliorated among Carolina slaves, it was the result of the efforts of the Society for the Propagation of the Gospel in Foreign Parts. SPG missionaries sought to raise the level of living among both whites and blacks. In some instances they met with considerable success. They suggested that slaves should be given time to study the Scriptures and to learn to read and write. In many cases they taught slaves themselves, and in one notable instance they fostered the establishment of a school for blacks in Charleston in which the teachers were slaves owned by the SPG. While these were significant ameliorations, they were also evidences of acceptance of the basic idea of enslavement, and with the religious sanction that the SPG gave to slavery, planters felt more secure than ever in their belief in the righteousness of the institution.

The presence of Quakers in North Carolina had a salutary effect on the conditions of slaves in the colony. They urged the establishment of regular meetings for slaves, and Quaker slaveholders were urged by their coreligionists to treat their blacks well. Before the end of the colonial period there was some sentiment among the Quakers to discourage members from purchasing slaves, and finally, in 1770, the organization described the slave trade as "an iniquitous practice" and sought its prohibition. Members of the SPG also sought to improve conditions among blacks as well as Indians and, as they had done in South Carolina, blacks encouraged masters to permit their slaves to attend religious services.

It is interesting to note that there was no real slave insurrection in North Carolina during the colonial period. The fact that the slave population was relatively small and that there was little impersonality on North Carolina plantations was doubtless responsible for this peaceful situation. In comparison with neighboring colonies, North Carolina presented a picture of remarkable calm in the period before the War for Independence.

Georgia was the only important New World colony to be established by England in the eighteenth century. It differed in several significant ways from the earlier English colonies: it was to grant no free land titles, to permit the use of no alcoholic beverages, and to allow no slavery. From the time of its establishment in 1733, however, each of these proscriptions was subjected to enormous pressure from the settlers, and one by one the restrictions collapsed. It was in 1750 that the third petition of the colonists brought about the repeal of the hated prohibition against slaves. From that point on the black population grew and slavery flourished. By 1760 there were 6,000 whites and 3,000 blacks. In 1773, when the last estimate was made before the War for Independence, the white population had increased to 18,000, while the black population numbered some 15,000.

Much of Georgia's slave code, adopted in 1755, was taken from the South Carolina code, and it reflected South Carolina's experience rather than Georgia's. For example, the interdiction against more than seven Negroes being out together without a white chaperone indicated South Carolina's general fear of black uprisings. Between Saturday evening and Monday morning, not even those slaves who were authorized to possess firearms were permitted to carry them on their persons. Under no conditions were they to be taught to read and write.

If the slaves of colonial Georgia did not actually engage in rebellion, they nevertheless resisted their enslavement by running away to Florida and by committing acts of sabotage. Strangely enough, Georgia displayed a relative indifference to insurrection by subjecting her slaves to service in the militia. Perhaps the service that Spanish Florida rendered as a place of escape for more discontented blacks made possible the paradoxical practice of using blacks as Georgia militiamen to assist in the return of fugitive slaves to Georgia.

■ The Middle Colonies

Although the Dutch were primarily interested in the slave trade and made great profits from transporting slaves to various colonies, they did not neglect their own New World settlements. There were large plantations in New Netherland, particularly in the valley of the Hudson River, and by 1638 many of them were cultivated largely with slave labor. The institution of slavery, as practiced by the Dutch in the New World, was relatively mild, with slaves receiving fairly humane treatment and many considerations as to their personal rights. The Dutch slave code was not elaborate, and manumission was not an uncommon reward for long or meritorious service. Although the demand for slaves always exceeded the supply, the number imported by the Dutch never reached such proportions as to cause serious apprehension or difficulty during the period of their domination.

The character of the institution of slavery changed when the English took over New Netherland in 1664. In 1665 the colonial assembly recognized the existence of slavery where persons had willingly sold themselves into bondage, and in the statute of 1684 slavery was recognized as a legitimate institution in the province of New York. In subsequent years the black population of New York grew substantially. In 1698 there were only 2,170 blacks in a total population of 18,067, while in 1723 the census listed 6,171 slaves. By 1771 the black population had increased to 19,883 in a total population of 168,007.

The slave code of New York became refined early in the eighteenth century. In 1706 the colony enacted a law stating that baptism of a slave did not provide grounds for a claim to freedom. A further and certainly significant provision was that a slave was at no time a competent witness in a case involving a freeman. In 1715 the legislature enacted a law providing that slaves caught traveling forty miles north of Albany, presumably bound for Canada, were to be executed upon the oath of two credible witnesses. Meanwhile, New York City was enacting ordinances for better control of slaves. In 1710 the city forbade blacks from appearing "in the streets after nightfall without a lantern with a lighted candle in it."

The concentration of an increasing number of slaves in the city of New York brought with it increased dangers to the white population. Blacks defied authority and disobeyed the laws. In 1712 the ungovernable temper of New York blacks flared up into a fully organized insurrection in which twenty-three slaves armed with guns and knives met in an orchard and set fire to a slaveholder's house. During the melee that followed nine whites were killed and six were injured. In the ensuing trial of the accused blacks twenty-one were found guilty and executed.

Almost thirty years later, in 1741, there was a rumor of an even larger insurrection. After a series of fires, the rumor spread that blacks and poor whites were conspiring to destroy law and order in the city and to seize control. After the city offered generous rewards for the apprehension of the conspirators, almost 200 whites and blacks were arrested and prosecuted. At least 100 blacks were convicted, 18 of whom were hanged, 13 burned alive, and 70 banished. Four whites, including 2 women, were hanged. There were no more serious outbursts during the colonial period, and by the time of the Revolution, New York had begun to recognize the moral and economic undesirability of holding human beings in bondage.

South of New York, the colonies of New Jersey, Pennsylvania, and Delaware each in its own way subscribed to the institution of slavery. After the English came to dominate New Jersey, they encouraged slavery in every way. Soon, the black population there was growing steadily: 2,581 in 1726, 3,981 in 1738, and 4,606 in 1745 out of a population of 61,000. In Pennsylvania the growth was not so rapid, largely because of the opposition to slavery by the Quakers. In 1688 Germantown Quakers issued their celebrated protest, and in 1693 George Keith remonstrated with Pennsylvanians for holding persons in perpetual bondage. But in 1685 no less a person than William Penn himself expressed the view that African slaves were more satisfactory workers than white servants, and this had the effect of greatly encouraging slavery in some quarters. In 1721 the black population of Pennsylvania was estimated at between 2,500 and 5,000. Thirty years later there were about 11,000 in the colony. In 1790 there were 10,274 blacks, of whom 3,737 were slaves and 6,537 were free.

In Pennsylvania there was some respect for blacks as human beings, and this attitude led to an early movement for manumission. Even those to whom the institution was acceptable shrank from the wholesale and indiscriminate enslavement of black people simply because it was possible to do so. Pennsylvania was not only relatively free from violence and interracial strife, but the blacks there made strides toward genuine accommodation to their new environment. The lines of communication between blacks and whites were not altogether closed, and the former gained much through these contacts. Schools and churches were a part of the lives of blacks, the institution of marriage was generally respected, and the black family achieved a stability unlike that reached by blacks in most English colonies.

Meanwhile, as early as 1636 slavery existed on the right bank of the Delaware. Since Delaware was a part of Pennsylvania until 1703, the laws of the latter colony applied to Delaware. After that date Delaware was on its own, and the slave population increased at a somewhat more rapid rate

TABLE 1
White and Black Population in the Colonies, 1750
(estimated)

COLONY	WHITE	BLACK
New Hampshire	26,955	550
Massachusetts	183,925	4,075
Rhode Island	29,879	3,347
Connecticut	108,270	3,010
New York	65,682	11,014
New Jersey	66,039	5,354
Pennsylvania	116,794	2,872
Delaware	27,208	1,496
Maryland	97,623	43,450
Virginia	129,581	101,452
North Carolina	53,184	19,800
South Carolina	25,000	39,000
Georgia	4,200	1,000

Source: U.S. Department of Commerce. Historical Statistics of the
United States: Colonial Times to 1970; Part 2. Bureau of the Census.
Washington, D.C. 1975.

than it did in Pennsylvania. As this occurred, Delaware drifted away from
the parent colony and became more closely identified with the interests of
the neighboring colonies to the south.

Slavery was never really successful in the Middle colonies. Their predominantly commercial economy, supplemented by subsistence agriculture, did
not encourage the large-scale employment of slave labor, and many of the
slaves that cleared through New York and Pennsylvania ports were later sent
into the Southern colonies. Even where there were extensive agricultural
enterprises there was no desire for slaves, for the Dutch, Swedes, and
Germans cultivated their farms with meticulous care and seemed to prefer to
do it themselves. There were those, moreover, who had moral scruples against
using slaves. Thus, many in the Middle colonies welcomed the arguments
against slavery that became more pronounced during the Revolutionary
period.

■ Blacks in Colonial New England

Although New England's primary interest in slavery was in the trade of
blacks, some were early introduced into Massachusetts and Connecticut. In
1638 a Salem ship unloaded several Africans in Boston, and in the following

year there were blacks in Hartford. Before a decade had passed, blacks were used in the construction of houses and forts in Connecticut. By the middle of the century the refugees who founded Rhode Island were using blacks to help establish that colony. While the status of these early New England blacks was rather uncertain, it gradually became clear in all New England colonies that slavery was a legitimate institution.

Whether slaves landing in New England were to be settled there or shipped to other colonies, they became important to the commercial life of the New England colonies. New England slave traders competed in the trade, although they were at a serious disadvantage compared to the powerful European trading companies. After England secured a monopoly of the slave trade to the New World in 1713, it welcomed New England merchants since there was more than enough for its own traders. In the first half of the eighteenth century New England traders thrived. Boston, Salem, Providence, and New London bustled with activity as outgoing ships were loaded with rum, fish, and dairy products, and as Africans, molasses, and sugar were unloaded from incoming ships. Up until the War for Independence the slave trade was vital to the economic life of New England.

The black population in New England grew slowly. In 1700, when the total population of the entire region was approximately 90,000, there were only 1,000 blacks. In the eighteenth century growth was more rapid. Massachusetts led with 2,000 blacks in 1715 and 5,249 by 1776. Connecticut was second with 1,500 blacks in 1715 and 3,587 by 1756. The largest percentage of blacks was to be found in Rhode Island, where in 1774 there were 3,761 blacks to 54,435 whites. The number in New Hampshire remained negligible all during the colonial period.

New England slavery needed little legal recognition for its growth and development. When the codes emerged late in the seventeenth century, slavery had already become well established. In 1670 Massachusetts enacted a law providing that the children of slaves could be sold into bondage, and ten years later it began to enact measures restricting the movement of blacks. In 1660 Connecticut barred blacks from military service, and thirty years later it restrained them from going beyond the limits of the town without a pass. The restrictions against the education of slaves were not as great as in other regions, and frequently blacks learned to read and write.

Since the number of slaves in New England remained relatively small throughout the colonial period, there was little fear of insurrections. Nevertheless, many slaves indicated their dislike of the institution by running away. Others attacked their masters and even murdered them. Still others plotted to rebel. In 1658 some blacks and Indians in Hartford decided to make a bid for their freedom by destroying several houses of their masters. In the eighteenth century there were a number of conspiracies to rebel in Boston and other towns in Massachusetts. The situation became so serious in Boston in 1723 that the selectmen found it necessary to take precautionary measures by forbidding slaves to be on the streets at night and to be "idling or lurking together."

Phillis Wheatley's "An Address to the Atheist"—1768

Thou who dost not daily feel his hand and rod
Darest thou deny the essence of a God!
If there's no heav'n, ah! whither wilt thou go
Make thy Ilysium in the shades below?
If there's no God from whom did all things spring?
He made the greatest and the minutest Thing.
Angelic ranks no less his power display
Than the least mite scarce visible to Day.

M. A. Richmond, *Bid the Vassal Soar, Interpretive Essays on the Life and Poetry of Phillis Wheatley and George Moses Horton* (Washington, 1974), p. 23.

Despite some restrictions, blacks in New England seemed to have been free to associate with each other and with peaceful Indians. The houses of some free blacks became a rendezvous where they danced, played games, and told stories. Slaves like Lucy Terry of Deerfield, Massachusetts, and Senegambia of Narragansett, Rhode Island, had a seemingly limitless store of tales about Africa and other faraway places that filled many an hour with excitement and pleasure. There was, moreover, ample opportunity for blacks to associate with whites, for hardly a house or church raising, an apple paring, or a corn husking took place without the presence of at least a portion of the slave population. On Guy Fawkes Day, Lorenzo Greene says, "Negroes joined in the boisterous crowds that surged through the streets of Boston, much to the annoyance of pedestrians."

Blacks in New England were in a unique position in colonial America. They were not subjected to the harsh codes or the severe treatment that their fellows received in the colonies of the South. Nevertheless, it is possible to exaggerate the humanitarian aspects of their treatment. Masters in New England held a firm hand on the institution and gave little consideration to the small minority that argued for the freedom of slaves. Although New Englanders took their religion seriously, they did not permit it to interfere with their appreciation of the profits of slavery and the slave trade. At the same time, they did not glut their home market with slaves and increase the number to the point where they would be fearful for their safety. There seemed to be the characteristic Yankee shrewdness in the New Englander's assessment of the importance of slavery to economic and social life.

CHAPTER 5

That All May Be Free

■ Slavery and the Revolutionary Philosophy

By the middle of the eighteenth century, slavery in the United States was an integral part of a maturing economic system. There had been protests against the slave trade, some colonies had imposed almost prohibitive import duties, and some religious groups, notably the Quakers, had questioned the right of one person to hold another in bondage. There had been, however, no frontal attack upon the institution, and even in the Northern colonies, where there was no extensive use of slaves, the majority of the articulate colonists paid little attention to slavery. Perhaps it was the colonists' preoccupation with their economic and political relations with England that accounted for the widespread indifference with which they regarded slavery. Colonial problems were so urgent that little time was left in which colonists could concern themselves with humanitarian matters. If there could be assurance that blacks would neither conspire to rebel nor offer aid and comfort to the French or the Indians, there seemed to be little reason to be concerned over this condition.

This general attitude prevailed up until the end of the French and Indian War in 1763. This significant year not only marked the beginning of a new colonial policy for England but also ushered in a new approach, on the part of the colonists, to the problem of slavery. There was, moreover, a discernible connection between the two developments. As colonists saw in England's new colonial policy a threat to the economic and political freedom that they had enjoyed for several generations, they also seemed to recognize a marked inconsistency in their position as oppressed colonists *and* slaveholders. John Woolman, a New Jersey Quaker, and Anthony Benezet, a Philadelphia Huguenot, had already begun their anti-slavery activities in the Middle colonies, and others, such as Benjamin Franklin and Benjamin Rush, had joined in the work to free the slaves. But there had been no dramatic denunciation of the institution by any outstanding political leader in the colonies. The resurrection of the hated navigation acts and the imposition of new regulations like the Sugar Act of 1764 brought forth eloquent defenses of the position of the colonists. One act of Parliament had, as James Otis declared, "set people a-thinking in six months, more than they had done in their whole lives before." They began to think of their dual role as oppressed and oppressor. Almost overnight the grave but quiet efforts of Benezet and Woolman bore fruit, as some colonial leaders began to denounce not only England's new imperial policy but slavery and the slave trade as well.

The Whig policy of "benign neglect" lent itself to the flow of ideas across the Atlantic as much as it winked at the clandestine flow of commerce in numerous directions. There is little reason to believe that the colonists were unaware of the revolutionary literature flowing from the pens of such French thinkers as Rousseau. There were enough revolutionary ideas in England, however, to inspire a movement against the proscribing policy of the parent country. Long before 1776 most Americans viewed John Locke's treatises on government as political gospel, and upon numerous occasions after 1763 they used these works to bolster their arguments. Locke's *Constitutions of Carolina* had recognized slavery in that colony, and his treatises on government defended the replacement of James II by William and Mary. If Locke could justify the revolution of 1688, certainly the same line of reasoning could justify the colonial action of the 1760s and 1770s.

It was almost natural for the colonists to link the problem of black slavery to their fight against England. The struggle of blacks to secure their freedom was growing. When James Otis was penning his eloquent protest in the *Rights of the British Colonies,* in which he affirmed the black's inalienable right to freedom, blacks themselves were petitioning the general court of Massachusetts for their freedom on the grounds that it was their natural right. The incident in Boston in March 1770 must have greatly impressed many of the colonists with the incongruity of their position. The presence of British soldiers in Boston excited the indignation of the people, and many wondered what could be done about it. The decision was made by a group, described by defense counsel John Adams at the trial of the British soldiers as "a motley rabble of saucy boys, Negroes and mulattoes, Irish Teagues and outlandish Jack Tars." Led by Crispus Attucks, a runaway slave, and shouting, "The way to get rid of these soldiers is to attack the main guard," they rushed into King Street to protest by action. They were fired upon by several men of Captain Preston's company. Attucks was the first to fall, two others were killed instantly, and two others later died from wounds.

Attucks could hardly be described as a saucy boy. Nor was he deserving of the other harsh things John Adams had to say about those who fell in the Boston Massacre. Attucks was more than forty-seven years old and had made his living during the twenty years after he ran away from his Framingham master by working on ships plying out of Boston harbor. As a seaman he probably felt keenly the restrictions that England's new navigation acts imposed. He had undertaken to make the protest in a form that England would understand. Attucks's martyrdom is significant not as the first life to be offered in the struggle against England. Indeed, there ensued almost five years of peace during which time it appeared as though Samuel Adams and his group would not get their war after all. The significance of Attucks's death seems to lie in the dramatic connection that it pointed out between the colonists' struggle against England and the status of blacks in America. Here was a fugitive slave who, with his bare hands, was willing to resist England to the point of giving his life. It was a remarkable thing, the colonists reasoned, to have their fight for freedom waged by one who was not as free as they.

In the years that followed the Boston Massacre, the colonists, as though pricked by conscience, frequently spoke against slavery and England at the same time. In 1773 the Reverend Isaac Skillman went so far as to assert that in conformity with the laws of nature, slaves should rebel against their masters. In 1774 Abigail Adams wrote her husband: "It always appeared a most iniquitous scheme to me to fight ourselves for what we are daily robbing and plundering from those who have as good a right to freedom as we have." About the same time, Thomas Jefferson wrote "A Summary View of the Rights of British America," in which he said that the abolition of slavery was the great object of desire in the colonies, but that it had become increasingly difficult because Britain had consistently blocked all colonial efforts to put an end to the slave trade.

In their thinking some colonists had thus moved from the position of acceptance of the institution of slavery to the position that it was inconsistent with their fight with England and finally to the view that England was responsible for the continuation of slavery. This view was translated into action in the fall of 1774 when the Continental Congress passed an agreement not to import any slaves after December 1, 1775. Georgia, the only colony not represented, adopted a similar measure in July 1775. These can hardly be regarded as antislavery measures, however. It must be remembered that there was general resentment against England's "Intolerable Acts," passed earlier in the year, and that many of the enactments of the first Continental Congress were retaliatory measures of a temporary nature.

The test of the colonists' regard for slavery came in their reaction to the Declaration of Independence, which was submitted to the Continental Congress by Thomas Jefferson. The formulation of a general political philosophy to justify the drastic step the colonists were taking was generally acceptable, even to the proposition that all people, being created equal, were endowed with "certain unalienable Rights . . . Life, Liberty, and the pursuit of Happiness." Jefferson's specific charges against the king were harsh and uncompromising. Among them were the following:

> He has waged cruel war against human nature itself, violating its most sacred rights of life and liberty in the persons of a distant people who never offended him, captivating and carrying them into slavery in another hemisphere, or to incur miserable death in their transportation thither. This piratical warfare, the opprobium of *infidel* powers, is the warfare of the Christian king of Great Britain. Determined to keep open a market where MEN should be bought and sold, he has prostituted his negative [veto] for suppressing every legislative attempt to prohibit or to restrain this execrable commerce; and that this assemblage of horrors might want no fact of distinguished die, he is now exciting these very people to rise in arms among us, and to purchase that liberty of which he deprived them, by murdering the people upon whom *he* also obtruded them; thus paying off former crimes committed against the *liberties* of one people, with crimes which he urges them to commit against the *lives* of another.

These charges, described by John Adams as the "vehement philippic against Negro slavery," were unacceptable to the Southern delegation at the Continental Congress and were stricken from the document.

The members of the Continental Congress doubtless realized that Jefferson's bold accusations of the king were at considerable variance with the truth. The slave trade had been carried on not only by British merchants but by colonists as well, and in some colonies no effort had been made even to regulate it. There was, moreover, much favorable disposition to slavery in the Southern colonies, an attitude shared by a larger number than the "few bold and persevering pro-slavery men" described by George Livermore. Those who favored slavery at all realized that if Jefferson's views prevailed in the Declaration of Independence, there would be no justification for the institution once the ties to England were completely cut. It would be better, therefore, to reject the strong language in which the complete responsibility was laid at the door of George III. In thus declining to accuse the king of perpetuating slavery and the slave trade, the colonists contented themselves with engaging in what Rufus Choate later called "glittering generalities" and in connecting all too vaguely the status of blacks with the philosophy of freedom for all people.

The silence of the Declaration of Independence on the matter of slavery and the slave trade was to make it equally difficult for abolitionists and proslavery leaders to look to that document for support. Even if Jefferson did say that all men were created equal, it could not be forgotten that the antislavery passages of the Declaration were ruled out altogether. By endowing all with inalienable rights superior to those of positive law, it was, however, a standing invitation to insurrection that few could accept. The implications of the Declaration, however vague, were so powerful that Southern slave owners found it desirable to deny the self-evident truths that it expounded and were willing to do battle with abolitionists during the period of strain and stress over just what the Declaration meant with regard to society in nineteenth-century America.

■ Blacks Fighting for American Independence

From the beginning of hostilities in 1775, the question of arming blacks, slave and free, consistently plagued the patriots who most of the time had trouble enough without this aggravating situation. The fear of slave insurrections had caused the colonists to exclude blacks from militia service even in Massachusetts in 1656, and in Connecticut in 1660. Despite this exclusion, blacks frequently participated in wars against the French and the Indians, thus developing a tradition of military service that was alive at the time of the War for Independence. As early as the battles of Lexington and Concord in April 1775, blacks took up arms against the British, and their presence at subsequent battles in the spring and summer of that eventful year is an important part of the military history of the struggle.

In May 1775, the Committee on Safety—commonly known as the Hancock and Warren Committee—took up the matter of the use of blacks in the armed forces and came to the significant conclusion that only freemen should be used since the use of slaves would be "inconsistent with the principles that are to be supported." It is doubtful that this policy was adhered to, for evidently slaves, as well as free blacks, fought in the Battle of Bunker Hill. Furthermore, many slaves were manumitted in order to serve in the army. Indeed, one of the outstanding heroes of the battle, Peter Salem, had shortly before the battle been a slave in Framingham, Massachusetts. One story, not thoroughly substantiated, says that Salem won the admiration of his comrades in arms by shooting the British Major Pitcairn. Mounting the redoubt and shouting, "The day is ours," Pitcairn, who displayed more valor than judgment, received the full force of Peter Salem's musket. The death of Pitcairn was a part of the moral victory won by the patriots on June 17, 1775.

Peter Salem was not the only black who succeeded in distinguishing himself at Bunker Hill. Another, Salem Poor, a soldier in a company and regiment made up largely of white men, won the praise of his superiors, who said that in the battle he "behaved like an experienced officer as well as an excellent soldier." In an official commendation presented to the general court of Massachusetts these military leaders said, "We would only beg leave to say, in the person of this said negro centres a brave and gallant soldier. The reward due to so great and distinguished a character, we submit to the Congress." While Peter Salem and Salem Poor stand out for their

AFRICAN-AMERICAN MASON. Prince Hall, fighter in the War for Independence, established Masonry among blacks after he was initiated by a British army lodge in 1775. *(Fisk Archives.)*

extraordinary feats of heroism, other blacks were integrated into the companies of whites and performed services for which they were later commended. Among these were Caesar Brown of Westford, Massachusetts, who was killed in action; Barzillai Lew, a fifer and drummer; Titus Colburn and Alexander Ames of Andover; Prince Hall, later an abolitionist and Masonic leader; and many other Massachusetts blacks: Cuff Hayes, Caesar Dickerson, Cato Tufts, Grant Cooper, and Sampson Talbert. While this is certainly not an exhaustive list, it is indicative of the early use of blacks in the War for Independence.

The black soldier had by no means won the right to fight for the independence of the United States. In the formulation of an overall policy for military service shortly after General Washington took command, it was decided that the services of blacks were not needed. Out of the council of war that Washington held on July 9, 1775, an order was sent to recruiting officers that they were not to enlist "any deserter from the ministerial army, nor any stroller, negro, or vagabond, or person suspected of being an enemy to the liberty of America nor any under eighteen years of age." It was a rather strange expression of gratitude for the services rendered by blacks that Washington and the high command found it desirable to exclude them from enlistment.

The ban on enlistment obviously did not affect blacks already in the service, but within a few months a movement was afoot to rid the army of all blacks. On September 26, 1775, Edward Rutledge of South Carolina moved in the Continental Congress to discharge all blacks in the army. Although he was strongly supported by many Southern delegates, he lost his point. On October 8, however, a council of war composed of Washington, Major Generals Ward, Lee, and Putnam, and several brigadier generals met and considered the use of blacks. It was agreed unanimously to reject all slaves and, by a large majority, to reject blacks altogether. Ten days later a group of civilians, among them Benjamin Franklin and Thomas Lynch, met with Washington and the deputy governors of Rhode Island and Connecticut to discuss plans for recruiting a new army. It was again agreed to reject blacks altogether. On November 12, 1775, General Washington issued an order instructing recruiters not to enlist blacks, boys unable to bear arms, or old men unable to endure the fatigues of campaign.

Thus, the new army under George Washington had settled the question of the black soldier by deciding not to permit any black, slave or free, to enlist. There is no indication that there would have been a change of policy had not the British made a political move that harassed the feeble Continental army almost as much as a significant military maneuver. On November 7, 1775, Lord Dunmore, the governor of Virginia, issued a proclamation that caused immediate concern among the patriots. In part, he said, "I do hereby . . . declare all indentured servants, Negroes, or others (appertaining to rebels) free, that are able and willing to bear arms, they joining his Majesty's troops, as soon as may be, for the more speedily reducing this Colony to a proper dignity." Had Washington known of this proclamation on November 12, he perhaps would not have issued his order prohibiting the enlistment of blacks. As soon as he learned of Dunmore's designs he manifested great concern. During the month of December he was most alarmed at what the consequences of the wholesale enlistment of blacks in the British army might mean in Virginia. In a letter to Richard Henry Lee on the day after Christmas, Washington asserted that if Dunmore was not crushed before spring, he would become the most formidable enemy to the cause of independence. His strength would increase "as a snowball, by rolling; and faster, if some expedient cannot be hit upon to convince the slaves and servants of the impotency of his design."

Washington had to act quickly. On December 31, he partially reversed his policy regarding the enlistment of blacks and in a report to the president of the Continental Congress said that he was permitting the enlistment of free blacks. He said that the free blacks who had served in the army were very much dissatisfied at being discarded. He further reported that it was feared that they would seek service in the British army if they were not permitted to serve with the patriots. On January 16, 1776, the Continental Congress approved a policy permitting free blacks "who had served faithfully in the army at Cambridge" to reenlist but made it clear that no others were to be received.

Virginians were alarmed. The hated Dunmore was openly soliciting support among their slaves. They felt constrained to counteract this bid with pleas and promises to blacks. On November 23, 1775, an article appeared in a Williamsburg paper severely criticizing Dunmore's proclamation and pointing out to blacks that the British motives were entirely selfish. Blacks were urged not to join Dunmore's forces and were promised good treatment if they remained loyal to the Virginia patriots. On December 13, the committee of the Virginia Convention officially answered the Dunmore proclamation. It not only denounced the British for enticing slaves away but also promised pardon to all slaves who returned to duty within ten days.

The alarm of the military high command and of Virginians was fully justified. Edmund Pendleton wrote Richard Henry Lee on November 27, 1775, that slaves were flocking to Dunmore in abundance. In March of the following year, Dunmore reported to the British secretary of state that the enlistment of blacks was proceeding very well, "and would have been in great forwardness, had not a fever crept in amongst them, which carried off a great many fine fellows." During the remainder of the war large numbers of blacks escaped to the British lines, seeking the freedom that had eluded them during their stay in the colonies. Wherever the British armies went they attracted many blacks, and Maryland, Virginia, and South Carolina were especially alarmed over the future of slavery regardless of the outcome of the war. As late as 1781 Richard Henry Lee would write his brother that two neighbors had lost "every slave they had in the world. . . . This has been the general case of all those who were near the enemy."

The presence of British troops in America and the war itself had an unsettling effect on slavery in general. Slaves ran away in large numbers even if they had no intention of reaching the British lines. Thomas Jefferson estimated that in 1778 alone more than 30,000 Virginia slaves ran away. David Ramsay, the South Carolina historian, asserted that between 1775 and 1783 his state lost at least 25,000 blacks. It has been estimated that during the war Georgia lost about 75 percent of its 15,000 slaves. How effective the British were in utilizing this manpower is not at all clear. Here and there, such as at Ft. Cornwallis, there are accounts of blacks serving in the British army. Perhaps their service was more valuable than has been believed, for in 1786 a corps of runaway blacks that had been trained by the British during the siege of Savannah were still calling themselves the "king of England's soldiers" and continued to harass the countryside of Georgia in an eighteenth-century resistance movement.

The British bid for blacks during the war had the effect of liberalizing the policy of the colonists toward them. Not only did Washington order the enlistment of some free blacks, but most of the states, either by specific legislation or merely by a reversal of policy, began to enlist both slaves and free blacks. In 1776 a New York law permitted the substitution of blacks for whites who had been drafted. In the same year Virginia went so far as to permit free mulattoes to serve as drummers, fifers, and pioneers, and in the following year Virginia merely required that all blacks who enlisted should furnish a certificate of freedom secured from a justice of the peace. In 1778 both Rhode Island and Massachusetts permitted slaves to serve as soldiers. In the same year North Carolina, in legislating against fugitive slaves, made it clear that the penalties under the law were not to be applied to liberated slaves in the service of North Carolina or the United States.

Under the more liberal laws of the states, blacks began to enlist in the state and Continental armies in large numbers. In 1778 Massachusetts and Rhode Island felt that enough black soldiers could be raised within their borders to form separate regiments. Indeed, it appeared as though states were now vying with each other in enlisting blacks. New Hampshire offered the same bounty to black soldiers that it was giving to whites, and masters were given bounties as payment for the freedom of their slaves. When the recruiting of white soldiers in Connecticut declined, a vigorous enlistment of blacks began. New York offered freedom to all slaves who would serve in the army for three years, while owners were given a land bounty for their slaves. Before the end of the war most states, as well as the Continental Congress, were enlisting slaves with the understanding that they were to receive their freedom at the end of their service.

Only two states, Georgia and South Carolina, continued to oppose the enlistment of black soldiers. It was a source of considerable embarrassment to Colonel John Laurens, who in 1778 was asked to raise several battalions of blacks in his native South Carolina. In 1779 the Continental Congress recommended that 3,000 blacks be recruited in Georgia and South Carolina. The Congress was to pay the owners not over $1,000 for each slave recruited, and at the end of the war the slave was to be set free and given $50. Georgia and South Carolina were alarmed over the plan and summarily rejected it. Despite several pleas from Laurens, neither state ever permitted such enlistment. By this time, Washington had so completely accepted the idea of blacks as soldiers that he could write of South Carolina and Georgia, "That spirit of freedom which at the commencement of this contest would have gladly sacrificed everything to the attainment of its object, has long since subsided, and every selfish passion has taken its place." Even in these states, however, slaves were running away—to fight with the British and win their own freedom or with the patriots and win the freedom of their country as well as their own.

Of the 300,000 soldiers who served the cause of independence, approximately 5,000 were blacks. Despite the fact that the bulk of the black population was in the South, the majority of black soldiers were from the North. They served in every phase of the war and under every possible condition. Some volunteered, others were drafted, while still others were substituted for white draftees. There were only a few separate black fighting groups. In Massachusetts two black companies were formed, one under Maj. Samuel Lawrence and the other—the Bucks of America—under Middleton, a black commander. Connecticut put a black company in the field under the leadership of Capt. David Humphreys, while the Rhode Island black company was under Col. Jeremiah Olney and later under Col. Christopher Greene. Some of these groups won the admiration and respect of their leaders and of the citizenry. Lawrence's company was described as a group "of whose courage, military discipline, and fidelity" their leader always spoke with respect. On one occasion his men rescued him after he was completely surrounded by the enemy.

The command of an all-black company was, at first, studiously avoided by most of the white officers. There was, therefore, some difficulty in securing a commander for the Connecticut company of blacks. Finally, Captain Humphreys volunteered his services, and under his leadership the group so distinguished itself that thereafter officers were said to have been as desirous of obtaining appointments in that company as they had previously been of avoiding them. In the Battle of Rhode Island, August 29, 1778, the black regiment under Colonel Greene "distinguished itself by deeds of desperate valor." On three occasions they repulsed the Hessian soldiers, who were charging down on them in order to gain a strategic position. In 1781, when Colonel Greene was surprised and killed near Points Bridge, New York, his black soldiers heroically defended him until they were cut to pieces, and the enemy reached him over the dead bodies of his faithful men. One white veteran described them as "brave, hardy troops. They helped to gain our liberty and independence."

The vast majority of black soldiers served in fighting groups made up primarily of white men. The integration of them was so complete that one Hessian officer, Schloezer, declared that "no regiment is to be seen in which there are not Negroes in abundance: and among them are able-bodied, strong, and brave fellows." Not only were they in the regiments of the New England and Middle Atlantic states, but they were also to be found fighting by the side of their white fellows in the Southern states. Hardly a military action between 1775 and 1781 was without some black participants. They were at Lexington, Concord, Ticonderoga, Bunker Hill, Long Island, White Plains, Trenton, Princeton, Bennington, Brandywine, Stillwater, Bemis Heights, Saratoga, Red Bank, Monmouth, Rhode Island, Savannah, Stony Point, Ft. Griswold, Eutaw Springs, and Yorktown.

As in any undertaking that involves large numbers of persons, most of the blacks who served in the War for Independence will forever remain anonymous. There were some, however, who by their outstanding service won recognition from their contemporaries and a conspicuous place in the history of the War for Independence. Two blacks, Prince Whipple and Oliver Cromwell, were with General Washington when he crossed the Delaware

Slaves Want Freedom, Too—1777

To the Honorable Counsel & House of [Representa]tives for the State of Massachusetts Bay in General Court assembled, January 13, 1777.

The petition of A Great Number of Blackes detained in a State of slavery in the Bowels of a free & Christian Country Humbly shuwith that your Petitioners apprehend that they have in Common with all other men a Natural and Unaliable Right to that freedom which the Grat Parent of the Unavers hath Bestowed equalley on all menkind and which they have Never forfuted by any Compact or agreement whatever—but thay wher Unjustly Dragged by the hand of cruel Power from their Derest friends and sum of them Even torn from the Embraces of their tender Parents—from A popolous Pleasant and plentiful contry and in violation of Laws of Nature and off Nations and in defiance of all the tender feelings of humanity Brough hear Either to Be sold Like Beast of Burthen & Like them Condemnd to Slavery for Life—Among A People Profesing the mild Religion of Jesus A people Not Insensible of the Secrets of Rational Being Nor without spirit to Resent the unjust endeavours of others to Reduce them to a state of Bondage and Subjection your honouer Need not be informed that A Life of Slavery Like that of your Petioners Deprived of Every social privilege of Every thing Requiset to Render Life Tolable is far worse than Nonexistance.

Collections, Massachusetts Historical Society, 5th Series, III (Boston, 1877), pp. 436–437.

on Christmas Day 1776. Tack Sisson, by crashing a door open with his head, facilitated the capture of the British general Richard Prescott, at Newport, Rhode Island, July 9, 1777. In the same year, Lemuel Haynes, who was later to become a distinguished minister in white churches, joined in the expedition to Ticonderoga to stop the inroads of Burgoyne's northern army. The victory of Anthony Wayne at Stony Point in 1779 was made possible by the spying of a black soldier by the name of Pompey. At the siege of Savannah in 1779, more than 700 Haitian free blacks were with the French forces that helped save the day. Among the wounded soldiers was Christophe, who was later to play an important role in the liberation of Haiti.

There are many instances of blacks serving in the navy during the War for Independence. Having piloted vessels in coastal waters before the war, their services were finally accepted during the dark days of the war. They were able and ordinary seamen, pilots, boatswain's mates, and gunner's mates. They were among the crews of the coastal galleys that defended Georgia, North Carolina, South Carolina, and Virginia. Luther P. Jackson has called attention to the service of Virginia blacks in the navy of the Revolution. He points out that black sailors fought on the *Patriot, Liberty, Tempest, Dragon, Diligence,* and many other vessels and indicates that some were enlisted for as many as ten or eleven years. In Connecticut and Massachusetts, blacks served in the navy, such as the three black seamen who were on Capt. David Porter's *Aurora* and the four who were on the crew of the privateer *General Putnam*. When he was but fourteen years old, James Forten was a powder boy on Stephen Decatur's *Royal Louis* and participated in the victory over several English vessels. Later, when he was captured and offered a home in England, he refused on the grounds that he felt that he should suffer the prisoner's lot in the cause of independence and to do less would be to betray his country.

Black patriots saw clearly the implications for their own future in their fight against England. They wanted human freedom as well as political independence. Even before Abigail Adams pointed to the inconsistency of fighting for independence while adhering to slavery, blacks spoke out. As early as 1766 they were seeking their freedom in the courts and legislatures. In January 1773 a group of "many slaves" asked the general court of Massachusetts to liberate them "from a State of Slavery." In 1774 a group of blacks expressed their astonishment that the colonists could seek independence from Britain yet give no consideration to the slaves' pleas for freedom. Blacks made literally scores of such representations and, in so doing, contributed significantly to broadening the ideology of the struggle to include at least some human freedom as well as political independence. The fact remained, as Edmund Morgan has observed, that to a large degree "Americans bought their independence with slave labor." It was yet to be seen if human freedom in general was as dear to them as political independence.

■ The Movement to Manumit Slaves

By the end of the War for Independence the ideology of the struggle that had been so clearly defined and so loudly proclaimed at the outset had been dimmed and muffled by the grim and practical realities of the war. Only the perspective of a brief period was needed to realize that the aims of the leaders were more political than social. And yet, some forces had been set in motion that operated to effect a change in the status of blacks. It is no mere coincidence that when the Battle of Lexington was fought the first antislavery society was just beginning to formulate its plans for action. This and similar organizations reflect the social implications of the Revolutionary philosophy. So powerfully did the philosophy act upon the minds of the people that almost every state enlisting slaves to serve in the army either freed them at the outset or promised manumission at the end of service. The records of several states in the 1780s abound in deeds of manumission of black soldiers and their families. While the number is undeterminable, it is not difficult to conclude that hundreds, if not thousands, of slaves secured their freedom at the end of the war.

The freedom that some black soldiers won for themselves did not go uncontested at the end of the war. Some masters sought to repossess slaves who had fought for freedom from Britain, and General Washington found it necessary to authorize several courts of inquiry to establish the validity of such claims. Finally, some states resorted to the enactment of laws such as the one that Virginia passed in 1783 granting freedom to all slaves "who served in the late war." A clear distinction was made, however, between those slaves who served in the army of the American states and those who merely ran away or who escaped to the British lines. Even General Washington expressed alarm at the news that blacks were embarking with the British fleet at various American ports, and he asked a friend in New York to help him retrieve some of his own runaways whom he suspected of being in that vicinity.

Other evidences, besides the manumission of soldier-slaves, that the Revolutionary philosophy was taking effect are seen in the activities of individuals immediately after the war. While no one as prominent as Thomas Jefferson took up the cudgel against slavery, numerous individuals of considerable stature spoke out against the institution. Samuel Hopkins of Rhode Island, Ezra Stiles of Connecticut, and Jeremy Belknap of Massachusetts were outstanding in the group of theologians who expressed antislavery views. In Virginia, St. George Tucker's *Dissertation on Slavery* was studied by the author's students at William and Mary and by Virginia slave owners as well. Other antislavery educators were Jedidiah Morse, the father of American geography, and William Rogers of the College of Philadelphia. Benjamin Franklin and Benjamin Rush continued to speak out against slavery, while the legal profession had outstanding spokesmen in Zepheniah Swift, Noah Webster, and Theodore Dwight.

Manumission and antislavery societies became more widespread after the war. The Quakers, who had organized the first society in 1775, were now joined by many other groups in this and other organizations. In 1785 the New York Society for Promoting the Manumission of Slaves was organized with John Jay as president. In Delaware a similar society was set up in 1788, and by 1792 there were antislavery societies in every state from Massachusetts to Virginia. Some sought to prevent the slave trade, while others were concerned with the deportation of blacks from the state. Most of them envisioned a scheme, however remote, of complete abolition of slavery. Local societies collected information on slavery and published reports on the progress of emancipation. Others published orations and addresses designed to arouse public sentiment against slavery.

The legislation against the slave trade, which began as a measure to combat England's commercial domination before the war, continued after hostilities were over. In 1783 Maryland prohibited the traffic in blacks. In 1786 North Carolina increased substantially the duty on every black imported. A duty of £15, for example, was levied on a black between twelve and thirty years of age imported directly from Africa. This law was repealed in 1790. In 1787 South Carolina prohibited the importation of slaves for several years, an act which was renewed from time to time until 1803, when it was repealed on the grounds that it was unenforceable.

Even before the surrender at Yorktown, the state of Pennsylvania in 1780 had made provisions for the gradual abolition of slavery. The law provided that no black or "Negro" born after that date should be held in bondage after he or she became twenty-eight year old and up to that time was to be treated as an indentured servant or an apprentice. In recalling the struggle against England, Pennsylvanians said that they felt they were called upon to manifest the sincerity of their professions of freedom, and to give substantial proof of gratitude, by extending a portion of their freedom to others, "who, though of a different color, are the work of the same Almighty hand." By 1783 the courts of Massachusetts had abolished slavery by asserting that the constitution of 1780 discountenanced the institution by saying that "all men are born free and equal." In 1784 Connecticut and Rhode Island passed acts that abolished slavery gradually. Manumission acts were passed in New York in 1785 and in New Jersey in 1786, though effective legislation was not achieved in those states until 1799 and 1804, respectively. While the Northern states were thus eradicating the institution, some of the Southern states, such as Virginia and North Carolina, were enacting legislation that facilitated the efforts of slave owners to manumit their human chattel. Perhaps the high-water mark of the postwar anti-slavery movement was reached in 1787 when the Congress added to the Northwest Ordinance the provision that neither slavery nor involuntary servitude should exist in the territory covered by it.

■ The Conservative Reaction

Despite the efforts of antislavery leaders to deal a death blow to slavery after the War for Independence, they were unable to do so. Resistance to abolitionist schemes hardened in the Southern states, where so much capital was invested in slaves and where a new economic importance was already being attached to the institution. In the 1780s, moreover, there was the sobering fear that the social program that grew out of the struggle against Britain would get out of hand and uproot the very foundations of social and economic life in America. As the plain people began to demand liberal and democratic land laws, moratoriums on their debts, and greater guarantees of human rights, they challenged the authority by which the select few ruled the American state. To this "horrid vision of disorder" which the leaders conjured up must be added the loud insistence of antislavery leaders for the destruction of property in human beings and the extension of liberty to all. Where would all this lead? The rebellion of Daniel Shays in Massachusetts suggested the answer: real revolution, pure and simple. The country's leaders had already planned their counterattack in the calling of a convention to meet in Philadelphia in 1787 to stabilize and strengthen the government and to stem the tide of social revolution.

It was only natural that slavery became an important consideration in the Constitutional Convention. In the heated debates over representation in the Congress, the question arose as to how slaves should be counted. Most of the Northern delegates could regard slaves in no light except as property and thus not deserving any representation. Georgia and South Carolina delegates were loud in their demands that blacks be counted equally with whites. Gouverneur Morris declared that the people of Pennsylvania would revolt on being placed on an equal footing with slaves, while Rufus King of Massachusetts flayed slavery in a fiery speech and condemned any proposal that would recognize it in the Constitution. The three-fifths compromise finally written into the Constitution was perhaps satisfactory to no one, but it demonstrates clearly the strength of the proslavery interests at the convention. It was inserted in Article I, Section 2, and reads as follows:

> Representatives and direct Taxes shall be apportioned among the several States which may be included within this Union, according to their respective Numbers, which shall be determined by adding to the whole Number of free Persons, including those bound to Service for a Term of Years, and excluding Indians not taxed, three fifths of all other persons.

It has been seen that several states had already acted to prohibit the slave trade. In 1787 the opponents of the traffic in human beings fervently hoped that the Constitutional Convention would act to stop this evil. To this end the Pennsylvania Abolition Society drafted a memorial imploring the convention to make the slave trade part of its deliberations and gave it to Benjamin Franklin to present. When it became obvious that the convention would consider the problem in any case, he decided not to present the memorial lest the suspicions of Southern members be aroused, thereby doing more harm than good. When the matter came before the convention, an argument ensued that was as fiery as any witnessed by the delegates. Young Charles Pinckney said that South Carolina could never accept a constitution that would prohibit the slave trade. Significantly, he added, "If the States be all left at liberty on this subject, South Carolina may perhaps by degrees do of herself what is wished, as Virginia and Maryland have already done." His cousin, Gen. C. C. Pinckney, was more severe on Virginia and Maryland. He asserted that these states would gain by stopping importations. Virginia's slaves would rise in value, and it would be "unequal to require South Carolina and Georgia to Confederate on such unequal terms." The fear of rupture at this critical moment led the states of the North and Upper South to compromise with the states of the lower South and to extend the slave trade for twenty years. The provision finally adopted in Article I, Section 9, reads:

> The Migration or Importation of such Persons as any of the States now existing shall think proper to admit, shall not be prohibited by the Congress prior to the Year one thousand eight hundred and eight, but a Tax or duty may be imposed on such Importation, not exceeding ten dollars for each Person.

It is significant that there was almost no opposition to the proposal that states give up fugitive slaves to their owners. The public obligation to return fugitive slaves, which had already been provided for in several Indian treaties between 1781 and 1786, was established in the Northwest Territory in 1787 in connection with the prohibition of slavery in that region. When the provision came before the convention for consideration, it was late, August 28, and the delegates were already impatient to return to their homes. Too, the slave owners had already won such sweeping constitutional recognition of slavery that the question of fugitive slaves was an anticlimax to the great debates. When Roger Sherman of Connecticut asserted that he saw "no more propriety in the public seizing and surrendering a slave or servant, than a horse," he found no support even among his New England colleagues. Without serious challenge, therefore, the provision was inserted in Article IV, Section 2:

> No Person held to Service or Labour in one State, under the Laws thereof, escaping into another, shall, in Consequence of any Law or Regulation therein, be discharged from such Service or Labour, but shall be delivered up on Claim of the Party to whom such Service or Labour may be due.

When the delegates to the Constitutional Convention returned to their homes in September 1787, they could look back on three months of political and economic wire pulling that was to check effectively the trend toward social upheaval. Perhaps in no area had there been greater success than in the matter of checking the antislavery movement. Quakers and other groups could view the new document as devoid of guarantees of human liberties, and zealous reformers could regard the Constitution as a victory for reaction; but their objections were silenced by the effective organization for ratification that was in operation even before the convention had adjourned. The fathers of the Constitution were dedicated to the proposition that "government should rest upon the dominion of property." For Southerners this meant slaves, just as surely as it meant commerce and industry for Northerners. In the protection of this property the Constitution had given recognition to the institution of human slavery, and it was to take seventy-five years to undo that which was accomplished in Philadelphia in 1787.

The adoption of the federal Constitution marks the end of an era not only in the political history of the United States but in the history of African Americans as well. With British domination at an end and stable government established, Americans could no longer lay the onus for slavery at the door of the parent country. They proudly accepted the challenge and responsibility of their new political freedom by establishing the machinery and safeguards that ensured the continued enslavement of blacks. Ironically enough, America's freedom was the means of giving slavery itself a longer life than it was to have in the British Empire. New factors on the horizon were about to usher in a new day for slavery as the old day passed away.

■

CHAPTER 6

Blacks in the New Republic

■ The Black Population in 1790

In the year following the inauguration of George Washington as president of the United States, foreign observers could view with a critical eye the low level of culture and the persistence of slavery in the new republic, but none could deny the happy prospect for permanence that stemmed from a continuously increasing population. There were nearly 4 million inhabitants in the United States, and the most casual observer could see signs of growth everywhere. Among these signs was the black population, which in 1790 numbered slightly more than 750,000. Of course, the vast majority, almost 89 percent, lived in the South Atlantic states where the plantation system was making the greatest demands for black labor. In 1790 Virginia had already taken the lead in black population, which it was to hold during the entire slave period. Virginia's 304,000 blacks were almost three times the number in South Carolina, Virginia's nearest rival. Most of the states in that region, however, presented a picture of an abundant black population. Only two, Georgia and Delaware, which no longer deserved to be classified with Pennsylvania, had less than 100,000 black residents. There were 641,691 slaves in the South Atlantic states and 32,048 free blacks.

Considering their location and economic interests, the Middle Atlantic states of New York, New Jersey, and Pennsylvania had substantial black

TABLE 2
Black Population Census of 1790

STATE	SLAVES	FREE
Maine		536
New Hampshire	157	630
Vermont		269
Massachusetts		5,369
Rhode Island	958	3,484
Connecticut	2,648	2,771
New York	21,193	4,682
New Jersey	11,423	2,762
Pennsylvania	3,707	6,531
Delaware	8,887	3,899
Maryland	103,036	8,043
Virginia	292,627	12,866
North Carolina	100,783	5,041
South Carolina	107,094	1,801
Georgia	29,264	398
Kentucky	12,430	114
Tennessee	3,417	361
Total	697,624	59,557

Source: Negro Population in the United States 1790–1915. *Arno Press and The New York Times (New York 1968), p. 57.*

populations. Of the 50,000 blacks in the region, approximately one-half lived in New York, while New Jersey followed with 14,000, and Pennsylvania with slightly more than 10,000. The decline of slavery in the region is revealed by the fact that by 1790 there were approximately 14,000 free blacks, comprising about 28 percent of the total black population. This figure is a silent tribute to the unobtrusive but effective work of the antislavery groups that made capital out of the Revolutionary philosophy that was in vogue for a few years following the War for Independence.

By 1790 slavery in New England was dying rapidly. The 3,700 slaves in the region were a mere one-fourth of the total black population of more than 13,000. Indeed, some states, Vermont and Massachusetts, reported no slaves at all. Connecticut, though, was holding on tenaciously to a slave population, and the 2,600 slaves in the state constituted the bulk of the New England slave population. The time was not distant, however, when all the New England states would report that only free blacks lived within their borders.

Although neither Kentucky nor Tennessee had become states in 1790, they were being rapidly settled and were soon to qualify for statehood. Among the inhabitants who were being counted in the quest for the new status were blacks who had been taken there by the Virginians and Carolinians who made their way across the mountains. In 1790 there were more than 12,000 slaves in Kentucky, while Tennessee had 3,400. Together these two prospective states could count only 475 free blacks. The migration of slaves to these new regions set the pattern that became so well established in the nineteenth century.

The black population in 1790 was essentially rural. Some cities and towns, however, could point to a substantial black population. Among these was New York City, which was already known for its heterogeneous population. There were 3,252 blacks, of whom 2,184 were slaves and 1,078 were free. Philadelphia had 1,630 blacks, but only 210 of them were slaves. At the other extreme was Baltimore with 1,578 blacks, of whom only 323 were free. Only one American city could boast that it had no slaves: all of Boston's 761 blacks were free.

There was hardly any indication that the black population would decline in the years following the first decennial census. Indeed, forces were already in operation to fasten slavery on the country with greater permanency and to increase, at least temporarily, slave importations into the country. Ira Berlin has shown that, by the end of the eighteenth century, there were three distinct African-American subcultures—in the North, in the Chesapeake area, and in the deep South—each with its own diverse patterns of black adjustment to, and differentiation from, the dominant white social order. In 1790 the center of black population was twenty miles west-southwest of Petersburg, Dinwiddie County, Virginia. Growth and migration were to cause it to shift with every passing decade. And this phenomenon alone was enough to indicate that the black population was among the most thriving of any of the ethnic groups in America.

■ Slavery and the Industrial Revolution

In the years immediately following the treaty of independence of 1783, the areas where slaves were concentrated experienced a severe depression. Tobacco plantations were plagued by two evils: soil exhaustion and a glutted market. Rice and indigo production brought little profit to the planters of these commodities. The price of slaves was declining, and there was reason to believe that the institution would deteriorate. The planters, however, would not have it so, and they did everything they could to sustain their losses until there was a better day. They did not have long to wait. Already the system of producing cotton textiles was undergoing revolutionary changes in England, and with the invention of spinning and weaving machinery, the manufacturing process was so cheapened that the demand for cotton goods was greatly stimulated. In turn, the demand for cotton fiber to feed the newly developed machinery seemed insatiable, this at a time when the planters of the United States were in desperate need for something that would inject new life into the sluggish plantation system.

For many years the manufacturers of the world had regarded cotton as among the most satisfactory textile materials. Technological difficulties, however, had stood in the way of its being more extensively produced. Now that it could be spun and woven easily, the twofold problem of discovering a variety that could be more easily separated from the seed and of inventing a machine to do this work was all that was left to be solved before cotton could become the world's greatest textile. As early as 1786 planters on the Georgia-Carolina coast began to experiment with growing a long, silky sea-island fiber that was quite superior to the green-seed, short-staple variety that had been cultivated on a small scale for many years. They found it highly satisfactory, and even without machinery to separate the seed from the fiber a greater quantity could be produced because of the ease with which the operation was effected. South Carolinians and Georgians began to plant larger cotton crops and to use slaves not only to cultivate the crops but to separate the fiber from the seeds as well. The areas in which sea-island cotton would grow were limited, however, and until some method was developed by which short-staple cotton, which could flourish in a variety of places, could be seeded there could be no wholesale expansion of cotton culture throughout the South.

Southern planters confidently hoped that in the near future an invention would relieve them of their anxiety. In 1792 Georgia went so far as to appoint a commission to look into the possibility of inventing a cotton gin. In the following year a young Yankee schoolteacher, Eli Whitney, visited the South in search of a position. The talk concerning the difficulties of seeding cotton interested him greatly. He soon grasped the problem and set out to find a solution to it. Within a few days he had made a model which gave promise of being satisfactory. It was only a matter of weeks before the major mechanical difficulties had been mastered, and Whitney and his host, Phineas Miller, began to make plans for the commercial manufacture of cotton gins. Whitney vainly attempted to establish a monopoly over the manufacture of cotton gins, but his failure simply meant that a larger number of these machines would be available at lower prices.

Within a few years after the invention of the cotton gin, the South was on its way to making the economic transition that the new development induced. Since the cultivation of cotton required no large capital, many farmers, even the poorer ones, began to shift from the cultivation of rice, indigo, or tobacco to cotton. Production increased, new lands were cleared, and black labor could now be employed exclusively in the cultivation of the crop instead of in the tedious task of seeding cotton. Exports mounted rapidly, but for many years England and the other manufacturing countries continued to receive, at high prices, all the cotton that the United States could furnish. In the beginning, it seemed that all the Southern farmers would prosper under the stimulation of cotton cultivation. As the years passed, however, and as the more economically resourceful planters began to purchase additional land and slaves, those without capital found themselves at a disadvantage and were forced to yield to those planters who were in a position to carry out large-scale cultivation.

The invention of the cotton gin and the extension of the area of cotton cultivation ushered in a period of economic change in the South that in degree compared favorably with any changes in the history of agriculture. One of the most important manifestations of this change was the increased demand for black slaves. Not only was there now a great opportunity to use the slaves that many had kept against their better judgment, but there was an opportunity to use even more if they could be secured. Thus, in the closing years of the eighteenth century and the opening years of the nineteenth century, the importation of slaves into the United States continued to flourish. In 1803, for example, it was estimated that no less than 20,000 slaves were imported into Georgia and South Carolina. As though they were racing against time, the merchants of New England sought to supply the planters of the South with the precious human cargo, the importation of which was to be outlawed within a few years.

■ Trouble in the Caribbean

While the United States was making an effort to stabilize its political life and the South was desperately attempting to salvage its economic system, there were rumblings not far off that disturbed both the political and the economic equilibrium of the United States. When the French Revolution broke out in 1789, blacks in the French possessions looked toward the prospect of securing for themselves the same elements of freedom for which Frenchmen at home were fighting. On the island of St. Domingue, even the people on the eastern, or Spanish, end of the island sought the equality that the French Revolution promised. When the whites on the island opposed the extension of these rights to blacks, there occurred an uprising in August 1791 which in magnitude and intensity demonstrated the blacks' determination to secure freedom and equality. Blacks so ruthlessly killed their white masters that the National Assembly in France felt compelled to withdraw the rights that it had extended and to send troops to quell the disturbance. The blacks were not awed by the appearance of soldiers from France, and there ensued a bitter struggle that lasted for more than two years. No semblance of order was restored until the French Republic issued a decree granting freedom to all slaves who supported its cause.

The intrepid leader of the black forces in Haiti was Toussaint L'Ouverture. An able and experienced soldier, he cast his lot with the forces of the Republic in 1794. For six years he was the dominant figure on the island, serving in successively higher military positions. By 1800 he was at the height of his power. Napoleon, however, regarded Toussaint as an obstacle to his plan to create a great French empire in the New World. With Louisiana in his hands and with St. Domingue as a key point in the Caribbean area, he could dominate the entire Western Hemisphere, or a substantial portion of it. He therefore dispatched a large army of 25,000 men under General LeClerc to subdue the island. Although the French were successful, by a series of tricks, in capturing Toussaint and taking him to France, they were not successful in subduing the island. Yellow fever and the bitter determination of the followers of Toussaint to be free conspired to defeat the aims of Napoleon.

The effect of these events on the course of American history was extremely important. Of Toussaint, W. E. B. Du Bois said, "He rose to leadership through a bloody terror, which contrived a Negro 'problem' for the Western Hemisphere, intensified and defined the anti-slavery movement, became one of the causes, and probably the prime one, which led Napoleon to sell Louisiana for a song, and finally, through the interworking of all these effects, rendered more certain the final prohibition of the slave-trade by the United States in 1807." Americans were terrified at the news of what was happening in Haiti. For more than a decade beginning in 1791 many Americans were more concerned with events in Haiti than with the life-and-death struggle that was going on between France and England. Despite the fact that Southern states wanted more slaves, they were afraid to import them. In 1792 South Carolina found it inexpedient to allow blacks "from Africa, the West India Islands, or other places beyond the sea" to enter for two years, but many entered illegally. In 1794 North Carolina passed an act "to prevent future importation and bringing of slaves." Virginia and Maryland strengthened their nonimportation laws. Though the Middle Atlantic and New England states did not seem as disturbed over Haiti as their Southern neighbors, there were attempts by Quakers and other humanitarian groups to take advantage of the situation and to strengthen various aspects of antislavery legislation. It would not be too much to say that the revolution in the West Indies did as much as anything else to discourage the importation of slaves into the United States.

As early as 1790 several organizations, including the Yearly Meeting of Friends in New York and the Pennsylvania Abolition Society, presented memorials to Congress requesting immediate legislation against the slave trade. The violent opposition of Southern representatives prevented decisive action. The antislavery organizations continued their activities during the succeeding years. The news from the Caribbean had the effect of hastening action by Congress. In 1794 a bill seeking to prevent slave trade to foreign ports and to prevent the fitting out of foreign vessels for the slave trade in the United States ports was passed by the Senate and the House. This was no victory for the antislavery forces in the United States. Instead, it merely represented the fear of many citizens that the revolution of the Haitian blacks might spread to the United States.

Closely allied with the slave trade was the question of fugitive slaves.

Blacks from the Caribbean had escaped to the United States during the conflict in Haiti and were moving rather freely from place to place. Slaves were escaping from plantations during this troubled period as they had always done. If these trends continued, it was within the realm of possibility that disaffected blacks might attempt some desperate measures to overthrow the institution of slavery. It was deemed wise, therefore, to institute legislation to implement the constitutional provision regarding fugitive slaves. In 1793 the first fugitive slave law was enacted. It empowered the master of an interstate fugitive to seize the slave wherever found, take him or her before any federal or state magistrate in the vicinity, and obtain a certificate warranting the slave's removal to the state from which he or she had fled. This law allowed no trial by jury and required conviction on only the oral testimony of the claimant or on an affidavit certified by a magistrate of the state from which the slave was alleged to have fled. Various groups protested the passage of the act, but to no avail. Although it proved to be exceedingly difficult to enforce, the measure remained part of the federal law and thus, to many, a manifestation of national approval of the institution of slavery.

The purchase of Louisiana was connected with both the trouble in the Caribbean and the institution of slavery in the United States. Louisiana had already become a center of sugarcane cultivation, whether it was in the hands of the French or the Spanish. Both these European groups lived in New Orleans and had spread up the river banks to cultivate the rich lands of the Mississippi delta. Black slaves were introduced into these areas by Creole planters, and by the late eighteenth century some were being brought into Louisiana from the Caribbean. The acquisition of Louisiana by France in 1800 greatly disturbed the United States, since in 1795 the new republic had negotiated a satisfactory arrangement with Spain for navigation of the Mississippi River. Representatives of the United States attempted to secure from France the promise that Western farmers could continue to navigate the river. Instead, the French offered them the whole of Louisiana, which the United States purchased in 1803. Perhaps several reasons caused Napoleon to decide to sell Louisiana. One important reason was his failure to hold Haiti and the consequent dark prospects that existed for his erecting a great empire in the New World with Louisiana and Haiti as important pivotal points. Thus it was the blacks of Haiti who were, to a large degree, responsible for the acquisition of Louisiana by the United States. The purchase of this new land made possible the extension of cotton and sugar culture by planters of the Southern United States and the greater entrenchment of slavery in the region.

■ The Closing of the Slave Trade

Despite the state laws prohibiting it, the African slave trade to the United States continued to flourish during the first decade of the national government. The slave interests were in a curious dilemma. On the one hand they feared the wholesale importation of raw and unruly blacks from Africa or the revolutionary and resourceful blacks from the Caribbean, while on the other hand they were in desperate need of a larger number of slaves to cultivate the cotton that was now in such great demand. The practicality, if not the venality, of merchants and planters compelled them to decide in favor of continued importation, hoping that the safeguards erected by the national and state governments would stem any tide of insurrection that might develop in the United States. In defiance of local laws, New England traders carried on an extensive traffic, while Southern planters were willing to receive slaves from whatever source possible.

Early in the nineteenth century antislavery groups resumed their efforts to secure stringent federal legislation against the slave trade. In January 1800, the free blacks of Philadelphia led the way by requesting Congress to revise the laws on the slave trade and on fugitives. When South Carolina reopened her ports to the trade in 1803, the antislavery forces began to press for action. Resolutions were introduced in the following Congress condemning the slave trade, but no conclusive steps were taken. In 1804 an attempt was made to prevent the importation of slaves into Louisiana, but the resolution presenting this matter received scant attention.

The question of the slave trade was brought dramatically before the country in December 1805, when Senator Stephen R. Bradley of Vermont introduced a bill to prohibit the slave trade after January 1, 1808. After a second reading, consideration of the measure was postponed. In February 1806, Representative Barnabas Bidwell of Massachusetts introduced a similar measure, but nothing was done about it. In his message to Congress on December 2, 1806, President Jefferson called the attention of Congress to the approaching date on which the slave trade could be prohibited. He suggested that measures be taken to "prevent expeditions to Africa that could not be completed before January 1, 1808." On March 2, 1807, the law prohibiting the African slave trade was passed. Persons convicted of violating the act were to be fined and imprisoned. The fines ranged from $800 for knowingly buying illegally imported blacks to $20,000 for equipping a slaver. The disposition of the imported blacks was left to the legislatures of the states. Finally, coastwise trade of slaves was prohibited if it was carried on in vessels of less than forty tons. Every provision of the bill was vehemently debated by representatives of slaveholding and non-slaveholding interests.

Antislavery interests both in England and the United States rejoiced in the year 1807. England had outlawed the slave trade, and in the same year the United States had followed. There was little real reason for rejoicing in the United States, however, for from the beginning, the law went unenforced. Responsibility for the enforcement of the act fell first to the secretary of the treasury, then to the secretary of the navy. At times, even the Department of State was given some duties in connection with its enforcement. In the midst of such shifting of responsibility it is not surprising to find the law poorly enforced. Some Southern states reluctantly passed supplementary acts disposing of illegally imported Africans, while others enacted no such legislation at all. Violations of the law were numerous. New England shipmasters, Middle Atlantic merchants, and Southern planters all disregarded the federal and state legislation when they found it expedient to do so. Those who had an unselfish interest in the closing of the slave trade could say, within a few years after 1808, that hardly anything had happened to the nefarious traffic except that it had been driven underground. The first underground railroad was not that established by abolitionists to transport slaves to freedom but the one used by merchants and others to introduce more blacks into slavery.

■ The Search for Independence

The Industrial Revolution in England, the invention of the cotton gin, the extension of slavery into the new territories, and the persistence of the slave trade into the nineteenth century all had the effect of establishing slavery in the United States on a more permanent basis than ever before. As the nineteenth century opened, there seemed little prospect that slavery would ever cease to exist in the United States. The atmosphere in which blacks lived, whether North or South, was charged with the permanent character of slavery in the United States. Even in the New England states, where laws were putting an end to the institution, blacks could not express much optimism or any great faith in the future, for it was well known that New England merchants were still taking slaves into the South and there was still no great moral indignation against the institution except in isolated areas and groups. Beginning with the Revolutionary period blacks had to seek ways not only of participating in the struggle to secure independence for their country but also to secure for themselves a measure of independence in an atmospehere laden with subordination, subservience, and disrespect for their individuality. This most difficult task involved the effort to forge separate institutions. This phase of black life and history constituted a significant step in the history of adjustment and acculturation in America.

One of the first blacks to make the search for intellectual and spiritual independence was Jupiter Hammon, a slave on Long Island. Growing into manhood during the years when the Wesleyan revival was strong both in England and America, Hammon was greatly influenced by the writings of Charles Wesley and William Cowper. In 1761 he published "An Evening Thought. Salvation by Christ, with Penitential Cries." In 1778 he published a twenty-one stanza poem "To Miss Phillis Wheatley." Other poems and prose pieces appeared in the next two decades. In "An Address to the Negroes of the State of New York," published in 1787, Hammon showed that he felt it his personal duty to bear slavery patiently, but at the same

PHILLIS WHEATLEY. Born in Africa about 1753 and brought to America as a young girl, Wheatley received wide recognition during her lifetime for her essays and poetry, as well as her mastery of Western manners and morals. In 1773 her owners manumitted her and she visited England, where her first book was published. *(The Schomburg Center For Research In Black Culture, The New York Public Library.)*

time he said that it was an evil system and that young blacks should be manumitted. He lived to see his master write a will ordering that certain of his slaves be set free at the age of twenty-eight, and in 1799, the year before his death, Hammon could rejoice that the state of New York had enacted legislation looking to the gradual emancipation of all slaves within the state.

BENJAMIN BANNEKER AND HIS VIRGINIA ALMANACK FOR 1794. Banneker, perhaps the most accomplished black in the early national period, published almanacs, was an astronomer, and served as a member of the commission to define the boundary line and lay out the streets of the District of Columbia. *(The Schomburg Center For Research In Black Culture, The New York Public Library.)*

Perhaps the best-known black of the period was Phillis Wheatley, born in Africa about 1753 and brought to America when still a little girl. In Boston she became the personal maid of Susannah Wheatley and apparently received kindly treatment and an opportunity to cultivate her mind. She rapidly learned to read the Bible and developed an appreciation for history, astronomy, geography, and the Latin classics. In 1770 her first poem, "On the Death of the Reverend George Whitefield," appeared. In 1773 she was manumitted and sent to England for her health. She met the Countess of Huntingdon, to whom one of her first poems was addressed, and rapidly gained popularity. Before leaving England, arrangements were made to have her first book published, *Poems on Various Subjects, Religious and Moral.* Upon her return she composed "His Excellency General Washington," "Liberty and Peace," and numerous other poems before her death in 1784. Phillis Wheatley attempted to write lyric poetry. She was not concerned with the problems of blacks or the country. Even the poem to General Washington is largely impersonal, while her "Liberty and Peace" is only remotely connected with the struggle against England. Her writings are perhaps a good example of the search for independence through the method of escape, which was to become a favorite device of blacks of a later century.

While Gustavus Vassa lived as much in England, Montserrat, and Jamaica as in the United States, the narrative of his life was so frequently printed and read in America that he can be said to represent the growing independence of spirit that blacks were manifesting at the end of the eighteenth century. Vassa was born in Benin in 1745. At the age of eleven he was kidnapped and taken to America. After working on a Virginia plantation he became the servant of a British naval officer. Later, while in the service of a Philadelphia merchant, he saved the money with which he purchased his freedom. Then he went to England, where he made his home between his extensive journeys. He joined in the antislavery movement, and in 1790 he presented to Parliament a petition for suppression of the slave trade. In 1789 he published, in two volumes, *The Interesting Narrative of the Life of Oloudah Equiano, or Gustavus Vassa.* It was immediately successful, and within five years eight editions had been issued. There can be no doubt about Vassa's resentment of slavery, for in his narrative he vigorously condemns Christians for their enslavement of blacks. Only one who had achieved a measure of personal independence could have condemned slavery in the following language:

> O, ye nominal Christians! might not an African ask you—Learned you this from your God, who says unto you, Do unto all men as you would men should do unto you? Is it not enough that we are torn from our country and friends, to toil for your luxury and lust of gain? Must every tender feeling be likewise sacrificed to your avarice? . . . Why are parents to lose their children, brothers their sisters, or husbands their wives? Surely, this is a new refinement in cruelty, which, while it has no advantage to atone for it, thus aggravates distress, and adds fresh horrors even to the wretchedness of slavery.

Perhaps the most accomplished black in the early national period was Benjamin Banneker. Born in 1731 in Maryland, of thrifty and industrious parents, Banneker attended a private school open to whites and blacks near Baltimore and developed a keen interest in science and mathematics. While still a young man he astounded his family and neighbors by constructing a clock from wooden materials. This display of mechanical genius attracted the attention of George Ellicott, a Quaker, who had moved into the neighborhood to establish a flour mill. Banneker frequently visited the Ellicott mills during their construction, and his general knowledge of the mathematical and engineering problems drew him and Ellicott closer together. Soon, Ellicott began to lend Banneker books on mathematics and astronomy. Within a few weeks Banneker had not only mastered the material in the books, but he had even discovered several errors in the calculations of the authors. By 1789 he had become so proficient in astronomy that he could predict a solar eclipse with considerable accuracy.

In 1791 Banneker began issuing his almanacs, a worthy undertaking that lasted until 1802. Among the prominent men attracted by this "black Poor Richard" was James McHenry, later the secretary of war in the cabinet of

Benjamin Banneker Writes to Thomas Jefferson—1791

Sir, I have long been convinced that if your love for yourselves, and for those inestimable laws, which preserved to you the rights of human nature, was founded on sincerity, you could not but be solicitous, that every individual, of whatever rank or distinction, might with you equally enjoy the blessings thereof; neither could you rest satisfied short of the most active effusion of your exertions, in order to the promotion from any state of degradation, to which the unjustifiable cruelty and barbarism of men have reduced them. . . .

Benjamin Banneker to Thomas Jefferson, August 19, 1791. Early American Imprints (Microprint), 1639–1800.

President John Adams. Through McHenry, Banneker was able to establish a number of important connections with officials of the national government. McHenry said that Banneker's work "was begun and finished without the least information or assistance from any person, or from any other books." He added that Banneker was "fresh proof that the powers of the mind are disconnected with the color of the skin, or, in other words, a striking contradiction to Mr. [David] Hume's doctrine, that the Negroes are naturally inferior to the whites, and unsusceptible of attainments in arts and sciences."

Banneker sent a manuscript copy of his first almanac to Thomas Jefferson, and in the accompanying letter he made a strong appeal for the exercise of a more liberal attitude toward blacks. He pointed to his own achievements as proof that the "train of absurd and false ideas and opinions which so generally prevails with respect to the Negro should now be eradicated." Jefferson warmly praised the almanac and sent it to Condorcet, the secretary of the Academy of Sciences in Paris, for, as he told Banneker, he considered it "a document to which your whole race had a right for its justifications against the doubts which have been entertained of them."

The most distinguished honor that Banneker received was his appointment to serve with the commission to define the boundary lines and lay out the streets of the District of Columbia. It was perhaps at the suggestion of his friend George Ellicott, himself a member of the commission, that Banneker's name was submitted to President Washington by Jefferson. When he arrived in the federal territory with Major L'Enfant and Ellicott, the Georgetown *Weekly Ledger* described him as "an Ethiopian whose abilities as surveyor and astronomer already prove that Mr. Jefferson's concluding that that race of men were void of mental endowment was without foundation." After his

PAUL CUFFEE AND HIS BRIG, "THE TRAVELLER." Cuffee, a successful businessman, derived his wealth from shipbuilding, a maritime trading fleet, real estate, and landholdings. Seeking to open new opportunities for freedom and economic mobility to his fellow blacks in the United States, he made visits to Africa and provided considerable financial support for African-American colonizationists. *(The Schomburg Center For Research In Black Culture, The New York Public Library.)*

work with the commission, he returned to his home in Maryland, resumed work on his almanacs, and continued his astronomical investigations.

The disastrous wars of 1793 greatly disturbed Banneker, and he devoted considerable attention to devising a means of putting an end to all wars. In his almanac in 1793 he carried a lengthy article by Benjamin Rush, who pointed out that one of the objections to the new government was that it did not have an office in the president's cabinet "for promoting and preserving perpetual peace in our country." Rush proposed the establishment of a secretary of peace, "who shall be perfectly free from all the present absurd and vulgar prejudices of Europe upon the subject of government." There can be no doubt that Banneker published the article by Rush because he subscribed so enthusiastically to the views of Rush on the subject of peace. He often opened the pages of his almanac to those who had constructive suggestions to make for the improvement of mankind. His life was a search for independence through his concern with problems that transcended race and even nation.

A distinguished contemporary of Banneker was James Derham, generally regarded as the first physician of African descent in the United States. Born into slavery in Philadelphia in 1762, Derham's master during his boyhood was a physician who taught him to read and write and to serve as his medical assistant. Later, during the War for Independence, Derham was the property of a British physician from whom he learned a great deal more about the practice of medicine. At the close of the war, he was purchased by a physician in New Orleans under whose tutelage he completed his medical training. He then purchased his freedom and set up his own practice, which soon was large and profitable. Fluent in French, Spanish, and English, Derham's reputation as an able physician spread to many groups. Benjamin Rush regarded Derham as an accomplished and learned practitioner from whom he himself learned much.

Among those who were searching for economic independence and group self-respect during the post-Revolutionary period, Paul Cuffe was one of the most outstanding. Very early in his life he developed an interest in commerce, and at sixteen years of age, in 1775, he secured employment on a whaling vessel. In the following year, during his second voyage, he was captured by the British and detained in New York for three months. During the war he and his brother refused to pay taxes in Massachusetts on the grounds that they were denied the franchise. Shortly thereafter Massachusetts passed a law allowing free blacks liable to taxation all the privileges belonging to other citizens. In 1780 Cuffe began to build ships of his own and to engage in commerce. As profits mounted, he expanded his seagoing activities and built larger vessels. By 1806 he owned one large ship, two brigs, and several smaller vessels, besides considerable property in houses and land. After joining the Society of Friends he became deeply interested, along with many other Quakers, in the welfare of blacks and wanted to engage in some activity that would improve their lot. In 1811 he went to Sierra Leone in his own vessel to investigate the possibilities of taking free blacks back to Africa. The war with England in the following year prevented his carrying out his plans. In 1815, however, he took thirty-eight blacks to Africa at an expense of $3000 or $4000 to himself. He learned, as colonizationists of a later day were to learn, that the expense of taking blacks back to Africa was so great as to be prohibitive.

The individual strivings of Jupiter Hammon, Phillis Wheatley, Gustavus Vassa, Benjamin Banneker, and Paul Cuffe not only represent the effort of blacks to secure a measure of independence for themselves in the post-Revolutionary period but are examples of the movement of Americans toward intellectual and economic self-sufficiency that was so characteristic of the period. Indeed, it can be said that these African Americans were, in a sense, leading the way since they overcame both the degraded position of their race and the psychological and intellectual disadvantage that all Americans of the period suffered. Their search for independence was matched only by the efforts of groups of blacks who found it necessary to forge separate institutions for their people during the same period.

In their efforts to elevate themselves intellectually in the post-Revolutionary period, blacks benefited from the general trend to establish and improve

Philadelphia Blacks Support Cuffe's African Colonization Plan—1815

Whereas Capt. Paul Cuffe, a citizen of the state of Massachusetts, made application to the Congress of the United States, at the session of 1814, for permission to make a voyage to Africa, for the purpose of aiding in the civilization and improvement of the inhabitants of that country and also to promote this desirable object, to take with him a few sober and industrious families, the situation of publick affairs at that period being unfavorable to the design, his proposition failed of success, but now under the blessing of Divine Providence, the causes of obstruction are removed, and he is again preparing to prosecute his voyage, accompanied by two families of this city, who have agreed to visit Africa and settle there.

The African Institution of Philadelphia, established for the promotion of this plan, feel it to be a duty to state, that it cordially unites with Paul Cuffe, in his disinterested and benevolent undertaking, and recommends the families of Anthony Survance and Samuel Wilson to the Friendly Society of Sierra Leone, as persons of good moral character, having satisfactorily settled their outward affairs as far as appears. The Institution likewise solicits on behalf of the adventurers, the friendly notice of all those among whom they may come.

Signed on behalf of the African Institution of Philadelphia

James Forten, Pres't
Russel Parrott, sec'ry

Poulson's American Daily Advertiser, September 20, 1815, from Lamont D. Thomas, *Rise to Be a People: A Biography of Paul Cuffe* (Urbana, Ill., 1986), p. 97.

schools in the new republic. There was also sentiment in favor of educating blacks, which the various abolition and manumission societies expressed before the turn of the century. The New England and Middle Atlantic states were especially active in this area. Whites in Boston were teaching black children both privately and in public institutions. In 1798 a separate school for black children was established by a white teacher in the home of Primus Hall, a prominent African American. Two years later blacks asked the city of Boston for a separate school, but the citizens refused. The blacks established the school anyway, and employed two Harvard men as instructors. The school continued to flourish for many years. Finally, in 1820, the city of Boston opened an elementary school for black children.

One of the best-known schools for blacks during the period was the New York African Free School established in 1787 by the Manumission Society.

When it began it had forty students, and the number never exceeded sixty in its first decade of existence. The opposition to the school was at first keen, but in 1800 constructive interest in the school was evident. New impetus for its continued growth came in 1810 when the state required masters to teach all slave children to read the Scriptures. By 1820 the institution was accommodating more than 500 black children.

New Jersey began educating black children in 1777. By 1801 there had been short-lived schools set up in Burlington, Salem, and Trenton. In addition Quakers and other religious and humanitarian groups were teaching black children privately. As early as 1774 the Quakers of Philadelphia established a school for black children, and after the war, thanks to funds provided by philanthropists like Anthony Benezet, the program was enlarged. In 1787 a school was built, and ten years later there were no less than seven schools for blacks in Philadelphia. This interest in the development of black education continued into the nineteenth century.

The interest in the South was not nearly as great. In 1801 a member of the Abolition Society of Wilmington, Delaware, conducted a school for black children on the first day of each week and taught reading, writing, and arithmetic. In 1816 a school and library were established with a black teacher. A few years later an academy for the instruction of young black women was established. In Maryland plans were made late in the eighteenth century for the opening of an academy, but the school never materialized. In Virginia, however, schools were set up in Richmond, Petersburg, and Norfolk. Quakers like Robert Pleasants offered land and money for the development of schools in Virginia and the Carolinas, but the insurrection of 1800 so frightened Southern planters that further expansion of the education program was discouraged. In the nineteenth century blacks in Southern states had to content themselves, for the most part, with clandestine schools and private teachers.

It was perhaps in the area of religion that African Americans showed the most determined efforts to secure real independence in the post-Revolutionary period. For a time, it seemed that the churches of the embryonic United States would insist upon complete integration of blacks into the religious life of the nation and would spearhead the attack against the institution of slavery. In 1784, for example, the Methodists declared that slavery was "contrary to the golden laws of God" and gave their members twelve months to liberate their slaves. This position proved to be somewhat premature, however, as Virginia and other Southern states forced a suspension of the resolution. In 1789 the Baptists said that slavery was a "violent depredation of the rights of nature and inconsistent with a republican government." Gradually, however, they were forced to recede from this position. After the war many churches accepted blacks, but whites were afraid that too liberal a policy would be disastrous to the effective control of slavery. Black ministers and church officials, it was thought, would exercise too much authority over their slave communicants and would perhaps cause trouble on the plantations.

RICHARD ALLEN. Allen was the leading figure in events that produced the independent black church movement and led to the establishment of the African Methodist Episcopal Church. He served as one of the early bishops of the A.M.E. Church. *(The Schomburg Center For Research In Black Culture, The New York Public Library.)*

American churches were having their own difficulties, and they found little time to devote any attention to the problems of blacks. The Toryism of a great number of the Anglican clergy caused many Americans to insist upon church disestablishment. Every denomination, except Roman Catholicism, moreover, was busy organizing a wing of its church that would be entirely separate from its European sponsor, and even the Catholics of the United States were to be set apart and controlled by a special Prefect Apostolic. These preoccupations tended to crowd the problem of blacks off the church scene and were in part the cause of the establishment of racially separate churches.

During the War for Independence, black Baptist churches began to spring up. George Liele, an industrious and resourceful black leader, founded a Baptist church in Savannah in 1779 before he finally left the country and settled in Jamaica. The work in Georgia was continued by his understudy, Andrew Bryan, who preached to whites as well as blacks. At the end of the war whites sought to close the church by whipping the members and imprisoning Bryan, but his benevolent master supported him, and finally Bryan's church became the nucleus for the organization of black Baptists in Georgia. Virginia blacks organized Baptist churches at Petersburg in 1776, at Richmond in 1780, and at Williamsburg in 1785. In some of these efforts they had the cooperation of white ministers.

It was in Northern communities that blacks went farthest in establishing independent churches. The best example of this trend was the work of Richard Allen and his followers in Philadelphia. This prospective leader demonstrated his industry and determination by saving enough money with which to purchase his freedom from his Delaware master in 1777, the year in which he also was converted. Within a few years he was preaching and winning the favor of Bishop Asbury. In 1786 he moved to Philadelphia, where he began to hold prayer meetings for his own people. His proposal to set up a separate place of worship for blacks was opposed by whites and some blacks. It was only after the officials of St. George's Church, where he frequently preached, proposed to segregate the large number of blacks who came to hear him that it became clear to him and others that blacks should have a separate church. The die was cast when, on one occasion, officials pulled Allen, Absalom Jones, and William White from their knees during prayer. Allen, with the help of Jones, immediately organized the independent Free African Society. Though Jones did not continue to cooperate with him and in 1801 became the first black Episcopal priest, Allen was able to organize and dedicate the Bethel Church in 1794. In 1799 Bishop Asbury ordained him deacon, and later he was elevated to the status of an elder. His church became known as the Bethel African Methodist Episcopal Church.

Branches of the AME church began to spring up in Baltimore, Wilmington, and various Pennsylvania and New Jersey towns, and a number of able persons, such as Daniel Coker, Nicholson Gilliard, and Morris Brown, came to Allen's aid. The church grew in strength until by 1816 it was possible to bind the various congregations together in a formal organization. The conference chose Daniel Coker as its bishop, but he resigned and Allen was elected to fill the position. It adopted a book of discipline similar to that of the Wesleyans and was thus launched on a career that was to make the AME church the leading organization among black Methodists. By 1820 there were 4,000 black Methodists in Philadelphia alone, while in the Baltimore district there were almost 2,000. The organization immediately spread as far west as Pittsburgh and as far south as Charleston. Only the strong opposition to black organizations, brought forth by the Vesey insurrection of 1822 (see Chapter 8), served to check the growth of black Methodism in the Southern states.

The white Methodists of New York had much the same attitude toward their black fellows as did their counterparts in Philadelphia. The result was a withdrawal of blacks from the John Street Methodist Episcopal Zion Church and the establishment of the African Methodist Episcopal Zion Church in 1796. Leading this movement were Peter Williams, James Varick, elected the first bishop in 1822, George Collins, and Christopher Rush. They could find no one in either the Episcopal or the Methodist church who would ordain and consecrate their elders, and finally they had to do it themselves. Overcoming schisms within and opposition without, the church was sufficiently stable by 1822 to elect a bishop and to set up a program of expansion.

The same trend toward independent organizations manifested itself among the Baptists. In 1809 thirteen black members of a white Baptist church in Philadelphia were dismissed to form a church of their own. Under the leadership of Reverend Burrows, a former slave, it became an important institution among the blacks of that community. The black Baptists of Boston, under the leadership of Reverend Thomas Paul, organized their church in 1809. At about the same time, he was assisting in organizing the church in New York that later came to be known as the Abyssinian Baptist Church. In each instance organization was brought about as a result of the separation of blacks from white congregations.

This establishment of separate houses of worship for African Americans, as inconsistent as it may seem with the teachings of the religion that they professed, gave blacks an unusual opportunity to develop leadership. Cut off from participation in the political life of the community and enjoying only very limited educational opportunities, their religious institutions served as a training ground for many types of activities. Although blacks frequently took the initiative in bringing about separation, it appears that such steps were not taken until it was obvious that they were not welcome in white churches. This keen sensitivity to mistreatment and the consequent organization of separate and independent religious organizations of their own were to be the reason for the church occupying such an important place in black life in the nineteenth and twentieth centuries.

Not only were blacks organizing separate churches, but they were also establishing other organizations of a benevolent and fraternal nature. On March 6, 1775, a British army lodge of Freemasons attached to a regiment under General Gage near Boston initiated fifteen blacks, including Prince Hall, a young man who had come to the mainland from Barbados ten years earlier. Hall was a minister and a recognized leader and spokesman of his people. He and his black brothers sought permission from white Americans to establish a chapter of black Masons, but their plea was rejected. In 1784 they applied to the Grand Lodge of England, and a warrant was immediately granted. The organization was not perfected, however, until 1787, with Hall as the master of African Lodge No. 459, located in Boston. In 1792 a black Grand Lodge was organized, with Hall as grand master. Five years later he issued a license to thirteen blacks, who had been initiated in England and Ireland, to set up a lodge in Philadelphia, and another was organized in Providence. Gradually, black Masonry spread over the land as three Grand Lodges came into existence by 1815. Although there was serious objection to black Masons in the beginning, white Masons were visiting the black lodges within a few years and cooperating in a number of ways.

In 1796 the African Society was organized by forty-four blacks in Boston. It declared its objectives to be benevolent and asserted that it would take "no one into the Society who shall commit any injustice or outrage against the laws of their country." It is said that this and similar organizations did much to bind blacks together and give them the experience of leadership and cooperation that was to mean much in a later day. They early sought integration into the political, social, and economic life of the nation. Having been generally rejected, there was no alternative except to forge out of their limited background and training institutions of their own. It is significant, moreover, that in the case of these institutions, just as in the case of individuals, considerable effort was made to share in the general development of the country and to contribute to its growth. The African American search for independence at the turn of the century was essentially, therefore, a struggle to achieve status in the evolving American civilization.

CHAPTER 7

Blacks and Manifest Destiny

■ Frontier Influences

Even before the turn of the century there were unmistakable evidences of profound economic and social changes taking place on the American scene. After 1800 the signs were much more discernible. Already there was talk about industrialization in the United States, and American businesspeople envied developments in England and Europe. Europeans were beginning to resume their migrations to the New World, once more hopeful about the bright future it held for them. The land beyond the areas of settlement was beckoning new settlers and began to exercise an influence on American life that seemed to increase with every passing year. This land beyond, the frontier land, rapidly became an influence in the evolution of the institution of slavery and, therefore, in the history of blacks in America.

In the early nineteenth century the United States could appraise its Western lands as one of its most valuable assets, especially after the purchase of Louisiana in 1803. Although it would be years before this area would be settled, Americans and Europeans were rapidly moving into the area beyond the mountains. Young, adventurous people from the seaboard states and Scotch-Irish and Germans from the Old World pushed back the frontier and became a part of the new states that were added to the American union.

Many of the settlers in the new West were affiliated with religions that emphasized equality and brotherly love, and those who were not ardent believers were without the means considered necessary to build a civilization based on slavery. Thus, a spirit of freedom was dominant on the frontier, but it was destined to be rendered unimportant and ineffective by the economic and social forces at work in the older states. Some residents of the seaboard states became attracted to the new lands because of their inability to adjust to the old environment. Others found it impossible to satisfy their economic needs in the areas already settled, where competition was keen and where the better opportunities were in the hands of a relative few. Still others, many of whom belonged to the upper class, sought new lands on which to grow the cotton for which there was now such a great demand. Frequently this last group had resources, occasionally slaves, with which to dominate the economic and social life of the frontier and to change the character of life there. The frontier, which had formerly been the haven to which social malcontents escaped and to which economic "ne'er do wells" retreated, now became the battleground on which lovers of freedom fought those who sought to entrench the institution of slavery.

It was not possible for the lovers of freedom to win their battle against the slaveholders. The Industrial Revolution and the invention of the cotton gin had already determined the course of events on the American frontier. The ideals of freedom succumbed before the powerful forces demanding slavery, and the attractive lands of the Southern Gulf states made inevitable the establishment of a cotton kingdom based on slavery. At first the frontier settlers fought the whole system of the East, but as the prospects of enrichment for all appeared, even they gradually gave their support to the institution.

Something may be said, moreover, of the manner in which frontier influences may have assisted in the westward march of slavery. The sentiment in favor of freedom and democracy in the West came as much from a new type of settler—German, Scotch-Irish, etc.—as it did from a transformation of the character of the people who moved from the seaboard to the back country. The greater portion of those who moved from the Atlantic coastal states were committed to the institution of slavery and, when possible, demonstrated this commitment by bringing slaves with them. If the spirit of freedom affected them at all, it was in the direction of confirming their right to control the lives of others and to engage in a ruthless exploitation of natural and human resources that was sanctioned by the frontier. The ideal of the West was not so much, as Frederick Jackson Turner, a historian of the frontier, has suggested, the right of everyone to rise to the full measure of his or her own stature. It was the right of everyone to take advantage of every opportunity that presented itself to gain the ends he or she desired and to ignore the basic ethical restraints that would have made some distinction between liberty and license. It was conceivable, therefore, that the frontier, with its attractive land and its spirit of ruthless freedom, may actually have encouraged the westward march of slavery in the early part of the nineteenth century.

■ Black Pioneers in the Westward March

All too frequently, students of history overlook the role of African Americans in the exploration and settlement of the American West. Whenever white Americans undertook the task of winning the West, there were black Americans, slave and free, who were involved in the process. Thus, when Meriwether Lewis and William Clark set out in 1803 under orders from President Jefferson, to explore the Louisiana Territory recently purchased from France, Clark took with him his trusted slave, York. A large and powerful man, York contributed to the success of the expedition by befriending and entertaining the Indians and providing sustenance for the explorers through his considerable skill in hunting and fishing. Upon completion of the expedition Clark emancipated York, and legend has it that York returned to the Western interior where he became a chief in an Indian tribe.

In the immensely profitable fur trade that followed in the wake of the Lewis and Clark expedition, there were black trappers who quite frequently were the most reliable liaison between white entrepreneurs and the Indians. While their reliability and integrity have often suffered at the hands of many recognized historians of the West, their presence and indeed their contributions can hardly be denied. In the 1820s, for example, Edward Rose served as a guide, hunter, and interpreter for the Missouri Fur Company. Despite the fact that Washington Irving was among those who spoke of his bad character and reputation, a contemporary, Col. Henry Leavenworth, wrote in 1823 that Rose had resided among the Indians for several years, "knew their language, and they were much attached to him." Leavenworth and, more recently, Kenneth W. Porter, have spoken of his invaluable services in the fur-trading activities in the West.

In the Minnesota Territory several blacks became prominent as trappers and traders. Among them was Pierre Bonga, a trusted slave of a Canadian fur trapper for the North West Company. Bonga was a skillful interpreter and did much of the negotiating with the Chippewas for his company. His son, George, became even more proficient, having learned English, French, Chippewa, and several other Indian languages. As an assistant and interpreter for Governor Lewis Cass of the Michigan Territory, George Bonga negotiated treaties with the Indians even while working as a voyageur for the American Fur Company. In time he became a free man and a "prominent trader of wealth and consequence." According to William L. Katz, Bonga Township in Cass County, Michigan, is named for his family.

Easily the most intrepid and remarkable of the black explorers of the American West was James P. Beckwourth. Born in 1798 of racially mixed parentage, Beckwourth served an apprenticeship to a St. Louis blacksmith. Desiring more freedom, he fled westward and secured employment with the Rocky Mountain Fur Company. Soon he became an accomplished wilderness fighter, equally skilled in the use of the gun, bowie knife, and tomahawk. In 1824 he was adopted by the Crow Indians, became their beloved "Morning

Star," and married the chief's daughter. He led the Crows in numerous bloody raids and, rising to the position of chief, was known as "Bloody Arm." He had a varied career, serving as a scout in the third Seminole war in Florida and trapping and prospecting for gold in California. In 1850 he discovered the pass in the Sierra Nevada near Reno that still bears his name.

There were others, including John Marsant and John Stewart, who served as missionaries to the Indians. Among other African Americans who participated in the westward march were those who had been emancipated by John Randolph of Virginia and who settled in Ohio; those who migrated from Northampton County, North Carolina, and settled in Indiana; and the celebrated sculptress Edmonia Lewis, part Chippewa, who attended Oberlin College before moving on to Boston, where she studied the art for which she later became famous. There were indeed hundreds of others—some obscure and others well known, at least in their time—who left their mark as black contributors in the winning of the West.

■ The War of 1812

The westward march was not seriously checked by the diplomatic stress and strain of the early nineteenth century or by the war in which it culminated. Indeed, it may be said that the War of 1812 was to some extent a part of the expansionist program of those who were moving westward. There were controversies over the impressment of American sailors by the British and the violation of neutral rights, but there was also the possibility that a war would result in the acquisition of new lands. If the newly acquired lands lay to the north, they could attract Northern settlers who otherwise might go into the emerging cotton kingdom and obstruct the extension of slavery. If, perchance, the expansionists could acquire more lands in the Southwest, it would help to satisfy the appetites of an economic system that was already showing signs of insatiability. In either case, a victorious war would encourage the extension of slavery, and the warhawks and expansionists knew it.

When war finally came in 1812, blacks had an opportunity once more to serve their country. The number who served, however, remained small, perhaps because the areas from which they naturally would have come— New England and the Middle Atlantic states—showed little enthusiasm for the war. There seemed to be no serious objections to blacks' serving in the armed forces of the United States, but there was little inclination to recruit them. New York, however, in 1814, passed an act providing for the raising of two regiments of men of color. Each regiment was to consist of slightly more than 1,000 men, who were to receive the same pay as other soldiers. If slaves enlisted with the permission of their masters, they were to receive their freedom at the end of the war. Doubtless these black soldiers served faithfully, for in 1854 at the New York State Convention of the Soldiers of

1812, a resolution was passed asking Congress to provide the officers, men, and their widows with a liberal annuity "and that such provisions should extend to and include both the Indian and African race . . . who enlisted or served in that war, and who joined with the white man in defending our rights and maintaining our independence."

Scattered through the white units were blacks who served largely in menial capacities. Some, however, fought gallantly, and the records testify to their heroism. One of the outstanding soldiers in the Battle of North Point was William Burleigh, a Philadelphia black. When the city of Washington was taken, Philadelphia and other Eastern cities were alarmed over the possibility of suffering the same fate. The Vigilance Committee of Philadelphia called on three leading black citizens, James Forten, Bishop Richard Allen, and Absalom Jones, and asked that blacks help erect adequate defenses for the city. More than 2,500 blacks met in the statehouse yard, went to Grays Ferry, and worked almost continuously for two days, after which they received the praise of a grateful city. A battalion of blacks was organized in Philadelphia and was on the verge of marching to the front when peace was announced.

A large number of blacks were enrolled in the navy, frequently without reference to race. It is estimated that at least one-tenth of the crews of the fleet on the Upper Lakes were blacks. Capt. Oliver H. Perry was not satisfied with the men, "blacks, soldiers, and boys," that were sent to him. Commodore Chauncey cautioned Perry that he should be proud of whomever he received and added that the fifty blacks on his ship were among the best men he had. Later, after the Battle of Lake Erie, Perry gave unstinted praise to the black members of his crew and declared that "they seemed absolutely insensible to danger." Other naval officers spoke of the gallantry of black seamen. Nathaniel Shaler, the commander of the *Governor Tompkins*, said that the name of John Johnson, a black seaman on his ship, should be registered in the book of fame. As Johnson lay dying after he had been struck by a twenty-four pound shot, he exclaimed, "Fire away my boys; no haul a color down." Another black, John Davis, who was struck in much the same way, begged to be thrown overboard, saying he was only in the way of the others.

It was with Gen. Andrew Jackson that blacks performed their most effective services during the War of 1812. Jackson, needing to augment his forces in the autumn of 1814, called upon the free blacks of Louisiana to answer the appeal from their country. He confessed that the policy of the United States in barring blacks from the service had been a mistake. He promised that all blacks who enlisted would receive the same pay and bounty as white soldiers and that although their officers would be white, their noncommissioned officers would be chosen from among them. Shortly before the Battle of New Orleans, after several units of black soldiers had been recruited and had served in the preliminary campaigns, Jackson told them that in their performance they had surpassed his hopes. He promised that the president would be informed of their conduct and that the "voice of the representatives of the American nation shall applaud your valor, as your general now praises your ardor."

In the Battle of Chalmette Plains, commonly known as the Battle of New Orleans, black soldiers occupied a position of strategic importance. They were very near Jackson's main forces—on the left bank of the Mississippi River, just at the right of the advancing left column of the British. One battalion, under Major Lacoste, was composed of men of color from New Orleans and numbered about 280. The other, under Major Daquin, was composed of blacks from St. Domingue and numbered about 150. These black soldiers erected the cotton-bag defenses for Jackson and contributed substantially to the American victory. As the British, under General Pakenham, attempted to take Jackson's position by assault, frontiersmen, blacks, regular army men, and others opened up a counterattack from behind their breastworks that was disastrous for the British. The war had already ended, but this belated victory for the Americans was significant psychologically as well as from a military viewpoint.

During the war blacks in search of freedom went over to the British. As in the War of Independence the British promised freedom to all fugitive slaves. It is impossible to make any estimate of the number who escaped to the British lines, but it is well known that some were later living in the British West Indies and in Canada. Some of those in the West Indies, however, had been sold into slavery. Many blacks entered the war on the side of America expecting to secure their freedom. Some did, but others were actually sent back to their masters at the end of the struggle. Thus, both sides betrayed, to some extent, the blacks who enlisted in the hope of getting their freedom. The Treaty of Ghent provided for the mutual restoration of properties. This applied to personal property—slaves—as much as to any territories that may have been won during the war. Since the British had been selling fugitive slaves in the West Indies, the Americans sought indemnities for this and other properties that were not restored by the British. It was not until 1828, however, that the British finally acceded to the demands of the United States and granted indemnities of more than $1 million.

■ Emergence of the Cotton Kingdom

The peace that settled over the United States in 1815 made possible the acceleration of the westward movement that was well under way before the war. The men of the South and West, the most enthusiastic supporters of the war, now felt that they had a right to move on to better lands. Many of the Indian dangers had been allayed, and the demand for cotton was increasing now that peace had come to the entire world. The years immediately following the close of the war witnessed an unparalleled movement of the population westward. Into the Gulf region went large numbers of settlers to clear the rich lands and cultivate extensive crops of cotton. Louisiana had become a state in 1812, and the population continued to increase as cotton and sugarcane became profitable crops of slaveholding planters. Mississippi and Alabama became states in 1817 and 1819, respectively. There had been only about 40,000 people in this area in 1810, but by 1820 there were 200,000 inhabitants, and twenty years later the population had almost reached the 1 million mark. The black population had also grown rapidly. In 1820 there were only 75,000 blacks in the Alabama-Mississippi region, while by 1840 almost half a million were in the area. The increase of the white population, coupled with the tremendous growth of the black population, largely slaves, is essentially the story of the emergence of the cotton kingdom.

A considerable number of planters from the seaboard states moved into the cotton kingdom, realizing that only in the new area could slavery have a possibility of becoming profitable. Attempts to grow cotton in Virginia and North Carolina had not been altogether satisfactory. At the beginning of the century the Southeastern states had grown most of the cotton. By 1821, however, the South Central states were producing over one-third of the cotton grown in the United States. By 1834 the coastal states produced 160 million pounds, while Alabama, Mississippi, Louisiana, and the other newly settled areas dominated production with 297.5 million pounds. Small wonder that slaveholders were going into the cotton kingdom. In 1832 the Lynchburg *Virginian* complained that "the constant emigration to the great West of our most substantial citizens, the bone and sinew of the country . . . is the daily subject of complaint among our mercantile men and of which our naked streets and untenanted houses are such emphatic evidence." Four years later a South Carolinian wrote: "The spirit of emigration is still rife in our community. From this cause we have lost many, and we are destined, we fear, to lose more, of our worthiest citizens."

As the income of planters in the new lands grew enormously and as the news of their prosperity found its way back to the seaboard, the wave of migration increased. The demand for slaves grew and, naturally, the prices of slaves went up. This mad scramble for land in the West, for slaves to cultivate the land, and for huge profits with which to expand were the ingredients that made the cotton kingdom one of the most dynamic areas of economic and social activity during the first half of the nineteenth century. The emergence of the cotton kingdom, in which the work was carried on primarily by black slaves, had the effect of committing the Gulf region to a regime of slavery and of unifying the South against any group or section that threatened to destroy those peculiar interests of the South and the cotton kingdom.

The acquisition of Florida in 1819, the settling of Missouri and its entrance into the Union as a slave state in 1821, and the movement culminating in the acquisition of Texas in 1845 were to a large extent a result of the forces that the emergence of the cotton kingdom let loose. In order to safeguard slaveholders against the possibility of losing their slaves through escape to Spanish soil, Florida was considered both desirable and necessary. The controversy over the entrance of Missouri into the Union demonstrated the determination of the South to secure, if possible, a political balance, and an equal determination on the part of the North to maintain political domination. The question of blacks was consequently catapulted into national prominence, and the incident seems to be symbolic of the irrevocable commitment of the South to the institution of slavery. Nothing more clearly demonstrates the insatiable appetite of plantation slavery for new lands than the generation-long struggle for the acquisition of Texas. It was perhaps the high-water mark in the effort of the South to absorb all the lands into which the cotton kingdom could be extended.

Shortly before the beginning of the War of 1812 the people of the West expounded the doctrine that later came to be known as Manifest Destiny. R. M. Johnson of Kentucky, for example, said that he would not die happy until all of Britain's North American possessions were incorporated into the United States. Points of view like this came to be expressed more and more by inhabitants of the slaveholding states, though it is true that many Northerners shared the same ideas. One of the most important motives for expansionism was declared to be the extension of the area of freedom. The area of the United States must be extended so as to make possible the development of a great "empire for liberty" in the New World. It was rather strange, therefore, to hear this doctrine expounded by those who held slaves and who saw little incongruity in their position as slaveholders and their pronouncements in favor of extending freedom and democracy.

It is safe to say that the extension of democracy was probably neither a primary motive of any of the Southern expansionists nor even a secondary motive of many of them. Their preoccupation was with extending the area not of freedom, but of slavery. Many Southerners called for the annexation of new areas as a means of defeating those who were antagonistic to the rights of Southern states. Thus, Manifest Destiny became a platform from which the slaveholder could plead for an extension of the institution of slavery. Southerners, in their thinking, had excluded blacks from their religious and moral conceptions of freedom and had evolved the new notion that the enslavement of blacks was essential to the freedom of whites. It is not too much to say, therefore, that Manifest Destiny, one of America's most dramatic shibboleths in the nineteenth century, contributed substantially to the extension of slavery during the generation immediately preceding the Civil War.

Blacks were not only moving involuntarily into the South Central states, where slavery was deeply entrenched, but they were also moving voluntarily into the North Central states, where presumably slavery would not exist. By 1830 there were more than 16,000 blacks in Ohio, Indiana, Illinois, and Michigan, and although under the Northwest Ordinance slavery was not permitted, there were no fewer than 788 slaves in the region at the time of the fifth census. Some of these migrants were runaway slaves, but others were ex-slaves who were seeking greater opportunities, as were the whites who moved into the North Central states after the War of 1812. An example of a fugitive slave moving into the region was William Trail, who in 1814 ran away from his Maryland master and with the aid of a forged pass went to Indiana. Although he was pursued and captured on two occasions, he finally won his freedom through court action and settled down to become a prosperous landowning farmer in Union County, Indiana. Another example of a free black on the frontier was an individual known as "Free Frank," who was born a slave in Kentucky but subsequently purchased his freedom as well as that of his wife and moved to Illinois. There, in Pike County, he founded the town of New Philadelphia and engaged in a variety of commercial enterprises. An outstanding citizen of Cleveland after 1830 was John Melvin, who moved to that community from Prince County, Virginia, where he was born of a slave father and a free mother. Melvin, through a succession of jobs, amassed sufficient money to purchase a lake vessel and engage in the carrying trade. He helped to organize the First Baptist Church and so vigorously opposed the segregation of blacks that the principle of free seating was adopted. He also assisted in organizing the first school for black children in Cleveland and sponsored the setting up of other such schools in Ohio. Thus, the same search for independence that characterized the efforts of blacks in the seaboard states was to be found in the activities of blacks in the newly settled states in the West.

■ The Domestic Slave Trade

One of the most important single factors augmenting the westward movement was the domestic slave trade. Although many migrants took slaves with them, others, less financially able, did not. Once in the South Central states and having realized some profits from their early ventures, the ambitious farmers began to seek slaves. Perhaps the best sources of supply were the states of the Atlantic seaboard that had found it increasingly difficult to maintain the institution at a profitable level. In the economic reorganization that circumstances forced upon Maryland, Virginia, and the Carolinas, slave trading took its place along with diversified farming as a solution to the difficult problems of economic readjustment. Even before 1800 the domestic slave trade in Maryland and Virginia was well developed. States like South Carolina that forbade importations from Africa permitted their citizens to purchase slaves from other states, thereby stimulating the domestic traffic considerably. Gradually, the interstate trade became profitable, and the consequent rising value of slave property had the effect of destroying much of the antislavery sentiment in Maryland and Virginia after the turn of the century.

With the official closing of the African trade in 1808 the domestic trade became more profitable, and by 1815, about the time of the great movement of the population into the cotton kingdom, it had become a major economic activity in the country. The machinery for handling the traffic developed rapidly, and before the very eyes of Americans there emerged an institution that served as a substitute, or a supplement, for the African trade, which was only slightly less obnoxious in its effects upon the social order. Many business firms that dealt in farm supplies and animals frequently carried a "line" of slaves. Auctioneers who disposed of real estate and personal property sold slaves along with their other commodities. Planters who were abandoning their farms or were undergoing some kind of retrenchment either passed the word around or advertised in the newspapers that they had slaves for sale. Benevolent organizations frequently sold slaves by lottery.

Almost every community in Maryland and Virginia had either traders or their agents scouring the countryside in search of slaves whom they could purchase at the lowest possible price and sell in the cotton kingdom at the highest possible price. Firms like Woolfolk, Saunders, and Overly of Maryland, and Franklin and Armfield of Virginia developed the slave-trading business to a point where it greatly enriched the members of the firm. Although they were generally held in low esteem, they were tolerated because they performed a service that was of great importance both to slaveholders and to those wishing to acquire slaves. Benjamin Lundy called Austin Woolfolk a "monster in human shape." When Woolfolk retaliated by beating Lundy mercilessly, the court fined him only $1, suggesting that the general disapproval of the traders was rather superficial. The newspapers cooperated with the traders in many ways. Not only did they serve them as advertising media, but they often received orders and acted as intermediaries between seller and purchaser.

The slave traders were a ubiquitous lot. They could be seen at general stores, at taverns, at county fairs, and on plantations. Wherever they heard of the possibility of the sale of slaves, they were there. When estates were to be probated or liquidated, they sought out the individuals involved and pressed them for whatever slaves were available. They could convincingly argue that a Virginian no longer needed his slaves, and then with equal firmness they could show a Mississippian that he needed at least ten new hands. Their advertisements are suggestive of twentieth-century methods. In 1834 Franklin and Armfield announced that they would pay cash for 500 blacks and would offer higher prices "than any other purchaser who is now, or may hereafter come into the market." Small wonder that these tycoons were able to move thousands of slaves each year from an area where they were not desired to a section where there was a pressing demand for them.

Baltimore, Washington, Richmond, Norfolk, and Charleston were the principal trading centers in the older states, while Montgomery, Memphis, and New Orleans were the outstanding marts in the newer areas. Although Washington was not the largest slave market, it was the most notorious until 1850 when the slave trade in the District of Columbia was brought to an end. Interstate traders headquartered in the District of Columbia operated in Maryland and Virginia. Alexandria, which was a part of the District of

Columbia until 1846, was, moreover, a good place from which to ship slaves by water or overland. The District of Columbia was aptly called, therefore, "the very seat and center of the slave trade." Foreign visitors to the nation's capital were puzzled at the sight of slave auction blocks, slave jails, and slave pens. Many of them, as well as many Americans, such as John Randolph of Roanoke, roundly condemned the practice of selling human beings in the capital of the world's most democratic nation. Washington was not alone, however, in possessing the various buildings and other symbols of the slave trade. Practically every city in the upper South and lower South had pens, jails, and other necessary accouterments for the effective prosecution of this profitable traffic. Who could deny, anyway, that jails were necessary? Were not some of the slaves unruly, indolent workers or, worse still, under suspicion as conspirators?

Some slaves were sold in the centers of the upper South and shipped to the cotton kingdom via the Atlantic Ocean. As far north as New York and Philadelphia slaves were loaded on cargo ships and sent into the lower South. Chesapeake ports, such as Baltimore, Washington, and Norfolk, were especially important in the slave-trading activity. New Orleans was, of course, the important port of entry and became the most important slave-trading center in the lower South. Other slaves were sent overland, through southwestern Virginia to Tennessee, thence into Alabama, Mississippi, and Louisiana. If they went by land, they frequently walked most of the way. When they reached the Ohio, Tennessee, or Mississippi River, they were placed on flatboats and shipped down the river like any other cargo. In most instances, whether by water or by land, they were taken in chains. More than one traveler was startled at the sight of migrating slaves who were either handcuffed or chained together or both. They were always under the watchful eye of the long-distance traders or their agents, who saw to it that none escaped, lest the profits be therefore proportionally reduced.

There was always a fear that the supply of slaves would become exhausted while the demand was still great. One of the ways in which the slaveholders guarded against this distressing eventuality was the systematic breeding of slaves, one of the most fantastic manipulations of human development in the history of humanity. Despite the denials and apologies of many students of the history of American slavery, there seems to be no doubt that innumerable slaveholders deliberately undertook to increase the number of saleable slaves by advantageously mating them and by encouraging prolificacy in every possible way. As early as 1796 a South Carolina slaveholder declared that the 50 slaves he was offering for sale were purchased for stock and breeding. In 1832 Thomas R. Dew admitted that Virginia was a "Negro raising state" and that it was able to export 6,000 per year because of breeding. Moncure Conway of Fredericksburg, Virginia, boldly asserted that "the chief pecuniary resource in the border states is the breeding of slaves; and I grieve to say that there is too much ground for the charges that general licentiousness among the slaves, for the purpose of a

William Wells Brown Tells about the Domestic Slave Trade—1847

In the course of eight or nine weeks Mr. Walker [slave trader] had his cargo of human flesh made up. There was in this lot a number of old men and women, some of them with gray locks. We left St. Louis in the steamboat Carlton, Captain Swan, bound for New Orleans. . . . I was ordered to have the old men's whiskers shaved off, and the gray hairs plucked out where they were not too numerous, in which case he had a preparation of blacking to color it, and with a blacking-brush we would put it on. This was new business to me, and was performed in a room where the passengers could not see us . . . and after going through the blacking process, they looked ten or fifteen years younger. . . .

The next day [after Natchez] we proceeded to New Orleans. . . . In a short time, the planters came flocking to the pen to purchase slaves. Before the slaves were exhibited for sale, they were dressed and driven out into the yard. Some were set to dancing, some to jumping, some to singing, and some to playing cards. This was done to make them appear cheerful and happy. My business was to see that they were placed in those situations before the arrival of the purchasers, and I have often set them to dancing when their cheeks were wet with tears. As slaves were in good demand at that time, they were all soon disposed of. . . .

William Wells Brown, *Narrative of William Wells Brown, A Fugitive Slave, Written By Himself*, in Gilbert Osofsky, *Puttin' On Ole Massa* (New York, 1969), pp. 191–194.

large increase, is compelled by some masters and encouraged by many." Experiments in slave rearing were carried on, albeit surreptitiously, in much the same way that efforts were made to discover new products that would grow on the exhausted soil. Slave rearing was another evidence of the desperation that gripped the upper South after it lost its economic leadership to the states of the cotton kingdom.

Slave breeding, strangely enough, was one of the most approved methods of increasing agricultural capital. Traders were castigated by the slaveholding gentry as being inhuman, vicious, and extremely venal, but slave-breeding owners were far more common and much more highly esteemed in the community. One respectable Virginia planter boasted that his women were "uncommonly good breeders" and that he never heard of babies coming so fast as they did on his plantation. Of course, the very gratifying thing about it was that "every one of them . . . was worth two hundred dollars . . . the moment it drew breath." Indeed, breeding was so profitable that many slave girls became mothers at thirteen and fourteen years of age. By the time they were twenty, some young women had given birth to as many as five children. Bounties and prizes were offered for great fecundity, and in some instances freedom was granted to mothers who had enriched their masters to the extent of bearing them ten or fifteen children. Arguments denying slave breeding by some recent students of slavery cannot successfully refute these and other contemporary testimonies regarding this practice.

Since the domestic slave trade and slave breeding were essentially economic and not humanitarian activities, it is not surprising to find that in the sale of slaves there was the persistent practice of dividing families. Husbands were separated from their wives, and mothers were separated from their children. This is not to say that there was never any respect manifested for the slave family. Here and there one can find sufficient respect for basic human rights or ample sentimentality to prevent the separation of families, but it was not always good business to keep families together. Since people sold and bought slaves largely for economic reasons, they eschewed the civilities that would have frowned upon separation. Louisiana law forbade separation of a mother from a child under ten years of age, and some other states discouraged the division of families. These laws, if enforced, would have done much to ameliorate the conditions of slavery; but they were almost wholly disregarded.

Few owners were sufficiently insensitive to human decency to admit that they were willing to divide slave families by sale. As a matter of fact, family members were frequently advertised as being for sale together, but they were not always sold together. Slaves often brought higher prices when sold separately. The large number of single slaves on the market bears testimony to the rather ruthless separation of families that went on during the slave period. Frederic Bancroft asserts that "the selling singly of young children privately and publicly was frequent and notorious." It was not unusual to see advertisements in which traders sought young blacks from eight to twelve years of age. Some traders, moreover, announced that they made a specialty of buying and selling young children.

In justification of the practice of separating families it was argued that family ties among slaves were either extremely loose or nonexistent and that slaves were, therefore, indifferent to separation. As Herbert Gutman has shown, this was not the case. Slaves responded to these assaults on familial relations by restructuring their social institutions into new forms, at times based on their African heritage, to establish distinctly African American relationships that often preserved their families in the face of the most adverse conditions. In every coffle of slaves shipped into the cotton kingdom by land or by water, slaves were handcuffed or chained, and hard-boiled traders often admitted that youngsters or oldsters, as the case might be, were unwilling to leave their families. Even more eloquent a denial of the claims of masters that ties of slave families were weak were the advertisements for runaways. All too frequently masters admitted that the fugitives had perhaps gone to a certain place where they were known to have had a wife, husband, or children. The frequency of such advertisements also belies the claim of many that slave families were hardly, if ever, separated.

TABLE 3
Average Prices of Prime Field Hands (young slave men,
able-bodied but unskilled)

	1800	1808	1813	1818	1828	1837	1843	1848	1853	1856	1860
Washington, Richmond, and Norfolk	$ 350	$ 500	$ 400	$ 700		$ 900			$1,250	$1,300	
Charleston, S.C.	500	550	450	850	$ 450	1,200	$ 500	$ 700	900		$1,200
Louisville, Ky.	400		550	800	500	1,200				1,000	1,400
Middle Georgia	450	650	450	1,000	700	1,300	600	900	1,200		1,800
Montgomery, Ala.				800	600	1,200	650	800			1,600
New Orleans, La.	500	600		1,000	700	1,300	800	900	1,250	1,500	1,800

Source: Ulrich Bonnell Phillips. The Slave Economy of the Old South: Selected Essays in Economic and Social History. Edited by Eugene D. Genovese. Louisiana State University Press (Baton Rouge 1968) p. 142.

The prices of slaves in the domestic trade reflected all the forces operating to create supply and demand. In the early nineteenth century, the prices of prime field hands were modest, ranging from $350 in Virginia to about $500 in Louisiana. Later, as the demand increased in the lower South, the prices on both the Northern and Southern markets tended to rise. The high point of the number of slaves sold in the domestic market was reached just before the panic of 1837 when Virginia reported that in the previous year no less than 120,000 slaves had been exported into the lower South. After the panic, the slump both in price and in demand became so pronounced that some traders were forced to return to Virginia and Maryland with their slaves and to sustain staggering losses. The forces that operated to increase slave prices in the last decade before the Civil War were largely political and social. In order to convince themselves and the abolitionists that slavery was a moral and economic good and to convince their neighbors of their affluence, planters continued to purchase all the slaves offered on the market. Prices skyrocketed, and by 1860 prime field hands were selling for $1,000 in Virginia and $1,500 in New Orleans.

Closely allied with slave trading was the practice of slave hiring. Owners had various reasons for hiring out their slaves instead of selling them. Some wanted to spread the income from the investment over a long period of time, others wanted to escape whatever stigma there might have been attached to being known as a slave seller, and still others wanted to keep the slaves either for the good of the latter or for the prestige that came from ownership. At any rate, there was almost always an opportunity to make a temporary disposition of slaves because of the constant demand for servants. Some whites hired slaves because the purchase was, for the moment, beyond their means; others merely had a temporary need for the services of a slave and saw no need to purchase one; still others reasoned that it was more economical in the long run to purchase services rather than titles, thereby escaping the responsibility that devolved on the owner during the slave's illness or old age.

Slaves were hired by the day, by the month, or by the year. The employer promised in the agreement to provide food, clothing, shelter, and medical care in addition to the stipulated wage. If the slave became ill or ran away, the wage continued. If the slave died, the wage ceased but the person who had hired the slave was usually compelled to show that he or she was not in any way responsible for the slave's death. Annual contracts ran for fifty-one weeks and did not cover the period from Christmas to New Year's Day. Hiring day was January 1 or some other day early in the new year. Some communities set aside a hiring day and gave all interested persons an opportunity to transact their business with great ease since the owners as well as the hirers would be able to find each other easily. On January 1, 1858, hiring day in Warrenton, Virginia, 500 slaves were advertised as being for hire.

The business of hiring was almost as highly organized as slave trading. There were hiring agents who prepared the papers, collected the money, and performed other similar services. At times these agents were also slave traders. In some instances, however, they were men without the resources necessary to engage in slave trading. Interestingly enough, there was no stigma attached to the business of serving as a hiring agent, and in their advertisements agents frequently proudly listed the names of their "patrons."

Slaves were hired to engage in all kinds of labor, but it was usually customary to state the nature of work in the agreement. They were hired by small farmers who needed a few extra hands at harvest time. They also worked in forests as woodcutters and turpentine hands. Hired slaves could also be found in factories and mines, on railroad construction jobs, and in canal digging. There were, of course, a considerable number in the towns serving as maids, porters, messengers, cooks, and the like. The rates of hire varied considerably depending on the skill of the slave as well as the supply. In 1800 a slave hand brought $100 per year in the lower South. By 1860 the price had increased to $200 or more. Toward the end of the period a young blacksmith in Mississippi was hired for $500, while several hands in Texas brought as much as $600.

Slave trading and hiring were thus essential parts of the economic and social fabric of the South. While practices that may have developed within the system were frowned upon, there was almost universal acceptance of the general principle of buying and selling human beings. To the owners of the upper South it meant the opportunity to dump on the market those individuals who were a serious burden in the period of economic transition. By breeding slaves for the market, moreover, the same owners could go far in the direction of reconstituting themselves economically. To traders it meant commissions and profits that ranged all the way from 5 to 30 percent of the sale price of the slaves, no mean return on a short-term investment. The social stigma of slave trading reduced competition and consequently increased the opportunity for profits. To the planters of the lower South the domestic slave trade provided an opportunity to secure the supply of labor necessary for the development and cultivation of new lands. Without the slaves of the upper South they felt stymied and frustrated. With them their opportunities for amassing wealth and influence were considered almost limitless.

■ Persistence of the African Trade

As the demand for slaves increased in the nineteenth century and as prices went up, merchants and traders experienced a great temptation to engage in the African trade, although it had been officially ended by federal legislation in 1808. The long, unprotected coast, the certain markets, and the prospect of huge profits were too much for American merchants, and they yielded to the temptation. After the War of 1812 it was generally admitted that American capital, American ships, and American sailors were carrying on an extensive slave trade between Africa and the New World. England was greatly distressed because she was committed to a program of eliminating the slave trade. In all her treaties with the new republics of Latin America, England forced them to promise not to engage in the slave trade. But it was embarrassing to England to observe that her recent enemy, with whom she was now on friendly terms, persisted in winking at gross violations of her own laws. There was little that England could do except to bring the pressure of world opinion to bear on the United States, but American citizens were not ashamed of their activities and so did not even heed the words of their own leaders.

In 1839 President Van Buren asked for an amendment of the law against the African slave trade in order to preserve the "integrity and honor of our flag." In June 1841, President Tyler said that there was every reason to believe that the traffic was on the increase. Almost every year witnessed an appeal of the president or some public leader for a more rigid enforcement of the law, but nothing was done. The most flagrant violations did not arouse public opinion to the point of bringing action against those who were profiting from the trade, and in this instance, it was not a sectional profit. New York merchants as well as those of New Orleans were benefiting from the illicit traffic. In 1836 the consul at Havana reported that whole cargoes of slaves fresh from Africa were being shipped daily to Texas in American vessels and that more than 1,000 had been sent within a few months. Two months later it was estimated that 15,000 Africans were annually taken to Texas. Bay Island, in the Gulf of Mexico, was a depot where at times as many as 16,000

Africans were on hand to be shipped to Florida, Texas, Louisiana, and other markets.

By 1854 those engaged in the African slave trade had become so bold as to advocate openly the official reopening of the trade. Between 1854 and 1860 every Southern commercial convention gave consideration to the proposition to reopen the trade. At the Montgomery convention of 1858 a furious debate was carried on over the problem. William L. Yancey, the Alabama "fire eater," argued, with considerable logic, that "if it is right to buy slaves in Virginia and carry them to New Orleans, why is it not right to buy them in Cuba, Brazil, or Africa and carry them there?" The following year, at Vicksburg, the convention voted favorably on a resolution recommending that "all laws, State or Federal, prohibiting the African slave trade, ought to be repealed." Only the states of the upper South, enjoying the profits reaped from the domestic slave trade, were opposed to reopening the African trade.

The federal law of 1808 was so weak and the enforcement of it so lax that a repeal was unnecessary to reopen the trade. When offenders were caught, they were placed under bond, which they promptly forfeited. Sometimes cases involving offenders were never brought before the courts. Thus, for all practical purposes the trade was open in the last decade before the Civil War, much to the distress of the Quakers and similar organizations. As the intersectional strife increased in intensity, importations into Southern ports became "bold, frequent, and notorious." Newly arrived blacks were openly advertised for sale, and most of the cities of the South had depots where they could be purchased if, for some reason, blacks from the upper South were not desired. In doing everything possible to keep the African trade open, Southerners were merely seeking to secure themselves against the possibility that the domestic slave trade would eventually go into a state of decline. There was the possibility, moreover, that if they could increase the supply of slaves, they would be able to secure them at lower prices.

Without slavery and the slave trade the westward movement on the Southern frontier would have been unsuccessful. It was the slaves, brought in either by settlers or traders, who transformed the Southern frontier from a wilderness into flourishing cotton and sugarcane farms and plantations. It was the slaves, moreover, who represented one of the most substantial forms of capital to be found in the cotton kingdom. Frederick Jackson Turner always described the trader as having preceded the farmer. He was, of course, referring to the person who carried on barter with the Indians. In this instance, however, the trader *followed* the farmer. It was the trader who brought the labor supply to the farmer. Although the order is in this case reversed, it would not be too much to say that slave traders with their black workers had a more profound effect on the history of the Southern frontier than Indian traders with their trinkets and fire water.

■

CHAPTER 8

That Peculiar Institution

■ Scope and Extent

Plantation slavery, as it developed in the cotton kingdom, was something of an anomaly on the American frontier. Although slavery was almost as old as the permanent settlements in America, not until the nineteenth century did it occupy so much of the attention and energy of the settlers as to threaten other forms of labor. The frontier had been a place where one could make or lose a fortune largely by one's own labors. The emergence of the great cotton plantation introduced a kind of exploitation of human and natural resources and fostered a type of discipline in rural areas that created what could at best be called a peculiar situation. Indeed, every aspect of agricultural life in the Southern United States underwent a complete transformation as a result of the new economic and social forces let loose by the Industrial Revolution. And what the Industrial Revolution did to the capitalistic system, new lands and the prospect of wealth from cotton culture did to the system of slavery. Large-scale operations were the order of the day. The farm became a plantation, which in turn became a rural factory with the impersonality of a large-scale economic organization. The face of the Southern frontier had been changed. Cotton and slavery were the great transforming forces.

One of the most rapidly growing elements in the population was the slaves. In 1790 there had been less than 700,000 slaves. By 1830 there were more than 2 million. The South Atlantic states, from Delaware to Florida, were still ahead in numbers, with 1,300,000, while the states of the lower South, none of which had been in the Union in 1790, now had 604,000 slaves. By the last census before the Civil War, the slave population had grown to 3,953,760! The states of the cotton kingdom had taken the lead, with 1,998,000 slaves within their borders. Virginia was still ahead in the number of slaves in a single state, but Alabama and Mississippi were rapidly gaining ground. As a matter of fact, the slave population of all the states of the lower South was increasing rapidly, while that of the upper South was either increasing very slowly or, as in the case of Maryland, was actually declining. The increase in the slave population to virtually 4 million by 1860 is an eloquent testimony to the extent to which slavery had become entrenched in the Southern states.

The impression should not be conveyed that the whites of the South, numbering about 8 million in 1860, generally enjoyed the fruits of slave labor. There was a remarkable concentration of the slave population in the hands of a relative few. In 1860 there were only 384,884 slave owners. Thus, fully three-fourths of the white people of the South had neither slaves nor an immediate economic interest in the maintenance of slavery or the plantation system. And yet, the institution came to dominate the political and economic thinking of the entire South and to shape its social pattern for two principal reasons. The great majority of the staple crops were produced on plantations employing slave labor, thus giving the owners an influence out of proportion to their number. Then, there was the hope on the part of most nonslaveholders that they would some day become owners of slaves. Consequently, they took on the habits and patterns of thought of slaveholders before they actually joined that select class.

While slaves were concentrated in areas where the staple crops were produced on a large scale, the bulk of the slave owners were small farmers. It is not too generally known that more than 200,000 owners in 1860 had five slaves or less. Fully 338,000 owners, or 88 percent of all the owners of slaves in 1860, held less than twenty slaves. (One must not be misled by these figures, however, for over one-half of the slaves were employed as field workers on plantations with holdings of more than twenty slaves, and at least 25 percent of the slave community lived on plantations where the number of slaves was in excess of fifty.) It is fairly generally conceded that from thirty to sixty slaves constituted the most profitable agricultural unit. If that is true, there were fewer plantations in the South that had what might be considered a satisfactory working force than has been generally believed. The concentration of 88 percent of all slaveholders in the small slave-owning group is significant for several important reasons. In the first place, it emphasizes the fact that the influence of large owners must have been enormous, since they have been successful in impressing posterity with the erroneous conception that plantations on which there were large numbers of slaves were typical. In the second place, it brings out the fact that the majority of slaveholding was carried on by yeomen rather than gentry. Finally, in a study of the institution of slavery, there is a rather strong indication that some distinction should be made between the possession of one or two slaves and the possession of, say, fifty or more.

But it was the tremendous productivity of the large plantations that placed the large slaveholder in a position of great influence. By 1860 Southern states were producing 5,387,000 bales of cotton annually. Four states, Mississippi, Alabama, Louisiana, and Georgia, produced more than 3,500,000 bales of this crop. It is no mere accident that these same states were also at the top of the list in the number of large slaveholders. Of the states having slaveholders with more than twenty slaves, Mississippi led, just as it did in productivity of cotton, followed by Alabama, Louisiana, and Georgia.

■ The Slave Codes

After the colonies secured their independence and established their own governments, they did not neglect the matter of slavery in the laws that they enacted. Where slavery was growing, as in the lower South in the late eighteenth and early nineteenth centuries, new and more stringent laws were enacted. All over the South, however, there emerged a body of laws generally regarded as the Slave Codes, which covered every aspect of the life of the slave. There were variations from state to state, but the general point of view expressed in most of them was the same: slaves are not people but property; laws should protect the ownership of such property and should also protect whites against any dangers that might arise from the presence of large numbers of slaves. It was also felt that slaves should be maintained in a position of due subordination in order that the optimum of discipline and work could be achieved.

The regulatory statutes were frankly repressive, and whites made no apologies for them. The laws represented merely the reduction to legal phraseology of the philosophy of the South with regard to the institution of slavery. Slaves had no standing in the courts: they could not be a party to a law suit; they could not offer testimony, except against another slave or a free black; and their irresponsibility meant that their oaths were not binding. Thus, they could make no contracts. The ownership of property was generally forbidden them, though some states permitted slaves to have certain types of personal property. A slave could not strike a white person, even in self-defense; but the killing of a slave, however malicious the act, was rarely regarded as murder. The rape of a female slave was regarded as a crime but only because it involved trespassing.

The greater portion of the Slave Codes involved the many restrictions placed on slaves to ensure the maximum protection of the white population and to maintain discipline among slaves. These rules were primarily negative. Slaves could not leave the plantation without authorization, and any white person finding them outside without permission could capture them and turn them over to public officials. They could not possess firearms, and in Mississippi they could not beat drums or blow horns. They could not hire themselves out without permission or in any other way conduct themselves as free people. They could not buy or sell goods. Their relationships with whites and free blacks were to be kept at a minimum. They could not visit the homes of whites or free blacks, and they could not entertain such individuals in their quarters. They were never to assemble unless a white person was present, and they were never to receive, possess, or transmit any incendiary literature calculated to incite insurrections.

Whenever there was an insurrection, or even rumors of one, it was usually the occasion for the enactment of even more stringent laws to control the activities and movements of slaves. For example, after the Vesey insurrection of 1822, South Carolina enacted a law requiring the imprisonment of all black seamen during the stay of their vessel in port. The Nat Turner insurrection of 1831 and the simultaneous drive of abolitionists against slavery brought forth the enactment of many new repressive measures in other parts of the South as well as in Virginia and neighboring states. Long before the end of the slave period the Slave Codes in all the Southern states had become so elaborate that there was hardly need for modification even when new threats arose to shake the foundations of the institution.

Ample machinery was set up to provide for effective enforcement and execution of the Slave Codes. In some states, slaves were tried in regular courts for infractions of the law. In other states, specially constituted slave tribunals had the responsibility of examining evidence and judging the guilt or innocence of slaves. Some states required trials by juries composed of slaveholders, while others merely required the cognizance of one, two, or three justices of the peace. Most petty offenses were punishable by whipping, while more serious ones were punishable by branding, imprisonment, or death. Arson, rape of a white woman, and conspiracy to rebel were capital crimes in all the slaveholding states. There was considerable reluctance to imprison a slave for a long period or to inflict the death penalty for the obvious reason that the slave represented an investment, and to deprive the owner of the slave's labor or life was to deprive the state of just that much wealth. Slaveholders were, therefore, extremely cautious about judging a slave offender hastily because of the danger of losing one of their own slaves through such a process at some later date. This is not to say that slaves enjoyed anything resembling due process of law or justice in any sense in which the term is applied to free persons. Since slaves were always regarded with suspicion and since some crimes were viewed as threats to the social order, they were frequently punished for crimes they did not commit and were helpless before a panic-stricken group of slaveholders who saw in the rumor of an insurrection the slow but certain undermining of their entire system.

One of the devices set up to enforce the Slave Codes and thereby maintain the institution of slavery was the patrol, which has been aptly described as an adaptation of the militia. Counties were usually divided into "beats," or areas of patrol, and free white men were called upon to serve for a stated period of time, one, three, or six months. These patrols were to apprehend slaves out of place and return them to their masters or commit them to jail, to visit slave quarters and search for various kinds of weapons that might be used in an uprising, and to visit assemblies of slaves where disorder might develop or where conspiracy might be planned. This system proved so inconvenient to some citizens that they regularly paid the fines that were imposed for dereliction of duty. A corrupted form of the patrol system was the vigilance committee, which came into existence during the emergencies created by uprisings or rumors of them. At such times, it was not unusual for the committee to disregard all caution and prudence and kill any blacks whom they encountered in their search. Committees like these frequently ended up engaging in nothing except a lynching party.

Despite the elaborateness of the Slave Codes both in the number of statutes and in the machinery of enforcement, there were innumerable infractions that went unpunished altogether. When times were quiet, there was an inclination to disregard the laws and to permit slaves to conduct themselves in a manner that would be regarded as highly offensive during an emergency. There was the desire, moreover, on the part of all masters to take all matters involving their slaves into their own hands and to mete out justice in their own way. The strong individualism that was bred on the frontier plantation and the planter's self-conception as the source of law and justice had the effect of discouraging conformity to statutes even when they were passed in the interest of the plantation system. Slaveholders always had the feeling that they could handle their own slaves, if only something could be done about those on the neighboring plantation. Such a point of view was not conducive to the effective enforcement of the Slave Codes.

■ Plantation Scene

The fact should not be ignored that the primary concern of owners was to get work out of their slaves. And the work of slaves was primarily agricultural. It is estimated that only 400,000 slaves lived in towns and cities in 1850. This left approximately 2.8 million to do the work on farms and plantations. The great bulk of them, 1.8 million, were to be found on cotton plantations, while the remainder were primarily engaged in the cultivation of tobacco, rice, and sugarcane. The cotton farm or plantation was, therefore, the typical locale of the slave. It must be recalled that when a farmer owned a few slaves, as was the case in a vast majority of instances, slaves and owners worked together in the fields and were compelled to engage in a variety of common tasks. On larger plantations, where the organization was so elaborate as to resemble a modern factory, there was extensive supervision by the owner or the overseer or both, and there was considerable division of labor among slaves. A large plantation always had at least two distinct groups of workers, house servants and field hands. The former cared for the house, the yards, and the gardens, cooked the meals, drove the carriages, and performed the other tasks expected of personal servants. The favored ones frequently traveled with their owners and enjoyed other advantages in the way of food, clothing, and education or experience.

Unfortunately, there are few records of the activities of slaves on smaller units. Therefore, a great deal has been made of the existence of a large force of house servants because a considerable number of large slaveholders kept diaries, journals, and other records that have given a clear picture of their activities. In some of these instances there were more house servants than necessary. If a planter could display a considerable number of house servants, he or she could convey the impression, frequently inaccurate, of having great affluence and living in a state bordering on luxury. The house servant group, moreover, tended to perpetuate and even to increase itself. Once a slave had served in a home, the prospect of working in the field was frowned upon and resisted with every available resource. House servants were even anxious to "work" their children into the more desirable situation and to marry them off to the children of other house servants. The result was that the group increased in numbers beyond the point necessary to maintain the average planter's home.

What may be termed the productive work was done in the fields by a force that constituted the principal group of slaves. Where there were not enough slaves to have house servants as well as field hands, agricultural activities seldom suffered. In such instances slaves found it necessary to do the chores around and in the house at times that ordinarily would have been their own time. The cultivation of a crop was a demanding undertaking, and the entire future of both slaves and owners depended on the success with which it was handled. Except on rice plantations, where slaves were given a specific assignment or task each day, the gang system was used. Literally, gangs of slaves were taken to the fields and put to work under the supervision of the owner or the overseer. The leader instructed them about when to begin work, when to eat, and when to quit. Slaves under this system were wholly without responsibility and had little opportunity to develop initiative. Consequently, the claim of some recent writers that owners could have made slavery more bearable to slaves by paying them for their work seems highly unlikely.

It was generally believed that one slave was required for the successful cultivation of three acres of cotton. The planting, cultivation, and picking of cotton required little skill, but a great deal of time. Men, women, and children could be used, though it is to be doubted if the very young and the very old were of any real value to the plantation. Aside from duties in connection with raising the crop, there were other things to do, such as clearing land, burning underbrush, rolling logs, splitting rails, carrying water, mending fences, spreading fertilizer, breaking soil, and the like. Small wonder that

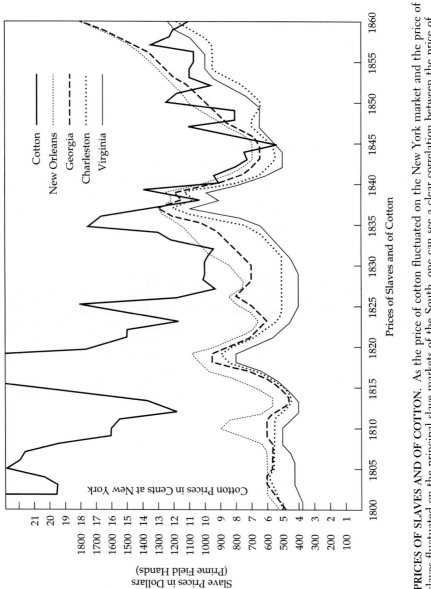

PRICES OF SLAVES AND OF COTTON. As the price of cotton fluctuated on the New York market and the price of slaves fluctuated on the principal slave markets of the South, one can see a clear correlation between the price of cotton and of slaves. *(Ulrich B. Phillips, American Negro Slavery, New York, 1966, p. 371.)*

many slaves worked not merely from sunrise to sunset but frequently long after dark. During harvest time the hours were longest since the planter was anxious to harvest the crop before it could be seriously damaged by inclement weather. Under such circumstances slaves were driven almost mercilessly. In 1830, for example, fourteen Mississippi slaves each picked an average of 323 pounds of cotton in one day. It was conceded that if an adult slave picked 150 pounds in one day it was a satisfactory performance. On Louisiana sugarcane plantations it was not unusual for slaves to work eighteen and twenty hours each day during the harvest season.

When there was no watchful supervision, little was accomplished in a slave system. Slaves felt no compulsion to extend themselves in their work unless the planter or overseer forced them. Their benefits would be the same, except on a few plantations where systems of rewards and bounties were developed, whether they worked conscientiously or whether they shirked at every opportunity. There was a great deal of complaining about the idleness and laziness of slaves, but this was inherent in a system of forced labor. On one occasion George Washington said that his slave carpenters were notorious piddlers and not even one of his house servants was worthy of trust. If slaves felt overworked, they frequently feigned illness or simply walked off for a day or so or, perhaps forever. The consistent evasion of work on the part of slaves was one of the reasons why planters always felt in need of more slaves to increase the productivity of their plantations.

In the effort to get work out of slaves the lash was frequently used. There was the general belief, born of a naive or sinister racial justification for the institution of slavery, that Africans were a childlike race and should be punished just as children were punished. Some planters went so far as to specify the size and type of lash to be used and the number of lashes to be given for certain offenses. Almost none disclaimed whipping as an effective form of punishment, and the excessive use of the lash was one of the most flagrant abuses of the institution. Many slaves fled because of brutal beatings by their owner or overseer. Unfortunately, the instances where one can determine the nature and extent of punishment are so few, if they exist at all, that efforts at statistical computation of whippings are pointless if not ridiculous.

The great majority of the plantations were managed by the planters themselves. An overseer was not needed unless there were more than twenty slaves or unless the planter was an absentee landlord. In many instances, moreover, planters worked in the fields and shared the experiences of their slaves. Under such conditions, there was likely to be less brutality on the part of management and more work on the part of the laboring force than under other circumstances. Southern planters were at the center of the economic, social, and political life of their community and naturally had the feeling that they should dominate the lives of their black property completely. If they were inclined to be benevolent and understanding, the slaves were fortunate indeed. If they were inclined to enjoy the exercise of authority and the cruelty that authority frequently fostered, then the slaves probably looked forward to either running away or being sold to a better owner.

It was on plantations where there were overseers that the greatest amount of cruelty and brutality existed. Since overseers came from a nonslaveholding and frequently landless group, they had no interest other than a temporary concern in the institution. Too frequently they hated the system and directed especial contempt toward slaves because they were of the opinion that slavery was responsible for their own unfortunate economic plight. They had the job of managing the entire plantation in the absence of the planter, or if it was too large for the planter to handle alone, the overseer was delegated a considerable portion of the responsibility. In any event, this authority over the slaves was almost unlimited. The owners demanded that the overseers get work out of the slaves and produce a superior crop. With such a mandate overseers were ruthless and excessively cruel in their treatment of slaves. Frequently, fights grew out of attempts of overseers to punish slaves, and in several instances overseers were run off the plantation by irate slaves. Before the planter had the opportunity to reprimand the overseer for his bestiality, he had often done irreparable damage. It must be remembered, moreover, that unless his cruelty bordered on the sensational, many planters were not concerned about it. On some plantations a slave called the driver was selected to assist the owner or overseer in getting work out of the slaves. The other slaves frequently resented this delegation of authority to one among them, and the driver was sometimes viewed as a traitor, especially if he took his duties seriously.

The responsibility of providing the necessities of life for slaves was a major one. The preoccupation with raising the staple crops was so great everywhere that insufficient attention was given to the very important matter of growing food. Charles S. Sydnor has observed that few Mississippi planters raised enough food to supply their needs. Consequently, many plantations were compelled to purchase foodstuffs and other supplies not only for the family of the planter but for the slaves as well. Whether grown on the plantation or brought in from other sections of the country, the fare was not a particularly exciting one, the principal items being meal and meat. On some of the larger plantations there was a central kitchen where the food was prepared, but on the average plantation each slave was responsible for the preparation of his or her own food. Each received a daily or weekly ration of meal and salt pork. For adult persons the weekly ration was about a peck of meal and three to four pounds of meat. This was at times supplemented with sweet potatoes, peas, rice, syrup, and fruit. Some slaves had their own gardens and chickens, but there was always the possibility of incurring the disfavor of the owner or overseer by spending too much time in this pursuit. A further supplement to one's diet could be made by hunting and fishing whenever possible.

It would be too much to suppose that slaves always resisted the temptation to take food from the owner's larder if the opportunity presented itself. The difficulty was that such supplies were locked up, and except for a few house servants, no slaves had access to them. But the house servants, who usually ate the same food as the whites whether they were permitted to do so or not, were perhaps not inclined to take food unless some kind of cabal had been formed for the systematic depletion of the owner's food supply. The break in the monotony of the unattractive fare came on holidays like Christmas when the owner sometimes provided items such as cheese, coffee, and candy as a contribution to the festive spirit.

The filching of perishable items like food was simple when compared with any efforts on the part of slaves to augment their supply of clothing. Some house servants were favored with the castoff garments of their owners, but the average slave wore what was generally described as "Negro clothes." They consisted of jeans, linseys, kerseys, and osnaburgs for the men and calico and homespun fabrics for the women. On some plantations slave women spun and wove the cloth out of which they made their dresses. Shoes, called "Negro brogans," were not provided except for the winter months. No more clothing was furnished than was absolutely necessary. Planters reasoned that slaves perhaps needed ample food in order to work efficiently, but they saw little connection between clothing and work. In a system as harshly materialistic as plantation slavery there was little or no inclination to indulge in any expenditures for slaves that were viewed as unnecessary for increased productivity.

Housing for slaves was especially poor. The small, rude huts were usually inadequate as well as uncomfortable. Windows and floors were almost unheard of. Frederick Olmsted was shocked when he viewed the slave cabins on some of the plantations he visited. They were small and dilapidated with no windows, unchinked walls, and practically no furnishings. One of the better ones had a bed, a chest, a wooden stool, some earthenware, and cooking vessels. Many cabins were wholly without beds, and slaves were compelled to sleep on quilts or blankets with only some straw or shucks between them and the earth. The inadequacy of space was, if possible, even worse than the absence of comforts and conveniences. One Mississippi planter had twenty-four huts, each measuring sixteen by fourteen feet, for his 150 slaves. Ulrich B. Phillips and others have defended the frightfully inadequate housing of slaves on the grounds that, first, the plantation was so close to the frontier that few planters could boast of entirely satisfactory living accommodations and, second, slaves were out of their cabins most of the time and, therefore, did not have a real need for greatly improved housing. In all fairness, these apologists could have added that these unfortunate living conditions go far to explain the crime, delinquency, and aversion to the "civilizing" tendencies of the plantation of which they so loudly accused slaves.

■ Nonagricultural Pursuits

In 1850 there were 400,000 slaves living in urban communities. It may be assumed that a majority were engaged in nonagricultural pursuits and that their number was augmented by plantation slaves whose owners hired them out to townspeople. There is no way of knowing how many such slaves were hired out, but there must have been thousands, especially in the period between the harvest and the new planting. It was in nonagricultural pursuits that slaves displayed the greatest variety of talent and training. Many plantations had slave carpenters, masons, and mechanics, but skilled slaves were to be most frequently found in towns. Indeed, a large number of town slaves possessed some kind of skill. In the Charleston census of 1848, for example, there were more slave carpenters than there were free black and white carpenters. The same was true of slave coopers. In addition, there were slave tailors, shoemakers, cabinetmakers, painters, plasterers, seamstresses, and the like. Many owners realized the wisdom of training their slaves in the trades, for their earning power would be greatly enhanced; and if the slaves were ever offered for sale they would perhaps bring twice as much as field hands of a similar age would bring.

White artisans were violently opposed, for the most part, to the teaching of trades to blacks. One white skilled worker in Mississippi, for example, said that he would starve before he taught a slave his trade. Most of the planters and proslavery leaders advocated training slaves in special skills, not only because it increased their value but because if slave labor were more extensively used, there would be wider and more enthusiastic support of the system. If towns as well as plantations became completely dependent on slave labor, whatever indifference there was to the institution would be transformed into warm advocacy.

Only the most demagogic of the Negrophobes contended that it was not possible to train blacks in artisanry. There were too many examples that belied such a contention. No state and few communities were without highly skilled slaves or slaves employed other than on a plantation. To be sure, the majority of slaves in nonagricultural pursuits found work as domestic servants, porters, or common laborers in towns. But there was a sufficient number of slave artisans to make it clear that they had the capacity to acquire skills. Frequently advertisements for a slave for sale or a runaway slave described him as a "first rate boot and shoe maker," an "experienced weaver and chair spinner," or an "excellent carpenter." In Virginia they were used in mills, iron furnaces, and tobacco factories. The Saluda textile factory in South Carolina at one time employed 98 slave operatives. They were also in the textile mills of Florida, Alabama, Mississippi, and Georgia. In Kentucky they were employed in the saltworks of Clay County and in the iron and lead mines of Caldwell and Crittenden counties. The Southern railroads also employed a considerable number for construction work. It is reported that in 1838 a corporation purchased 140 slaves at a cost of $159,000 to work on the construction of a railroad between Jackson and Brandon, Mississippi. For ten years a slave was the engineer on the West Feliciana Railroad, one of the oldest in the Southern United States. Finally, slaves were frequently employed in river transportation and at docks. Despite Olmsted's observation that Irish workers were employed to unload boats on the Mississippi River because slaves were too valuable, slaves were extensively used in such work. They worked on the docks at New Orleans, Savannah, Charleston, Norfolk, and other Southern ports.

There were even slave inventors. In 1835 and 1836 Henry Blair, designated in the records as a "colored man" of Maryland, received patents for two corn harvesters he had developed. By 1858, however, the attorney general had ruled that since a slave was not a citizen, the government could not enter into an agreement with him by granting him a patent, nor could the slave assign the invention to his owner. Benjamin Montgomery, a slave owned by Jefferson Davis, invented a boat propeller toward the end of the slave period. Davis made an attempt to have it patented, but failed. This perhaps accounts for the passage of a law by the Confederate Congress in 1861 providing that if the owner took an oath that his or her slave had actually invented a device, the patent would be issued to the owner. It was not until after the Civil War that blacks were able to secure patents for their inventions without any difficulty.

■ Social Considerations

It has been assumed too frequently that slavery provided an idyllic existence not only for owners but for slaves as well. The fact is, however, that even for the planter life was not always pleasant. There was little in the way of recreation and other diversions to foster a zest for living either on the plantation or in the Southern towns. Life was so barren generally that it can hardly be described as "the good life" even under the most favorable circumstances. The plantation, with its inherent isolation and consequent social and cultural self-sufficiency, frequently bordering on stagnancy, tended to perpetuate the barrenness. For slaves there was little in the way of enjoyment and satisfaction during the moments or hours they were off the job. It must be remembered that for the most part slaves had no time they could call their own, and not infrequently they worked such long hours that periods of free time necessarily had to be used for rest. Even if there was no work and even if an opportunity for diversion presented itself, slaves could never escape the fact that they were slaves and that their movements as well as their other activities were almost always under the most careful surveillance. If they found it possible to enjoy the periods when they were not on the job, they either possessed a remarkable capacity for accommodation or were totally ignorant of the depth of their degraded position.

Most slave children had the run of the plantation and played with the white children in and out of the "big house," in and out of the cabins, and through the yards without any inhibitions. When blacks reached the useful age, which was very early, much of the playing was over. When they reached the social age, interracial playing was over altogether, and they settled down to the existence that was the inevitable lot of a slave. There was almost nothing of a day-to-day nature for slaves to do in the way of recreation. If the plantation was near a stream it might be possible for them to make it through the woods and spend an hour or so fishing, but not infrequently this was for the specific purpose of supplementing their food supply instead of for recreation. When whites went hunting at night they usually took some slave men, but on a large plantation there were many who never got this opportunity. Races, fairs, militia muster, and election days were occasions for the relaxation of rules on the plantation. Some slaves were favored by being given permission to attend these events. Even if they did not go, there was an opportunity for them to sing, dance, and visit because of the festive spirit that such occasions brought to the plantation.

There were two periods to which slaves could look forward as periods of recreation and relaxation: the summer lay-by and Christmas. At the end of the cultivation period, there was a considerable reduction of duties, which gave slaves an opportunity either to work for themselves or to engage in some kind of recreation. The Christmas season brought a complete suspension of work, except the bare essentials such as cooking and washing, and for one week both town and plantation slaves had a period of merrymaking. On the Atlantic seaboard much of the festivities centered around the John Canoe celebration, a custom practiced in the Caribbean and perhaps in Africa in which slaves engaged in singing, dancing, drinking, and visiting the whites and asking for Christmas presents. Weddings, anniversaries, and the like, whether of whites or blacks, were other opportunities for merrymaking. Some planters even gave dances for their slaves. Doubtless these were exceptions. Few of the 4 million slaves in 1860 led anything except the most barren existence in which their only moments of pleasure were in singing a plaintive melody, strumming a banjo, telling a tale, or playing a game.

As long as proper precautions were taken there was little opposition to some form of religious activity among slaves. Owners had reason to be suspicious if the emphasis was on instruction or if there were slave leaders. Otherwise there was either support of a religious program for slaves or passive indifference. There were some black congregations on the larger plantations and in the towns. Richmond, Charleston, and Lexington, Kentucky, are examples of cities in which churches for slaves were located. One Mississippi planter erected a small Gothic church and paid a clergyman $1,500 to preach to him and his slaves. The number of black preachers was always considerable, and few plantations were without at least one.

When the abolitionists began their crusade against slavery, planters became more cautious regarding religious activities among slaves and undertook to control them more effectively. In most states black preachers were outlawed between 1830 and 1835, and thereafter slave religious services were presided over by a white person. More and more, however, slaves were required to attend the churches of their masters. This ambivalent attitude toward autonomous religious activity reflected whites' fears that it would be difficult, if not impossible, to control and monitor the beliefs and practices of slaves who were devout Christians. Such fears proved accurate, for many of the most pious and influential slaves had a keen understanding of the difference between the gospel of proslavery preachers and the Christian scriptures' message of divine punishment for oppressors and liberation for the faithful. Albert Raboteau has traced some of the numerous ways in which slaves blended their African religious culture with selected aspects of Christianity to produce a sustaining, and at times defiant, religious community—"the invisible institution in the ante-bellum South."

The invitation to slaves to attend white churches, which bordered on compulsion, did not represent a movement in the direction of increased fellowship. Rather, it was the method that whites employed to keep a closer eye on their slaves. It was believed that too many conspiracies had been planned at religious gatherings and that such groups gave abolitionists an opportunity to distribute incendiary ideas and literature. When Bishop Atkinson of North Carolina raised the question "Where are our Negroes," he not only implied that they were in churches other than the Episcopal church but that they were beyond the restraining influence of the conservative element of white society. When slaves attended the churches of planters, they usually sat either in the gallery or in a special section. The earliest examples of racial segregation could be found in churches. In one instance the white congregation constructed a partition several feet high to separate the masters from the slaves.

In the states of the lower South the Baptist and Methodist denominations had the greatest influence on plantation slaves. These were evangelical churches that moved with the population and adjusted their program to the needs of the people. The Methodist camp meetings and the Baptist "protracted" meetings were opportunities not only for religious refreshing but for social intercourse as well. They were the most effective means of releasing the pent-up emotions that the monotonous life of the rural South created. Thus, whites attended in large numbers, and, as Gilbert Seldes has pointed out, they were "times of refreshing." Under such circumstances, whites and Negroes sang together, shouted together, and spent themselves emotionally together. It was the nearest thing to interracial religious fellowship that the South produced.

Once planters were convinced that conversion did not have the effect of emancipating their slaves, they sought to use the church as an agency for maintaining the institution of slavery. Ministers were encouraged to instruct slaves along the lines of obedience and subserviency. Bishops and other high church officials were not above owning slaves and fostering the continuation of slavery. In Louisiana the Episcopal Bishop Polk owned 400 slaves, and although he regularly gave them religious instruction, there is no indication that he attempted to set them free. The Presbyterians and Quakers seemed to have been the most liberal in their attitude toward blacks, but they were not the large slaveholders. The latter were to be found in the Episcopal church

FAMILY WORSHIP ON A SOUTH CAROLINA PLANTATION. This drawing from the *Illustrated London News* for December 5, 1863, was made by an English artist while visiting a plantation near Port Royal, South Carolina. The "state of almost patriarchal simplicity" that characterizes the planter's position reflects the sympathetic attitude that many Englishmen had toward the Confederacy during the Civil War.

on the Atlantic seaboard and in the Baptist and Methodist churches in the cotton kingdom. In the last three decades before the Civil War the church became one of the strongest allies of the proslavery element. Slaves who had found refuge and solace in the religious instructions of the white clergy had reason to believe that they were now trapped by an enemy who had once befriended them.

Despite legal restrictions and despite contentions on the part of Southerners like John Calhoun that Africans could not absorb educative experiences, slaves were receiving education in various parts of the South. It is remarkable how generally the laws against the teaching of slaves were disregarded. Planters became excited over the distribution of abolition literature in the South, but they gave little attention to preventing the training of slaves to read, which would have rendered abolition literature ineffective to a large extent. Indeed, some masters themselves taught their slaves. William Pease of Hardman County, Tennessee, was taught by his owners. There was one strange case in which a planter taught his slaves to spell and read but not to write. One planter in northern Mississippi boasted that all twenty of his slaves could read and that they purchased their own books. The case of Frederick Douglass having been taught by his mistress is perhaps the best-known instance of an owner teaching a slave. In some cases, even when masters were opposed to their slaves receiving instruction, the children of masters would teach slaves to read and write. There are records of hirers and even overseers giving instruction to slaves.

The instruction of one or two slaves, though a violation of the law, was not regarded as serious, and there was hardly any danger of prosecution. But the instruction of slaves in schools was another thing. Even this was undertaken in various parts of the South. Naturally, more care had to be exercised in the selection of students and in the dissemination of information concerning the schools, but there were blacks and whites who were willing to run the risk of legal prosecution and social disapprobation in order to teach slaves. Schools for blacks are known to have existed in Savannah, Georgia; Charleston, South Carolina; Fayetteville, New Bern, and Raleigh, North Carolina; Lexington and Louisville, Kentucky; Fredericksburg and Norfolk, Virginia; and various other cities in Florida, Tennessee, and Louisiana. Francis Cardozo attended school in Charleston until he was twelve years of age. After searching for some time, Frederika Bremer, a European visitor, finally found one of the schools in Charleston and visited it. In 1847 there was a school in Louisville, Kentucky, which slaves were allowed to attend upon presenting permits from their masters.

There is no way of knowing the extent to which blacks attended white schools. In 1840 they were permitted to attend school with white children in Wilmington, Delaware. There is the interesting account, though perhaps fictional, of Julius Melbourn who was sent to a white academy near Raleigh, North Carolina, by his mistress and supposedly remained there until it was discovered that he was not white. Other mulattoes may well have had more success than Melbourn. Nor is there any way of ascertaining with any degree of accuracy the extent of education among slaves. Some Southern whites said that blacks did not have the capacity to learn. Some Northern abolitionists said conditions in the South were so bad that almost no blacks had the opportunity to learn. Amos Dresser believed that 1 out of every 50 slaves in the Southwest could read and write. C. G. Parsons estimated that 5,000 of Georgia's 400,000 slaves were literate. Whatever the number, it represented a clear-cut step in the direction of Americanization and made, at least for some, the process of adjustment to freedom somewhat less difficult.

The slave family experienced great difficulty in maintaining itself on a stable basis in a system where so little opportunity for expression was possible. Too seldom did the owner recognize the slave family as an institution worthy of respect, and frequently the blind forces inherent in the

Harriet Jacobs Remembers Her Life as a Young Slave Girl

But I now entered on my fifteenth year—a sad epoch in the life of a slave girl. My master began to whisper foul words in my ear. Young as I was, I could not remain ignorant of their import. I tried to treat them with indifference or contempt. The master's age, my extreme youth, and the fear that his conduct would be reported to my grandmother, made him bear this treatment for many months. He was a crafty man, and resorted to many means to accomplish his purposes. Sometimes he had stormy, terrific ways, that made his victims tremble; sometimes he assumed a gentleness that he thought must surely subdue. Of the two, I preferred his stormy moods, although they left me trembling. He tried his utmost to corrupt the pure principles my grandmother had instilled. He peopled my young mind with unclean images, such as only a vile monster could think of. I turned from him with disgust and hatred. But he was my master. I was compelled to live under the same roof with him—where I saw a man forty years my senior daily violating the most sacred commandments of nature. He told me I was his property; that I must be subject to his will in all things. My soul revolted against the mean tyranny. But where could I turn for protection? No matter whether the slave girl be as black as ebony or as fair as her mistress. In either case, there is no shadow of law to protect her from insult, from violence, or even from death; all these are inflicted by fiends who bear the shape of men. The mistress, who ought to protect the helpless victim, has no other feelings towards her but those of jealousy and rage.

Harriet A. Jacobs, *Incidents in the Life of a Slave Girl Written By Herself.* (Cambridge, Mass., 1987), pp. 27–28.

system operated to destroy it. Courtship and the normal relationships preliminary to marriage seldom existed. Only when owners manifested some real interest in the religious and moral development of their slaves was there an effort to establish slave families on a stable basis. There are instances where planters insisted on religious ceremonies to unite slave couples, and there is one case of a mistress insisting upon "passing" on all the suitors of her female slaves. One thing that distressed almost all slaveholders was the desire of slaves to marry slaves on other plantations. Such a union, planters knew, would involve one or the other of the slaves being away from his or her own plantation at various times and reduced efficiency as a worker. Slaves were, therefore, encouraged to marry on the plantation if at all possible, and when this was not possible masters sought either to purchase the spouse of their slave or sell their slave to the owner of the spouse.

The permanency of a slave marriage depended on the extent to which the couple had an opportunity to work and live together so that through common experiences they could be drawn closer together. There are numerous examples of the emergence of a stable slave family, especially where there were children to strengthen the bond and where they were not divided through sale. It has been well said by E. Franklin Frazier that the economic interests of the masters were often inimical to the family life of the slaves, but John Blassingame and Herbert Gutman have shown that the slave family was frequently a viable institution.

The bearing of children was often extremely hard for the slave women. Lack of adequate medical care had a particularly negative impact on the health of slave women during pregnancies, childbirths, and the period immediately thereafter, and the high death rate of slave infants in many ways was a reflection of this. Although having learned, by observing the white family unit, certain elements of so-called decency and self-respect, the slave woman was frequently forced into cohabitation and pregnancy by her master. Obviously in such cases the family was established on a very tenuous basis. She may have learned to care for her husband, who had been forced upon her, but the likelihood was not very great. Nor did she have much opportunity to develop any real attachment for her children. Little time off was given for childbearing, and child rearing was of course a haphazard arrangement in which the mother, just like everyone else, was relieved of any responsibility. Nevertheless, the slave mother did what she could to stabilize her family and to keep it together. Division by sale was fiercely resisted. J. W. Loguen's mother, for example, had to be tied to a loom when her children were taken from her to be sold, and Josiah Henson's mother looked on "in an agony of grief" as she saw her children sold one by one.

Sir Charles Lyell said that "one of the most serious evils of slavery is its tendency to blight domestic happiness; and the anxiety of parents for their sons, and constant fear of licentious intercourse with slaves is painfully great." This "evil" not only blighted the happiness of the white family but was one of the powerful forces operating to weaken the slave family altogether. The extensive miscegenation that went on was largely the result of people living and working together at common tasks and the subjection of slave women to the whims and desires of white men. There was some race mixture that resulted from the association of black men and white women, but this was only a small percent of the total. Despite all the laws against the intermingling of the races, the practice continued, and its persistence is another example of the refusal of the members of the dominant group to abide by the laws that they themselves created.

In cities like Charleston, Mobile, and New Orleans there was widespread intermixture. In New Orleans the practice of young white men maintaining young black women in a state of concubinage became so common as almost to gain social acceptability. Some relationships were the result of physical compulsion on the part of the white man, and if resistance was offered it was frequently beaten back in the most vicious manner. Many slave women carried to their graves scars that had been inflicted by their owners or other whites when resistance was offered to their advances. Other slave women did not resist, either because of futility, the prestige that such a relationship could bring, or because of the material advantages that might accrue from it. Children born of such unions were slaves, and the result of such extensive mixing was that by 1850 there were 246,000 mulatto slaves out of a total slave population of 3.2 million. By 1860 there were 411,000 mulatto slaves out of a total slave population of 3.9 million. The number may well have been greater, for census takers counted as mulattoes only those who appeared to be of mixed parentage, but there were many mulattoes who did not appear to be.

The reactions of white fathers to their black progeny were varied. Some had no feeling for them at all and sold them when the opportunity presented itself, just as they would sell any other slave. Not infrequently they were encouraged to do this by their wives, who resented the presence of slave children who had been fathered by their husbands. Other men, however, developed a great fondness for their slave children and emancipated them and provided for them. Frequently, old, repentant men atoned for their youthful waywardness by freeing their mulatto children and giving them land and money. Few, however, bestowed as much as John Stewart of Petersburg, who left to his "natural colored daughter" a house, a lot, and all of his money, which amounted to $19,500.

■ The Slave's Reaction to Bondage

Owners of slaves almost always sought to convey the impression that their human chattel were docile, tractable, and happy. This effort became a part of their defense of the institution, and they went to the extreme in this representation. Frequently, also, the antislavery forces contended that slaves were easily controlled and that was the explanation for their exploitation by their owners. Each group in its own way, therefore, was inclined to overstate the case and to refuse to make a realistic appraisal of a slave's true reaction to his or her status. There is no reason to conclude that the personality of a slave was permanently impaired by engaging in duplicity in the slave-master relationship. It must be remembered that some of the actions of slaves were superficial and were for the purpose of misleading their owners regarding their true feelings. In the process of adjustment innumerable techniques to escape work as well as punishment were developed and in many instances were successful. Any understanding of reactions to slave status must be approached with the realization that the slave at times was possessed of a dual personality and could be one person at one time and quite a different person at another time.

It cannot be denied that as old as the institution of slavery was, human beings had not, by the nineteenth century, brought themselves to the point where they could be subjected to it without protest and resistance. Resistance could be found wherever slavery existed, and slavery in the United States was no exception. Too frequently, misunderstanding, suspicion, and hatred were mutually shared by master and slave. Indeed, they were natural enemies, and on many occasions they conducted themselves as such. There are, of course, numerous examples of kindness and understanding on the part of owners as well as docility—which may be more accurately described as accommodation—and tractability on the part of slaves. But this was an unnatural relationship and was not, by the nature of things, inherent in the system.

The brutality that apparently was indigenous in a system of human exploitation existed in every community where slavery was established. The wastefulness and extravagance of the plantation system made no exception of human resources. Slaves were for economic gain, and if beating them would increase their efficiency—and this was generally believed—then the rod and lash should not be spared. Far from being a civilizing force, moreover, the plantation bred indecency in human relations, and the slave was the immediate victim of the barbarity of a system that commonly exploited the sex of the women and the work of everyone. Finally, the psychological situation that was created by the master-slave relationship stimulated terrorism and brutality because masters felt secure in their position and interpreted their role as calling for that type of conduct. Many masters as well as slaves got the reputation of being "bad," and this did nothing to relieve the tension that seemed to be mounting everywhere as the institution developed.

The laws that were for the purpose of protecting slaves were few and were seldom enforced. It was almost impossible to secure the conviction of a master who mistreated a slave. Knowing that, the owner was inclined to take the law into his or her own hands. Overseers were generally notorious for their brutality, and the accounts of abuse and mistreatment on their part as well as on the part of hirers are numerous. Masters and mistresses were perhaps almost as guilty. In 1827 a Georgia grand jury brought in a true bill of manslaughter against a slave owner for beating his slave to death, but he was acquitted. Several years later Thomas Sorrell of the same state was found guilty of killing one of his slaves with an axe, but the jury recommended him to the mercy of the court. In Kentucky a Mrs. Maxwell had a wide reputation for beating her slaves, both men and women, on the face as well as the body. There is also the shocking account of Mrs. Alpheus Lewis, who burned her slave girl around the neck with hot tongs. Drunken masters had little regard for their slaves, the most sensational example of which is a Kentucky man who dismembered his slave and threw him piece by piece into the fire. One Mississippi master dragged from the bed a slave whom he suspected of theft and inflicted over 1,000 lashes. Repeated descriptions of runaways contained phrases such as "large scar on hip," "no marks except those on his back," "much scarred with the whip," and "will no doubt show the marks of a recent whipping." They suggest a type of brutality that doubtless contributed toward the slave's decision to abscond.

To the demonstrations of brutality as well as to the very institution of slavery itself, slaves reacted in various ways. Thanks to the religion of their masters they could be philosophical about the whole thing and escape through ritual and song. The emphasis on otherworldliness in slave songs certainly suggested grim dissatisfaction with their worldly status. "Dere's a Great Camp Meetin' in de Promised Land," "Look Away in de Heaven, Lord," "Fo' My Soul's Goin' to Heaven Jes' Sho's You Born," and "Heaven, Heaven, Everybody Talkin' 'Bout Heaven Ain't Goin' There" are only a few of the songs that slaves sang in the hope that their burdens would be relieved in the next world. As long as they were in this world they had to make the most of a bad situation by loafing on the job, feigning illness in the fields and on the auction block, and engaging in an elaborate program of sabotage. Slaves were so hard on farming tools that special ones were developed for them. They drove the animals with a cruelty that suggested revenge, and they could be so ruthless in destruction of the fields that the most careful supervision was necessary to ensure survival of the crops until harvest time. Forests, barns, and homes were burned to the extent that members of the patrol were frequently fearful of leaving home lest they be visited with revenge in the form of destruction of their property by fire.

Self-mutilation and suicide were popular forms of resistance to slavery. Slaves cut off their toes and hands and mutilated themselves in other ways so as to render themselves ineffective as workers. One Kentucky slave carpenter, for example, cut off one of his hands and the fingers of the other when he learned that he was to be sold down the river. There were several instances of slaves having shot themselves in the hand or foot, especially upon being recovered from running away. The number of suicides seems relatively high, and certainly the practice was widespread. Slaves fresh from Africa committed suicide in great numbers. In 1807 two boatloads of Africans newly arrived in Charleston starved themselves to death. When his slave woman was found dead by her own hanging in 1829, a Georgia planter was amazed since he saw no reason why she should want to take her own life. When two Louisiana slaves were returned to their master after having been stolen in 1858, they drowned themselves in the bayou. One of the South's wealthiest planters, Charles Manigault, lost a slave by a similar act when the overseer threatened him with punishment. Sometimes slave mothers killed their own children to prevent them from growing up in slavery.

Much more disturbing to the South were the numerous instances of slaves doing violence to the master class. Poisoning was always feared, and perhaps some planters felt a real need for an official taster. As early as 1761 the Charleston *Gazette* remarked that the "Negroes have begun the hellish act of poisoning." Arsenic and other similar compounds were used. Where they were not available, slaves are known to have resorted to mixing ground glass in the gravy for their masters' tables. Numerous slaves were convicted of murdering their masters and overseers, but some escaped. In 1797 a Screven County, Georgia, planter was killed by his newly imported African slave. Another Georgia master was killed by a slave who stabbed him sixteen times.

The slave was later burned alive. The slave of William Pearce of Florida killed his master with an axe when Pearce sought to punish him. Carolina Turner of Kentucky was choked to death by a slave whom she was flogging. Though the citizenry had long complained of the woman's merciless brutality in dealing with her slaves, her killer was summarily hanged for his deed. The times that overseers and masters were killed by slaves in the woods or fields were exceedingly numerous, as the careful reading of almost any Southern newspaper will reveal.

Every Southern community raised its annual crop of runaway slaves. There was both federal and state legislation to aid in their recovery, but many slaves escaped forever. The practice of running away became so widespread that every state sought to strengthen its patrol and other safeguards, but to little avail. Hardly a newspaper went to press without several advertisements listing runaways, and sometimes there were several columns of such advertisements. The following is typical:

> Absconded from the Forest Plantation of the late William Dunbar, on Sunday the 7th instant, a very handsome Mulattress called Harriet, about 13 years old, with straight dark hair and dark eyes. This girl was lately in New Orleans, and is known to have seen there a man whom she claims as her father and who does now or did lately live on the Mississippi, a little above the mouth of the Caffalaya. It is highly probable some plan has been concocted for the girl's escape.

Long before the Underground Railroad was an effective antislavery device (see Chapter 10) slaves were running away: men, women, and children, singly, in pairs, or in groups. At times they went so far as to organize themselves into groups called Maroons and to live in communities, on the order of Palmares in Brazil. The forests, mountains, and swamps of the Southern states were their favorite locations, and they proved to be troublesome to the masters who sought to maintain strict order on their plantations.

Some slaves disguised themselves or armed themselves with free passes in their effort to escape. Others simply walked off, apparently hoping that fate would be kind and assist in their permanent escape. Some were inveterate runaways such as the North Carolina woman who fled from her master's plantation no less than sixteen times. Others were not as daring and gave up after one unsuccessful attempt. While there is no way of even approximating the number of runaways, it is obvious that fleeing from the institution was one of the slaves' most effective means of resistance. It represented the continuous fight that slaves carried on against their masters.

The most sensational and desperate reaction of slaves to their status was the conspiracy to revolt. To those who could summon the nerve to strike for their freedom in a group, it was what might be termed "carrying the fight to the enemy" in the hope that it would end, once and for all, the degradation of human enslavement. To whites it was a mad, sinister act of

Henry Bibb Writes to His Former Master—1844

You may perhaps think hard of us for running away from slavery, but as to myself, I have but one apology to make for it, which is this: I have only to regret that I did not start at an earlier period. I might have been free long before I was. But you had it in your power to have kept me there much longer than you did. I think it is very probable that I should have been a toiling slave on your property to-day, if you had treated me differently.

To be compelled to stand by and see you whip and slash my wife without mercy, when I could afford her no protection, not even by offering myself to suffer the lash in her place, was more than I felt it to be the duty of a slave husband to endure, while the way was open to Canada. My infant child was also frequently flogged by Mrs. Gatewood, for crying, until its skin was bruised literally purple. This kind of treatment was what drove me from home and family, to seek a better home for them. But I am willing to forget the past. I should be pleased to hear from you again, on the reception of this, and should also be very happy to correspond with you often, if it should be agreeable to yourself. I subscribe myself a friend to the oppressed, and Liberty forever.

Narrative of the Life and Adventures of Henry Bibb, an American Slave, in Gilbert Osofsky, ed., *Puttin' on Ole Massa* (New York, 1969), pp. 155–156.

desperate savages, in league with the devil, who could not appreciate the benign influences of the institution and who would dare shed the blood of their benefactors. Inherent in revolts was bloodshed on both sides. Blacks accepted this as the price of liberty, while whites were panic-stricken at the very thought of it. Even rumors of insurrections struck terror in the hearts of slaveholders and called forth the most vigorous efforts to guard against the dreaded eventuality.

Revolts, or conspiracies to revolt, persisted down to 1865. They began with the institution and did not end until slavery was abolished. It can, therefore, be said that they were a part of the institution, a kind of bitterness that whites had to take along with the sweetness of slavery. As the country was turning to Jeffersonian Republicanism at the beginning of the nineteenth century, many people believed that a new day had arrived for the common person. Some blacks, however, felt that they would have to force their new day by breaking away from slavery. In Henrico County, Virginia, they resolved to revolt against the institution under the leadership of Gabriel Prosser and Jack Bowler. For months they planned the desperate move, gathering clubs, swords, and the like for the appointed day. On August 30, 1800, over 1,000 slaves met six miles outside of Richmond and began to march on the city, but a violent storm almost routed the insurgents. Two slaves had already informed the whites, and Governor Monroe, acting promptly, called out more than 600 troops and notified every militia commander in the state. In due time scores of slaves were arrested, and 35 were executed. Gabriel Prosser was captured in late September, and after he refused to talk to anyone he too was executed.

Whites speculated extravagantly over the number of slaves involved in this major uprising. The estimates ran all the way from 2,000 to 50,000. The large numbers, together with the total disregard slaves seemed to have for their own lives, caused the whites to shudder. The "high ground" that slaves took in maintaining silence added to the stark terror of the whole situation. When one was asked what he had to say, he calmly replied:

> I have nothing more to offer than what General Washington would have had to offer, had he been taken by the British officers and put to trial by them. I have ventured my life in endeavouring to obtain the liberty of my country-men, and am a willing sacrifice to their cause; and I beg, as a favour, that I may be immediately led to execution. I know that you have predetermined to shed my blood, why then all this mockery of a trial?

The unrest among slaves, even in Virginia, continued into the following year, and plots were reported in Petersburg and Norfolk and in various places in North Carolina. The latter state became so excited that many slaves were lashed, branded, and cropped, and at least 15 were hanged for alleged implication in conspiracies. In the following years before the war with England there were reports of insurrection up and down the Atlantic seaboard. Conspiracy had crossed the mountains, for in 1810 a plot was uncovered in Lexington, Kentucky. The following year, more than 400 rebellious slaves in Louisiana had to be put down by federal and state troops. At least 75 slaves lost their lives in the encounter and in the trials that ensued. There was another uprising in New Orleans in the following year.

Following the War of 1812 the efforts of slaves to revolt continued. In Virginia in 1815 a white man, George Boxley, decided to attempt to free the slaves. He made elaborate plans, but a slave woman betrayed him and his conspirators. Although Boxley himself escaped, six slaves were hanged and another six were banished. When the revolutions of Latin America and Europe broke out, Americans could not restrain themselves in their praise and support of the fighters for liberty. The South joined in the loud hosannas, while slaves watched the movements for the emancipation of the slaves in Latin America and the Caribbean. Perhaps all these developments had something to do with what was the most elaborate, though not the most effective, conspiracy of the period: the Denmark Vesey insurrection.

Vesey had purchased his freedom in 1800 and for a score of years had made a respectable living as a carpenter in Charleston, South Carolina. He was a sensitive, liberty-loving person and was not satisfied in the enjoyment of his

NAT TURNER EXHORTING HIS FOLLOWERS. The 1831 revolt of Nat Turner and his followers in Virginia resulted in the deaths of his master and numerous other whites. Once the revolt was crushed, dazed whites strengthened slave codes and redoubled vigilance. The artist's depiction reflects whites' fears of the consequences of blacks meeting without the supervision of their masters. *(Culver Pictures.)*

own relatively comfortable existence. He believed in equality for everyone and resolved to do something for his slave brothers and sisters. Over a period of several years he carefully plotted his revolt and chose his assistants. Together they made and collected their weapons: 250 pike heads and bayonets and 300 daggers. Vesey also sought assistance from Haiti. He set the second Sunday in July 1822 for the day of the revolt; and when the word leaked out, he moved it up one month, but his assistants, who were scattered for miles around Charleston, did not all get the word. Meanwhile, the whites were well aware of what was going on and began to round up suspects. At least 139 blacks were arrested, 47 of whom were condemned. Even 4 white men were fined and imprisoned for encouraging them in their work. Estimates of the number of blacks involved in the plot ran as high as 9,000.

The following decade saw the entire South apprehensive over possible uprisings. The revival of the antislavery movement and the publication of such incendiary material as David Walker's *Appeal* put the South's nerves on edge. Several revolts were reported on Louisiana plantations in 1829, and in 1830 a number of citizens of North Carolina asked their legislature for aid because their slaves had become "almost uncountroulable." The panic of the 1820s culminated in 1831 with the insurrection of Nat Turner. This slave from Southampton County, Virginia, was a mystical, rebellious person who had on one occasion run away and then decided to return to his master. Perhaps he had already begun to feel that he had been selected by some divine power to deliver his people from slavery.

Upon the occasion of the solar eclipse in February 1831, Turner decided that the time had come for him to lead his people out of bondage. He selected the Fourth of July as the day, but when he became ill he postponed the revolt until he saw another sign. On August 13, when the sun turned a "peculiar greenish blue," he called the revolt for August 21. He and his followers began by killing Turner's master, Joseph Travis, and his family. In rapid succession other families fell before the blows of the blacks. Within twenty-four hours 60 whites had been killed. The revolt was spreading rapidly when the main group of blacks was met and overpowered by state and federal troops. More than 100 slaves were killed in the encounter, and 13 slaves and 3 free Negroes were immediately hanged. Turner was captured on October 30, and in less than two weeks, on November 11, he was executed.

The South was completely dazed by the Southampton uprising. The situation was grossly exaggerated in many communities. Some reports were that whites had been murdered by the hundreds in Virginia. Small wonder that several states felt it necessary to call special sessions of the legislature to consider the emergency. Most states strengthened their Slave Codes, and citizens literally remained awake nights waiting for slaves to make another break. The uprisings continued. In 1835 several slaves in Monroe County, Georgia, were hanged or whipped to death because of implication in a conspiracy. In the following decade there were several uprisings in Alabama, Louisiana, and Mississippi. In 1853 a serious revolt in New Orleans involving 2,500 slaves was aborted by the informing of a free black. In 1856 the Maroons in Bladen and Robeson counties, North Carolina, "went on the warpath" and terrorized the countryside. Up until and throughout the Civil War, slaves demonstrated their violent antipathy for slavery by continuing to rise against it.

One little-known sidelight of slave revolts is the encouragement and assistance that whites gave to blacks. Two Frenchmen were said to have been involved in Gabriel Prosser's plot. In 1802 a Virginia slave confessed that some white men had promised to help him secure arms and ammunition for an uprising. It will be recalled that four white men were convicted for encouraging Denmark Vesey's uprising. In Mississippi in 1835, twenty-one "bleached and unbleached" conspirators were hanged. In the same year white men in Georgia were involved in a plot, and two whites were hanged in Louisiana for helping to plan an uprising. There were always reports that whites, whose names were most difficult to obtain, were assisting in some way with slave plots. It is not at all strange that some whites sou' encourage the revolts. When consideration is given to the large nur whites in the South who could have traced their economic and soci directly to slavery, it is surprising to find that there was not a large involved in attempts to wipe out the institution of slavery.

CHAPTER 9

Quasi-Free Blacks

■ American Anomaly

With the prohibition of slavery in several Northern states and with programs for gradual emancipation in others before the end of the eighteenth century, it was only natural that free blacks would in due time become a substantial element of the population. Slavery, moreover, had been excluded from the Northwest Territory, though it persisted there for several decades after 1787. There had been some free blacks during the entire colonial period, but for the most part they were inconsiderable in number and inconsequential in influence. The Revolution, with its philosophy of egalitarianism, had served to increase the number of free blacks not only in the North but in the South too, where some masters put the philosophy into practice. But in the South the existence of a large group of free blacks proved to be a source of constant embarrassment to slaveholders, for it tended to undermine the very foundation on which slavery was built. The perpetuation of relations between the whites and blacks in the South was predicated upon the indisputable control of the latter by the former. Free blacks, regardless of what their rights were theoretically, could not be an exception. It became necessary, therefore, for Southerners to carry on a campaign of vilification against free blacks in order to "keep them in their place." In the heat of this campaign one antagonist went so far as to describe free blacks as "an incubus upon the land."

Despite Southern opposition to the presence of free blacks, white people themselves were frequently responsible for the increase. Masters, stricken by conscience, impelled by affection, or yielding to the temptation to evade responsibility, manumitted their slaves in large numbers until legislation either discouraged or prevented them from doing so. Many slaves were freed by their masters through deeds of manumission. In some instances the manumitted were children of a master by one of his slaves. Others were manumitted through wills, like the slaves of John Randolph, numbering more than 400, who were set free upon his death in 1833. There were stipulations in some wills that slaves should be set free upon reaching a certain age or upon the death of the testator's heirs. Either individual owners or the state manumitted slaves occasionally for meritorious service. The slave who saved the Georgia capitol from destruction by fire was set free in 1834. Pierre Chastang of Mobile was bought and freed by popular subscription because of his outstanding service in the War of 1812 and in the yellow fever epidemic of 1819.

Enterprising slaves were able to amass sufficient capital to purchase their freedom, especially if their masters were willing to cooperate. There are several examples of masters who set up programs of self-hire for slaves who looked toward purchasing themselves. Some slaves, regardless of their masters' attitude, saved enough money to purchase their freedom. Lunsford Lane of Raleigh, for example, spent his spare time making pipes, raising chickens, and engaging in other tasks in order to realize his ambition of becoming free. A slave could not always trust an owner who promised freedom upon the payment of a certain amount of money, as one of Lane's friends found out after he had given his owner $800 and then had had to run away. Indeed, thousands of slaves secured their freedom by running away.

As the number of free blacks increased by these various methods of obtaining freedom, it also multiplied through the natural excess of births over deaths. Children born of free black mothers were also free, and as the free black family achieved a degree of stability, children became an important factor in adding to their numbers. There was some increase, moreover, from the birth of mulatto children to white mothers. The practice of white women mixing with black men was fairly widespread during the colonial period and had not entirely ceased by 1865.

There were 59,000 free blacks in the United States at the time of the first decennial census in 1790. Slightly more than 27,000 were in the Northern states, and 32,000 in the South. In the next decade they increased by approximately 82 percent, and in the following decade by 71 percent. After 1810 the rate of increase fell sharply, a trend that continued up until 1860. This decline was due largely to laws against manumission and to the opposition of those who viewed their increase with great alarm. Many states required blacks to leave the state upon being manumitted. By 1830 there were 319,000 free blacks in the United States, and thirty years later the number had climbed to 488,000, of whom 44 percent lived in the South Atlantic states and 46 percent in the North. The remainder were to be found in the South Central states and the West. Maryland led all other states with

DEED OF MANUMISSION. Ebenezer Rothwell of Newcastle County, Delaware, promised to set free his twenty-year-old slave, Isaac, when he reached the age of thirty-two. Other popular forms of emancipation were by will and by legislative act. *(Original ms. The Moorland-Spingarn Research Center, Howard University.)*

83,900 free blacks in 1860, a figure only slightly smaller than the slave population. Virginia was next with 58,000, followed closely by Pennsylvania with 56,000, its entire black population.

By 1860 free blacks were concentrated in six areas: the tidewater counties of Virginia and Maryland; the Piedmont region of Virginia and North Carolina; the Southern cities of Baltimore, Washington, Charleston, Mobile, and New Orleans; the Northern cities of Boston, New York, Cincinnati, and Philadelphia; isolated areas in the old Northwest like Cass County, Michigan,

Hammond County, Indiana, and Wilberforce, Ohio; and communities in which blacks had mixed freely with Indians, such as those in Massachusetts, North Carolina, and Florida. Free blacks were inclined to be urban. In 1860 there were 25,600 in Baltimore, 22,000 in Philadelphia, 12,500 in New York, 10,600 in New Orleans, and 3,200 in Charleston. The greater opportunities, both economic and social, doubtless accounted for their tendency to concentrate in cities.

Wherever free blacks settled, they lived somewhat precariously upon the sufferance of the whites. Their legal status was fairly high during the colonial period and was strengthened somewhat during the Revolutionary period. After that time, however, their status deteriorated, until toward the end of the slave period the distinction between slaves and free blacks had diminished to a point where in some instances it was hardly discernible. Free blacks found it especially difficult to maintain their freedom. A white person could claim, however fraudulently, that a black person was a slave, and there was very little he or she could do about it. There was, moreover, the danger of the black person's being kidnapped, as often happened. The chances of being reduced to servitude or slavery by the courts were also great. A large majority of free blacks lived in daily fear of losing what freedom they had. One slip or ignorance of the law would send them back into slavery. Several states, such as Virginia, Tennessee, Georgia, and Mississippi, required registration. Florida, Georgia, and several other states compelled free blacks to have white guardians. All Southern states required them to have passes, and if one was caught without a certificate of freedom, he or she was presumed to be a slave.

The controls that the state and the community exercised over free blacks mounted year by year. One especially annoying regulation limited their movement. In no Southern state could they move about as they wished, and in some Northern communities it was dangerous to try, lest they be thought fugitive slaves. North Carolina prohibited free blacks from going beyond the county adjoining the one in which they resided. As early as 1793 Virginia barred them from entering the state, and by 1835 most of the Southern and several Northern states had restricted or prohibited free black immigration. Penalties for violations of these laws were severe. In Georgia, for example, the offender was fined $100, and failing to pay it—which could be expected—was sold into slavery. There were also laws against free blacks leaving the state for any length of time, such as sixty or ninety days, and returning.

There was a mass of legislation designed to insure the white community against any threats or dangers from free blacks. Virginia, Maryland, and North Carolina were among the states forbidding them to possess or carry arms without a license. This permit was issued annually, and only to those whose conduct was above reproach. By 1835 the right of assembly had been taken away from almost all free blacks in the South. They could not hold church services without the presence of a licensed and respectable white minister. Benevolent societies and similar organizations were not allowed to

CERTIFICATE OF FREEDOM. Most communities required free blacks to carry such a certificate on their person at all times. Not all of them provided printed forms such as this one, which was issued by the court clerk of Chesterfield County, Virginia. (*Original ms. The Moorland-Spingarn Research Center, Howard University.*)

convene. In Maryland they could not have "lyceums, lodges, fire companies, or literary, dramatic, social, moral, or charitable societies." In many communities contact with slaves was kept at a minimum, and laws against entertaining slaves or visiting them were among those most strenuously enforced.

A number of proscriptions made it especially difficult for free blacks to make a living. In 1805 Maryland prohibited them from selling corn, wheat, or tobacco without a license. In 1829 Georgia made it illegal for them to be employed as typesetters. Two years later North Carolina required all black traders and peddlers to be licensed, while South Carolina forbade the employment of free blacks as clerks. A large number of states made it illegal for them either to purchase or to sell alcoholic beverages. Georgia free blacks could not make purchases on credit without the permission of their guardians. Despite these restrictions every state required free blacks to work, and their means of support had to be visible. As early as 1725 Pennsylvania had set the pattern by ordaining that "if any free negroe, fit to work, shall neglect so to do and loiter and misspend his or her time . . . any two Magistrates . . .

are . . . impowered and required to bind out to service, such negroe, from year to year, as to them may seem meet." Other states passed similar laws during the national period, some going so far as to require free blacks to post bonds as security against becoming public charges. Not only were adult free blacks hired or bound out, but their children were taken and placed in the care of white persons. Illegitimate children whose parents had violated some law or were without means of supporting them were apprenticed out to be taught a trade and to be given moral instruction.

In some states the constitutions written during the Revolutionary period did not exclude free blacks from voting. They voted to a considerable extent in Maryland, North Carolina, New York, and Pennsylvania for several years. All Southern states entering the Union after 1789, except Tennessee, excluded Negroes from the franchise. In a bill signed by President Jefferson in 1802 they were excluded from the franchise in the nation's newly established capital, Washington, D.C. Shortly after the beginning of the nineteenth century, as the campaign to reduce the free black's status got under way, states both in the North and South began to disfranchise them. Maryland's free blacks lost the ballot in 1810. Those in Tennessee were disfranchised in 1834, and in the following year those in North Carolina lost the ballot. Even Pennsylvania confined the privilege to white males in 1838. In its constitution of 1821, New York set up a property qualification of $250 for blacks and a residence requirement of three years for free-black suffrage. Meanwhile, whites had no property requirements for voting and could qualify with only a one year's residency. In states that did not disfranchise blacks, their political influence was taken lightly and there was no extensive voting by blacks anywhere after 1830.

Despite these significant reductions in status, free blacks were expected to bear the burdens that other citizens bore, and in some instances they were expected to do even more. In Pensacola, Florida, they had to pay a tax of $2 for putting on entertainments. In Baltimore in 1859 and in other places as well, they were expected to pay school taxes, but their children were not allowed to attend publicly supported schools. In general they were barred from serving in a state militia except as musicians or servants. Two significant exceptions were the New York law of 1814 raising two black regiments and the Louisiana laws of 1812 authorizing a militia corps of free men of color and, in Natchitoches, a police corps of free blacks.

The right to own and dispose of property was generally conceded to free blacks. When Texas was a republic there was some question as to whether they could own land there, but their right had at least been partially recognized by the time Texas entered the Union in 1845. Only Georgia, in 1818, forbade free blacks to own any real estate or slaves, but the following year the act was repealed, except for Savannah, Augusta, and Darien.

In courts of law the testimony of free blacks was not admissible in cases where whites were parties. Perhaps the clearest example of the disesteem in which free blacks were held was the general policy of permitting slaves, viewed as wholly irresponsible before the law, to testify against them. In practice, however, the courts were fairly lenient toward them. Indeed, from the courts, especially the higher ones, they received the greatest protection. In rejecting the claims of a white person that a black person should be thrown out of court because he had not proved that he was free, the Maryland Court of Appeals said that, in pleading, he did not have to prove his freedom. A justice of the North Carolina Supreme Court went so far as to say that a free black could strike a white man in self-defense: "A free negro, however lowly his condition, is in the 'peace of the State,' and to deprive him of this right would be to put him on the footing of an outlaw."

Slaveholding states had a rather peculiar way of demonstrating their interest in the welfare of free blacks. Since their life was especially difficult, legislators were of the opinion that this class of people should be given the opportunity to choose their masters and reenslave themselves. In 1857 Tennessee enacted a law to facilitate reenslavement. In the following year Texas enacted such a law, and in 1859 and 1860, respectively, Louisiana and Maryland passed similar legislation. Several other states, including North Carolina, seriously considered such statutes, but for various reasons failed to enact them. Perhaps Arkansas went farthest: in 1859 the legislature passed an act to remove free blacks and mulattoes by compelling those who remained in the state at the end of a year to choose masters "who must give bond not to allow such negroes to act as free."

■ Economic and Social Development

It was only natural that free blacks should experience great difficulty in achieving anything resembling economic stability and independence. There was, first of all, the considerable psychological adjustment that had to be made in the transition from enslavement to freedom for all except those who were born free. The success and rapidity of this transition frequently depended upon the responsibility a person had been able to assume while still a slave. Another difficulty, almost insurmountable in some places, was the strong opposition of many white workers to blacks, especially in the artisan class. Whites sought legislation barring them from certain trades; failing in this, they frequently resorted to intimidation and violence in order to eliminate the competition of free blacks. Finally, there was legislation that restricted the movements of free blacks, barred them from certain occupations, and placed them at a disadvantage in other ways. The vast majority were without any special skills and had to content themselves with being agricultural workers or, in urban communities, common laborers. Thanks to the apprenticing system established in some states and to the practice of training many slaves as artisans, a considerable number of free blacks possessed skills that enabled them to achieve a degree of economic independence and affluence before the Civil War.

TABLE 4
Free Black Real Estate Ownership in Fourteen Cities in 1850

CITIES	VALUE OF REAL ESTATE	NUMBER OF OWNERS	AVERAGE VALUE OF HOLDING
New Orleans	$2,354,640	650	$3,623
Philadelphia	327,000	77	4,248
Cincinnati	317,780	118	2,693
Charleston	200,600	47	4,268
Brooklyn	145,785	98	1,488
Baltimore	137,488	101	1,361
New York	110,010	71	1,549
Washington	108,816	178	611
Louisville	95,650	63	1,518
Pittsburgh	74,200	38	1,953
Buffalo	57,610	41	1,405
St. Louis	49,650	16	3,103
Albany	44,400	32	1,388
Boston	41,900	13	3,223

Source: Leonard P. Curry. The Free Black in Urban America 1800–1850: The Shadow of the Dream. *The University of Chicago Press (Chicago, Ill. 1983), p. 267. Reprinted by permission.*

Despite the strong opposition of white workers, urban blacks followed their trades if they had any. Even the unskilled found some kind of work to do because they were concentrated in areas that were losing white workers to the West, and in the shortage that prevailed even the labor of the despised black was welcomed. In Charleston, Charles H. Wesley found free blacks engaged in more than 50 occupations, many of them requiring a high degree of skill. They worked in the building trades, made clothing and foods, operated machines, and piloted ships. There were more than 70 occupations in North Carolina in which they were engaged. Among those working in Baltimore in 1860 were several confectioners, druggists, and grocers. Though there were only slightly more than 2,000 free blacks in Boston in 1860, they were scattered among nearly 100 occupations, including paperhanging, engraving, quarrying, photography, and tailoring. They were also in the professions of the ministry, teaching, law, and dentistry. Practically the same can be said for those in New York City and, to a lesser extent, in Cincinnati. In Philadelphia in 1859, they engaged in more than 130 occupations, all of which involved the exercise of skills. Even in the deep South there were free blacks working in occupations and professions that would have disturbed those who were opposed to their progress and surprised those who were convinced of their improvidence. In Atlanta, for example, Roderick Badger was practicing dentistry in 1859. In New Orleans, where in 1845 Norbert Rillieux had invented a vacuum pan for evaporating syrup in the manufacture of sugar, there were teachers, jewelers, architects, and lithographers in 1860. Almost every community had its free black carpenters, barbers, cabinetmakers, and brickmasons; many had shopkeepers, salespeople, and clerks, even where it was in violation of the law.

Aid given by some owners as well as by organizations such as the Society of Friends, the Pennsylvania Society for the Abolition of Slavery, and the North Carolina Manumission Society helped free blacks get a start, and this assistance frequently amounted to enough for them to acquire their first piece of property, usually personal. One benevolent master in Baltimore gave his manumitted slave a house and a lot worth more than $12,000 in 1859. Several gave their freed chattel as much as 100 acres of land. From these benevolences and from their own efforts, free blacks gradually accumulated property. As early as 1800 those in Philadelphia owned nearly 100 houses and lots. By 1837, in New York City, they owned $1.4 million worth of taxable real estate and had $600,000 on deposit in savings banks. In Cincinnati, the property of free blacks was valued at more than $500,000. These evidences of economic stability caused one European observer to describe them as "shrewd and sensible blacks."

Free blacks in the Southern states also accumulated property. In Maryland they paid taxes on more than $1 million of real property in 1860, and 12 owned property valued in excess of $5,000. Luther P. Jackson found that in Virginia in 1860 they owned more than 60,000 acres of farmland and their city real estate was valued at $463,000. In North Carolina they owned $480,000 worth of real property and $564,000 worth of personal property in 1860. In Charleston, 352 blacks paid taxes in 1859 on property valued in excess of $778,000. Tennessee's free blacks owned about $750,000 worth of real and personal property in 1860. The affluence of a large number of free blacks in New Orleans is well known. They owned more than $15 million worth of property in 1860. Small wonder that in the preceding year the *Daily Picayune* was moved to describe them as "a sober, industrious, and moral class, far advanced in education and civilization."

The extent of slaveholding among free blacks has been a matter of only recent concern to the student of history. The majority of black slave owners had some personal interest in their property. Frequently the husband purchased his wife, or vice versa; or the slaves were the children of a free father who had purchased his wife; or they were other relatives or friends who had been rescued from the worst features of the institution by some affluent free black. There were instances, however, in which free blacks had a real economic interest in the institution of slavery and held slaves in order to improve their own economic status. This was true of Cyprian Ricard, who purchased an estate with ninety-one slaves in Louisiana, and of Charles Rogues and Marie Metoyer, who had forty-seven and fifty-eight slaves, respectively. In the Charleston area, as well as around New Orleans, there were several free Negroes who had slaves in such great numbers as to indicate an economic interest in the institution. Free blacks on occasion also employed white people to work for them. Thomas Day, North Carolina's best-known cabinetmaker, employed a white journeyman for several years. Jim Dungey, a wagoner of Nashville, Tennessee, had labor-management problems of his own, for in October 1859 the *Republican Banner* reported that he "got into a fight with a white man in his employ."

Individual cases of affluence among free blacks are numerous. Solomon Humphries of Macon, Georgia, was a leading grocer in the city; before his death he accumulated property worth more than $20,000, including several slaves. Jehu Jones, proprietor of one of Charleston's best hotels, amassed a fortune of more than $40,000 and sent his son to Amherst. James Forten, who had started out as an errand boy on the docks of Philadelphia, became a sailmaker and accumulated a fortune of more than $100,000. Thomy Lafon, the tycoon of New Orleans, was worth $500,000 at his death. He had contributed so much to the development of the city that the state legislature ordered a bust of Lafon to be carved and set up in some public institution in New Orleans. Much closer to the average was James Boon, a North Carolina artisan who, despite his excellence as a carpenter, spent most of his time trying to remain solvent and whose property, what little there was, was in the hands of his creditors more often than in his own.

In the beginning little social distinction was made in America on account of race. As the racial justification for slavery developed, there began to creep into the mores of American society a distinction between blacks and whites. One of its first manifestations was the passage of laws against intermarriage. More and more, however, the real distinction came to be that between whites and those blacks who had some claim to freedom. In the nineteenth century, as the slaveholding class found it necessary to establish safeguards for effective control of free blacks, a veritable wall was erected around the blacks, who found it necessary to develop their own lives and institutions. There existed between them and the rest of the world a minimum of communication, and even this communication steadily decreased.

The free black family evolved as a result of three lines of social relations: marriage within the group; marriage to slaves; and relations, legal or clandestine, with whites and Indians. The free black was not always subjected to the social controls that affected the rest of society. As a result, the relations out of which the free black family sprang were frequently judged immoral and uncivilized according to prevailing social conventions. When free blacks married one another, however, they usually secured licenses and went through a civil or religious ceremony. The marriage of a free black to a slave, which could not be effected without consent of the slave's owner, was more frequently a rather informal union for which no license was secured. Relations with white people were equally informal and consisted of a free black "taking up" with a white person or, as in New

Orleans, a well-to-do white man maintaining a free black woman under a system of *placage,* or concubinage. These relations, together with the manumission of black children by white fathers, accounted for the 159,000 free mulattoes in the United States in 1850.

There was little in the way of organized recreation for free blacks. Their pleasures came from the rather simple experiences of visiting, singing, or attending meetings of organizations to which they belonged. There was considerable drinking, though hardly as much as many whites claimed. Gambling among themselves, with slaves, or with whites, all of which were criminal offenses, was another recreation for them. In urban areas they enjoyed the dances given by various societies and benevolent organizations. Cakewalks and balls were events in Baltimore to which many free blacks looked forward. The best known of the dances were the quadroon balls in New Orleans and a few other Southern cities. These can hardly be called recreation for them, however, since white men were the only males in attendance. Quadroons were either young women whom white men were keeping as concubines or those who were eligible for such relations. Only New York blacks could boast of an "African Theater," which flourished for several years after it was founded in 1821.

Free blacks held their fraternal organizations and benevolent societies in high esteem. The Masons continued to flourish during the generation immediately preceding the Civil War. In Maryland, for example, by 1845 they had grown to the point where it became desirable to form the First Colored Grand Lodge, and two years later another was set up. In 1843, under the leadership of Peter Ogden, a group of them organized the Grand United Order of Odd Fellows, which became one of the major black fraternal organizations. They found it desirable to bind themselves together for social and cultural uplift, economic advancement, and mutual relief. Thus, a large number of benevolent societies sprang into existence, some of which were secret. In Baltimore, there was one as early as 1821, composed of young men, and by 1835 there were thirty-five. The Friendship Benevolent Society for Social Relief, the Star in the East Association, and the Daughters of Jerusalem were some of the more prominent organizations with substantial savings accounts in Baltimore banks. In other cities there were benevolent associations of mechanics, coachmen, caulkers, and other workers, suggesting that blacks were organizing themselves into unions at about the same time as whites. In the deep South such organizations were frowned upon by most whites and were outlawed altogether in many communities. They persisted, however, in some places. As late as 1860 they were being organized in New Orleans, where the Band Society, with the motto Love, Union, Peace, had bylaws requiring its members "to go about once in a while and see one another in love" and to wear the society's regalia on special occasions.

Important to the free black, as to the slave, was the church. Religious services offered opportunities for social intercourse as well as spiritual uplift.

The independent church movement of the North continued to grow. The African Methodist Episcopal Zion church increased its membership and extended its areas of operation. As blacks moved west they founded new congregations of these religious communities. In 1847 the African Methodist Episcopal church began the publication of a weekly magazine, *The Christian Herald,* which was changed to *The Christian Recorder* in 1852. By maintaining national organizations black Methodists were able to make their influence felt through important institutions in American life.

More free blacks belonged to Baptist churches, but because their churches were decentralized, their influence was not as great as that of the Methodists. Where a black Baptist church was associated with other churches, it was usually with white churches in the same area rather than with black churches elsewhere. While this was an important step in Americanization, it left black Baptists without much force among their own people. There were strong Baptist churches in many Northern cities, including Philadelphia, New York, and Boston, and in some towns in the West, such as Cleveland, Cincinnati, Detroit, and Chicago.

The South generally proscribed religious life among blacks between 1820 and 1860. Although the African Methodist Episcopal church had made considerable headway in Charleston, for example, the organization was crushed by the weight of public opinion in 1822. Whites generally believed that black Methodists were implicated in the Denmark Vesey plot. Realizing the futility of trying to carry on against such odds, the Reverend Morris Brown, who later became a bishop, led his flock to the North. Other free black preachers in the South experienced even greater hardships. Although John Chavis was one of North Carolina's most beloved Presbyterian ministers, he was not allowed to preach after 1831. Henry Evans, who organized the first Methodist church in Fayetteville, North Carolina, would doubtless have been evicted from his post had he been alive in 1831. Ralph Freeman, a well-known Baptist minister, was so determined to preach after 1831 that the Pee Dee Baptist Association of North Carolina felt compelled to publish a notice warning him to "refrain from making evening appointments of his own." White Episcopalians and Presbyterians solved the problem of free blacks by admitting them to worship, usually in segregated sections of their churches. As an effective independent institution among free blacks, the church declined before the outbreak of the Civil War.

One unique service that black religious leaders rendered was ministering to whites. Lemuel Haynes, the Revolutionary soldier, had set the example by his long service to white congregations in several Northern towns. Others were Samuel Ringgold Ward, pastor of a white congregation in Cortlandville, New York, and Henry Highland Garnet, who served a white church in Troy, New York. Many Southern black ministers, such as Freeman, Evans, and Chavis, preached to white congregations before the proscriptive laws of the 1820s and 1830s.

In Northern communities the opportunities for blacks to secure an education widened in the nineteenth century. In many places, however, separate schools were maintained. Boston established them for black children in 1820, followed closely by other Massachusetts towns. Antislavery sentiment soon attacked the practice, and by 1855 both Boston and New Bedford permitted black children to attend white public schools. Rhode Island and Connecticut maintained separate schools, but in the last decade before the Civil War, larger funds were given to them. Not until 1824 did the New York Common Council begin to support African Free Schools (see Chapter 6). The city took them over altogether in 1834. Although some communities in the state permitted black children to attend white schools, the legislature made it clear in 1841 that any district could establish separate schools. New Jersey also maintained schools for black children. The citizens of Pennsylvania continued to give both public and private support to schools for blacks as they increased in number, particularly in the western part of the state.

In the West, as more and more blacks migrated, the citizens there were also faced with the problem of education. Ohio excluded them from public schools by law in 1829. Twenty years later the state provided for separate schools, but never appropriated enough funds to set up anything creditable. Citizens of Indiana and Illinois were equally indifferent. Michigan and Wisconsin adopted more democratic policies, but most blacks in the West had to wait until after the Civil War before they could be educated in considerable numbers at public expense.

Free blacks in the South experienced far greater difficulty. Public interest in education was extremely low. Since the responsibility for educating youth was largely a private one, free blacks who would not have benefited directly from public education, did not receive even the indirect benefits of contact with a more educated white populace. There was, moreover, very strong sentiment against educating them. It was believed that they were likely to imbibe seditious and incendiary doctrines through their reading. All the Southern states made it very difficult for them to secure an education by passing laws making it unlawful to instruct free blacks. A surprisingly large number of them nevertheless learned at least the fundamentals. In Baltimore, for example, there were almost 200 adult blacks studying in 1820. Five years later a day and night school was being maintained where many subjects were taught, including Latin and French. The Bethel Charity School, founded by Daniel Coker in 1816 as a part of the enlarged program of the African Methodist Episcopal church, continued to flourish for a number of years. There were several other such schools in Maryland.

Shortly after the settlement of the District of Columbia, several white teachers, including Henry Potter and one Mrs. Haley, taught black children. Later, Maria Billings established a school in Georgetown. In 1807 several free blacks, among them George Bell, Nicholas Franklin, and Moses Liverpool, built the first schoolhouse for blacks in the District of Columbia. It was not until 1824, however, that there was a black teacher, John Adams, in the District. Then schools for blacks began to increase in number, and within a few years

James Thomas, Free Black, Attends School in Tennessee—1830s

A portion of the year (some years) the authorities allowed a school to be kept for teaching the children of Free persons. In that school I learned to read and write. It was surprising to a great many whites to see a colored boy or man with a newspaper. Often they would ask, "Can you read?" It was a question with many people whether it was the proper thing to have a school for the free people for two reasons. First they might write passes for the slaves. Second it might cause the slave to want the same. The law forbid the teaching of the slaves, but many families had servants that were taught by the children and the heads of the family made no objection, rather encouraged it. . . .

School was kept occasionaly. It was regarded a great favor to have it allowed at any time. Each pupil or scollar paid one dollar per month. Often there was no school because there was no teacher. When I was quite young there was a colored man who taught school and was a fine scollar himself. One night he was taken out by what was termed the slicks and whipped pretty near to death. The leader of the gang was a son of the most distinguished Jurist in the state. . . . After that the colored teachers were afraid to try it. Finaly a white man came in and taught. When Mother could spare me from her work I went to school.

From Tennessee Slave to St. Louis Entrepreneur: The Autobiography of James Thomas, ed. by Loren Schweninger (Columbia, Mo., 1984), pp. 31–32.

some of the best were to be found in Washington. Black students came there from Maryland and Virginia to study under teachers of their own race.

Free blacks in Virginia and North Carolina received private instruction from whites and other free blacks, but very little in schools. For almost thirty years John Chavis of Raleigh, North Carolina, maintained a school in which he taught whites during the day and free blacks in the evening, but after 1831 he confined his teaching to white children. The blacks of Fredericksburg, Virginia, sought permission from the state legislature in 1838 to send their children to school out of the state, but their plea was summarily rejected. There is plenty of evidence, however, that many free blacks in Virginia and North Carolina towns were being educated right up until the Civil War. In South Carolina their best opportunity to secure an education was provided in Charleston. As early as 1810 blacks had organized the Minor Society school for orphans, and others also attended. In Florida some free blacks sent their children away to school, while others hired teachers to instruct them, as in St. Augustine and Pensacola. New Orleans had several schools for free blacks. The *Ecole des Orphelins Indigents,* set up in 1840, was generously supported by such wealthy free blacks as Thomy Lafon, Madame Couvent, and Aristide Mary, who bequeathed $5,000 to the school. Some went to France for an education, such as Edward Dede, who studied music in Paris.

From all this educational activity a better trained free black citizenry emerged. There is little doubt that they were eager to secure an education. Of 2,038 in Boston in 1850, almost 1,500 were in school. There were 1,400 at schools in Baltimore and 1,000 in New Orleans. In the states and territories as a whole 32,629 were in school in 1860. In every community they were studying, with an apparent belief that education would solve some of their problems. Where opportunities did not exist, they sought to create them and gave enthusiastic support to their institutions. Just as Lafon and Madame Couvent set examples of philanthropy in New Orleans, so did free blacks in other parts of the country. In several communities they organized Phoenix Societies with the special object of promoting the improvement of "Morals, literature and the mechanic arts." The "Mental Feast," a social occasion, survived thirty years later in the interior towns of Pennsylvania and the West. It was a sign that blacks were part of the great awakening that swept American education in the generation preceding the Civil War.

They also made a start in higher education. In 1826 Edward Jones and John Russwurm graduated from Amherst College and Bowdoin College, respectively, and before the Civil War blacks were attending Oberlin, Franklin, and Rutland colleges, Harvard Medical School, and other institutions of higher learning. The doors of several institutions that were to become predominantly black colleges opened during this period. In 1851 a young white woman from New York, Myrtilla Miner, went to Washington to establish an academy for black females. So much opposition developed that the school was maintained only with difficulty. At the outbreak of the Civil War, it was still a small institution, but the idea had already been conceived for the college in Washington that long bore her name. In 1839 plans were made for an Institute for Colored Youth in Philadelphia. The school was incorporated in 1842 and began to flourish ten years later under the leadership of Charles L. Reason of New York. A bequest for $300,000 by the Reverend Charles Avery led to the establishment in 1849 of a college for blacks in Allegheny City, Pennsylvania, that bore the benefactor's name. With enough funds and an efficient faculty of both races, the institution flourished. Meanwhile, Reason, William G. Allen, and George B. Vashon each taught for a time at Central College, a white institution in McGrawville, New York.

Two denominational institutions founded during the period that have continued to grow are Lincoln University in Pennsylvania and Wilberforce University in Ohio. Lincoln, beginning as Ashmun Institute under Presbyterian sponsorship, was incorporated in 1854 and admitted its first students two years later. In 1855 the Cincinnati Conference of the Methodist Episcopal church decided to raise money to establish a college for black youth which was incorporated the following year as Wilberforce University. Its early students were mainly the mulatto children of Southern planters. After a brief suspension at the beginning of the Civil War, it was reopened under the sponsorship of the African Methodist Episcopal church.

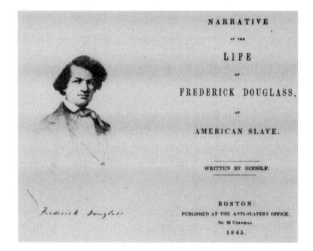

THE NARRATIVE OF FREDERICK DOUGLASS. This is one of many slave narratives written in the antebellum period. Douglass wrote two other autobiographies: *My Bondage and My Freedom* (1855) and *The Life and Times of Frederick Douglass* (1881). *(Courtesy The Schomburg Center for Research in Black Culture, The New York Public Library, Astor, Lenox, and Tilden Foundations.)*

Blacks became much more articulate in the antebellum years than they had been during the previous century. There were poets, playwrights, historians, newspaper editors, and others who provided a black perspective to the world. In North Carolina, George Moses Horton, who was virtually free, wrote poems that were widely read. In 1829 he published a volume entitled *The Hope of Liberty,* and for the next thirty years wrote for students at the University of North Carolina and for various newspapers. Unfortunately, his interest in poetry diminished as he took to drink; perhaps he realized that for him there was no hope of liberty. Daniel A. Payne, who had a brilliant career as a bishop in the African Methodist Episcopal church, published a small volume in 1850 entitled *Pleasures and Other Miscellaneous Poems.* Though they reveal little imagination, a critic said that "with his love of order and precision he had a sense of versification . . ." Frances Harper, whose *Poems on Miscellaneous Subjects* appeared in 1854, made her most significant contributions after the Civil War. *Our Nig; Or Sketches From the Life of a Free Black,* the first novel by an African American and by an African-American woman appeared in 1859; its author, Harriet E. Wilson, a free black, probably lived in Massachusetts. In the words of its discoverer, Henry Louis Gates, Jr., *Our Nig* "stands as a 'missing link' . . . between the sustained and well developed tradition of black autobiography and the slow emergence of a distinctive black voice in fiction." The cultural life of blacks in New Orleans was best represented by a group of seventeen poets who issued a volume in 1845 entitled *Les Cenelles.* The editor, Armand Lanusse, and several contributors had lived or studied in France, and their work clearly shows the influence of Lamartine and Béranger.

The largest and perhaps most significant group of black writers consisted of ex-slaves—fugitive or manumitted—who told the stories of their experiences in narratives. Frequently they were inspired and assisted by abolitionists who desired to use their writings as arguments against slavery. Some narratives, however, were the work solely of former slaves who had received the rudiments of an education. Because of the content of these works, most of them have a dramatic quality that the imagination alone, untutored by experience, would have difficulty in achieving. Among former slaves who published their narratives between 1840 and 1860 were William Wells Brown (1842), Lunsford Lane (1842), Moses Grandy (1844), Frederick Douglass (1845), Lewis Clarke (1846), Henry Bibb (1849), J. W. C. Pennington (1850), Solomon Northup (1853), Austin Steward (1857), and J. W. Loguen (1859). Many more narratives were published during and after the Civil War. Despite their subjectivity, they are an important source for the study of slavery in America.

Some of these writers made other contributions. William Wells Brown described his foreign travels vividly in *Three Years in Europe* (1852) and was the first black person to write a play, *The Escape* (1858), and a novel, *Clotel; or the President's Daughter* (1853). J. W. C. Pennington, even before he published his narrative, had written a *Textbook of the Origin and History of the Colored People* (1841). A more capable historian was William C. Nell, whose *Services of Colored Americans in the Wars of 1776 and 1812* first appeared in 1852. Three years later it was issued in a substantially revised edition under the title *The Colored Patriots of the American Revolution with Sketches of Several Distinguished Colored Persons to Which Is Added a Brief Survey of the Condition and Prospects of Colored Americans.* Martin R. Delany, a leading black physician who had studied at Harvard Medical School, published in 1852 *The Condition, Elevation, Emigration and Destiny of the Colored People of the United States.* Seven installments of his novel, *Blake; or the Huts of America,* appeared in *Anglo-African* magazine in 1859. Similar books on the condition of blacks indicated that they were becoming introspective and self-critical, an unmistakable sign of maturity and adjustment. In a class by itself, perhaps, was the work of James McCune Smith of New York. In 1846 this graduate of the medical college at the University of Glasgow published a paper entitled "Influence of Climate on Longevity, with Special Reference to Life Insurance."

Most black newspapers of the period were concerned mainly with the antislavery crusade. Best known were the first one, *Freedom's Journal,* started by Samuel Cornish and John Russwurm in 1827, and the *North Star,* first published by Frederick Douglass in 1847. With its name changed in 1850 to *Frederick Douglass's Paper,* the latter enjoyed wide circulation for several years. Other short-lived periodicals were the *Mystery* (Pittsburgh, 1843), the *Colored Man's Journal* (New York, 1851), the *Mirror of the Times* (San Francisco, 1855), and the *Anglo-African* (New York, 1859).

■ The Struggle in the North and West

For thirty years before the Civil War, blacks were migrating north and west from the South. Not only were slaves running away, but those already free were looking northward in the hope of finding greater opportunities and better treatment. They went to cities in the Northeast in large numbers and also to the old Northwest along with white immigrants from Europe. Between 1850 and 1860, for example, Michigan's black population jumped from 2,500 to 6,700, Iowa's more than tripled, and California's increased from 962 to 4,086. The reaction to this wholesale migration was not pleasant. Northern whites had shown no unusual hostility to blacks who were already in their midst, but they did not welcome the crude, rough type that came from the South. Indeed, they hoped to keep the North and West free not only of slavery but of blacks as well.

Racial animosity grew in both the North and West, and in many instances manifested itself in physical violence. In Philadelphia in 1819, three white women stoned a black woman to death. A few years later, the citizens adopted a policy of driving blacks away from Independence Square on the Fourth of July, since they were considered not to have had any part in establishing the nation. In 1831 the people of New Haven, Connecticut, became alarmed over the proposal of abolitionist Simeon Jocelyn to establish a college for blacks, and they resolved to oppose it with all their resources. When John Randolph's manumitted slaves were taken to Ohio, German settlers opposed their presence so vigorously that Randolph's executor had to find another place for them to settle. More than one interracial fight on the California mining frontier grew out of white resentment at blacks being there.

Sometimes violence reached the proportions of riots. In 1830 a mob drove eight blacks out of Portsmouth, Ohio. For three days in 1829, bands of white ruffians in Cincinnati took the law into their own hands and ran out of the city those blacks who did not have the bonds required by law. More than 1,000 found it advisable to leave. Blacks were also victims of the riot that occurred when the proslavery element of Cincinnati destroyed the office in which James G. Birney had published an antislavery newspaper, the *Philanthropist*. Defenseless blacks were attacked in their homes, and many left the city. The fugitive slave riot in 1841 also involved many blacks who were in no way connected with harboring fugitives.

In New York there were riots in Utica, Palmyra, and New York City in 1834 and 1839. The most serious antiblack outbreaks, however, took place in Pennsylvania. On August 12, 1834, a mob of whites marched into the black section of Philadelphia and committed numerous acts of violence. The following day they wrecked the African Presbyterian Church, burned homes, and mercilessly beat up several blacks. This reign of terror entered its third day before the police put an end to it. Similar uprisings occurred in 1835 and 1842. By the latter year a large number of whites were out of work because of the severe depression, and when blacks were celebrating the abolition of slavery in the West Indies, the unemployed broke up their parade, attacked scores of them, and burned the New African Hall and Presbyterian Church. State troops had to be called to assist the police in quieting the city. In 1839 there had been an outbreak in Pittsburgh during which whites did considerable damage to the black section of the city by burning and tearing down houses.

The South enjoyed playing up Northern hostility toward blacks. When an observer said that in New York and Philadelphia blacks were noted chiefly for their "aversion to labor and proneness to villainy," he was quoted extensively in the Southern press. Southerners recounted with pleasure how a Georgia black returned after attempting to live in Ohio and Canada for two years, learning to dislike each place thoroughly. They also told of the Louisiana blacks who suffered so much in New York City that they begged visiting Southerners to take them back with them. When a North Carolina free black remarked that he had been kicked about and abused so much in Cincinnati that he would like to return to the South, a Greensboro paper not only reported the incident but reprinted the article five years later as though it had just happened.

There can be no doubt that many blacks were sorely mistreated in the North and West. Observers like Fanny Kemble and Frederick L. Olmsted mentioned incidents in their writings. Kemble said of Northern blacks, "They are not slaves indeed, but they are pariahs, debarred from every fellowship save with their own despised race. . . . All hands are extended to thrust them out, all fingers point at their dusky skin, all tongues . . . have learned to turn the very name of their race into an insult and a reproach." Olmsted seems to have believed the Louisiana black who told him that they could associate with whites more easily in the South than in the North and that he preferred to live in the South because he was less likely to be insulted there. Such points of view delighted slaveholders and confirmed their belief that slavery was better than freedom for blacks.

Southerners did not seem to realize, however, that the essential difference between the South and the North and West was that in the latter sections blacks had more of the law on their side and could therefore resist encroachments on their rights. Northern blacks could organize and fight for what they believed to be their rights, and there was a substantial group of white citizens who gave them both moral and material support. In 1830 a convention of blacks with delegates from New York, Pennsylvania, Maryland, Delaware, and Virginia, met in Philadelphia "to devise ways and means for the bettering of our condition." James Forten, John B. Vashon, Samuel Cornish, and other leaders were present. They considered raising funds to establish a college and to encourage blacks to migrate to Canada. Many blacks were opposed to these measures as unsound solutions to their problems, and indeed there were some who opposed the idea of a black convention at all.

For several years, however, these conventions met regularly, and such leading white citizens as Arthur Tappan, John Rankin, and William Lloyd Garrison met with them. In 1847 several delegates, including William C. Nell, met in Troy, New York, and urged that blacks seek admission to white colleges. Nell believed that diligent and outstanding black students would win the respect of enemies and convert them into friends. In 1850 a convention at Columbus, Ohio, resolved to resist all forms of oppression, promote universal education, and encourage blacks to aspire to mechanical, agricultural, and professional pursuits.

In the decade preceding the Civil War, there were more black conventions than ever before. They met in Rochester, Cleveland, New York, Philadelphia, and other cities. One of the most important, held at Rochester in 1853, saw the formation of a National Council of Colored People. A stirring memorial, signed by Frederick Douglass among others, was issued to the American people, asserting that "with the exception of the Jews, under the whole heavens, there is not to be found a people pursued with a more relentless prejudice and persecution, than are the free colored people of the United States." After reciting various ways in which they had been mistreated and humiliated, the memorial declared that no other race could have made more progress "in the midst of such an universal and stringent disparagement. It would humble the proudest, crush the energies of the strongest, and retard the progress of the swiftest. In view of our circumstances, we can, without boasting, thank God, and take courage, having placed ourselves where we may fairly challenge comparison with more highly favored men."

There were also conventions of special groups. In 1848 the Citizens Union of Pennsylvania was organized to fight for first-class citizenship for blacks. In 1850 the American League of Colored Laborers was formed in New York to promote cooperation and to foster the education of young blacks in agriculture, the mechanical arts, and commerce.

■ Colonization

The problem of what to do with blacks who would not "adjust" to American life was an old one. It arose shortly after the arrival of the first Africans in America. Banishment was an early punishment for the crimes of both whites and blacks. As the number of free blacks increased, it was felt that they must be sent out of the country if property in slaves was to be secure. Certainly there could be no complete discipline of slaves as long as free blacks were in their midst. Even Northern communities felt that emancipation and concessions of equality were insufficient because the two races could not always live together in harmony. The prevailing point of view was aptly summed up by J. C. Galloway of North Carolina, who said, "It is impossible for us to be happy, if, after manumission, they are to remain among us."

As early as 1714 a "native American," believed to be a resident of New Jersey, had proposed sending blacks back to Africa. The idea did not die. Just after the War for Independence, Samuel Hopkins and the Reverend Ezra Stiles discussed the possibility of putting this notion into practice. In 1777 a Virginia legislative committee, headed by Thomas Jefferson, set forth a plan of gradual emancipation and deportation. Several organizations for manumission, such as the Connecticut Emancipation Society, had as one of their objectives the colonization of free blacks. Perhaps nothing brought colonization before the country more dramatically than the transporting of thirty-eight blacks to Africa in 1815 by Paul Cuffe, at his own expense. His act suggested what might be done if more people, or even the government, became interested. It suggested, too, that some blacks were indeed interested in leaving the United States.

Within two years after Cuffe's voyage, the American Colonization Society was organized, with Bushrod Washington as president and Henry Clay and John Randolph of Roanoke among its prominent members. Plans were immediately made to establish a colony in Africa, with the aid of federal and state governments, and to educate public opinion to support the project. Agents were sent out to raise funds and to interest free blacks in emigrating to Liberia, whose capital was honored with the name of President Monroe. Soon, thousands of dollars flowed into the society for the purchasing and chartering of ships to transport blacks. By 1832 more than a dozen legislatures had given official approval to the society—even slaveholding states like Maryland, Virginia, and Kentucky. North Carolina, Mississippi, and other states had local colonization societies. At first, only free blacks were transported to Africa. After 1827 some slaves who were manumitted expressly for this purpose were taken to Liberia. By 1830 the society had settled 1,420 blacks in the colony.

The society's first ten years were its best. In 1831 the abolitionists, led by Garrison, who was once a friend of colonization, renounced the scheme. Arthur Tappan, Gerrit Smith, and James G. Birney joined in the attack. Many auxiliary societies, desiring greater autonomy, seceded from the parent organization, which became insolvent in 1834. In Liberia, where the cost of living was high and the colony's affairs were mismanaged, many settlers were unhappy. Dark days thus descended upon the American Colonization Society, but it managed to struggle along for several years before it became moribund in the decade before the Civil War.

Although the American Colonization Society comprised the largest group of individuals interested in deporting blacks, there were other groups and individuals no less interested. Southern newspapers, for example, did what they could to banish free blacks. One Mississippi paper ran an advertisement of how pleasant a place Haiti would be for blacks emigrating from the United States. Indeed, the Haitians were anxious to attract free blacks to their island. A North Carolina newspaper urged free blacks to solve their problems by emigration. It suggested that they go to Canada, Mexico, South America, or the American West. Few whites, however, supported the idea that they should move west after white migration began at the close of the War of 1812.

Despite all the schemes to deport free blacks from the United States, not more than 15,000 migrated. The American Colonization Society was responsible for most of them—approximately 12,000. To places other than Liberia there was less than a trickle. For several reasons all these schemes failed. In the first place, it was not economically feasible to send hundreds of thousands of blacks to Africa or anywhere else. The cost of transporting and maintaining several hundred thousand people would run far into millions if not billions of dollars, and there were not enough supporters of the idea to give it anything like a fair chance of success. In the second place, those who did support it were such a heterogeneous lot that in the long run they could not develop a program agreeable to all. Some advocates of colonization hoped to see an end to slavery and a return of all blacks to their native land. Others supported the schemes because of their conviction that blacks were basically incapable of adjusting to Western civilization and would be better off in their original habitat. Still others saw in colonization an opportunity to carry Christianity and civilization to Africa. Slaveholders hoped, of course, to drain off the free black population, thereby giving great security to the institution of slavery. Motives as varied as these doomed colonization. The attitude of blacks themselves had a great deal to do with its failure.

Shortly after formation of the American Colonization Society a group of free blacks had met in Richmond and mildly approved of the idea of colonization, but they preferred to live elsewhere in the United States, possibly in the Missouri River valley, rather than in Africa. Farther south, free blacks who were weary of fighting a hopeless battle resigned themselves to colonization. The great majority of those who went to Africa were from the slaveholding states. In the North, however, there was almost universal opposition to colonization, particularly in Africa. In Philadelphia 3,000 blacks, led by Richard Allen and James Forten, met in 1817 and registered their objections to colonization, urging the "Humane and Benevolent Inhabitants of Philadelphia" to reject the scheme altogether. They branded it as an "outrage, having no other object in view than the benefit of the slaveholding interests of the country."

Within ten years black opposition had risen to fever pitch. Meetings were held in Baltimore, Boston, New York, Hartford, New Haven, Pittsburgh, and many other cities. New York blacks referred to the supporters of colonization as "men of mistaken views," while those of Lyme, Connecticut, described colonization as "one of the wildest projects ever patronized by enlightened men."

Every convention of blacks opposed colonization, and the leaders spoke and wrote against the scheme. Martin R. Delany was especially hostile to the American Colonization Society, which he described as "anti-Christian in its character and misanthropic in its pretended sympathies." He denounced the leaders as "arrant hypocrites" who were conducting an organization that was obviously "one of the Negro's worst enemies." The main motive of colonization, he claimed, was to eliminate blacks from the United States, and for that purpose a government had been set up in Africa that was "not independent—but a poor *miserable mockery*—a burlesque on a government."

But not all Northern blacks were opposed to colonization. Even Martin Delany thought that blacks would prosper in Central and South America, and on one occasion he described these places as their future home in the New World. He also thought that Canada West (upper Canada) would be a satisfactory home if it were not annexed to the United States. Such an eventuality, he said, would mean that the "fate of the colored man, however free before, is doomed, doomed, forever doomed." Several outstanding ministers supported colonization on the ground that it would extend Christianity to heathen lands. Among them were Daniel A. Payne and Alexander Crummell, who went to Africa in the interest of Christianity and colonization. Lott Cary and Colin Teague went to Liberia in 1821 under the auspices of the Richmond African Baptist Missionary Society and the General Baptist Missionary Convention. While Cary showed no enthusiasm for the policies of the American Colonization Society, he labored among the African settlers until his death in 1828. But colonization itself was doomed: African Americans were as permanent a fixture as there was in America.

Thus blacks went through the terrible ordeal of moving toward freedom. It cannot be said even of the most fortunate that they were entirely free. They suffered indignitites and insults, legal disabilities and economic privations, and violent physical and verbal calumniations. Their reactions, even when sober and considered, were the reactions of a frustrated, stricken people. The mistreatment of free blacks was not sectional. At best the situation in the North was tolerable, but only in a relative sense: it was better than in the South. Small wonder there was so much despair. Small wonder, too, that in the South a few who were free became slaves again. Too few of them saw that in the growing intersectional strife between North and South there was opportunity for the downtrodden and hope for the faint-hearted.

■

CHAPTER 10

Slavery and Intersectional Strife

■ The North Attacks

The antislavery sentiment generated by the humanitarian philosophy of the eighteenth century never completely died out in America. To be sure, there was a period of quiescence as the South found new opportunities for the profitable employment of slaves and as the North became concerned with its own economic and political problems. But some people continued to oppose slavery as an institution, and long before militant abolitionists appeared on the scene around 1830 the most convincing arguments against slavery had already been developed. Soon after the War of 1812 sectionalism was apparent as the North swung to manufacturing and the South, still wedded to agriculture, came to see clearly that the interests of the two sections were becoming antagonistic. Indeed, the industrial development of the North changed the point of view of that section. As people there were brought closer together, they sought to solve their pressing problems through cooperation. In the South, however, the plantation system tended to preserve frontier independence: there was little communal life, only slight civic responsibility, and little interest in various programs for the improvement of humanity. The contest over Missouri, moreover, crystallized the sectional conflict and emphasized the importance of slavery as a national issue.

Antislavery sentiment in the North increased steadily after 1815 as more ministers, editors, and other leaders of public opinion spoke out against the evils of the institution. Several years passed before almost all these critics were confined to the North. In 1817 Charles Osborn published the *Philanthropist*, an antislavery paper, in Ohio, but two years later he moved to Tennessee and published the *Manumission Intelligencer*. In 1820 Elihu Embree was publishing the *Emancipator* in Jonesboro, Tennessee, while William Swaim was expressing the opposition of Quakers to slavery in his *Patriot*, published at Greensboro, North Carolina. In 1821 the itinerant Benjamin Lundy began editing the *Genius of Universal Emancipation*, in which he set forth a complete program for the emancipation and colonization of blacks. Although he lacked the emotional fervor of later abolitionists, he was not without courage and devotion to the cause of freeing the slaves.

Within ten years after the beginning of Lundy's work, three events indicated that the age of the militant abolitionists had arrived. These were the publication of David Walker's "Appeal," the appearance of William Lloyd Garrison's *Liberator*, and the insurrection of Nat Turner, which many incorrectly thought was inspired by the activities of men like Garrison (see Chapter 8). David Walker was a North Carolina free black who had moved to Boston where he engaged in selling secondhand clothes. His bitter hatred for slavery was not diminished by his leaving the South. If anything, it was increased. In September 1829 his essay appeared: "Walker's Appeal in Four Articles, Together with a Preamble to the Colored Citizens of the World, But in Particular and very Expressly to those of the United States of America." It was one of the most vigorous denunciations of slavery ever printed in the United States. In unmistakable language he called upon blacks to rise up and throw off the yoke of slavery:

> Are we men!! I ask you . . . are we MEN? Did our creator make us to be slaves to dust and ashes like ourselves? Are they not dying worms as well as we? . . . How we could be so *submissive* to a gang of men, whom we cannot tell whether they are as good as ourselves or not, I never conceive. . . . America is more our country than it is the whites—we have enriched it with our *blood and tears*. The greatest riches in all America have arisen from our blood and tears: And they will drive us from our property and homes, which we have earned with our blood.

Walker closed his appeal by quoting the Declaration of Independence to show that blacks were justified in resisting, with force if necessary, the oppression of white masters. A startled country read the words of this black man who called for militant action.

In January 1831 the first issue of Garrison's *Liberator* appeared. Garrison had served his novitiate as Lundy's assistant on the *Genius of Universal Emancipation* and in jail for libelous words against a ship captain who had transported slaves to New Orleans. He was finished with gradualism; he had shifted from supporting colonization to opposing it. In the first issue of his newspaper he also invoked the Declaration of Independence, claiming that the black man was as much entitled to "life, liberty and the pursuit of happiness" as the white man. Immediate and unconditional abolition of slavery was, from his point of view, the only solution. He laid down his challenge to slavery in most dramatic language when he said:

> I *will* be as harsh as truth, and as uncompromising as justice. On this subject, I do not wish to think, to speak, or write, with moderation. . . . I am in earnest—I will not equivocate—I will not excuse—I will not retreat a single inch—AND I WILL BE HEARD.

Thus Garrison became the country's most articulate spokesman for nonviolent militant abolition. For a whole generation he was one of the most important forces working for the freedom of slaves. It was an auspicious beginning for an exciting career. Small wonder that people in the South connected the so-called incendiary writings of Walker and Garrison with the insurrections of Nat Turner and of others; but Garrison always followed a policy of nonviolent, passive resistance.

The militant antislavery movement that had developed by 1831 was in itself a powerful religious crusade—part of the larger humanitarian movement sweeping Europe and the Northern United States. It stemmed from the growing popular concern for the welfare of underprivileged persons, which manifested itself in the antislavery movement, the crusade for better working conditions in England, and the search for a better life in America. It was closely connected, in many respects, with movements for peace, women's rights, temperance, and other reform programs that developed simultaneously. In the West, it was connected with the Great Revival, of which Charles G. Finney was the dominant figure, emphasizing the importance of being useful and thus releasing a powerful impulse toward social reform. The young converts joined Finney's Holy Band, and if the abolition of slavery was a way of serving God, they were anxious to enter into the movement wholeheartedly.

Abolitionists worked out an elaborate argument against the perpetuation of slavery. In the first place, they insisted that it was contrary to the teachings of Christianity, since Jesus taught the doctrine of universal brotherhood and one of the cardinal principles of Christianity was that all men were created in the image of God. James G. Birney's *Letter to the Ministers and Elders* (1834) and Theodore Weld's *The Bible Against Slavery* (1837) carried these religious arguments against slavery to their conclusion. In the second place, abolitionists contended that slavery was contrary to the fundamental principles of the American way of life, which valued freedom as an inalienable right of the individual. Slaves were denied this right: they had no freedom in seeking employment, no religious freedom, no marriage or family rights, no legal protection, and few opportunities to secure an education. They also contended that slavery was economically unsound because the workers could

David Walker Calls for Justice—1829

I ask every man who has a heart, and is blessed with the privilege of believing—Is not God a God of justice to *all* his creatures? Do you say he is? Then if he gives peace and tranquillity to tyrants, and permits them to keep our fathers, our mothers, ourselves and our children in eternal ignorance and wretchedness, to support them and their families, would he be to us a God of *justice?* I ask, O ye *Christians!!!* who hold us and our children in the most abject ignorance and degradation, that ever a people were afflicted with since the world began—I say, if God gives you peace and tranquillity, and suffers you thus to go on afflicting us, and our children, who have never given you the least provocation—would he be to us *a God of justice?* If you will allow that we are MEN, who feel for each other, does not the blood of our fathers and of us their children, cry aloud to the Lord of Sabaoth against you, for the cruelties and murders with which you have, and do continue to afflict us.

Walker's Appeal in Four Articles, Together with a Preamble to the Coloured Citizens of the World, But in Particular, and very Expressly, to those of the United States of America (Boston, 1830), p. 68.

not be expected to be efficient and there was such a waste of physical and human resources in the plantation economy. The culture and civilization of the South suffered, moreover, for the master-slave relationship did not produce a gentility of spirit but brought out instead the baser aspects of the nature of both. Theodore Weld expressed this view succinctly, pointing out that domination of one person by another is essentially uncivilized, when he said, "Arbitrary power is to the mind what alcohol is to the body; it intoxicates." Finally, abolitionists condemned slavery as a menace to the peace and safety of the country. The South was becoming an armed camp where whites lived in constant fear of a widespread uprising of slaves. This fear, it was contended, generated violence and was the cause of bloodshed.

Although antislavery forces had for years believed that colonization was one way of relieving the country of its dreaded "Negro problem," militant abolitionists were on the whole unalterably opposed to colonization. They were suspicious of it because of the support it received from slaveholders, who could not be interested in putting an end to slavery as an institution. Abolitionists felt, as the great majority of blacks did, that colonization was primarily for the purpose of draining off the free black population in order to make slavery even more secure. Garrison said that the American Colonization Society had "inflicted a great injury upon the free and slave population; first by strengthening the prejudices of the people; secondly, by discouraging the education of those who are free; thirdly, by inducing passage of severe legislative enactments; and, finally, by lulling the whole country into a deep sleep." Even more vigorous denunciations appeared in his *Thoughts on Colonization*, published in 1832.

With principles of their own, not necessarily egalitarian, abolitionists were now ready to organize and to wipe out the institution of slavery. In 1831 the New England Anti-Slavery Society was formed. Beginning with a small group of fifteen, Garrison imbued his followers with the idea of immediate emancipation. As their numbers grew, they became more radical and vociferous, the very voice of Garrison. Some, especially in New York and Philadelphia, were from the beginning opposed to Garrison's radical views. Encouraged by the abolition of slavery in the British Empire, this moderate group did much to bring about the organization of the American Anti-Slavery Society in Philadelphia in 1833. Arthur Tappan, a wealthy New York merchant, was the first president. Other important leaders were Theodore Weld, James G. Birney, William Goodell, Joshua Leavitt, Elizur Wright, Samuel May, and Beriah Green, most of whom had been active in local antislavery societies. The organization was dominated by Garrison, however, and when it issued a declaration of sentiments he was successful in getting his views incorporated into the document. A publicity program was drawn up and carried out largely by the New York group. Four periodicals were published: *Human Rights, Anti-Slavery Record, Emancipator,* and *Slave's Friend.* Pamphlets were distributed throughout the North and, when possible, in the South. Through its many agents, local units were organized and money was raised to further the program of emancipation. In 1836 there were seventy lecturers in the field, drawn largely from the ministry, theological seminaries, and colleges.

In the West the antislavery movement had become a crusade by 1830. Most of the leaders who left the South went West. James G. Birney went from Alabama to Kentucky and thence to Ohio. Levi Coffin left North Carolina and carried on his abolition activities in Indiana. Later, these men were joined by others who had found the atmosphere of their home communities peculiarly hostile to antislavery ideas. After Theodore Dwight Weld arrived at Lane Theological Seminary in Cincinnati, the students there were encouraged to discuss the problem of slavery, and the free and open debates won many people, including Southerners, to the cause of abolition. The students put their views into practice by going out into the community to organize groups to assist slaves, and they instructed black youth and participated in the dangerous activities of the Underground Railroad. When the students withdrew from Lane rather than submit to a conservative administration, they went in large numbers to Oberlin College, where a theology department was established with funds provided by such antislavery philanthropists as Arthur and Lewis Tappan of New York. From that time on Oberlin became an important center of antislavery activity. Western Reserve was another college from which students went forth imbued with antislavery ideas. At no other time in American history had colleges played such an important part in a program of social reform.

The zealous Garrison was impatient even with a national organization like the American Anti-Slavery Society, all of whose members were committed to a crusade for the immediate abolition of slavery. They did not press hard enough, they were unwilling to concede equality to women as leaders of the movement, and they hesitated to criticize the churches for not taking an unequivocal stand. In 1839 Garrison and his followers decided to seize control of the national organization. At a convention the following year Garrisonians were elected to the important offices, and women were given positions of responsibility. The New York group, opposed to this bid by Garrison for power, organized under Lewis Tappan the American and Foreign Anti-Slavery Society. It was friendly to churches and sought to use them to end slavery. It believed that political action was necessary to overcome constitutional and legal obstructions to emancipation.

The members of this new society became the nucleus of the Liberty party, which was organized in 1840. In two successive presidential campaigns they nominated James Birney, but at the peak of their strength in 1844 he polled only 60,000 votes. The dismal results proved conclusively that, although millions of people were opposed to slavery, a political party had to offer more than an antislavery platform in order to win support. The Republican party was to demonstrate in the next decade that it had learned this lesson.

By 1840, when the energies of the abolitionists were split into two national bodies, effective work was done by state and local organizations. They maintained agents in the field, published newspapers, and distributed antislavery literature throughout the country. Garrison remained strong to the end in New England. Among his followers he could list John Greenleaf Whittier, the poet of abolition; Wendell Phillips, "abolition's golden trumpet"; and women like Lucretia Mott, Lydia Maria Child, and Maria Weston Chapman. In the border states and the West, however, Birney and Weld were strong, and unlike Garrison they continued to counsel moderation and to insist upon political action.

While "Garrisonism" met with more opposition than other forms of abolition, there was always much sentiment, even in the North, against any kind of antislavery agitation. David M. Reese, for example, called the American Anti-Slavery Society the "purest of all humbugs"; Episcopal Bishop John H. Hopkins of Vermont opposed it because he was convinced that blacks were better off as slaves than as free men. The opposition to abolition frequently became violent. Elijah P. Lovejoy was run out of St. Louis for criticizing the leniency of a judge in the trial of whites accused of burning a black man alive. Later, in Alton, Illinois, he was killed when a mob destroyed for the fourth time the press on which he printed the *Alton Observer*. In Cincinnati a mob destroyed James Birney's press in 1836, and he barely escaped with his life.

Antislavery lecturers often found it difficult to rent halls in which to speak. Even if they succeeded, they could not be certain that their program would go off as planned, for many a meeting was broken up by mobs. Even women who supported the antislavery crusade were in danger of suffering insults and indignities. When Prudence Crandall, a Quaker teacher, admitted a black girl to her school in Canterbury, Connecticut, white patrons boycotted it. After she decided to open a school for black girls, with the aid of abolitionists like Garrison and Lewis Tappan, the citizens broke windows, insulted the teacher, and had her arrested for violating a state law that forbade the teaching of blacks who were not residents of the state.

Abolitionists could expect little help or protection from the federal government. As early as 1828 they submitted a petition to Congress to abolish slavery in the District of Columbia, but nothing was done about it. As petitions against slavery began pouring in, the House of Representatives adopted a rule in 1836 providing that such petitions were to be received and laid on the table. This "gag rule," as abolitionists dubbed it, was vigorously opposed by men like John Quincy Adams of Massachusetts and Joshua Giddings of Ohio, but it was not rescinded until 1845. As long as it stood, abolitionists complained that the sacred right of petitioning the legislature for a redress of grievances was being denied.

It was the countenancing of violence by abolitionists that caused many law-abiding citizens to oppose them and rendered utterly hopeless their schemes to obtain government support. Convinced that slaveholders had the law of the land on their side, abolitionists resorted to the principle of a higher law, which they felt justified their circumventing or breaking the law. Garrison and his followers, although nonviolent, pointed out the inevitability of the violence of the Nat Turner insurrection. In 1839 Jabez Hammond of New York said that only force would end slavery and that military schools for blacks should be set up in Canada and Mexico. When slaves revolted aboard the *Creole* on a voyage from Hampton Roads to New Orleans, Representative Joshua Giddings not only opposed treating the slaves as common criminals but even praised them for seeking freedom. The House of Representatives, shocked by his open defiance of the law, censured Giddings. Forthwith he resigned, went home to Ohio, and was immediately returned to Congress by his antislavery constituency. The redoubtable Giddings later praised other blacks and whites for seeking to abolish slavery, and finally the House became accustomed to his tirades against the institution. By 1850 the philosophy of force was so integral a part of abolitionist doctrine that many viewed it as a movement toward anarchy.

■ Black Abolitionists

Whites were not alone in their opposition to slavery. From the beginning, blacks, who suffered most from the subjugation of their race, gave enthusiastic support to abolition. Indeed, strong abolitionist doctrine had been preached by blacks long before Garrison was born. Before the War for Independence, slaves in Massachusetts brought actions against their masters for the freedom that they regarded as their inalienable right. During and after the Revolutionary War, blacks sought the abolition of slavery by petitioning the state and federal governments to outlaw the slave trade and to embark upon a program of general emancipation. Prince Hall, Benjamin Banneker, Absalom Jones, and Richard Allen issued strong denunciations of slavery before 1800, and organizations like the Free African Society of Philadelphia passed resolutions calling for its abolition. In the nineteenth century blacks organized antislavery societies. By 1830 they had fifty groups, one that was very active in New Haven, and several in Boston, New York, and Philadelphia. One of the strongest was located in New York and named for the famous English antislavery leader Thomas Clarkson.

The year 1829 was especially significant for black abolitionists. Out of Boston came David Walker's *Appeal,* a blast against slavery, and out of Raleigh, North Carolina, came the protest of George Moses Horton in his *Hope of Liberty.* Horton cried out:

> Bid Slavery hide her haggard face,
>   And Barbarism fly:
> I scorn to see the sad disgrace
>   In which enslaved I lie.

It was in 1829, too, that Robert A. Young published his *Ethiopian Manifesto, issued in defence of the black man's rights, in the scale of universal freedom.* He prophesied, like Walker, that from blacks there would arise a messiah with the strength to liberate his people. Young did not create as much alarm as Walker, although he advocated measures fully as drastic to end slavery.

When the period of militant abolitionism began, black people were ready to join whites in fighting the hated institution. They organized their first national convention in the year before the publication of Garrison's *Liberator* and issued strong denunciations of colonization and slavery that left no doubt in the minds of Americans where they stood. The eagerness of black abolitionists to join the movement for liberation is demonstrated by their reaction to the appearance of the *Liberator.* Of the 450 subscribers in the first year, 400 were blacks, and one enthusiastic, affluent black abolitionist sent Garrison a gift of $50. Such contributions helped to make possible his first trip to England.

Blacks were especially active in organizing the American Anti-Slavery Society. Members whose duty it was to draw up the declaration of sentiments met in Philadelphia at the home of a black man, Lewis Evans. Five leaders served on the first board of managers: Peter Williams, Robert Purvis, George B. Vashon, Abraham Shadd, and James McCrummell. These black "founding fathers" were men of many interests and talents. Purvis, born in Charleston of a well-to-do white father who generously provided for him, had attended Amherst College and was active in many local causes, including the

LEADERS OF THE FREE BLACK COMMUNITY: WILLIAM WELLS BROWN, MARTIN
R. DELANEY, HENRY HIGHLAND GARNET, ROBERT PURVIS, SOJOURNER TRUTH
(ISABELLA BAUMFREE), AND HARRIET TUBMAN. These brave men and women challenged the mistreatment and humiliation to which their people were subjected. In doing
so they refuted the arguments for black inferiority, affirmed the legitimacy of blacks'
claims to the rights and privileges of citizenship, and were influential examples to other
members of their race. *(The Schomburg Center For Research In Black Culture, The New
York Public Library. Sojourner Truth courtesy of Sophia Smith Collection, Smith College.)*

SARAH PARKER REMOND. Abolitionist of Salem, Massachusetts, she lectured against slavery in the United States and Europe. After studying medicine, she married an Italian and settled in Florence, where she practiced medicine until her death at the age of 68. *(Courtesy, Peabody and Essex Museum, Salem, MA.)*

Underground Railroad. Vashon, a graduate of Oberlin College, was a poet, lawyer, and teacher. At most of the annual meetings there were black delegates who spoke out frequently. When the American and Foreign Anti-Slavery Society was organized, blacks were no less active in that body.

Among those who joined in promoting the organization that was committed to political action were Christopher Rush, Samuel Cornish, Charles B. Ray, and James W. C. Pennington.

To local and regional antislavery organizations, which carried the burden of the work, blacks gave their time, energy, and money. The first presiding officer of the Philadelphia Female Anti-Slavery Society was a local dentist, James McCrummell. Frederick Douglass was elected president of the New England Anti-Slavery Society in 1847. Vigilance committees, set up to raise funds to help slaves escaping to freedom, were frequently dominated by blacks. In 1835 David Ruggles became secretary of the New York committee and remained active until his eyesight failed him. In Philadelphia, Robert Purvis had charge of the first vigilance committee, which was headed several years later by William Still.

Blacks were also prominent in the abolition movement as agents and speakers for various societies. Several were full-time employees of local or national bodies. Among the better-known agents were Frederick Douglass, Theodore S. Wright, William Jones, Charles Lenox Remond and his sister Sarah, Frances E. W. Harper, Henry Foster, Lunsford Lane, Henry Highland Garnet, Charles Gardner, Andrew Harris, Abraham Shadd, David Nickens, James Bradley, and William Wells Brown. A notable black abolitionist was Isabella Baumfree, better known by her adopted name Sojourner Truth. From New York she traveled through New England and the West, moving audiences by her quaint speech, a deep, resonant voice, and a hatred for slavery, which she expressed with a unique religious mysticism.

White abolitionists took great pride in introducing black agents to doubting audiences to demonstrate what they could do if given the opportunity. They were among the best speakers. On one occasion, after Douglass had electrified an audience with his remarkable eloquence, Garrison rose to his feet and flung out the question, "Is this a man or a thing?" Henry Highland Garnet spoke with a "terrible pride," and William Wells Brown is reputed to have made a favorable impression wherever he went. Small wonder that many of these speakers were encouraged to carry the message of American abolition to Europe. More than a score of black abolitionists went to England, Scotland, France, and Germany. Among them were Douglass, Brown, Remond, Pennington, Garnet, Nathaniel Paul, Ellen and William Craft, Samuel Ringgold Ward, Sarah Parker Remond, and Alexander Crummell. They were received with enthusiasm almost everywhere and were instrumental in linking up the humanitarian movement in Europe with various reform movements on this side of the Atlantic.

Black abolitionists wrote as well as spoke in favor of emancipation. Most of the black newspapers founded before the Civil War were abolitionist sheets. Perhaps the outstanding journalist was Samuel Cornish, who with John Russwurm had established the first black newspaper, *Freedom's Journal*, in 1827. Two years later, Cornish began his second venture, *Rights of All*, an extremely radical but short-lived paper. In 1836 he published the *Weekly Advocate*, and in the following year, with the help of Charles B. Ray and

Frederick Douglass at Rochester's Independence Day—1852

I am not included within the pale of this glorious anniversary! Your high independence only reveals the immeasurable distance between us. The blessings in which you, this day, rejoice, are not enjoyed in common. The rich inheritance of justice, liberty, prosperity and independence, bequeathed by your fathers, is shared by you, not by me. The sunlight that brought light and healing to you, has brought stripes and death to me. This Fourth July is *yours*, not *mine. You* may rejoice, *I* must mourn. To drag a man in fetters into the grand illuminated temple of liberty, and call upon him to join you in joyous anthems, were inhuman mockery and sacrilegious irony. Do you mean, citizens, to mock me, by asking me to speak to-day? If so, there is a parallel to your conduct. And let me warn you that it is dangerous to copy the example of a nation whose crimes, towering up to heaven, were thrown down by the breath of the Almighty, burying that nation in irrevocable ruin! I can to-day take up the plaintive lament of a peeled and woe-smitten people!

"By the rivers of Babylon, there we sat down. Yea! we wept when we remembered Zion. We hanged our harps upon the willows in the midst thereof. For there, they that carried us away captive, required of us a song; and they who wasted us required of us mirth, saying, Sing us one of the songs of Zion. How can we sing the Lord's song in a strange land? If I forget thee, O Jerusalem, let my right hand forget her cunning. If I do not remember thee, let my tongue cleave to the roof of my mouth."

Philip S. Foner, *The Life and Writings of Frederick Douglass*, II (New York, 1950), pp. 181–204.

Phillip A. Bell, he edited the *Colored American*. Other black abolitionist newspapers were the *National Watchman*, edited by William G. Allen and Henry Highland Garnet; the *Mirror of Liberty*, a quarterly issued by David Ruggles; and, of course, the *North Star* of Frederick Douglass.

Douglass was the outstanding black abolitionist. A fugitive slave, he was first introduced to the movement when in 1841 he attended an antislavery convention in Nantucket, Massachusetts. After speaking there he was employed by several societies and rapidly became one of the best-known orators in the United States, lecturing in the North and East, and in England. A narrative of his life was published in 1845. Two years later he started the *North Star*, an incident that led to his break with Garrison, previously one of his chief sponsors. Douglass was active in black conventions, the Underground Railroad, and many other efforts to improve the conditions of his race. He was endowed with the physical attributes of an orator: a magnificient, tall body, a head crowned with a mass of hair, deep-set, flashing eyes, a firm chin, and a rich, melodious voice. Few antislavery leaders did so much to carry the case of the slave to the people of the United States and Europe in the generation before the Civil War.

In their militant bitterness black abolitionists equaled and sometimes surpassed their white brethren. David Walker was by no means alone in demanding violence. In 1844 the Reverend Moses Dickson established in Cincinnati an "order of Twelve of the Knights and Daughters of Tabor" to help overthrow slavery. Two years later he organized the Knights of Liberty in St. Louis. In 1843 Henry Highland Garnet made an address to the Buffalo Convention of Colored Citizens that shocked even many abolitionists: "Brethren, arise, arise! Strike for your lives and liberties. Now is the day and the hour. Let every slave throughout the land do this and the days of slavery are numbered. Rather die freemen than live to be slaves. . . . Awake, Awake, millions of voices are calling you! Let your motto be resistance; no oppressed people have secured their liberty without resistance." Although many blacks viewed his utterances with alarm, by 1854 the black conventions were ready for violence. A resolution adopted at that time declared that "those who, without crime, are outlawed by any Government can owe no allegiance to its enactments [and] . . . we advise all oppressed to adopt the motto, 'Liberty or Death.'" Indeed, black abolitionists had become as ardent in their Garrisonism as any follower of the high priest of abolitionism.

■ The Underground Railroad

Perhaps nothing did more to intensify the strife between North and South, and to emphasize in a most dramatic way the determination of abolitionists to destroy slavery, than the Underground Railroad. Slaves who ran away were irritating and troublesome enough, and the South had been plagued with them from the earliest days of slavery. But when free blacks and whites, fired with an almost fanatical zeal, undertook systematically to wreak havoc on an institution that meant so much to the South, it was almost too much to bear. It was this organized effort to undermine slavery, this manifestation of the workings of a presumably higher law, that put such a strain on intersectional relations and sent antagonists and protagonists of slavery scurrying headlong into the 1850s determined to have their uncompromising way.

The origin of the Underground Railroad goes back to the eighteenth century. Perhaps there were people to help fugitives as early as there were runaway slaves. By the end of the War for Independence, however, organized resistance seemed to be taking shape. At least George Washington thought so when he complained in 1786 of a slave, escaping from Alexandria to Philadelphia, "whom a society of Quakers, formed for such purposes, have attempted to liberate." By the following year Isaac T. Hopper had settled in Philadelphia, and though still in his teens he began to develop a program for the systematic assistance of slaves escaping from the South. Within a few years they were being helped in a number of towns in Pennsylvania and New Jersey. Slowly these antislavery operations spread in various directions.

Henrietta Buckmaster gives 1804 as the year of "incorporation" of the Underground Railroad. It was then that General Thomas Boude, an officer during the Revolution, purchased a slave, Stephen Smith, and brought him home to Columbia, Pennsylvania, followed by Smith's mother, who had escaped to find her son. The Boudes took her in. Within a few weeks the woman who owned Smith's mother arrived and demanded her property. Not only did the Boudes refuse to surrender the slave, but the town supported them. The people of Columbia resolved to champion the cause of fugitives. By 1815 this sentiment was expressed in Ohio. And by 1819 underground methods were used to spirit slaves out of North Carolina. Even before the period of militant abolitionism, the movement that was to be known as the Underground Railroad had grown into a widespread institution.

The name "Underground Railroad" was probably coined shortly after 1831 when steam railroads became popular. There are several versions of how the movement got its name. A plausible one concerns a slave, Tice Davids, who escaped from his Kentucky master in 1831 and got across the Ohio River. Although the master was in hot pursuit, he lost all trace of the slave after crossing the river and was so confounded that he declared the slave must have "gone off on an underground road." That was entirely possible, for by 1831 there were plenty of "underground" roads on the Ohio River, and they had stations, conductors, and means of conveyance. From that time, which coincided exactly with the emergence of Garrison and his militant followers, up until the outbreak of the Civil War, the Underground Railroad operated in flagrant violation of federal fugitive slave laws. It was the most eloquent defiance of slaveholders that abolitionists could make.

In the case of anything so full of adventure and danger as the Underground Railroad, it is difficult to separate fiction from fact. There are stories of breathtaking escapes and exciting experiences that would be quite incredible save for unquestionable verification by reliable sources. After the Railroad had developed an efficient organization, there was a generality of practice that makes possible a brief description of its operation. All, or almost all, of the operations took place at night, for that was the only time when the fugitives and their helpers felt even partially secure. Slaves prepared to make their escape by taking supplies from their masters and, if necessary, by disguising themselves. Those of fair complexion frequently passed as white people and sometimes posed as their own masters. Darker ones posed as servants on their way to meet their owners. There are several cases on record where fugitives were provided at crucial moments with white babies in order to make their claims of being nurses appear more convincing. At times men posed as women and women as men.

In the early days of the Underground Railroad most of the fugitives were men, and they usually traveled on foot. Later, when the traffic was heavy and women and children were fleeing, escorts and vehicles were provided.

The conductors carried their human cargo in covered wagons, closed carriages, and farm wagons specially equipped with closed compartments. Blacks were sometimes put in boxes and shipped as freight by rail or boat. Thus Henry Box Brown was shipped from Richmond to Philadelphia by the Adams Express Company. When traveling by land—and at night—conductors and fugitives were guided by the North Star, by tributaries of the Ohio or other rivers, and by mountain chains. On cloudy nights, when there were no other means of finding directions, they even resorted to feeling the moss on tree trunks and moving north upon discovering it.

Since travel was almost exclusively at night, it was necessary to have stations rather close together, from ten to twenty miles apart, where fugitives could rest, eat, and wait for the next night's journey. During the day they were hidden in barns, in the attics of homes, and in other out-of-the-way places. Meanwhile, the word was passed to succeeding stations, by what was called "the grape vine telegraph," that fugitives were on their way. One ambiguous message mailed by a conductor to the next stationmaster in 1859 gave much more information than a casual glance revealed. It read, "By to-morrow evening's mail, you will receive two volumes of 'The Irrepressible Conflict' bound in black. After perusal, please forward and oblige."

All Underground Railroad lines led north. They began on various plantations in the South and ran vaguely—and dangerously—up rivers and valleys and across mountains to some point on the Ohio or upper Mississippi River in the West, and to points in Pennsylvania and New Jersey in the East. Once the North had been reached, the route was much clearer, though traversed with only slightly less danger, for planters, traders, and sheriffs pursued fugitives relentlessly and resorted to the most desperate means to recover them.

Even if the Underground Railroad did not need papers of incorporation, it needed capital. The fugitives required food and clothing, and frequently there were unexpected expenses such as boarding a train in order to evade a pursuing owner or displaying affluence to convey the impression that one had been free long enough to accumulate wealth. Quakers and similar groups raised funds to carry on the work. The vigilance committees of Philadelphia and New York solicited money. Philanthropists contributed, as did the conductors and other "officials" of the Railroad. Harriet Tubman, one of the greatest of all conductors, would take several months off whenever she was running low in funds and hire herself out as a domestic servant in order to raise money for conveying slaves to freedom.

The Underground Railroad did not seem to suffer for want of operators. Wilbur H. Siebert has catalogued more than 3,200 active workers, and there is every reason to believe that there were many more who will remain forever anonymous. Outstanding among the white workers was Levi Coffin, a Quaker and the so-called president of the Underground Railroad. His strategic location in southern Indiana, as well as his remarkable zeal, made it possible for him to help more than 3,000 slaves escape. Calvin Fairbanks,

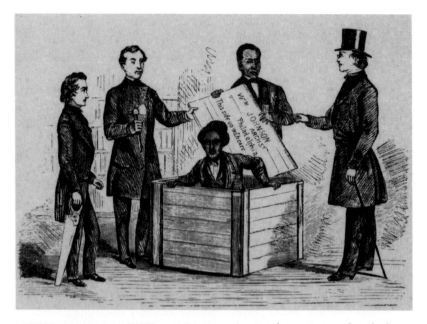

RESURRECTION OF HENRY BOX BROWN. Among the many ways by which slaves escaped to the North was shipment as merchandise. Brown was shipped from Richmond to Philadelphia, a trip requiring twenty-six hours. The white men in the drawing are J. M. McKim, C. D. Cleveland, and Lewis Thompson; the black man is William Still. From William Still, *The Underground Railroad.*

who had learned to hate slavery as a student at Oberlin College, began to travel in the South in 1837 on the dangerous business of freeing slaves. In Kentucky he engaged in a regular business of transporting slaves across the Ohio River. On one occasion, with a teacher from Vermont known as Miss Webster, he helped three slaves escape by posing as her servants. It was said that not one of his fugitives was ever recaptured, though he spent many years in jail because of his work.

In many respects the most daring white conductor on the Underground Railroad was John Fairfield. Son of a Virginia slaveholding family, he would have nothing to do with the institution and decided to live in a free state. Before going north, he helped a slave who was his friend escape to Canada. News of his exploit spread: not only did the whites of his community seek to find and arrest him, but slaves sought his aid to escape. He could not refuse to help, and thus began his career as a conductor on the Underground Railroad. He delivered slaves "on order." Blacks in the North and in Canada would give him money and a description of their friends or relatives and he would deliver them. At times he conveyed as many as fifteen. He posed as a slaveholder, a slave trader, or a peddler of eggs and poultry in Louisiana, Alabama, Mississippi, Tennessee, and Kentucky in order to gain the confidence of slaveholders. He was so convincing in each role that he was seldom suspected of being implicated in a slave's escape. Those that he did not take to Canada he delivered to Levi Coffin, who arranged the rest of their journey. His greatest triumph was in conveying twenty-eight slaves to freedom by organizing them into a funeral procession. He suffered in his work from privation and exposure and one time he was shot, but he persevered in his missions of freedom until his death in 1860, when he is believed to have been killed in an insurrection of slaves in Tennessee. John Brown, dashing from Missouri with twelve slaves and later attacking Harpers Ferry in an attempt at insurrection, has received more notice from historians, but Fairfield was as effective a fighter of slavery as any man who lived before the Civil War.

There were many black officials on the Underground Railroad. Jane Lewis of New Lebanon, Ohio, rowed fugitives regularly across the Ohio River. John Parker, who purchased himself for $2,000, was in league with John Rankin and other white workers on the Railroad. Josiah Henson, born a slave, escaped with his wife and two children to Canada, learned to read and write, and returned south often to assist slaves in their escape. Once he went to Kentucky by a circuitous route through New York, Pennsylvania, and Ohio in order to avoid suspicion. He took 30 refugees out of Kentucky and led them to Toledo within a period of two weeks. Elijah Anderson has been called the general superintendent of the Underground Railroad in northwestern Ohio. From 1850 until his death seven years later in the Kentucky state prison, he worked arduously in behalf of fugitive slaves. By 1855 he had led more than 1,000 to freedom. John Mason, himself a fugitive slave from Kentucky, was one of the most astute conductors. According to William Mitchell, a black missionary in Canada, Mason brought 265 slaves to his home in the course of nineteen months. On one occasion he was captured and sold back into slavery, but again he made good his escape. In all he delivered about 1,300 slaves into free territory.

Easily the most outstanding conductor on the Underground Railroad was Harriet Tubman. Although frail of body and suffering from recurrent spells of dizziness, she not only escaped from slavery herself but also conveyed many others to freedom, including her sister, her two children, and her aged mother and father. She is said to have gone south nineteen times and to have emancipated more than 300 slaves. Unable to read or write, she nevertheless displayed remarkable ingenuity in the management of her runaway caravans. She preferred to start the journey on Saturday night, so that she could be well on her way before the owners had an opportunity the following Monday to advertise the escape of their slaves. She tolerated no cowardice and threatened to kill any slave who wished to turn back. Well known in Philadelphia, New York, and Boston, where she frequently delivered escaped slaves, she preferred to lead them all the way to Canada after the passage of the Fugitive Slave Law in 1850, explaining that she could not trust Uncle Sam with her people any longer.

The very nature of the institution prevents any accurate estimate of the number of slaves who found freedom by the Underground Railroad. Governor Quitman of Mississippi declared that between 1810 and 1850 the South lost 100,000 slaves valued at more than $30 million. This is a much larger figure than the census gives for blacks in the North who were born in slaveholding states, but Wilbur H. Siebert believes that it is fairly accurate. He is certain, for example, that approximately 40,000 passed through Ohio alone.

The Underground Railroad intensified the resentment that the South felt toward outside interference. It was not realized that the Railroad ran inside the South. Not only Northerners participated in its management, but Southern whites and blacks were among its most valuable engineers and conductors, and all the passengers were blacks desperately anxious to get away from the peculiar institution of the South.

■ The South Strikes Back

Despite the fact that there was considerable Southern sentiment against slavery during the colonial and early national periods, the institution always had its defenders. Almost from the beginning no attack on slavery went unanswered. When Samuel Sewall wrote *The Selling of Joseph,* John Saffin answered his attack on slavery with an enthusiastic rebuttal in 1701. Persons of no less stature than George Whitefield, the great evangelist, and his friend James Habersham sprang to the defense of slavery in the middle of the eighteenth century. When there was some doubt regarding the future of slavery under the new national government, most of the Southern congressmen made it clear that they would tolerate no interference with the institution. From the time that Jefferson's *Notes on Virginia* was made public, Southern leaders did not hesitate to use his work to strengthen their contention that blacks were by nature an inferior race and therefore should be enslaved. Some Southerners conceded that slavery was a political evil, but almost none agreed with antislavery antagonists that it was also a great moral evil.

In the early nineteenth century the question of slavery was overshadowed by other problems of a political and economic nature. Foreign relations were strained, and the nation's energies were directed toward trying to stay out of the Napoleonic Wars in Europe. America's preoccupation with becoming more self-sufficient economically caused the North to turn its attention to shipping and, later, manufacturing, while the South made the transition from a tobacco and rice slave economy to one in which cotton was dominant. It would not be accurate, however, to describe sectional attitudes toward slavery during this period as altogether indifferent. As some people continued to attack slavery, its defenders spoke up, gradually developing the classic defense that was to be reiterated with so much feeling in the period ahead.

Even before the great debate over the admission of Missouri, the antislavery movement had assumed something of a sectional character. Emancipation of the slaves in Northern states had proceeded at a time when the institution was becoming more deeply entrenched in the South with the development of the cotton kingdom. Emigration of the majority of antislavery men and women from the slave states, moreover, deprived the South of an opportunity to hear the other side of the argument from its neighbors. Dwight L. Dumond insists that this migration deprived the South of men and women "whose combined intelligence, moral courage, and Christian benevolence would have gone far toward modifying the harsher features of slavery, toward preventing so great a unanimity of opinion in that section in support of slavery as a positive good, and toward keeping alive the spirit of free discussion." Later, as antislavery men and women withdrew from the colonization movement and organized militant antislavery societies, the South found that it could no longer tolerate any enemies of slavery in its midst. The debate over Missouri, the insurrection of Denmark Vesey, and the increased activity of the abolitionists all convinced the residents of the South that they must give more attention to the defense of their institution. When the call went out for defenders, they were sufficient both in number and in zeal. They began to strike back at their Northern traducers, blow for blow.

Southerners were now determined not to apologize for slavery. They stopped thinking of it as having any undesirable aspects. They evolved the idea, and clung to it with ferocious tenacity, that slavery was a positive good. In 1826 Edward Brown brought out *Notes on the Origin and Necessity of Slavery*, which drew heavily from a pamphlet published the previous year by Whitemarsh B. Seabrook. Brown declared that "slavery has ever been the stepping ladder by which countries have passed from barbarism to civilization. . . . It appears . . . to be the only state capable of bringing the love of independence and of ease, inherent in man, to the discipline and shelter necessary to his physical wants." A few months later Thomas Cooper of South Carolina published his first proslavery pamphlet. One by one, Southern educators and ministers joined in the defense of slavery, and the war of words was on.

The proslavery argument was based on a theory of the racial inferiority and biological inequality of blacks. There were four main postulates of the theory. In the first place, it was contended that slave labor was absolutely essential to the economic development and prosperity of the South. Governor Hammond of South Carolina expressed this point of view clearly:

> In all social systems there must be a class to do the menial duties, to perform the drudgery of life. . . . Its requisites are vigor, docility, fidelity. Such a class you must have or you would not have that other class which leads progress, civilization, and refinement. It constitutes the very mud-sill of society and of political government; and you might as well attempt to build a house in the air, as to build either the one or the other, except on this mud-sill.

In the second place, it was asserted that blacks were inferior and destined to occupy a subordinate position. In *Southern Institutes*, George S. Sawyer forcefully stated this point of view:

The social, moral, and political, as well as the physical history of the negro race bears strong testimony against them; it furnishes the most undeniable proof of their mental inferiority. In no age or condition has the real negro shown a capacity to throw off the chains of barbarism and brutality that have long bound down the nations of that race; or to rise above the common cloud of darkness that still broods over them.

Doctors like John H. Van Evrie, Josiah Clark Nott, and many others published works in which they subscribed to an ethnological justification of African slavery.

Another argument of proslavery leaders was that through the ages the church had sanctioned slavery as a means of converting the heathen to Christian civilization. There was, of course, some conflict between the theory that blacks were incapable of improvement and the notion that they could be civilized and Christianized in slavery; but little attention was paid to this apparent contradiction, and each argument was used where it would do the most good. The Reverend James Henley Thornwell, Bishop Stephen Elliott, and Dr. B. M. Palmer were only three among many Southern religious leaders who held fast to this point of view and expressed it in their sermons and writings. With many Northern religious leaders holding opposite points of view, an intersectional clash of denominations was inevitable. Thus fifteen years before the Civil War the Baptists, Methodists, and Presbyterians had each split into two groups.

Finally, the proslavery argument ran, the white race had not degenerated because of slavery but had developed a unique and high degree of culture. George Fitzhugh, Beverly Tucker, and others claimed that a society in which everyone was free was a failure and that the South had solved its problems by acknowledging the fact that culture and civilization could advance only if slaves were available to do the work.

This war of words became so bitter, and the atmosphere in the South so tense, that free inquiry and free speech disappeared. People with points of view at variance with the accepted proslavery creed were run out of the South. Colleges became hotbeds of secession, and every agency in the community was employed to defend slavery. Even men of letters, like William Gilmore Simms, wrote proslavery essays, poems, and songs. In words the South struck back with a vengeance.

The South loved action too well, however, to let the conflict remain on an academic level. It was a practical matter too: the vociferous antislavery preachers must be silenced if they were not to do irreparable damage to Southern institutions. In October 1831, the Georgia legislature offered $4,000 for the arrest of Garrison. There was a price on the head of Arthur Tappan, $12,000 in Macon and $20,000 in New Orleans. The vigilance committee of South Carolina offered $1,500 for the arrest of any person distributing the *Liberator* or Walker's *Appeal*. Most of the leading participants in the abolition movement and the activities of the Underground Railroad could boast that they were officially wanted in the South.

Pushing their program of resistance a step further, Southern leaders were resolved to keep the writings of abolitionists out of their communities, by force if necessary. They worked up such popular resentment to the circulation of abolitionist literature in the South that citizens took the matter into their own hands. In July 1835 a group broke into the Charleston post office, seized antislavery newspapers, and made a bonfire out of them in the public square. Many other cities followed this example. When it appeared that the federal government would not punish them for their actions, Southern postmasters of their own accord began to take abolitionist literature out of the mails.

People living in the South, whether natives or from the North, found it desirable to speak with extreme caution on the question of slavery. One white man was lashed in Petersburg, Virginia, and ordered to leave the town for expressing the view that "black men have, in the abstract, a right to their freedom." A Georgian who subscribed to the *Liberator* was dragged from his home by a mob, tarred and feathered, set afire, ducked in the river, and then tied to a post and whipped. Amos Dresser, a former student at Lane Seminary, went into Tennessee to sell Bibles. When it could not be proved in court that he was spreading abolitionist doctrine, a mob lashed him one midnight in a public square, with the hearty approval of several thousand onlookers. Whites who associated with blacks on any basis that suggested equality were severely dealt with. Several, for example, were murdered in Georgia and South Carolina for the "crime" of mixing with blacks in public.

Proslavery leaders even carried the fight into enemy territory. They not only went North in pursuit of their runaway slaves, but they sought to spread proslavery doctrine and to spy on abolitionists. A Kentucky slaveholder, dressed in the garb of a Quaker, went to Indiana to get information on the Underground Railroad. Because he knew so little about Quaker speech and customs, he was soon discovered. Another went so far as to pose as an antislavery lecturer. Visiting several communities in Indiana and Ohio, he discovered that fugitives were hiding out and notified their masters, who promptly came and claimed their property. He was in a community, however, that was hostile to slavery, and the citizens insisted that the slaves be given a hearing. In court it was decided that the masters' claims were invalid, and the slaves were set free.

In the decade before the Civil War intersectional strife reached a new peak. There was division and dissension among abolitionists with regard to policy, but there was more unity than ever among proslavery leaders. In both sections the war of words had failed to bring satisfactory results. In the North the practical abolitionists resolved to destroy slavery by perfecting the Underground Railroad and delivering slaves into free territory. In the South the practical proslavery leaders resolved to keep the institution of slavery inviolate by destroying every vestige of thought that was at variance with it. If conformity involved burning books or newspapers, spying on the enemy in order to be able to counterattack successfully, or even killing blacks or whites, then in a situation where so much was at stake it simply had to be done.

■ Stress and Strain in the 1850s

Perhaps no decade in the history of the United States has been so filled with tense and crucial moments as the ten years leading to the Civil War, and closely connected with most of these crises was the problem of slavery. The period was ushered in by the controversy over slavery in the newly acquired territory in the Southwest. With the discovery of gold in California in 1848 and with the rapid peopling of many areas in the Mexican cession, a policy had to be decided upon. Some leaders held that the new territory should be divided into slave and free sections as in the Missouri Compromise. The abolitionists, of course, and many others in the North, wanted a total exclusion of slavery from the territories, a point of view expressed in the Wilmot Proviso. Still others were of the opinion that the question should be decided by the people who lived in the new territories, an approach to the problem which was popularized by Stephen A. Douglas. Finally, there were those who insisted that slavery could not be legally excluded anywhere, a view vigorously advanced by John C. Calhoun. The question of fugitive slaves, moreover, was very much alive. Southern owners had never had too much luck in recovering them. In 1842, in the case of *Prigg v. Pennsylvania,* the Supreme Court ruled that state officials were not required to assist in the return of fugitives, and the decision did much to render ineffective all efforts to recover slaves.

In 1850 these questions were thoroughly aired in Congress, and a desperate effort was made to work out a solution that would diminish intersectional strife. After considerable debate by Clay, Calhoun, Douglas, Seward, and Chase, an agreement was reached which provided that (1) California should enter the Union as a free state; (2) the other territories would be organized without mention of slavery; (3) Texas should cede certain lands to New Mexico and be compensated; (4) slaveholders would be better protected by a stringent fugitive slave law; and (5) there should be no slave trade in the District of Columbia. The Compromise of 1850 was by no means satisfactory to all, and Georgia, Mississippi, Alabama, and South Carolina seriously considered secession. Southerners said they would remain in the Union only as long as there was strict adherence to the compromise, especially in enforcing the fugitive slave act.

It soon became clear that neither section was seriously reconciled to the Compromise of 1850 as a final settlement of the slavery question. Militant abolitionists were still determined to assist runaways, and new federal legislation could not deter them. In 1851 they went so far as to rescue a slave, Shadrach, from a United States marshal in Boston who was preparing to return him to his owner. It was the zeal of the slaveholders that especially irritated the abolitionists. With the new law against fugitives, slaveholders put on intensive hunts, determined to drive back into slavery even those fugitives who had lived free for years. For example, they seized Jerry McHenry, who had lived in Syracuse for several years and was regarded as a substantial citizen; but members of the Liberty party convening there were led by Gerrit Smith and William Seward to rescue McHenry and send him on his way. These are merely two examples of what came to be open defiance of the law on the part of militant abolitionists. Their attitude convinced the South that the North was not willing to abide by the Compromise of 1850.

The appearance of *Uncle Tom's Cabin* in 1852 increased the strain on intersectional relations. This novel by Harriet Beecher Stowe sold more than 300,000 copies in the first year of publication and was soon dramatized in theaters throughout the North. Its story of abject cruelty on the part of masters and overseers, its description of the privation and suffering of slaves, and its complete condemnation of Southern civilization won countless thousands over to abolition and left Southern leaders busy denying the truth of the novel. The damage had been done, however, and when Southerners counted their losses from this one blow, they found them to be staggering indeed.

The sectional truce brought about by the Compromise of 1850 was at an end, but if it needed a legislative act to destroy it, the Kansas-Nebraska Act of 1854 was precisely the thing. Introduced into the Senate by Stephen A. Douglas of Illinois, the act provided that Kansas and Nebraska should be organized as territories and that the question of slavery should be decided by territorial legislatures. Whatever the motives of Douglas may have been, the passage of the act precipitated a desperate struggle between North and South for the control of Kansas. The Missouri Compromise had been in effect repealed, and those forces that mustered the greatest strength in Kansas could win it. In the ensuing years abolitionist and proslavery factions fought and bled for Kansas, and the land became a preliminary battleground of the Civil War. No longer was there much semblance of intersectional peace. Although the climate of Kansas would have prevented any extensive development of plantation slavery there, the principle was important to both sides, and they conducted themselves accordingly.

The Kansas-Nebraska Act persuaded many antislavery leaders that political action was necessary to combat the relentless drive of proslavery forces to extend slavery. Northern Whigs, Free Soilers, and Democrats who had fought the passage of the act came together, and out of their discussions arose the Republican party. This new political organization, unalterably antislavery in its point of view, profited by the mistake of earlier antislavery parties and evolved a program broad enough to attract voters who were indifferent to slavery. Southerners, meanwhile, sought to counteract this new party by demanding further extension of slavery and the reopening of the African slave trade.

The significance of these trends had hardly become apparent when the

JOHN BROWN MEETING THE SLAVE MOTHER. Brown was hanged in 1859, following his unsuccessful attempt to launch an assault on slavery by seizing the federal arsenal at Harper's Ferry. On his way to the place of execution, he greeted a slave mother and her child. *(John Hope Franklin Collection.)*

Supreme Court in 1857 handed down a decision in the case of *Scott v. Sanford* that had the effect of widening the breach between North and South. Dred Scott was a Missouri slave whose master had first taken him to live in free Illinois and subsequently to a fort in the northern part of the Louisiana purchase, where slavery had been excluded by the Missouri Compromise. Upon his return to Missouri, Scott sued for his freedom on the ground that residence on free soil had liberated him. The majority of the Court held that Scott was not a citizen and therefore could not bring suit in the courts. Chief Justice Roger B. Taney, speaking for the Court, added that since the Missouri Compromise was unconstitutional, masters could take their slaves anywhere in the territories and retain title to them. The decision was a clear-cut victory for the South, and the North viewed it with genuine alarm. With the highest court in the land openly preaching the proslavery doctrine, there was little hope that anything short of a most drastic political or social revolution would bring an end to slavery. All abolitionists were not as optimistic as Frederick Douglass, but they hoped with him that "The Supreme Court . . . [was] not the only power in this world. We, the abolitionists and colored people, should meet this decision, unlooked for and monstrous as it appears, in a cheerful spirit. This very attempt to blot out forever the hopes of an enslaved people may be one necessary link in the chain of events preparatory to the complete overthrow of the whole slave system."

Indeed, only two more links were needed to bring on the bitter war that gave freedom to the slaves: one was the raid of John Brown, and the other was a Republican victory at the polls in 1860. Brown had worked in the cause of freedom for many years. He had done his part to aid the antislavery forces in Kansas, and he had worked on the Underground Railroad out of Missouri. By 1859 he was anxious to strike a more significant blow for the freedom of slaves. He traveled through the North raising money and talking with white and black abolitionists. Finally, he laid his plans to attack slaveholders and liberate their slaves. On Sunday night, October 16, with a small band of less than fifty men he seized the federal arsenal at Harpers Ferry, Virginia, in the hope of securing sufficient ammunition to carry out a large-scale operation against the Virginia slaveholders. Immediately the countryside was alerted, and both federal and state governments dispatched troops which overwhelmed Brown and his men. Among those with Brown were several blacks, including Lewis Sheridan Leary, Dangerfield Newby, John Anthony Copeland, Shields Green, and Osborn Perry Anderson. Leary and Newby were killed; Copeland and Green were hanged; and Anderson escaped.

The effect of this raid on the South was electrifying. It made slaveholders think that abolitionists would stop at nothing to wipe out slavery. No one felt secure because there were rumors of other insurrections to come and widespread complaints that slaves were insolent because they knew their day of liberation was near. The whole South was put on a semi-war footing, with troops drilling regularly as far south as Georgia and with increasing demands for arms and ammunition by the militia commanders of most states.

On December 2, 1859, John Brown was hanged, but not before he had dazzled the country by his words and his conduct after the trial. He told a reporter from the *New York Herald*, "I pity the poor in bondage that have none to help them; that is why I am here; not to gratify any personal animosity, revenge or vindictive spirit. It is my sympathy with the oppressed and wronged, that are as good as you and as precious in the sight of God. ... You may dispose of me easily, but this question is still to be settled—the negro question—the end of that is not yet." Upon hearing his sentence he calmly said, "Now, if it is deemed necessary that I should forfeit my life for the furtherance of the ends of justice, and mingle my blood further with the blood of my children and with the blood of millions in this slave country whose rights are disregarded by wicked, cruel, and unjust enactments, I say, let it be done."

Some people said that Brown was a madman, but few who saw him and listened to him thought so. Governor Wise of Virginia said, "They are themselves mistaken who take him to be a madman. ... He is a man of clear head, of courage, of fortitude and simple ingenuousness." He terrified the South and captivated the North by his deed. Many had died fighting for freedom, but none had done it so heroically or at such a propitious moment. The crusade against slavery now had a martyr, and nothing wins followers to a cause like a martyr. Literally thousands of people who had been indifferent were now persuaded that slavery must be abolished. There can be no doubt that many voted for the Republican ticket in 1860 because of this conviction.

When it became clear that the Republican candidate would stand on an antislavery platform, the South began once more to utter threats of secession. But with the nomination of Abraham Lincoln, instead of a pronounced abolitionist like Seward of New York or Chase of Ohio, it was the abolitionists who were worried. They were not sure how far Lincoln would go to put an end to slavery. And yet, as Dwight Dumond has pointed out, his words and deeds for twenty years had clearly been antislavery. He had said many times that slavery was hostile to the poor man. During his one term in Congress he had done what he could to keep the territories free, so that poor people could feel secure there. He had said that blacks should be protected in their right to the enjoyment of the fruits of their own labor, and he had vigorously denounced the Dred Scott decision. Nevertheless, Garrison, Phillips, Sumner, and other abolitionists were skeptical of him because he was not one of them.

Lincoln's election, which many Democrats conceded after they split into factions at the Charleston and Baltimore conventions, marked the elevation to power of a party whose philosophy was, from the Southern point of view, revolutionary and destructive. There was no place in the Union for states unalterably committed to the maintenance and extension of slavery. The November election returns, which gave victory to the Republicans, were the signal for calling conventions in the South to take the step that fire-eaters and proslavery leaders had already decided upon.

It was in an atmosphere of slavery that the weapons for waging the Civil War were sharpened. It was the question of slavery that sundered the sections and forced them to settle the question by a bloody war. The humanitarian reform movement would have proceeded apace had there been no slaves, for temperance, women's rights, and the like would have received generous support in communities where there was a tendency to assume civic responsibility. It was the question of slavery, however, that intensified the reform crusade and brought the country to the impasse of 1860. Without slavery the question of the extent of federal authority in the territories would have remained academic and could have been debated openly and peaceably. Without slavery the South would have remained a land where freedom of thought could command respect and where all institutions would not feel compelled to pursue a course of action prescribed by the planting aristocracy. Just as the antislavery movement had its roots deep in the liberal philosophy of the Revolutionary period, so intersectional strife and the Civil War itself had their roots in the question of the future of black people in the United States.

CHAPTER 11

Civil War

■ Uncertain Federal Policy

When President-Elect Lincoln arrived in Washington late in February 1861, the nation he was to administer during the next four years was rapidly falling apart. Seven states in the lower South had already seceded, and there was talk of the same momentous step being taken in each of the other slave states. Even before his inauguration Lincoln perceived that his most important and difficult task was stemming the tide of national disintegration. In his carefully worded inaugural address he condemned the Southern citizens—not the states—who were in insurrection, and thus he may have won friends in the doubtful border states. But his words were hardly encouraging to abolitionists, who felt that the time for words was over. Action was needed, in their opinion, to bring an end to an institution against which the Republican party had taken a stand during the election campaign. But Lincoln had to move cautiously lest he offend the eight slave states that still remained in the Union. No amount of caution, however, could maintain peace indefinitely without surrendering the authority of the federal government in the South. When the time came to defend Fort Sumter, Lincoln acted promptly, but the defense of the fort cost him four more slave states and plunged the country into civil war.

Even if there had not been the problem of keeping the remaining slave states—Delaware, Maryland, Kentucky, and Missouri—in the Union, there were still many people in the North who would have recoiled from a war against slavery. Lincoln not only had to mollify the border slave states but also had to avoid any policy offensive to thousands throughout the North who had grown weary of the abolition movement. He could hope in the meantime to soften the attacks that abolitionists were bound to make on him by giving ground to them on less dangerous matters.

When blacks rushed to offer their services to the Union, they were rejected. In almost every town of any size there were large numbers of blacks who sought to serve in the Union army. Failing to be enlisted, they bided their time and did whatever they could to assist. In New York they formed a military club and drilled regularly until the police stopped them. Several Philadelphia blacks offered to go south and organize slave revolts, but this was unthinkable. In the nation's capital they made repeated requests of the War Department to be received into the army. At a meeting in Boston they passed a resolution urging the government to enlist them: "Our feelings urge us to say to our countrymen that we are ready to stand by and defend our Government as the equals of its white defenders; to do so with 'our lives, our fortunes, and our sacred honor,' for the sake of freedom, and as good citizens; and we ask you to modify your laws, that we may enlist,—that full scope may be given to the patriotic feelings burning in the colored man's breast."

Abolitionists began to wonder if they had supported the wrong candidate in Lincoln. They were filled with even greater despair when they observed the vacillating policy adopted by the government with reference to slaves who escaped to federal lines. Indeed, there was no policy; each commander used his own discretion. In the spring of 1861, blacks sought refuge within federal lines near Fortress Monroe in Virginia. When General Butler learned that slaves had been employed in erecting Confederate defenses, he immediately declared that they were "contraband of war" and should not be returned to their owners. Instead, they were put to work for the Union forces. For several months it was not at all clear that the authorities in Washington would endorse his action, and several replies from the War Department to his requests for a clarification of policy were evasive.

In June 1861 several military officers spoke out in favor of returning all fugitives. In the West, General Halleck adopted this policy. But the lack of any uniform policy was clearly indicated by two developments in July 1861. On July 9 the House of Representatives passed a resolution declaring it was not the duty of federal troops to capture or return fugitive slaves. One week later, General Winfield Scott wrote Brigadier General McDowell, in the name of President Lincoln, asking him to allow owners of fugitive slaves in Virginia to cross the Potomac and recover runaways who had taken refuge behind Union lines. Small wonder that there was so much dissatisfaction among abolitionists with regard to federal policy. Phillips, Sumner, and Garrison openly attacked the government and demanded a more forthright stand on fugitives and emancipation. It was not until the passage of the Confiscation Act of August 6, 1861, that anything resembling uniform treatment was applied to fugitives by the federal government. The act provided that any property used with the owner's consent and with his or her knowledge in aiding or abetting insurrection against the United States was the lawful subject of prize and capture wherever found. When the property consisted of slaves, they were to be forever free.

As Union armies pushed into the South, blacks poured over Union lines by the thousands. Yet federal policy regarding their relief and employment was hardly more clear-cut than it had been when the legality of receiving them at all was doubtful. Again each commanding officer seemed to use his own discretion. In western Tennessee, General Grant found it necessary to appoint John Eaton to take charge of all fugitives in his area in November 1862. A special camp was set up for blacks at Grand Junction, Tennessee, where Eaton supervised the hiring out of these ex-slaves, leased abandoned plantations to whites who hired them, and saw to it that they were paid for their work. In Louisiana, General Benjamin Butler leased blacks to loyal planters who paid them $10 a month. It was most difficult to secure the cooperation of soldiers and officers, who did not want to appear to be serving with blacks. The transition period for them was extremely difficult, and because of the confused and changing federal policy, they endured at times both hunger and exposure. While they did not suffer cruel punishment, there were many instances of unfair treatment, a most perplexing problem to the officers whose principal responsibility was to take the war to the enemy.

In December 1862 Rufus Saxton, head of the Department of the South, sought to reduce the confusion involving the employment and relief of fugitives by issuing an order for a general plan to be followed everywhere. Abandoned lands were to be used for the benefit of ex-slaves. Black families were allotted two acres for each working hand. They were to plant corn and potatoes for their own use, with tools to be furnished by the government, and the plowing was to be done by those assigned to that task. All blacks were required to raise a certain amount of cotton for government use. In many areas superintendents of "Negro affairs" were appointed, whose duties were to take a census of the black population, see that blacks were employed and had the necessaries of life, take charge of land set aside by the government for their use, and protect those who had hired themselves out to white employers. Some superintendents, like the Reverend Horace James of the North Carolina area, performed their duties conscientiously, but others did not show much interest in the problems of blacks.

Relief was almost always difficult because of the small amount of land available for the use of blacks. In his report in 1864 the Reverend Mr. James said, "We control indeed a broad area of navigable waters, and command the approaches from the sea, but have scarcely room enough on land to spread our tents upon." The government was selling much of the land held for nonpayment of taxes to private parties. Eastern capitalists and philanthropists bought most of the available land in South Carolina, and frequently, though not always, these new owners had little interest in the plight of blacks.

Another difficulty arose out of the fact that the Treasury Department contested the right of the War Department to administer the affairs of black people. Although the secretary of war desired the Treasury to control all confiscated property, except that used by the military, officers in the field were of the opinion that they could best handle everything. While the controversy raged during 1863 and 1864, blacks suffered for want of any coordinated supervision. In his message to the Confederate Congress in the fall of 1863, President Davis excoriated Northern conduct of black affairs. After describing the starvation and suffering among blacks in contraband camps, he said that "there is little hazard in predicting that in all localities where the enemy have gained a temporary foothold, the negroes, who under our care increased sixfold in number . . . will have been reduced by mortality during the war to not more than one-half their previous number." While his criticism was by no means objective, there was indeed much suffering and death among blacks. In 1864 a Union official admitted that mortality in black camps was "frightful" and that "most competent judges place it at not less than twenty-five percent in the last two years."

The federal policy for relief of former slaves developed so slowly that private citizens, both black and white, undertook to supplement it. As early as February 1862 meetings were held in Boston, New York, and other Northern cities for the express purpose of rendering more effective aid to Southern blacks. On February 22 the National Freedmen's Relief Association was organized in New York, and soon thereafter came the Contraband Relief Association in Cincinnati, which later changed its name to the Western Freedmen's Aid Commission. The Friends Association for the Relief of Colored Freedmen was established in Philadelphia, and a group of Chicago citizens formed the Northwestern Freedmen's Aid Commission. In 1865 all were united in the American Freedmen's Aid Commission. Religious organizations, such as the United States Christian Commission and the American Missionary Association, joined in providing relief for blacks. Collections were taken up, clothing and food solicited, and agents sent south to minister to the needs of ex-slaves.

A significant contribution of private agencies toward the adjustment of former slaves to their new status was in education. Although the federal government had no policy in this matter, it was not averse to cooperating with philanthropic organizations. Their work in educating blacks began in 1861 when Lewis Tappan, treasurer of the American Missionary Association, wrote General Butler to offer the services of his organization. Butler welcomed such aid, and the Reverend L. C. Lockwood was sent to develop a program. On September 15, 1861, he opened a Sunday School for blacks in the home of former President Tyler, and two days later he began the first day school, with Mary S. Peake as the teacher. Within a few months the American Missionary Association had established schools for blacks at Hampton, Norfolk, Portsmouth, and Newport News, Virginia, and on several plantations. By 1864 more than 3,000 blacks were in school with 52 teachers, of whom at least 5 were black. They were paid by the associations, but the government furnished subsistence.

Several schools were established in Washington for refugees, and the freedmen's relief associations of Boston and Philadelphia supplied teachers. In North Carolina, the chaplains of Northern regiments took an early interest in the education of blacks, and later the American Missionary Association and relief organizations extended their programs into this area. The first day schools were set up in July 1863. One year later there were schools at Beaufort, Washington, Plymouth, Morehead, and other places, with 3,000 students and 66 teachers. Evening schools were also established for adults. General Butler took great interest in this work and sponsored the erection of a large building at Hampton to accommodate 800 students.

The New England Freedmen's Aid Society started education for blacks in South Carolina in 1862 when 31 men and women arrived as teachers. Schools were established on larger plantations and in towns, and by June 1863 it was estimated that 5,000 blacks were in school. Gradually education for blacks was extended to most areas occupied by Union troops. In 1863 General Banks established a system of public education under the Department of the Gulf, and a Board of Education for Freedmen supervised the schools. By the end of the next year ninety-five schools had been set up under the department, with 162 teachers, of whom 130 were Southerners including several blacks. There were 9,571 students in day schools, and another 2,000 in evening schools.

The enthusiasm of Northerners for the education of blacks was tremendous. In the last year of the war at least 1,000 young Northern men and women were teaching and caring for ex-slaves. They brought with them slates, pencils, spelling books, readers, blackboards, and chalk. While they met strong opposition from a majority of Southern whites, there were some who not only favored but contributed to the success of schools for blacks. All through the South were to be found native whites teaching blacks before the close of the war.

Some blacks established schools for their own people. In Natchez, for example, three schools were started during the war by black women. In Savannah, blacks could boast not only of two large schools that they had founded, but also of a black board of education to determine their policies. Most schools for blacks had poor facilities, inadequate supplies, and insufficient teachers, but African Americans attended them in larger and larger numbers. The people responsible for establishing these schools—Northerners and Southerners, whites and blacks—made a most significant contribution to the adjustment of a people emerging from slavery.

The opposition of the government early in the war to using black soldiers evoked unfavorable criticism from abolitionists. There was considerable agitation for arming blacks. Garrison and Phillips believed that it was cruel to deprive blacks of the opportunity to fight for the freedom of their brothers. White Northerners who were not abolitionists objected to fighting for the freedom of blacks when blacks themselves were not fighting. There were many, however, including some soldiers, who did not want blacks to wear the uniform of the Union, feeling that it should be reserved for those whose citizenship was unquestioned. Lincoln feared that the border states would take exception to a policy of arming blacks and that it would seriously alienate support in the North. He therefore gave no serious consideration to arming them until the spring of 1862, and then it was forced on him.

As a result of considerable pressure from officers in the field, the acting secretary of war authorized Gen. Thomas W. Sherman in October 1861 to "employ fugitive slaves in such services as they may be fitted for . . . with such organization as you may deem most beneficial to the service; this, however, not being a general arming of them for military service." While Sherman did not take advantage of this authorization to arm some slaves, his successor, David Hunter, sent out a call in May 1862 for blacks to serve in the army. Within a few months enough had responded for the First South Carolina Volunteer Regiment to be activated, but almost immediately Hunter was forced to disband the group, and the men were sent home unpaid and dissatisfied. In the autumn of 1862, however, Lincoln permitted the enlistment of some blacks. General B. F. Butler mustered a whole regiment of free blacks in Louisiana, and Hunter's South Carolina regiment was reorganized by General Saxton. In December, Gen. Augustus Chetlain assumed control of blacks volunteering in Tennessee, and thereafter the program was definitely considered a successful venture.

Machinery for recruiting black soldiers in the South was set up in the spring of 1863 by Adj. Gen. Lorenzo Thomas, who was sent to the Mississippi Valley to put it into operation. A special bureau was established in his office for the "conduct of all matters referring to the organization of Negro troops." Recruiting agents were selected and stations established in Maryland, Tennessee, Missouri, and at other strategic points. All able-bodied black men were eligible for military employment. Where loyal masters consented to the enlistment of their slaves, the masters were to receive $300 for each one. If sufficient recruits were not obtained in an area within thirty days, slaves were taken without consent of loyal owners. Although two years had elapsed before the federal government adopted a clear-cut policy regarding black soldiers, it demonstrated that when the circumstances were favorable, it could pursue a policy vigorous enough to satisfy even the most zealous abolitionists.

These months of vacillation on the treatment of runaway slaves, the relief of blacks, and their military service had a disquieting effect on their status during the Civil War. If the federal government would not take a stand to uphold them, they could expect little from private citizens. White reformers joined with such black leaders as Douglass, Langston, Remond, and Brown in fighting for recognition, but they achieved small results. Newspapers in the North opposed to the Lincoln administration complained that the government had plunged the country into a costly war to help undeserving

Susie King Taylor Wishes to See the Yankees—1862

. . . I had been reading so much about the "Yankees" I was very anxious to see them. The whites would tell their colored people not to go to the Yankees, for they would harness them to carts and make them pull the carts around, in place of horses. I asked grandmother, one day, if this was true. She replied, "Certainly not!" that the white people did not want slaves to go over to the Yankees, and told them these things to frighten them. . . . I wanted to see these wonderful "Yankees" so much, as I heard my parents say the Yankee was going to set all the slaves free. Oh, how those people prayed for freedom! I remember, one night, my grandmother went out into the suburbs of the city to a church meeting, and they were fervently singing this old hymn,

> Yes, we all shall be free,
> Yes, we all shall be free,
> Yes, we all shall be free,
> When the lord shall appear.

when the police came in and arrested all who were there, saying they were planning freedom, and sang "the lord," in place of "Yankee," to blind any one who might be listening.

Susie King Taylor, *Reminiscences of My Life in Camp* (Boston, 1902), pp. 7–8.

blacks. The Philadelphia *Age* said that abolitionists had brought on the war to fulfill their "ebony ideals," ignoring the interests of millions of free white men. The editors of these papers strove to create unfavorable public opinion, and not infrequently they succeeded. They headlined any allegations of the rape of white women by black men and insisted that abolitionists were encouraging miscegenation. This sensational and irresponsible journalism had the desired effect: hostility toward blacks actually increased in many Northern communities during the war.

Such hostility was most clearly shown by white workers of the North. They feared that emancipation of the slaves would cause a general exodus of former slaves to the North and that the ensuing competition for work would depress wages and create unemployment. White laborers in many places sought to raise their wages by striking, but the willingness of employers to use black strikebreakers convinced them that competition with black workers had already materialized. The result was that fights and riots occurred where blacks sought work. In New York in 1862, a group of black women and children who worked in a tobacco factory were mobbed. The use of black workers on the Camden and Amboy Railroad in New Jersey caused considerable agitation and threats of reprisals by unemployed whites. Longshoremen in Chicago, Detroit, Cleveland, Buffalo, New York, and Boston fought black workers whenever they were brought on the job.

The New York draft riots of 1863 were closely connected with the competition between whites and blacks for work. Shortly before the riots began, 3,000 longshoremen went on strike for higher wages. Blacks, with police protection, took their places. When the government began drafting unemployed whites, they looked upon it as adding insult to injury: they had been displaced on their jobs by blacks and were now being sent off to fight in a war to set more of them free. Consequently, they resisted conscription to the point of violence. During the riots in July, many homes and business places of blacks were burned, and freedmen's associations, organized to help in the relief of Southern blacks, found it necessary to aid blacks in New York. Perhaps it is not too much to suggest that there was a discernible correlation between the uncertainty of federal policy and the hostile attitude of many white citizens in the North toward their darker fellows.

■ Moving toward Freedom

From the very beginning of the war there had been speculation as to whether or when the slaves would be emancipated. Most Northern Democrats were opposed and said unequivocally that slavery was the best status for blacks. Abolitionists supported the Republicans in 1860 principally because their platform was antislavery, and they demanded that the party fulfill its pledge by setting the slaves free. Lincoln had to move cautiously, however, for constitutional, political, and military reasons. His views on emancipation were well known. As early as 1849 he had introduced a bill in Congress for the gradual emancipation of slaves in the District of Columbia, and in the ensuing decade he stated his position on several occasions. For the abolitionists, gradual emancipation was bad enough, but not even to take definite steps in that direction was unforgivable.

The whole matter caused Lincoln grave concern. As he evolved his plan of emancipation, he was viewed all the more unfavorably because he felt it necessary to restrain enthusiastic officers who emancipated slaves without his authorization. In 1861 Gen. John C. Frémont proclaimed military emancipation in Missouri, but Lincoln had to modify his action in keeping with the Confiscation Act. In 1862 Gen. David Hunter proclaimed that slaves in Georgia, Florida, and South Carolina were to be forever free. When Lincoln learned of this order ten days after it was announced, he immediately issued a proclamation nullifying it and reminding slaveholders that they could still adopt his plan of compensated emancipation.

President Lincoln was going ahead with this plan for solving the problem of blacks in America. He hoped to achieve emancipation by compensating owners for their human property, and then he looked forward to colonizing them in some other part of the world. In the fall of 1861 he attempted an experiment with compensated emancipation in Delaware. He urged his friends there to propose it to the Delaware legislature. He went so far as to write a draft of the bill, which provided for gradual emancipation, and then he composed another, which provided that the federal government would share the expenses of compensating masters for their slaves. Although these bills were much discussed, there was too much opposition to introduce them.

More definite steps in the direction of emancipation were taken in the spring of 1862. In a special message to Congress, President Lincoln recommended that a resolution be passed announcing that the United States would cooperate with any state adopting a plan of gradual emancipation together with satisfactory compensation of the owners. He urged the congressional delegations from Delaware, Maryland, West Virginia, Kentucky, and Missouri to support his policy. They opposed it, however, because their constituents were unwilling to give up their slaves. A joint resolution introduced by Roscoe Conkling nevertheless passed both houses and was approved by the president on April 10, 1862. The abolitionists were furious; they felt that Southern slaveholders should not be paid to surrender property they did not rightfully possess. Wendell Phillips, speaking in Cincinnati before a crowd hostile to his views, criticized the administration, declaring that the right hand of Southern aristocracy was slavery and the left hand the ignorant white man. All over the North abolitionists denounced Lincoln's plan of compensated emancipation.

Another of Lincoln's recommendations, which became law in April 1862, provided for the emancipation of slaves in the District of Columbia. There would be compensation, of course, but not exceeding $300 for each slave. A significant feature was the provision of $100,000 to support the voluntary emigration of freedmen to Haiti and Liberia. Colonization seemed almost as important to Lincoln as emancipation. In August 1862 he called a group of prominent free blacks to the White House and urged them to support colonization. He told them, "Your race suffer greatly, many of them, by living among us, while ours suffer from your presence. In a word we suffer on each side. If this is admitted, it affords a reason why we should be separated." Perhaps some of them pledged their support, for in his second annual message he was able to say that many free blacks had asked to be colonized. Largely at Lincoln's suggestion, the State Department made inquiries of South American governments and of some insular and African governments concerning the possibility of colonizing black Americans. Only two replies were entirely satisfactory to Lincoln; they suggested that colonies of former slaves be established in Panama and on the Ile à Vache, in the Caribbean. Up until the end of the war Lincoln held out hope for colonizing at least some of the slaves who were being set free.

From June 1862 the policy of the government toward emancipation took shape rapidly. On June 19 the president signed a bill abolishing slavery in the territories. On July 17 a measure became law setting free all slaves coming from disloyal masters into Union-held territory. Lincoln again called together congressmen from the border slave states and told them that since slavery would be destroyed if the war lasted long enough, they should accept his plan of compensated emancipation. His plea fell on deaf ears. Having gone as far as he had, however, Lincoln considered emancipating by proclamation all slaves in rebellious states, an idea that he discussed with his secretaries of state and navy, Seward and Welles.

For two days, July 21 and 22, the cabinet debated the draft of an emancipation proclamation that Lincoln read to them. Rebels were to be warned of the penalties of the Confiscation Act and reminded of the possibility of emancipating their slaves and receiving compensation. All slaves were to be set free on January 1, 1863. Only two cabinet members, Seward and Chase, agreed even in part with Lincoln's proposed proclamation, and Seward strongly advised him not to issue it until the military situation was more favorable. Apparently there was some hope, based on rumor, that the president would issue the proclamation in August. When it was not forthcoming, advocates of emancipation were sorely disappointed. Horace Greeley, writing in the *New York Tribune,* urged Lincoln to proclaim emancipation. Antislavery delegations called upon him. Interestingly enough, the president told one delegation that he could not free slaves under the Constitution because it could not be enforced in the rebel states. Any proclamation would be about as effective, from Lincoln's point of view, "as the Pope's bull against the comet."

It was the Union victory at Antietam on September 17, 1862, that caused Lincoln to act. Five days later he issued a preliminary proclamation. In this document he revived the possibility of compensated emancipation and said that he would continue to encourage the voluntary colonization of blacks "upon this continent or elsewhere." The time had come, however, when more direct action was needed. So he proclaimed that on January 1, 1863, "all persons held as slaves within any State, or designated part of the State, the people whereof shall be in rebellion against the United States, shall be then, thenceforward, and forever free."

The general reaction in the North was unfavorable. Many whites felt that the war was no longer to save the Union but to free the slaves, and some soldiers resigned rather than participate in such a struggle. The Peace Democrats accused the administration of wasting the lives of white citizens in a costly abolitionist war. Abolitionists hesitated to condemn the proclamation since it was better than nothing, but to them it seemed at best very poor compensation for all the struggles and sacrifices they had made for more than a generation. Furthermore, what if the war should end and there were no rebellious states on the first of January 1863? The prospect sent cold shivers through every ardent abolitionist. The real reaction was seen at the November elections. Although the Republicans maintained a majority in

Congress, the Democrats won in many Northern communities and gained substantially in both the House and Senate.

The preliminary proclamation, despite this critical reaction, captured the imagination of workers in many parts of the world, who viewed it as a great humanitarian document, and whenever slaves learned of it they laid down their tools and took on the mantle of their newly found freedom. By the end of December 1862, the suspense attending the final proclamation was so great that even before it was read it had assumed the significance of one of the great documents of all times. On December 31 watch meetings were held by blacks and whites in many parts of the country at which prayers of thanksgiving were offered for the deliverance of the slave. At Tremont Temple in Boston, Frederick Douglass, William Wells Brown, William Lloyd Garrison, Harriet Beecher Stowe, Charles B. Ray, and other fighters for freedom heard on January 1 the words that emancipated more than three-fourths of the slaves. President Lincoln set free all slaves except those in states or parts of states not in rebellion against the United States at that time. These exceptions, in addition to the four loyal slave states, were thirteen parishes of Louisiana, including the city of New Orleans; the forty-eight counties of Virginia, which had become West Virginia; and seven counties in eastern Virginia, including the cities of Norfolk and Portsmouth.

Lincoln left no doubt of his justification for the Emancipation Proclamation. Twice he mentioned the *military* necessity of pursuing this course. He described it as a "fit and necessary war measure" for suppressing the rebellion which he could take by virtue of the power vested in him as commander in chief of the army and navy. In the last paragraph of the proclamation he said that it was "sincerely believed to be an act of justice, warranted by the Constitution upon military necessity." He counseled slaves, however, to abstain from all violence except in self-defense and to work faithfully for reasonable wages.

If the Emancipation Proclamation was essentially a war measure, it had the desired effect of creating confusion in the South and depriving the Confederacy of much of its valuable labor force. If it was a diplomatic document, it succeeded in rallying to the Northern cause thousands of English and European laborers who were anxious to see workers gain their freedom throughout the world. If it was a humanitarian document, it gave hope to millions of blacks that a better day lay ahead, and it renewed the faith of thousands of crusaders who had fought long to win freedom in America.

During the war years slaves had moved significantly toward freedom. Many of them were among the first, however, to realize that it had not been achieved. Even after the proclamation was issued there were more than 800,000 slaves in the border states untouched by it, to say nothing of the hundreds of thousands if not millions in the Confederacy who were not even to hear about the proclamation until months later. Political and economic freedom, moreover, blacks had neither in the South nor in the North. Their leaders were concerned about these matters. The National Convention of Colored Men, which met at Syracuse in October 1864, discussed the questions of employment, enfranchisement, and the extension of freedom. If blacks had no answers to these questions, it was because of the complexity and magnitude of the problems involved in adjusting more than 4 million people to a new climate of freedom.

■ Confederate Policy

One of the greatest anxieties of the South at the beginning of the war was the conduct of slaves. The reaction of slaves to their status involved not only the security of the white civilian population but also the maintenance of a stable economic system without which there was no hope of prosecuting the war successfully. The owners took no chances. It was all right to talk about the love of slaves for their masters during times of peace, but in war idle talk and wishful thinking were not the stuff of victories. There was widespread sentiment for much closer control of slaves. Patrol laws all over the Confederacy were strengthened. Instead of biweekly patrols, Florida in 1861 required them to make their rounds once a week, and even more often "when informed by a creditable citizen of evidence of insubordination or threatened outbreak, or insurrection of slaves." In 1862 Georgia canceled exemptions from patrol duty, and Louisiana imposed a fine of $10 or twenty-four hours' imprisonment for failure to perform it.

The fears of white Southerners appeared to be fully justified. Ordinary emergencies might not excite the slaves, but gradually they became aware that in this war their freedom was at stake. To be sure, there were slaves who remained on the plantation, worked faithfully for their masters, and protected their mistresses, but as Bell I. Wiley has pointed out, "these acts of loyalty, in the light of contemporary evidence, must be considered as exceptional." The most widespread form of disloyalty was desertion. It could hardly be called running away in the sense that it was before the war. Between 1861 and 1865 black men and women simply walked off plantations, and when Union forces came close, they went to their lines and got food and clothing. In Arkansas, according to Thomas Staples, "whenever federal forces appeared, most of the able-bodied adult Negores left their owners and sought refuge within the Union lines." Almost the entire slave population of the Shirley plantation in Virginia deserted to the Union lines. In August 1862 a Confederate general estimated that slaves worth at least $1 million were escaping to the federals in North Carolina.

Confederate and state officials sought to halt the wholesale exodus of slaves by having planters engage in what was called "running the Negroes." When an area was threatened with invasion by federal troops, the planters would remove their slaves to safety, usually in the interior. More than 2,000 were transferred from Washington and Tyrell counties to the interior of

ROBERT SMALLS. Smalls, a slave pilot in Charleston, became a Civil War hero when he sailed with his family out of the harbor aboard a Confederate steamer, *The Planter,* of which he had taken control, and delivered it to the Union squadron that was blocking the harbor. After the Civil War, Smalls served five terms in the United States House of Representatives as a member from South Carolina. *(Schomburg Center For Research in Black Culture, New York Public Library.)*

North Carolina in the autumn of 1862. It was an interesting sight to see planters moving with "black capital," sometimes on foot, sometimes by wagon or cart, but always in haste. Not all blacks were amenable to the idea of "refugeeing," at least not with their masters, and at times they openly resisted them and went off in the opposite direction—toward Union troops.

Slaves were often insolent toward whites, especially when their lands were being invaded by Union armies. In 1862 a Mississippi citizen wrote the governor that "there is greatly needed in this county a company of mounted rangers . . . to keep the Negroes in awe, who are getting quite impudent. Our proximity to the enemy has had a perceptible influence on them." The situation became so disturbing in Georgia that a bill was introduced in the legislature "to punish slaves and free persons of color for abusive and insulting language to white persons." The Richmond *Enquirer* reported that a coachman, upon learning that he was free, "went straightly to his master's chamber, dressed himself in his best clothes, put on his best watch and chain, took his stick, and returning to the parlor where his master was, insolently informed him that he might for the future drive his own coach." A North Carolina citizen summed up the prevailing white point of view in 1864: "Our Negroes are beginning to show that they understand the state of affairs, and insolence and insubordination are quite common."

As the war entered its more desperate stages, many slaves refused to work or to submit to punishment. A South Carolina planter complained in 1862 that "we have had hard work to get along this season, the Negroes are unwilling to do any work, no matter what it is." Another exasperated planter said, *"I wish every negro would leave the place* as they will do only what pleases them, go out in the morning when it suits them, come in when they please, etc." Some Louisiana slaves demanded wages for their labor. In Texas, a slave cursed his master "all to pieces" when the latter attempted to punish him. Relations became so strained in some areas that masters and mistresses stopped trying to punish their slaves, lest they resort to desperate reprisals.

Other acts of slave disloyalty were giving information and guidance to federal troops, seizing the master's property upon arrival of these troops and helping to destroy it, and inflicting bodily harm upon white civilians. Most white Southerners lived in constant fear of slave uprisings during the war, especially after the Emancipation Proclamation. Rumors of uprisings became common, and slaveholders were so terrified at the prospect of bloody insurrections that they frequently appealed to Union troops for protection.

One of the main objections of white Southerners to conscription was that it would drain off the white male population and encourage blacks to revolt. In 1864 the Richmond *Whig* said, "Take away all, or nearly all the vigorous whites, and leave the negro to the feeble control of women, children, and old men, and the danger is that famine will be superadded to insurrection." In several Alabama and Georgia towns slaves were hanged for plotting insurrection; many were committed to jail for implication in these plots. The number of actual insurrections was relatively small because slaves were able to secure their freedom without committing violence. The practice in the South, moreover, was to act summarily in the case of people suspected of insurrection in order to discourage any large-scale revolt.

Since Southern agriculture had been based on staple crops, there was great difficulty in making the transition to a wartime economy that would provide the food necessary for the fighting forces. In most places cotton acreage was forcibly reduced by law, and there was a wholesale conversion of land to corn, wheat, and other cereal grains. The laboring force was the greatest problem. The supervision of slaves, who knew little about grain production and were not interested in it, fell into the hands of white women, disabled white men, and faithful slaves.

Slaves were employed not only on farms but in factories as well. The ironworks of Virginia and Alabama used them throughout the struggle. In 1862 the famous Tredegar Works advertised for 1,000 slaves. At the ironworks they cut the wood for charcoal, hauled iron to shipping points, and engaged in various types of skilled labor. In 1864 there were 4,301 blacks and 2,518 whites in the iron mines of the Confederate states east of the Mississippi. Slaves were also to be found mining coal and working in salt factories. Historian James Brewer has shown how indispensable they were in Virginia's war effort. Relying on the skills of slaves could be a dangerous business, however. Robert Smalls, a slave pilot in Charleston, sailed with his family out of the harbor aboard a Confederate steamer, *The Planter,* of which he had taken control, and delivered it to the Union squadron that was blocking the harbor.

Confederate and state governments relied on slave and free black labor to do much of the hard work involved in prosecuting the war. Slave laborers were secured by contracts with their masters, by hiring them for short periods, and by impressment. By the fall of 1862 the labor shortage was so acute in the South that most states had authorized the impressment of slaves. In 1863 a desperate Confederate government passed a general impressment law, and one year later voted to impress 20,000 slaves. Up until the close of the war President Davis constantly urged that more slaves be impressed. The results were not at all gratifying. In the first place, the owners of slaves did not like the principle of impressment, by which their property could be seized at a price set by the government. Consequently, they simply refused to cooperate in many instances. Slaves did not like impressment, because to work for military authorities involved vastly more strenuous work than what they were accustomed to doing for their own masters, if they chose to work at all. With master *and* slave opposed to impressment, there was little chance for its success.

Even without it Confederate and state governments were able to secure the services of thousands of slaves who performed many important tasks. Most of the cooks in the Confederate army were slaves, and the government recognized their value to the morale and physical fitness of the soldiers by designating four cooks for each company and providing that each one should receive $15 a month as well as clothing. There were also slave teamsters, mechanics, hospital attendants, ambulance drivers, and common laborers. Much of the work in the construction of fortifications was done by slaves. As Union armies invaded the South, tearing up railroads and wrecking bridges, gangs of slave and free black workers repaired them. They were also extensively employed in the manufacture of powder and arms. Of 400 workers at the naval arsenal in Selma, Alabama, 310 were black in 1865.

Affluent Confederates took their body servants to war with them. These workers kept the quarters clean, washed clothes, groomed uniforms, polished swords, buckles, and spurs, ran errands, secured rations, cut hair, and groomed the animals. Some even took part in fighting. In November 1861 it was reported that one servant "fought manfully" and killed four Union soldiers. As the fighting grew desperate, and rations shorter, most servants were sent home. The Confederate soldiers had come to realize that outside medieval romances there was no place for body servants on the field of battle.

It was one thing to have blacks performing all types of work, even with the army, and quite another to put weapons in their hands. Some white Southerners had wanted to arm blacks from the beginning, and local authorities had permitted free blacks to enroll for military service. In 1861 the Tennessee legislature authorized the governor to enlist all free blacks between fifteen and fifty years of age in the state militia. Memphis went so far as to open a recruiting office for them. Public opinion, however, was generally against arming blacks. There was, of course, the fear that they would turn on their masters. To accept them for military service, moreover, would be an acknowledgment of their equality with whites. When a company of sixty free blacks presented themselves for service at Richmond in 1861, they were thanked and sent home. A company of free blacks in New Orleans was allowed to parade but not to go into battle.

Despite the stern opposition of Southern leaders to enlisting blacks, agitation in favor of it continued throughout the war. After reverses in the autumn of 1863 the debate increased, and the Alabama legislature recommended arming a large number of slaves. In 1864 Gen. Patrick Cleburne proposed to officers in the Tennessee army that they organize a large force of slaves and promise them freedom at the end of the war. This proposal, coming from a high army official, provoked considerable discussion, and President Davis, fearing that it did the Confederate cause no good, ordered that no such force of slaves be organized. Discussion continued, however, and at a meeting of the governors of North and South Carolina, Georgia, Alabama, and Mississippi in October 1864, a resolution was adopted suggesting the use of slaves as soldiers. Davis was still opposed to the proposition. In his message to the Confederate Congress the following month he said as much but added: "Should the alternative ever be presented of subjugation or of the employment of the slave as a soldier, there seems no reason to doubt what should then be our decision."

The Confederate Congress in the winter of 1864–1865 openly debated arming the slaves. A representative from Mississippi deplored any suggestion that slaves should be armed and cried out, "God forbid that this Trojan horse should be introduced among us." The outspoken editor of the Charleston *Mercury* declared that South Carolina would no longer be interested in prosecuting the war if slaves were armed.

A bill was introduced in the Confederate Senate in 1865 providing for the enlistment of 200,000 blacks and their emancipation if they remained loyal through the war. Advocates of the measure sought the approval of Gen. Robert E. Lee. The South's most respected soldier said that the measure was not only expedient but also necessary, that blacks would make efficient soldiers, and that those who served should be freed at the end of the war. On March 13, 1865, a bill was signed by President Davis which authorized him to call on each state for its quota of additional troops, irrespective of color, on the condition that the slaves recruited from any state should not exceed 25 percent of the able-bodied male slave population between eighteen and forty-five. Recruiting officers were immediately appointed to enroll blacks for the Confederate army.

The enlistment of blacks was very slow in the West. A Mississippian wrote his governor that they were fleeing to avoid conscription. Enlistment went better on the Eastern seaboard, where officers resorted to dances and parades to work up enthusiasm among blacks for the Confederate cause. It was too late, however, for the Confederacy had already been destroyed by the onslaught of Union forces and by its own internal strife and disorganization. There are unconfirmed reports that some black troops saw action on the side of the Confederacy, but if they did, their number was very small. Had the Confederacy reached a decision to use black troops two years earlier, a considerable force might have been enlisted. But in view of so much slave disloyalty, there is little reason to believe that they would have fought effectively for the Confederate cause.

■ Blacks Fighting for the Union

When blacks were finally permitted to enlist in the Union army, they did so with alacrity and enthusiasm. In the North leading blacks like Frederick Douglass served as recruiting agents. Rallies were held at which speakers urged blacks to enlist, and in Boston, New York, and Philadelphia blacks went to recruiting stations in large numbers. In the South, too, there were many who enlisted, but not all saw the necessity of fighting when they were winning their freedom without it. Enlistment of blacks was, however, a notable success: more than 186,000 had enrolled in the Union army by the end of the war. From the seceded states came 93,000, and from the border slave states, 40,000. The remainder, approximately 53,000, were from free states. It is possible that the total figure was larger, for some contemporaries insisted that many mulattoes served in white regiments without being designated as blacks.

Black troops were organized into regiments of light and heavy artillery, cavalry, infantry, and engineers. To distinguish them from white soldiers, they were called United States Colored Troops, and for the most part they were led by white officers with some black noncommissioned officers. At first it was difficult to secure white officers for black outfits, because regular army men were generally opposed to having blacks in the service. Joseph T. Wilson says that West Pointers were especially averse to the idea of commanding black troops and ostracized their fellows who undertook the task. There were those, however, who enthusiastically assumed the responsibility and made such a reputation for themselves and their men that it was not difficult to secure white officers for black outfits toward the close of the war. Among those who were outstanding as leaders were Col. Thomas Wentworth Higginson of the First South Carolina Volunteers, Col. Robert Gould Shaw of the Fifty-fourth Massachusetts Regiment, and Gen. N. P. Banks, who for a time had the First and Third Louisiana Native Guards under his command.

Some blacks held commissions in the Union army. Two regiments of General Butler's *Corps d'Afrique* were entirely staffed by black officers, including Maj. F. E. Dumas and Capt. P. B. S. Pinchback. An independent battery at Lawrence, Kansas, was led by Capt. H. Ford Douglass and 1st Lt. W. D. Matthews. The 104th Regiment had two black officers, Maj. Martin R. Delany and Capt. O. S. B. Wall. Among the black surgeons who received commissions were Alexander T. Augusta of the 7th Regiment and John V. DeGrasse of the 35th. Charles B. Purvis, Alpheus Tucker, John Rapier, William Ellis, Anderson Abbott, and William Powell were hospital surgeons in Washington. Among the black chaplains with commissions were Henry M. Turner, William Hunter, James Underdue, Williams Waring, Samuel Harrison, William Jackson, and John R. Bowles.

At the beginning there was discrimination in the pay of white and black soldiers. The Enlistment Act of July 17, 1862, provided that whites with the rank of private should receive $13 a month and $3.50 for clothing, but blacks of the same rank were to receive only $7 and $3, respectively. Black soldiers and their white officers objected vigorously to this discrimination. The Fifty-fourth Massachusetts Regiment served a year without pay rather than accept discriminatory wages and went into battle in Florida in 1864 singing "Three cheers for Massachusetts and seven dollars a month." In the Third South Carolina Regiment, Sgt. William Walker was shot, by order of court martial, for "leading the company to stack arms before their captain's tent, on the avowed ground that they were released from duty by the refusal of the government to fulfill its share of the contract." After many protests the War Department, beginning in 1864, granted equal pay for black soldiers.

Blacks performed all kinds of services in the Union army. Organized into raiding parties, they were sent through Confederate lines to destroy fortifications and supplies. Since they knew the Southern countryside better than most white soldiers and could pass themselves off as slaves, they were extensively used as spies and scouts. White officers relied upon information secured by black spies. Harriet Tubman was a spy for Union troops at many points on the eastern seaboard.

Black soldiers built fortifications along the coasts and up the rivers. They were engaged so much in menial tasks, instead of fighting, that their officers made numerous complaints. One said that he would rather carry his rifle in the ranks of fighting men than be overseer to black laborers. In 1864 Adj. Gen. Lorenzo Thomas took notice of the situation and issued an order that there should be no excessive impositions upon black troops and "that they will be only required to take their fair share of fatigue duty with white troops. This is necessary to prepare them for the higher duties of conflicts with the enemies."

The "higher duties of conflicts" had already begun, for blacks saw action against Confederate forces as early as the fall of 1862. Hardly a battle was fought up to the end of the war in which some black troops did not meet the enemy. They saw action, according to George Washington Williams, in more than 250 skirmishes. In the Battle of Port Hudson, eight black infantry regiments fought.

Naturally the Confederacy was outraged by the Northern use of black troops. The question immediately arose as to whether they should be treated as soldiers of the enemy or slaves in insurrection. The vast majority of white Southerners viewed black soldiers as rebellious slaves and insisted that they should be treated as such. In 1862 President Davis ordered that all slaves captured in arms were to be delivered to the state from which they came, to be dealt with according to state laws. Union officials insisted that captured blacks should be treated as prisoners of war, but the Confederates did not accept that point of view until 1864.

Some captured blacks, perhaps not many, were sold into slavery. Others were killed. The Confederate secretary of war countenanced the killing of some black prisoners in order to make an example of them. In 1864 a Confederate officer, Col. W. P. Shingler, told his subordinates not to report the capture of any more blacks. The worst case was the Fort Pillow affair. On April 12, 1864, the fort fell to Confederate forces under the command of Gen. Nathan B. Forrest. Blacks who were there were not permitted to surrender; they were shot, and some were burned alive. Yet many black troops were captured and held as prisoners of war by the South. In 1863 General Butler reported that 3,000 black troops were prisoners of the Confederates. Late in 1864 nearly 1,000 black prisoners worked on Confederate fortifications at Mobile.

Blacks saw action in every theater of operation during the Civil War. They were at Milliken's Bend in Louisiana, at Olustee in Florida, at Vicksburg in Mississippi, and at the siege of Savannah. They fought in Arkansas, Kentucky, Tennessee, and North Carolina. They played a part in the reduction of Petersburg and were at Appomattox Court House, April 9, 1865. Congress awarded a medal to Decatur Dorsey for gallantry while acting as color-sergeant of the Thirty-ninth United States Colored Troops at Petersburg on July 30, 1864. James Gardner, of the Thirty-sixth, received a medal for rushing in advance of his brigade to shoot a Confederate officer leading his men into action. Four men of the Fifty-fourth Massachusetts Infantry earned the Gilmore Medal for gallantry in the assault on Fort Wagner, in which their commanding officer, Col. Robert Gould Shaw, lost his life. Maj. Gen. Gilmore issued the following order to commend black soldiers under his command for a daring exploit:

On March 7, 1865, a party of Colored soldiers and scouts, thirty in number . . . left Jacksonville, Florida, and penetrated into the interior through Marion County. They rescued ninety-one Negroes from slavery, captured four white prisoners, two wagons, and twenty-four horses and mules; destroyed a sugarmill and a distillery . . . and burned the bridge over the Oclawaha River. When returning they were attacked by a band of over fifty cavalry, whom they defeated and drove off with a loss of more than thirty to the rebels. . . . This expedition, planned and executed by Colored men under the command of a Colored noncommissioned officer, reflects credit upon the brave participants and their leader.

ROBERT GOULD SHAW AND THE MEN OF THE FIFTY-FOURTH MASSACHUSETTS INFANTRY. This monumental frieze by Augustus Saint-Gaudens on the Boston Commons commemorates the heroic service during the Civil War of the all-black army unit and its commanding officer. It has come to symbolize the contributions of all the blacks who fought for the freedom of their people and to ensure the preservation of the Union. *(Courtesy Barbara W. Moore.)*

Testimonies similar to this were given by Maj. Gen. E. R. S. Canby, Godfry Weitzel, James G. Blunt, S. A. Hurlbut, Alfred H. Terry, and W. F. Smith, as well as by men of other ranks. The most significant thing about their words of praise is that they bear witness to the fact that black soldiers did what they could to save the Union and secure their freedom.

More than 38,000 black soldiers lost their lives in the Civil War. It has been estimated that their rate of mortality was nearly 40 percent greater than that among white troops. In the Fifth United States Colored Heavy Artillery, for example, 829 men died, the largest number of deaths in any outfit in the Union army. The Sixty-fifth Colored Infantry lost more than 600 men from disease alone. The high mortality rate among blacks is to be explained by several unfavorable conditions. Among them were excessive fatigue details, poor equipment, bad medical care, the recklessness and haste with which they were sent into battle, and the "no quarter" policy (namely, the refusal to regard them as soldiers fighting under the accepted rules of war) with which Confederates fought them. It is impossible to estimate the number of blacks who died at the hands of their enemy, but it must have run into many thousands. There can be no doubt, therefore, that blacks contributed heavily to the victory of Union forces in the second great war for freedom.

■ Victory!

The surrender of the Confederate army in 1865 meant victory not only for the powerful military forces of the North but also for an indestructible Union. Once and for all the question of whether states had a right to secede from the Union was settled. The question of the exact relation of a state to the federal government could arise again, but all states were bound henceforth to recognize the superior sovereignty of the federal government.

The surrender of the Confederacy was also a personal victory for President Lincoln and his policies. It was he who evolved the theory that the states had not seceded but that rebellious citizens had gotten out of hand. Now he could use this theory, magnanimous as it was, to hasten binding up the nation's wounds. Almost as long as any man in public life, Lincoln had spoken out against slavery. Now he could view with satisfaction its abolition, which began with his war proclamations and ended with the adoption of the Thirteenth Amendment late in 1865.

The end of the war marked a victory for the abolitionists. At no time in the nation's history had a pressure group done so much to shape public opinion and then to move opinion to action. For a generation they had labored tirelessly, suffering abuse and even bodily harm. With them, however, it was a moral crusade and they were blind to personal indignities and insensible to suffering. More effectively than ever before in our history they had roused the nation's conscience to its sins and misdeeds. Up until the present day, Americans still feel the effects of the morality in human relations which was the creed of abolitionists.

For blacks, Lee's surrender was a victory. At last they had achieved what human beings everywhere have always wanted—freedom. The end of the war brought to a close a period of enslavement that had lasted for almost 250 years. The desire for freedom had been kept alive through the centuries by those blacks who demonstrated by their conduct that freedom and the right to it transcended racial lines. The victory was won in part by their struggles through the centuries as well as by their service in the final battles.

Paradoxically, the end of the war was also a victory for the South. To be sure, it had suffered military reverses and lost much. But it had been delivered from the domination of an institution that had stifled its economic development and rendered completely ineffective its intellectual life. Opportunities for extensive development in new areas of economic activity had hardly existed in the South, and because it was sensitive to criticism of slavery, the region had expelled both freedom of speech and the talents that flourish only in freedom. It was a great day for the South when at last it could be realistic in economic life and its churches, schools, and writers could face the truth and express it as they saw it. At least, no system of slavery any longer demanded that they do otherwise.

The end of the war was, moreover, the beginning of a new era in the history of the United States. The economic revolution ushered in by the

COMPANY E, 4TH UNITED STATES COLORED INFANTRY. Over 186,000 blacks fought under the Union flag during the Civil War. Company E was one of the detachments assigned to guard the nation's capital. *(Library of Congress.)*

tremendous forces let loose in war was to transform every phase of American life and to create new problems and injustices for reformers to solve. In the new era the Republicans would have to find a new faith for their party, and the abolitionists new social ills to eradicate. Blacks would have to perfect their freedom in a society that was changing so rapidly that adjustment would be difficult even for the best educated of them. For all Americans, perhaps the greatest problem that arose out of the Civil War and its economic aftermath was to find a way to retain freedom, the desire for which had become almost an obsession, and yet at the same time to enjoy security, which was becoming more precarious in the new economic order. As black people and white people set out to find the perfect balance between freedom and security in post-Civil War America, democracy faced a new test.

CHAPTER 12

The Effort to Attain Peace

■ Reconstruction and the Nation

In few periods of our history has the whole fabric of American life been altered so drastically as during the Civil War and the period immediately following it. To be sure, there were the social and economic changes arising from the emancipation of 4 million slaves in the South, but these changes were so completely interwoven with other consequences of the war as to make them wholly inseparable. Although the South, for example, did not experience great industrial development during the war, the North did; and the forces let loose were so powerful that they affected the entire course of Reconstruction. The political changes that began with the secession of the Southern states affected the whole nation, but the economic transformation brought on by numerous changes in production and distribution demanded the attention of every practical-minded person in the United States.

It must be remembered, as Howard K. Beale has pointed out, that there is no way of understanding Reconstruction unless an attempt is made to study it in its setting. It is not a history of "Negro rule," as many historians have dubbed the period of Radical Reconstruction, nor is it merely Southern history, however much students in the past have approached it from a regional point of view. It is an integral part of the national history, and one may find an explanation for strange events in Alabama not only in the activities of people in that state but in the movements and transactions of citizens in Boston, New York, or Philadelphia as well. From 1865 to the end of the century, the United States was picking up the threads of its social, political, and economic life, which were so abruptly cut in 1861, and attempting to weave them into a new pattern. South Carolina's political life after 1865 was affected by more than the presence of blacks in the state legislature or in other positions of public trust. It was affected, as well, by the dynamic changes of economic reconstruction. Reconstruction in 1865 was indeed nationwide.

White Southerners who traveled in the North after the Civil War were amazed at the changes that a few years had wrought in the economic life of the section. The pressing military needs, the extensive inflation of Union currency, and the stimulating effect of protective tariff legislation had all conspired to industrialize the North. Steel factories were producing much more than what was needed for the prosecution of war; railroads were rapidly connecting the North and West in one large community. Hundreds of technological developments made possible the production of commodities, the conception of which would have strained the imagination two decades earlier. New forms of economic organization emerged whose possibilities for expansion throughout the nation and the world were almost unlimited and whose leaders were filled with a desperate anxiety to create monopolies and reap huge profits. Northerners were as anxious to sell to ex-Confederates as they were to Northerners. The most discerning white Southerners must have seen that the new order of things was the result of the triumph of industrialism over the agrarian way of life. The new and old bustling cities were symbols of the triumph, while the wasted and abandoned lands of the South signified the defeat of the old agrarianism. White Southerners could also see that if their section was not careful, its economic and psychological defeat would be as complete as its military downfall.

The political situation was much disturbed in the period after the Civil War, and the problem of the reorganization of the seceded states was only part of the unsettled state of political affairs. During the war the president had wielded many powers that would not be tolerated in peace, and even before the war's end Congress signified by its choleric temper that it was anxious to restore the balance of the three branches of government. From the point of view of many men in Congress, the pendulum had to swing back, and not even a Lincoln should obstruct the delicate operations of constitutional government. The unexpected accession to the presidency of Andrew Johnson merely complicated matters and made Congress more determined than ever to have a full share in governing the country. The fear of Republicans that they would lose political control, the pressure of new industrialists for favorable legislation, and conflicting philosophies of Reconstruction are all considerations that cannot be overlooked in studying the politics of the period.

The political chaos that followed in the wake of war carried with it the inherent element of corruption. There was an extravagance in wartime spending that encouraged corruption, and the beneficiaries of graft and bribery had no intention of retiring at the end of the war. Indeed, many wartime profiteers kept within the bounds of respectability, but in the postwar period adhering to the restraints of respectability was no longer desirable. As the more able men went into industry and other economic activities, incompetent people, the easy prey of cunning industrialists and unscrupulous politicians, took over the management of political affairs. Sound economic and political reconstruction became all the more difficult, and the United States became a prime example of corruption during the postwar years.

The problem of American political immaturity after the Civil War cannot be dismissed merely by observing that there were 4 million blacks who were without any experience in public affairs. To these must be added the millions of Europeans who poured into the country and muddied the political waters considerably. Many of them had not participated in any kind of government, and most of them had no understanding of the workings of representative government. The vast majority, moreover, spoke "strange" languages and were poorly educated. These factors, in addition to their low standard of living, made adjustment in the New World even more difficult. They were, of course, exposed to venal and corrupt politicians and frequently became unwitting accessories to the crimes of corrupt governments. Towns were attracting millions of people from the country. Although they were for the most part American citizens, they were so ignorant of the ways of urban life that they fell victims of scheming city politicians. All these elements added to the political chaos of Reconstruction and made it more difficult.

The immediate problems of Reconstruction were numerous. One of the most important was the rebuilding of the war-torn South and the restoration of its economic life on the basis of free labor. At the end of the war there was no civil authority in the Carolinas, Georgia, Florida, Alabama, Mississippi, and Texas. Many despondent Southerners abandoned their farms or left the South altogether. Others, willing to start over again, did not know where to begin. Much of the countryside had been devastated by Union armies. Public buildings and private homes had been burned. The lands had deteriorated under poor cultivation or none at all, and titles to lands and crops in many areas were in dispute. Everywhere there was suffering from starvation and disease. Many former slaves, homeless and without jobs, wandered from place to place, much to the disgust and fear of whites. The ideological aberrations of whites were disturbing: they had difficulty in thinking of a black as a free person, and this problem of reconciling themselves to this new status loomed larger and larger before their vision, blinding them to an objective consideration of other pressing problems.

The needs of the South were great, both in number and variety. There was the important problem of finding a way to restore the seceded states to their places in the Union. It was not as simple as welcoming a prodigal back into the family. Precautions had to be taken to make sure that state governments did not fall into the hands of irreconcilable ex-Confederates who might undo the accomplishments of the war. Involved in this problem were the questions of how much punishment the leaders of the Confederate states should suffer and whether their states had indeed seceded at all. Tedious as the problem was, it appeared that it might soon be solved, and that the United States would once more be truly united.

Inseparably connected with the problems of rebuilding the South and bringing it back into the Union was the question of ex-slaves. There was no dispute over the fact that they were in dire need, but there was serious debate over who could best serve their needs. There was no question of their status as free individuals but conflict arose over the possible distinctions between them and white people. Even more serious was the problem of whether their status should be settled and their condition improved before the Southern states were permitted to return to the Union.

A barrier to the solution of these pressing postwar troubles was the legacy of hate inherited from a generation of bitter intersectional strife. Perhaps this animosity was the most grievous wound to heal, for it lay deep in the hearts of whites, North and South, and none knew how to attend it. There was no hope of solving any problem until a new spirit of conciliation and good will could be created. In this intangible and elusive area lay the key to intersectional peace.

Thus Reconstruction was essentially a national, not merely a sectional or racial, problem. The major obstacles in the way of a satisfactory settlement grew out of developments that were for the most part national. With the perspective of more than 100 years it becomes increasingly clear today that few crises in the history of the United States have so urgently demanded national action. Almost as obvious is the fact that the problem of Reconstruction was essentially the problem of how to move the nation toward greater economic and political democracy.

■ Conflicting Policies

Lincoln early saw the need for a policy of dealing with the states of the South as they capitulated to the Union army and of handling the large number of blacks who came under the control of the United States before the end of the war. Since he had insisted that the war was a rebellion of Southern citizens rather than a revolt of the states, he could deal with citizens of the Confederacy on the assumption that they had misled their state governments. It was the function of the president, he believed, to undertake whatever measures were necessary to reorganize the states in the South. As states collapsed, Lincoln appointed military governors who had complete power until civil authority could be established. In December 1863 he outlined to Congress his comprehensive plan for Reconstruction and issued a proclamation containing its essential features.

Acting on the assumption that Reconstruction was an executive problem, President Lincoln extended general amnesty to the people of the South, except for certain high Confederate civil and military officials, and called on them to swear allegiance to the United States. When as many as one-tenth of the people of a state as had cast votes in the election of 1860 complied with the proclamation, a government could be established that would be recognized by the president. Although his proclamation was generally well received and the Southern states proceeded to reconstruct themselves under its provisions, some members of Congress were of the opinion that the president was too lenient and that Reconstruction was a matter to be handled by Congress. They enacted their own measure, the Wade-Davis Bill, which disfranchised a larger number of ex-Confederates, delayed action until a majority of whites had qualified as loyal voters, and required greater assurances of loyalty from reconstructed governments. The president refused to sign the bill but granted that it provided one way for a state to reorganize if it chose to do so.

As far as the former slaves were concerned, Lincoln realized that there must be a satisfactory settlement of their status if peace was to be secured in the South. All during the war Lincoln had entertained the hope that a substantial number of blacks would choose to emigrate from the United States, and he had tried to secure congressional cooperation in encouraging them to do so. It must have become obvious to him that the problem could not be solved in this way, and he was faced with having to reach some solution based on the continued presence of blacks in the United States and in the South. He permitted the establishment of a number of departments of "Negro affairs," which assumed responsibility for administering to the needs of blacks in the early years of the war. Gradually, the work of these departments was taken over by the Freedmen's Bureau.

Concerning the recognition of black citizenship, Lincoln was of the opinion that with education blacks would qualify for it, at least on a restricted basis. In 1864 he wrote to Governor Georg M. Hahn of Louisiana asking "whether some of the colored people may not be let in [to the elective franchise] as, for instance, the very intelligent, and especially those who have fought gallantly in our ranks." Doubtless he was disappointed when the new legislature met in the fall of 1864 and failed to extend the franchise to any Louisiana blacks, despite the fact that many of them were individuals of considerable intellectual and economic achievement.

There was some evidence of a conflict between the president and Congress over the policy of reconstructing the South before the death of Lincoln in April 1865. Shortly after Andrew Johnson took office as president, he made it clear that he would follow essentially the plan of Reconstruction outlined by Lincoln. There were some signs that he might go beyond it. When Charles Sumner, the ardent protagonist of black rights, conferred with Johnson shortly after he became president, Johnson assured him that they were agreed on black suffrage. In his proclamation of May 1865, he called for complete abolition of slavery, repudiation of Confederate war debts, nullification of the ordinances of secession, and disqualification of the people Lincoln had disfranchised as well as all Southerners worth $20,000 or more. He appointed provisional governors in the Southern states, and legislatures, based on white suffrage, were called to modify their constitutions in harmony with that of the United States.

Through 1865 and 1866 Southern whites gradually assumed the responsibility of governing their people. The greatest concern of Southerners was the problem of controlling blacks. There were all sorts of ugly rumors of a general uprising in which blacks would take vengeance on whites and dispossess them of their property. Most Southern whites, although willing to concede the end of slavery even to the point of voting for adoption of the Thirteenth Amendment, were convinced that laws should be speedily enacted to curb blacks and to ensure their role as a laboring force in the South. These laws, called Black Codes, bore a remarkable resemblance to the antebellum Slave Codes (see Chapter 8) and can hardly be described as measures that respected the rights of blacks as free individuals. Several of them undertook to limit the areas in which blacks could purchase or rent property. Vagrancy laws imposed heavy penalties that were designed to force all blacks to work whether they wanted to or not. The control of blacks by white employers was about as great as that which slaveholders had exercised. Blacks who quit their jobs could be arrested and imprisoned for breach of contract. They were not allowed to testify in court except in cases involving members of their race. Numerous fines were imposed for seditious speeches, insulting gestures or acts, absence from work, violating curfew, and the possession of firearms. There was, of course, no enfranchisement of blacks and no indication that in the future they could look forward to full citizenship and participation in a democracy.

As it became clear to Northern protagonists of blacks that the Reconstruction policy of President Johnson sanctioned white home rule in the South in ways strikingly similar to those existing before the Civil War, they became furious. Friends of blacks refused to tolerate a policy that would nullify the gains made during the war. Abolitionists, roused again to their crusade, demanded that blacks be enfranchised and a harsher policy adopted toward the South. Practical Republicans, fearful of the political consequences of a South dominated by Democrats, became convinced that black suffrage in the South would aid in the continued growth of the Republican party. Industrialists with an eye on markets and cheap labor in the South, were fearful that the old agrarian system would be resurrected by the Democrats. These groups began to pool their interests in order to modify substantially the Johnson policy of Reconstruction.

When Congress met in December 1865, it was determined to take charge of Reconstruction. If there had been any doubt as to the direction in which the South was moving, it was dispelled by the character of the representatives sent to Congress. One had been vice president of the Confederacy, and there were four Confederate generals, five Confederate colonels, six Confederate cabinet officers, and fifty-eight members of the Confederate Congress. Although none could take the oath of office, their election indicated that the South stood solidly behind its defeated leaders. Thaddeus Stevens, a wily Republican leader and vigorous supporter of a stern policy toward the South, was exasperated. He proposed that Congress assume control of Reconstruction, asserting that the president's policy had been essentially provisional. Congress adopted a Stevens resolution creating the Joint Committee on Reconstruction to inquire into the condition of the Southern states and to make recommendations for a new policy.

In two bills, one to strengthen the Freedmen's Bureau and extend its life and the other to guarantee civil rights to blacks, Congress sought to exercise its influence in behalf of blacks. President Johnson vetoed the Freedmen's Bureau bill on the grounds that it was unconstitutional and proposed to do more for blacks than had ever been done for whites. The attempt to override the veto failed. He likewise vetoed the civil rights bill and declared that blacks were not yet ready for the privileges and equalities of citizens. Johnson's veto of these two bills, his condemnation of the proposed Fourteenth Amendment, and his attack on Stevens, Sumner, and other Northern leaders, put Congress in an angry mood. Consequently, on April 9, 1866, it passed the civil rights bill over his veto.

The fight between the president and Congress was now out in the open. Both believed that they could muster enough strength to have their way. Johnson was so confident that he decided to carry the fight to the people and call on them to return men to Congress in the fall of 1866 who would support his program. His conduct during the well-known "swing around the circle" was so unbecoming and his utterances so indiscreet that the entire country was outraged. He was soundly repudiated at the polls when the nation elected to Congress an overwhelming majority to oppose him and his Reconstruction program.

The rejection of the Fourteenth Amendment by the Southern states, their enactment of Black Codes, the widespread disorder in the South, and President Johnson's growing obstinacy persuaded many people that the South had to be dealt with harshly. Consequently, the Joint Committee presented to Congress a measure that ultimately was the basis of the principal Reconstruction Act of 1867. Through this measure the ex-Confederate states except Tennessee, where Reconstruction was moving satisfactorily, were divided into five military districts in which martial law was to prevail. On the basis of universal male suffrage a convention in each state was to draw up a new constitution acceptable to Congress. No state was to be admitted until it ratified the Fourteenth Amendment. Former rebels who could not take the ironclad oath were of course disfranchised. President Johnson vetoed the bill, contending that it was unconstitutional, that it was unfair to the states that had been reorganized, and that blacks, not having asked to vote, did not even understand what the franchise was. Congress overrode the veto and proceeded to enact other measures in the new program of Reconstruction.

The victory of Congress over the president was complete. It had enfranchised blacks in the District of Columbia, put the Freedmen's Bureau on a firm footing, carried forward its program of reconstructing the South through stern and severe treatment, and laid plans for subordination of the presidency by removal of its incumbent. The victory of Congress not only marked the beginning of a harsh policy toward the South but also signified the triumph of a coalition of interests—crusaders, politicians, and industrialists—all of whom hoped to gain something substantial through congressional reconstruction. It produced new conflicts, more bitter than preceding ones, and created so much confusion and chaos in almost every aspect of life that many of the problems would persist for more than a century.

■ Relief and Rehabilitation

In the closing months of the war and afterward, the South suffered acutely. The abandoned lands, the want of food and clothing, the thousands of displaced persons, and the absence of organized civil authority to cope with the emergency merely suggest the nature of the disorder and suffering. A most interesting and poignant feature of the time was ex-slaves searching for husbands, wives, or children who years earlier had been separated by sale or other transactions. As Herbert Gutman stated so pointedly, nothing better illustrated the remarkable stability and resiliency of the black family than their efforts to reunite and, in many instances, their taking steps to make their marriages and children legitimate after years and decades of living together as slaves with no marriage contract. Blacks were distressed, moreover, not only because they lacked the necessaries of life but also because they genuinely feared, especially after the death of President Lincoln, that they would gradually slip back into a condition hardly better than that of slaves. Leon Litwack indicated in *Been in the Storm So Long* that ex-slaves were constantly facing the question of what it meant to be free; indeed, how free was free? In those early days following the close of the war, they found it increasingly difficult to live out their notions of freedom as they had dreamed of it during slavery. In the summer and fall of 1865 they held several conventions, all looking toward an improvement in their condition. A black convention in Nashville protested seating the Tennessee delegation to Congress because the legislature had not passed just laws for African Americans. It also demanded that Congress recognize black citizenship. A group of 120, meeting in Raleigh, North Carolina, declared that they wanted fair wages, education for their children, and repeal of the discriminatory laws passed by the state legislature. Mississippi blacks protested reactionary policies in their state and asked Congress to extend the franchise to them. It was the same thing in Charleston and

North Carolina Blacks Seek Relief—1865

We are fully conscious that we cannot long expect the presence of Government agents, or of the troops to secure us against evil treatment from unreasonable, prejudiced, and unjust men. We have no desire to look abroad for protection and sympathy. We know we must find both at home, among the people of our own State, and merit them by our industry, sobriety and respectful demeanor, or suffer long and grievous evils. . . .

We most earnestly desire to have the disabilities under which we have formerly lived removed; to have all the oppressive laws which make unjust discriminations on account of race or color wiped from the statutes of the State. We invoke your protection for the sanctity of our family relations. Is this asking too much? . . . .

Though associated with many memories of suffering as well as of enjoyment, we have always loved our homes, and dreaded, as the worst of evils, a forcible separation from them. Now that Freedom and a new career are before us, we love this land and people more than ever before. Here we have toiled and suffered; our parents, wives and children are buried here, and in this land we will remain, unless forcibly driven away. . . .

"Address from the Convention of the Colored People of North Carolina," New York, *Daily Tribune*, October 7, 1865.

Mobile: blacks were demanding suffrage, the abolition of Black Codes, and measures for the relief of suffering.

While the pleas of blacks were largely ignored in the South, there were Northerners of both races who worked to relieve their distress. Private organizations had taken up this work during the war, and considerable pressure was applied to Congress as early as 1863 to assume responsibility for the welfare of needy whites and blacks in the South. Military commanders did whatever they could or wanted to do with regard to relief.

The need, however, was for a comprehensive and unified service for freedmen. It was not until March 1865 that the Bureau of Refugees, Freedmen, and Abandoned Lands, better known as the Freedmen's Bureau, was established. With officials in each of the Southern states, the bureau aided white refugees and former slaves by furnishing supplies and medical services, establishing schools, supervising contracts between ex-slaves and their employers, and managing confiscated or abandoned lands, leasing and selling some of them to former slaves.

The atmosphere in which the Freedmen's Bureau worked was one of hostility. Many white Northerners looked upon it as an expensive agency, the existence of which could not be justified in time of peace. In the South opposition to the bureau was vehement. There was serious objection to

CHARLOTTE FORTEN, TEACHER AMONG FLORMER SLAVES. Born in Philadelphia and educated in Salem, Massachusetts, Charlotte Forten began her teaching
career in St. Helena's Island, South Carolina, in 1862. *(Moorland Springarn Research Center, Howard University.)*

federal interference with the relations between worker and employer. It was
believed, moreover, that the bureau had a political program for enfranchising
blacks and establishing a strong Republican party in the South.

There can be no doubt that the Freedmen's Bureau relieved much
suffering among blacks and whites. Between 1865 and 1869, for example, the
bureau issued 21 million rations, approximately 5 million going to whites
and 15 million to blacks. By 1867 there were forty-six hospitals under the
bureau staffed by physicians, surgeons, and nurses. The medical department
spent over $2 million to improve the health of ex-slaves and treated more
than 450,000 cases of illness. The death rate among former slaves was
reduced, and sanitary conditions were improved.

The bureau undertook to resettle many people who had been displaced
during the war. Because of the urgent need for labor to cultivate the land,
free transportation was furnished ex-slaves to leave congested areas and to
become self-supporting. By 1870 more than 30,000 had been moved. Al-

though abandoned and confiscated lands were generally restored to their owners under the amnesty proclamations of Lincoln and Johnson, the bureau distributed some land to former slaves. Colonies of infirm, destitute, and vagrant blacks were set up in several states. Small parcels of land were first allotted and then leased to them for management and cultivation.

The bureau sought to protect blacks in their freedom to choose their own employer and to work at a fair wage. Both parties were required to live up to their contract. Agents of the bureau consulted with planters and ex-slaves, urging the former to be fair in their dealings and instructing the latter in the necessity of working to provide for their families and to achieve independence and security. Thousands of blacks returned to work under conditions more satisfactory than those that had existed before the bureau supervised their relations with employers. Gen. Oliver Otis Howard, the bureau's commissioner, reported that "in a single state not less than fifty thousand [labor] contracts were drawn." Even when they did not know all the stipulations of the contracts, many former slaves suspected that their employers would not live up to them. The "fust dif'culty," a South Carolina freedman said, was that "we gits no meat," although he assumed from the contract that they would.

When it was felt that the interest of blacks could not be safely entrusted to local courts, the bureau organized "freedmen's" courts and boards of arbitration. They had civil and criminal jurisdiction over minor cases where one or both parties were ex-slaves. Frequently an expression of the bureau's interest was sufficient to secure justice for former slaves in the regular courts. In Maryland, for example, the case of a white physician who assaulted a black without provocation was taken by the bureau agent to the state supreme court, which admitted the testimony of blacks and convicted the physician.

The bureau achieved its greatest successes in education. It set up or supervised all kinds of schools: day, night, Sunday, and industrial schools, as well as colleges. It cooperated closely with philanthropic and religious organizations in the North in the establishment of many institutions. Among the schools founded in this period that received aid from the bureau were Howard University, Hampton Institute, St. Augustine's College, Atlanta University, Fisk University, Storer College, and Biddle Memorial Institute (now Johnson C. Smith University). The American Missionary Association and the Baptists, Methodists, Presbyterians, and Episcopalians were all active in establishing schools. Education was promoted so vigorously that by 1867 schools had been set up in "the remotest counties of each of the confederate states."

Teachers came down from the North in large numbers. Besides Edmund Ware at Atlanta, Samuel C. Armstrong at Hampton, and Erastus M. Cravath at Fisk, there were hundreds whose services were not as widely known. In 1869 there were 9,503 teachers in schools for former slaves in the South. Although some of the white teachers were Southerners, a majority of whites came from the North. In *Reading, 'Riting, and Reconstruction*, Robert Morris reminds us that many white teachers discriminated against their black colleagues. Noticing the obvious differences in how the white veteran antislavery leader, the Reverend Sela G. Wright, treated white and black teachers under his supervision, a black resident of Natchez, Mississippi, referred to him as a "copperhead preacher." The number of black teachers nevertheless was growing, and gradually they took over supervision of some schools.

By 1870, when the educational work of the bureau stopped, there were 247,333 pupils in 4,329 schools. Reports from all quarters "showed a marked increase in attendance, and advance in scholarship, and a record of punctuality and regularity which compared favorably with the schools in the north." The bureau had spent more than $5 million in schooling ex-slaves. The shortcomings in the education of blacks arose not from a want of zeal on the part of teachers but from ignorance of the needs of blacks and from the necessary preoccupation of students with the problem of survival in a hostile world.

Despite Southern hostility to the bureau and the inefficiency of many officials, it performed a vastly important task. As a relief agency it deserves to be ranked with the great efforts of recent depressions and wars. It demonstrated that the government could administer an extensive program of relief and rehabilitation and suggested a way in which the nation could grapple with its pressing social problems. To be sure, there was corruption and inefficiency, but not enough to prevent the bureau from achieving notable success in ministering to human welfare.

Another agency that offered both spiritual and material relief during Reconstruction was the black church. The end of the war led to the expansion of independent churches among blacks. There were no longer Southern laws to silence black preachers and proscribe separate organizations. Blacks began to withdraw from white churches once they had secured their freedom, and consequently the black church grew rapidly after the war. In 1865 black members of the white Primitive Baptist churches of the South established a separate organization called the Colored Primitive Baptists in America. In 1869 the General Assembly of the Cumberland Presbyterian church organized its black members in the Colored Cumberland Presbyterian church. One of the most important separate churches emerged in the Colored Methodist Episcopal church. By 1870, when blacks had organized five conferences, the first general conference was held, and white bishops came to consecrate W. H. Miles and R. H. Vanderhorst as the first black bishops, to be followed three years later by L. H. Holsey, J. A. Beebe, and Isaac Lane.

Older black churches entered a new stage of growth. The African Methodist Episcopal church, which had only 20,000 members in 1856, boasted 75,000 ten years later. In 1876 its membership exceeded 200,000, and its influence and material possessions had increased proportionally. The Baptists likewise enjoyed phenomenal growth. Local churches sprang up overnight under the ministry of unlettered but inspired preachers. In 1866 the black Baptists of North Carolina organized the first state convention. Within a few years every Southern state had a large black Baptist organization. Total membership increased from 150,000 in 1850 to 500,000 in 1870. As the first social institution fully controlled by blacks in America, these churches gave them an opportunity to develop leadership, and it is no coincidence that many outstanding Reconstruction leaders were ministers. Bishop H. M. Turner of Georgia, the Reverend R. H. Cain of South Carolina, and Bishop J. W. Hood of North Carolina were a few of the political leaders who gained much of their experience in the black church.

■ Economic Adjustment

It was one thing to provide temporary relief for former slaves and another to guide them along the road to economic stability and independence. The release from bondage of 4 million persons had serious implications for the economic structure of the South at a time when it could least afford to be disturbed. To be sure, many ex-slaves would not work, at first, because they were exhilarated by their new liberty, and still others scorned low wages and lacked confidence in their employers. But many were active, and all were potential competitors in the labor market. To white workers the situation was extremely disturbing. White planters, however, in an effort to reestablish themselves, were anxious to secure labor at the lowest possible price, and if in their own minds they conceded the right of blacks to be free, they were seldom able to realize that blacks also had a right to refuse work. Many prospective employers therefore sought to force blacks to work. The Black Codes were in many instances formulated with this specific end in view.

The Black Codes represented the effort of the South to solve problems created by the presence of former slaves, as the Freedmen's Bureau represented the efforts of the federal government to achieve the same end. Establishment of the Freedmen's Bureau and of Radical Reconstruction governments did not mean that the Black Codes had failed, but rather that political power over the South had been transferred to Washington. In the final analysis, neither the Black Codes nor Radical Reconstruction solved the economic problems of ex-slaves. What solution there was, however unsatisfactory, came by negotiations between the white employer and the black worker, in some instances under the supervision of the Freedmen's Bureau. Because the federal government failed to give blacks much land, they slowly returned to the farms and resumed work under circumstances scarcely more favorable than those prevailing before the war. Black agricultural workers found themselves at the mercy of white planters. Labor contracts drawn up to bind both parties were frequently disregarded, employers failing to pay stipulated wages and workers failing to perform tasks outlined in their contracts.

Once blacks were back on the farm as workers, they were paid either in

Dr. Norton Discusses
Ex-Confederates—1866

Washington, February 3, 1866

Dr. Daniel Norton (colored) sworn and examined.
By Mr. [Jacob M.] Howard, [Senator from Michigan]

Question. Where do you reside?
Answer.   I reside in Yorktown, Virginia.

Question. How old are you?
Answer.   About 26 years old.

Question. Are you a regularly licensed physician?
Answer.   I am.

Question. Where were you educated?
Answer.   In the State of New York. I studied privately under Dr. Warren. . . .

Question. Are you a native of Virginia?
Answer.   Yes, sir. I was born in Williamsburg, Virginia.

Question. What is the feeling among the rebels in the neighborhood of Yorktown
           towards the government of the United States?
Answer.   They do not manifest a very cordial feeling toward the government of
           the United States. There are some, of course who do, but the majority
           do not seem to manifest a good spirit or feeling. . . .

Question. How do the colored people feel toward the government of the United
           States?
Answer.   They feel determined to be law-abiding citizens. There is no other
           feeling among them.

Question. Are you a delegate sent to the city of Washington by some association?
Answer.   I am. I was sent by three counties; I represent, perhaps, something like
           fifteen or twenty thousand people. The great trouble, in my opinion, is
           that the colored people are not more disposed to return to their former
           homes on account of the treatment which those who have gone back
           have received.

Question. State generally whether or not the treatment which those colored people
           receive at the hands of their old white masters is kind or unkind.
Answer.   It is not what I would consider kind or good treatment. . . .

Question. In case of the removal of the military force from among you, and also
           of the Freedmen's Bureau, what would the whites do with you?
Answer.   I do not think that the colored people would be safe. They would be in
           danger of being hunted and killed. The spirit of the whites against the
           blacks is much worse than it was before the war. . . .

Report of the Joint Committee on Reconstruction (Washington, 1866), pp. 51–52.

monthly wages or a share of the crop. Plantation wages ranged from $9 to $15 a month for men and from $5 to $10 for women, in addition to food, shelter, and fuel. Where the sharecropping system prevailed, former slaves were allowed from one-quarter to one-half of the cotton and corn; they were also provided with a house, fuel, and in some cases food. There was every opportunity for the contracting parties not to live up to their word; good faith was the only effective way to keep agreements. It need not be added that where hatred and bitterness prevailed, as in so many parts of the South, relations between employer and worker often militated against efficient production.

There can be no question that the majority of blacks worked, despite Southern doubts of their efficiency as free laborers. Many of them resented the suggestion that they would not work. The editor of a black newspaper declared in 1865 that black people need not be reminded to avoid idleness and vagrancy. After all, he concluded, "the necessity of working is perfectly understood by men who have worked all their lives." The same could be said of women. They had no other choice but to cast their lot with their former masters and assist them in restoring economic stability to the rural South. By 1870 the cotton kingdom had retrieved much of its losses, and by 1875 the white South had come to realize that cheap labor could be the basis for a profitable agricultural system. The cotton crop of 1870 had not reached the level of production achieved just before the war, but by 1880 the South was producing more cotton than ever. While the sugar crop recovered more slowly, its continued improvement was marked. Thus black farm workers contributed greatly to the economic recovery of the South. As free workers, however, they gained but little. The wages paid them in 1867 were lower than those that had been paid to hired slaves. In the sharecropping system the cost of maintenance was so great that at the end of the year ex-slaves were indebted to their employers for most of what they had made and sometimes more than they had made. The white South generally recovered much more rapidly than the former slaves.

Many former slaves had received the impression that abandoned and confiscated lands were to be distributed to them in lots of forty acres by January 1866. This impression stemmed from the Confederate apprehension during the war that the Union government planned to seize their land and convey it to ex-slaves, and from the bill creating the Freedmen's Bureau, which gave tacit encouragement to such a plan. Although nothing came of it, the federal government sought to encourage the dispersion of populations from congested centers by opening public lands, under the Southern Homestead Act of 1866, in Alabama, Mississippi, Louisiana, Arkansas, and Florida to all settlers regardless of race. Eighty acres were available for the head of each family. Within a year ex-slaves secured homesteads in Florida covering 160,960 acres, and in Arkansas they occupied 116 out of 243 homesteads. By 1874 blacks in Georgia owned more than 350,000 acres of land. "Forty acres and a mule" as a gift of the government had not been realized, but wherever possible blacks were acquiring land in their effort to achieve economic security.

Neither white nor black Southerners were fully aware of the revolutionary implications of the industrial changes taking place. While the South was preoccupied with the restoration of an agricultural regime, the rest of the country responded to the quickened pace of living ushered in by industrialization. Most blacks remained in rural areas, but a considerable number joined their fellows in the urban centers of both the North and South. They migrated to the cities not because they knew of their industrial development but because of a repugnance for plantation life, which they still associated with slavery. The war was hardly over before the sharp cleavage between white and black workers became apparent. White artisans and factory hands were keenly aware of the same threat to their security that had embittered the landless whites of the South before the war. African-American blacksmiths, bricklayers, pilots, cabinet makers, painters, and other skilled workers met stern opposition from white artisans wherever they sought employment. In many instances the opposition led to violence, in the North as well as in the South.

The use of black labor had the curious effect of making it more difficult for black workers to achieve security and respectability in the world of labor. Manufacturers and entrepreneurs did not hesitate to employ blacks in order to undermine white labor unions. In 1867, for example, black ship caulkers were brought from Portsmouth, Virginia, to Boston to defeat white workers' efforts to secure an eight-hour day. Operators of iron and cotton mills and railroad builders all looked south for cheap labor, even if it meant the displacement of workers with a much higher standard of living. The deliberate degradation of black labor by white employers in all sections of the country made it impossible for black and white workers to join hands or to present a solid front to management.

On the whole blacks were not welcomed into labor organizations in the postwar period. Some local unions admitted them, like the carpenters and joiners in Boston in 1866, but most locals would not. The locals, moreover, prevented national unions from adopting a nondiscriminatory policy on the grounds that local autonomy must be preserved. When the National Labor Union was organized in Baltimore in 1866, blacks were invited to cooperate in the general movement, but it was made clear that if they were to be regarded as trustworthy, they must adhere to the true principles of labor reform. It looked as though blacks were to be effectively barred from the white labor movement, and as a result a group of black workers met in December 1869 to organize the National Negro Labor Union. During the next few years this organization sought affiliation with white labor, but without much success. Local black organizations advanced the cause of the black worker. But white workers did everything possible to retard the growth of a black labor movement, and black leaders too frequently sought to use their organizations for political purposes. Until after 1880 black workers remained, involuntarily, outside the organized labor movement. Meanwhile, as victims of ruthless and unscrupulous employers, they acquired the reputation of being strikebreakers who worked for lower wages than whites. This reputation was to follow them for several generations after the Civil War.

Since Reconstruction was a period in which efforts were made by citizens everywhere to achieve economic independence through various forms of business enterprise, blacks did likewise. Lack of capital was an obstacle to their success in business. In 1865 blacks in Baltimore organized the Chesapeake and Marine Railway and Dry Dock Company, capitalized at $40,000 with the stock divided into 8,000 shares. At the end of five years the company purchased a shipyard and was apparently prospering, but profits began to decline in 1877, and in 1883 the company went out of existence. In Savannah, blacks invested $50,000 in a business venture that proved worthless. They also failed in an effort to run a land and lumber enterprise in which they had invested $40,000. There were other groups and individuals who sought to make a living by opening shops, but many of them failed, for they had no knowledge of how to operate a business, and those who knew how were caught in the depression following the panic of 1873.

One effort to assist former slaves in their economic adjustment was the encouragement given them to save their money. There had been several experiments with savings banks for blacks during the war. After the allotment system was developed, many soldiers saved regularly in banks established for that purpose. Outstanding were the Free Labor Bank set up by General Banks at New Orleans, and another established by General Butler at Norfolk. Toward the end of the war, blacks were given an opportunity to save at the Freedmen's Savings and Trust Company, which was chartered by the federal government in 1865. The business of the organization, with William Booth as president, was confined to the black race, and two-thirds of the deposits were to be invested in securities of the United States.

On April 4, 1865, the headquarters of the Freedmen's Bank, as it was called, was opened in New York. Within the next few months branches were started in Washington, New Orleans, Nashville, Vicksburg, Louisville, and Memphis. By 1872 there were thirty-four branches, with only the New York and Philadelphia offices in the North; by 1874 the deposits in all branches totaled $3,299,201.

But unmistakable evidences of failure were apparent: there was inaccurate bookkeeping, and some of the cashiers were incompetent. There had been almost no black employees at the beginning, but gradually they were hired. Some, but not all, proved able to perform their tasks. Political influence was used to secure loans. At a time when his business was tottering, Jay Cooke borrowed $500,000 at only 5 percent interest, and Henry Cooke together with other financiers unloaded bad loans on the bank. After the big financial houses failed in 1873, there was a run on the bank, and many speculating officials resigned, leaving blacks to take the blame. In March

1874 Frederick Douglass was made president, but the bank was already a failure, although neither he nor the public was aware of the fact. When he realized the truth, he resorted to desperate means to save the bank, using his own money and appealing to the Senate Finance Committee for more. The bank was placed in liquidation by Congress so that it could be reorganized, but it was too late. Confidence in the bank had been completely shattered, and on June 28, 1874, it closed. Thousands of black depositors suffered losses they could ill afford. Black leaders, some of whom were blameless, were castigated by their fellows, while the Cookes and others, who benefited most, escaped without public censure.

Perhaps the greatest failure of Reconstruction was economic. At the end of the period both white and black workers in the South were suffering from want and privation. In the North, where their lot was substantially better, they had not yet learned to cope with the powerful industrialists who were using political agencies as their most reliable allies and bribing officials with greater regularity than they paid their employees. While the white leaders of the South were preoccupied with opposing black suffrage and civil rights, Northern financiers and industrialists took advantage of the opportunity to impose their economic control on the South, and much of it endured for generations. The inability of blacks to solve their problems was not altogether to their discredit. It was merely a symptom of the complexity of the new industrial America, which baffled even the most astute of its citizens.

■ Political Currents

The Reconstruction Act of 1867 imposed on the white South a regime more difficult to bear than defeat. Vast numbers of white Southerners were to be disfranchised; blacks and their allies, loyal whites and those from the North who apparently had come to stay, were to enjoy the ballot. Constitutional conventions were called for the express purpose of eradicating the last vestiges of the old order. From the white Southerners' point of view all power was to be placed in the hands of those least qualified to control their destiny. Two years of white home rule were discredited because it was said that white Southerners had tried to turn the clock back to the years before the war. White Southerners thought the clock was now being turned back to the days of barbarism.

The constitutional conventions called in pursuance of the Reconstruction Act all contained black members. Only in South Carolina did they make up a majority of delegates, and in Louisiana they were equal to the whites, each having forty-nine delegates. In some states the ratio of blacks to whites was small, as in Texas where only nine out of ninety members of the convention were black. In most states blacks constituted only a respectable minority of the delegates. In six states native white Southerners were in the majority. Some black members had been slaves, but others had always been free, and among them were emigrants from the North. Some blacks were of considerable intellectual stature. In Florida it was generally conceded that Jonathan Gibbs was "the most cultured member of the convention." For the most part, the black members of the conventions were men of moderation. A generous appraisal of the personnel of a black delegation was made by the Charleston *Daily News:* "Beyond all question, the best men in the convention are the colored members. Considering the influences under which they were called together, and their imperfect acquaintance with parliamentary law, they have displayed, for the most part, remarkable moderation and dignity. . . . They have assembled neither to pull wires like some, nor to make money like others; but to legislate for the welfare of the race to which they belong." Typical of the magnanimity of the black members are the words of Beverly Nash before the constitutional convention of South Carolina:

> I believe, my friends and fellow-citizens, we are not prepared for this suffrage. But we can learn. Give a man tools and let him commence to use them, and in time he will learn a trade. So it is with voting. We may not understand it at the start, but in time we shall learn to do our duty. . . . We recognize the Southern white man as the true friend of the black man. . . . In these public affairs we must unite with our white fellow-citizens. They tell us that they have been disfranchised, yet we tell the North that we shall never let the halls of Congress be silent until we remove that disability.

The state constitutions drawn up in 1867 and 1868 were the most progressive the South had ever known. Most of them abolished property qualifications for voting and holding office; some of them abolished imprisonment for debt. All of them abolished slavery, and several sought to eliminate race distinctions in the possession or inheritance of property. Although the planters of Louisiana thought their constitution was the "work of the lowest and most corrupt body of men ever assembled in the South," the laws codified on the basis of this constitution, together with laws adopted later in three codes, remain even today the basic law of the state. In every state the ballot was extended to all male residents, except for certain classes of Confederates, and it is significant that some blacks, like Nash of South Carolina and Pinchback of Louisiana, were vigorously opposed to any disqualification of Confederates.

The conservative elements of the South almost unanimously denounced the new constitutions and fought to defeat their ratification. When they gained power at the end of Reconstruction, however, they seemed anxious to rewrite only those clauses of the constitutions that had enfranchised blacks. Florida finally adopted a new constitution in 1885, Mississippi in 1890, South Carolina in 1895, Louisiana in 1898, and Virginia in 1902. Like those written soon after the overthrow of Reconstruction, they were remarkably similar to the documents that had been so roundly condemned. Victors in the campaigns for white supremacy were wise enough to retain the public school systems, the modernized machinery of local government, and other measures

FIRST AFRICAN-AMERICAN GOVERNOR.
P. B. S. Pinchback, the elected lieutenant governor
of Louisiana, served as governor for forty-one days
when H. C. Warmoth was removed from office.
(Culver Pictures.)

in the Reconstruction constitutions that pointed toward a more progressive South.

During Reconstruction, blacks held public offices in Southern states. They sat in the legislatures and assisted in enacting laws that won both the praise and the condemnation of bitter partisans. It was in South Carolina that they wielded the greatest influence. In the first legislature there were eighty-seven blacks and forty whites. From the outset, however, the whites controlled the state senate, and in 1874 the lower house as well. At all times there was a white governor. It can be said, therefore, that at no time were blacks in control of South Carolina. There were two black lieutenant governors, Alonzo J. Ransier in 1870 and Richard H. Gleaves in 1872. Samuel J. Lee was speaker of the house in 1872, and Robert B. Elliott occupied that position in 1874. Francis L. Cardozo, an accomplished black who had been educated at the University of Glasgow and in London, was secretary of state from 1868 to 1872 and treasurer from 1872 to 1876. He was regarded by friends and enemies, says A. A. Taylor, as one of the best-educated men in South Carolina, regardless of color.

The blacks of Mississippi were not as largely represented in their new government. In the first Reconstruction legislature there were forty black members, some of whom had been slaves. In 1873 they held three significant positions: A. K. Davis was lieutenant governor; James Hill, secretary of state; and T. W. Cardozo, superintendent of education. On the whole, blacks took little part in legislation, but a few were chairmen of important legislative committees. In 1872 John R. Lynch was Speaker of the House, and at the end of the session a white Democrat praised him "for his dignity, impartiality, and courtesy as a presiding officer."

Between 1868 and 1896 Louisiana had 133 black legislators, of whom 38 were senators and 95 were representatives. At no time did they approach control of public affairs. John W. Menard was elected to Congress but was denied a seat. Three blacks, Oscar J. Dunn, P. B. S. Pinchback, and C. C.

SOUTH CAROLINA'S SUPREME COURT JUSTICE. Jonathan Jasper Wright, the first African American elected to the Pennsylvania bar (1866). He went to South Carolina, was elected to the state supreme court in 1870 and served until 1876. (*Courtesy of the South Carolina Library, University of South Carolina.*)

Antoine, served as lieutenant governor, and Pinchback was acting governor for forty-three days in the winter of 1873 when Henry C. Warmoth was removed from office. Although blacks were not in control, they sought to improve political conditions. Oscar J. Dunn, for example, led the fight against corruption and extravagance.

Blacks were not significant in the leadership of Alabama during Reconstruction. They were in both houses of the legislature, but not in sufficient numbers to secure positions of power. They helped to adopt the Fourteenth and Fifteenth Amendments, however, and put a state system of schools into operation.

Although blacks were elected to the first Reconstruction legislature of Georgia, they had difficulty in securing and retaining their seats. In September 1868 the legislature declared that all black members were ineligible, and not until almost a year later, when the state supreme court declared them eligible, were they able to regain their seats. The black members introduced many bills on education, the jury system, city government reform, and women's suffrage. Two able black legislators, Jefferson Long and H. M. Turner, sought better wages for black workers but got little support from their colleagues, who in many instances supported the industrialists seeking to exploit all forms of natural and human resources.

In Florida and North Carolina black members of the Reconstruction government were primarily interested in relief, education, and suffrage. In

MISSISSIPPI'S SPEAKER OF THE HOUSE. Elected to the State legislature in 1869, John Roy Lynch became speaker in 1872 before going on to serve three terms in the United States House of Representatives. *(Culver Pictures.)*

Jonathan Gibbs, superintendent of public instruction from 1872 to 1874, they had an able leader, a champion of equal rights. H. S. Harmon led the fight for a satisfactory school law. With other black legislators he supported a homestead law and such measures as would provide greater economic security for the mass of citizens. North Carolina blacks helped to inaugurate a system of public schools. An outstanding worker in the field of education was the Reverend J. W. Hood, who had helped write the constitution of 1868 and served as assistant superintendent of education.

Very few blacks held office in the new government of Virginia. Twenty-seven sat in the first legislature, and others served in minor posts. They were never powerful enough to determine any policy of the government except, as A. A. Taylor says, on a few occasions where they held the balance between militant white factions. So far as the exercise of influence is concerned, the same thing can be said of blacks in Tennessee, Arkansas, and Texas.

An important way in which blacks participated in politics was by election to Congress. Between 1869 and 1901, two served in the Senate and twenty in the House of Representatives. The two senators were Hiram R. Revels and Blanche K. Bruce, both representing Mississippi. Revels was a North Carolina free black who had migrated to Indiana, Ohio, and Illinois, receiving his education at a seminary in Ohio and at Knox College in Illinois. By the time of the Civil War he had been ordained a minister in the African Methodist Episcopal church and had taught school in several places. During the war he recruited blacks for the Union army, founded a school for freedmen in St. Louis, and joined the army as chaplain of a black regiment in Mississippi. After the war he settled in Natchez and became prominent in state politics. In 1870 he was elected to the United States Senate to fill the seat previously occupied by Jefferson Davis. He favored the removal of all disqualifications on ex-Confederates and worked diligently in the interest of his state. He admitted that during his year in the Senate he received fair treatment even in the matter of patronage.

In 1874 Blanche K. Bruce was elected to the Senate, the only black to be elected to a full term until the election in 1966 of Edward Brooke, a Republican from Massachusetts. Bruce had been born a slave in Virginia. When the war came, he escaped from St. Louis to Hannibal, Missouri, and established a school for blacks. After the war he studied in the North for several years. In 1869 he went to Mississippi, entered politics, and worked up through a succession of offices from tax collector to sheriff and then superintendent of schools. In the Senate he usually voted with his party and introduced a number of bills to improve the conditions of blacks. When P. B. S. Pinchback was denied a seat in the Senate, to which he had been elected from Louisiana, Bruce spoke for him in vain. He succeeded in having some pension bills passed, but his chief work was with the Manufactures, Education, and Labor Committee and the Pensions Committee. As chairman of the select committee on the Freedmen's Bank, he conducted a thorough investigation of the causes for its failure. His wide range of interests as a lawmaker is seen in the introduction of bills on the Geneva award for Alabama claims, another for aid to education and railroad construction, and one for reimbursement of depositors in the Freedmen's Bank.

Of the twenty blacks who served in the House of Representatives, South Carolina sent the largest number, eight, and North Carolina followed with four, three of whom served after Reconstruction. Alabama sent three, and Georgia, Mississippi, Florida, Louisiana, and Virginia, one each. It was in the Forty-first Congress, in 1869, that blacks, three of them, first made their appearance in the federal legislature. In the next Congress there were five. The peak was reached in the Forty-third and Forty-fourth Congresses when seven black men sat in the House of Representatives. In length of service, J. H. Rainey and Robert Smalls, both of South Carolina, led with five terms for each. John R. Lynch of Mississippi and J. T. Walls of Florida both served three terms, and six others served two terms each.

Most of the blacks in Congress had had some experience in public service before going to Washington, as delegates to constitutional conventions, as

AN EARLY MIXED JURY IN THE UNITED STATES. This group of men was impanelled to serve on a jury to try Jefferson Davis, the president of the Confederacy. Although he had been held in prison since his capture, he was released without trial shortly after the impanelling had been made. *(Courtesy The Moorland-Springarn Research Center, Howard University.)*

state senators and representatives, or as state or local officials. While they were chiefly concerned with civil rights and education, their efforts were not by any means confined to problems of blacks. Many fought for local improvements such as new public buildings and appropriations for rivers and harbors. Several, like Walls of Florida and Lynch of Mississippi, promoted protective tariffs for home products. Walls was also interested in the recognition of Cuba. Hyman of North Carolina advanced a program for relief of the Indians, and Nash of Louisiana uttered a plea for intersectional peace.

Concerning the work of black members of Congress, the white historian James Ford Rhodes wrote: "They left no mark on the legislation of their time; none of them, in comparison with their white associates, attained the least distinction." It must be remembered, however, that if few measures introduced by blacks were enacted into law, there were other ways in which as members of Congress they served effectively. Many bills that they introduced were deemed unworthy of serious consideration, but this was also true of a majority of the bills presented to Congress. Others died a natural death on the tortuous road from one house to the other and to the president's desk. None of the black members enjoyed the prestige of chairing important committees, and they had great difficulty in winning the respect even of colleagues in their own party. At a time when Congress could count among its members men affiliated with the most scandalous and corrupt deals in the history of the country, it was not without significance that a former

FIRST AFRICAN AMERICAN IN THE UNITED STATES SENATE. Hiram R. Revels was elected in 1870 to fill the seat previously occupied by confederate President Jefferson Davis. *(Bettmann Archive.)*

congressman and ex-Confederate general, Roger A. Pryor, was moved to say in 1873: "We have not yet heard that a Negro congressman was in any way implicated in the Credit Mobilier scandal." To James G. Blaine, who knew most of the black congressmen, "the colored men who took seats in both Senate and House did not appear ignorant or helpless. They were as a rule studious, earnest, ambitious men, whose public conduct . . . would be honorable to any race."

More important than the men, white or black, who held office during Reconstruction were the forces operating to influence their actions. Although blacks were members of Congress, lieutenant governors, sheriffs, prosecuting attorneys, and recorders of deeds, at no time was there black rule anywhere in the South. Indeed, it can be said with some reason that there was no carpetbag rule as the term is commonly understood. The South, as well as the North, was subject to the most dynamic political and economic currents that had ever stirred American life. Economic revolution, not Reconstruction,

BLANCHE KELSO BRUCE—MISSISSIPPI TEACHER, PLANTER, AND POLITICIAN.
Bruce was the first African American to win a full term in the United States Senate.
(Moorland Spingarn Research Center, Howard University.)

determined the pattern of public action after 1865. Tariff legislation was more important than civil rights; railroad subsidies were more important than the suffrage. The industrialists of the North, who had come to control the Republican party, wanted a satisfactory settlement of the Southern problem in order to hasten the exploitation of Southern resources and to capture Southern markets. When the Radical Reconstruction program served their purposes, they cooperated, as in the period when they sought favorable consideration from the Southern legislatures; but when the program failed to bring peace and order, thereby postponing prosperity, they helped to restore home rule to the South.

It is significant that Northern industrialists were active in the South throughout Reconstruction. As Horace Mann Bond points out, William D. Kelly and other Northern capitalists were so anxious to exploit the rich resources and cheap labor of Alabama that they used their influence to bring about a hasty, if not satisfactory, reconstruction of the state. Iron and railroad interests were powerful in Alabama, and many Northern capitalists worked behind the scenes, manipulating the actors on the Reconstruction stage. In

1867, for example, the legislature granted $12,000 a mile to companies building railroads and later increased this sum to $16,000. Between 1867 and 1871 the Louisville and Nashville Railroad and the Alabama and Chattanooga Railroad received $17 million in endorsements and loans. These subsidies became part of the Reconstruction debt.

It has been estimated that of $305 million owed by eleven Southern states in 1871, at least $100 million of the debt consisted of contingent and prospective liabilities incurred by the issue of railroad bonds. Southerners and Northerners, Republicans and Democrats, had cooperated in lending the credit of these states to railroad investments. A survey of the Reconstruction debt shows clearly that Southern legislatures were not as extravagant in the purchase of whiskey and cigars for their members as in yielding to the pressure of Northern money interests for favorable and costly legislation. In addition, the expenses of carrying out legitimate programs for improved roads, public education, and other social services accounted for much of the Reconstruction debt.

The graft and corruption of the period were neither new nor peculiar to the South. Public office has been used for personal gain too frequently to ascribe the practice to any particular group, section, or period. The Southern land agents who stole public funds during Van Buren's day would qualify as excellent thieves today. The North descended to a new level of public immorality after the Civil War. Bribery and thievery were rampant in the South during Reconstruction, but doubtless they stemmed from the same forces that made the Tweed Ring in New York and numerous scandals in the Grant administration disgraces to the whole nation. Similar forces have created similar situations in the America of later days.

From a national point of view Reconstruction was a period in which the country moved steadily toward a more powerful position in the world economy, thereby making possible the exercise of tremendous influence on world affairs in succeeding years. The Fourteenth Amendment gave Americans their first clear-cut definition of citizenship and strengthened their position as individuals in a complex social order. It also gave corporations an opportunity to flourish under the broad interpretation that the Supreme Court soon put upon the amendment. In the Fifteenth Amendment, a wider exercise of the franchise was guaranteed along with the removal of race as a disability. In the South, Reconstruction laid the foundations for more democratic living by sweeping away all qualifications for voting and holding office and by establishing a system of universal free public education. In failing to provide adequate economic security for former slaves, Reconstruction left them no alternative but to submit to their old masters, a submission that made easier the efforts of Southern whites to overthrow Reconstruction and restore a system based on white supremacy.

CHAPTER 13

Losing the Peace

■ The Struggle for Domination

The war was hardly over before the victors found out that it was easy to sit in Washington and proclaim peace by presidential decree or legislative enactment but very difficult to establish peace in a country so recently torn apart by civil conflict. Despite the fact that General Grant thought that the South would accept the verdict of the battlefield, there were others who believed that the South was irreconcilable. Carl Schurz returned from a tour of the region with the verdict that the South had submitted only because it saw no alternative. He was alarmed at having found "no expression of hearty attachment to the great republic." To his horror, treason was not odious in the South. The tragic dispersion of the Confederate troops at the end of the war contrasted miserably with the presence of Northern invaders—not only white soldiers but also black troops, in fact, far fewer than the former Confederates claimed—stationed at strategic points to maintain the peace. This was evidence of the North's conviction that the South was barbarous and that the spirit of slavery had "debased the Southern mind, destroyed liberty and law, and vitiated all white elements upon which a restored union might be erected." Each section was thoroughly convinced that the other was wicked and, under the circumstances, not to be trusted to do the right thing.

The Republicans, having the upper hand even in the early years of Reconstruction, were determined to strengthen their position and perpetuate their power. They had effective propaganda for these purposes. They could remind the country that it was the South which had treasonably fought to destroy the Union, that old slaveholders were only waiting for an opportunity to reenslave blacks, and that the Republican party had saved the nation from complete ruin at the hands of Democrats, North and South. The vulnerable position of the Democrats was summed up by Schurz: "There is no heavier burden for a political party to bear, than to have appeared unpatriotic in war." To be sure, the Democrats claimed they were dedicated to peace and union, but it was a modest claim compared to the extravagant and righteous pretensions of the Republicans. Many Republicans, whatever their altruistic motives, were moved to adopt the cause of blacks almost solely by considerations of political expediency and strategy. It would have been unnatural for them not to have strengthened their party by enfranchising African Americans and enlisting them as loyal voters. It would have been equally unnatural for the Democrats, especially the Southern wing, to have abided this clever political maneuver.

The struggle of these two parties to dominate national politics shaped the history of Reconstruction and led to the final defeat of both in attaining peace. Democrats generally opposed all Republican measures regardless of their merits. Republicans, convinced of the perfidy if not downright treason of the Democrats, sought to create a coalition that was too self-centered to be either altruistic or effective. To each party must be ascribed some share of the guilt for their utter failure to establish peace between the sections and the races.

With Union troops in the South and an increasing number of federal officials, most of whom were loyal Republicans, the latter sought to build up a strong Southern wing of their party. Many Freedmen's Bureau officials were interested not only in the welfare of the freedman but in the growth of the Republican party as well. Moreover, missionary groups and teachers from the North, who saw in the Republican party an instrument by which the South could be saved from barbarism, supported it enthusiastically. It would be incorrect, however, to conclude that these groups were primarily political in their motives or activities. But the special agency that recruited Republicans, primarily among blacks, was the Union League.

The Union League of America was organized in the North during the war. It did an effective job in rallying support for the war wherever there was much opposition. Later it branched out into the South to protect the fruits of Northern victory. As a protective and benevolent society, it welcomed black members and catechized them on political activity. As the Freedmen's Bureau and other Northern agencies grew in the South, the Union League became powerful, attracting a large number of blacks. With the establishment of Radical Reconstruction, the league became the spearhead for Southern Republicanism. Since blacks were the most numerous enfranchised group in many areas, the league depended on them for the bulk of Republican strength.

By the fall of 1867 there were chapters of the league all over the South.

South Carolina alone had eighty-eight, and it was said that almost every black in the state was enrolled. Ritual, secrecy, night meetings, and an avowed devotion to freedom and equal rights made the league especially attractive to blacks. At elections they looked to their chapters for guidance on voting. If they had any doubt about the straight Republican ticket, the league had only to remind them that this was the party of Abraham Lincoln and of deliverance. A vote for Democrats, they said, was a vote for the return of slavery. During most of Reconstruction, the Union League and such smaller organizations as the Lincoln Brotherhood and the Red Strings delivered the black vote to the Republican party in national as well as state and local elections.

As long as Lincoln and Johnson permitted some Southern whites to participate in Reconstruction, the whites believed that they could handle blacks and resurrect the Democratic party. Even when the presence of black troops outraged them, they could protest vigorously to the president, as Wade Hampton did in 1866, and expect quick relief. These white Southerners were determined to guide their own destiny and control blacks. When Radical Reconstruction made this impossible, in 1867 they struck with fury and rage.

The violence, which culminated in the Ku Klux Klan movement, did not arise solely, however, from the establishment of Radical Reconstruction and the consequent elimination of many Southern white men from public life. As early as 1866, when Southern whites had almost complete charge of Reconstruction, a kind of guerrilla warfare was carried on against both blacks and whites who represented the Washington government in the South. The head of the Freedmen's Bureau in Georgia, for example, complained that bands of men calling themselves Regulators, Jayhawkers, and the Black Horse Cavalry were committing the "most fiendish and diabolical outrages on the freedmen" with the sympathy not only of the populace but of the reconstructed governments too. There were scores of these coercive organizations all over the South. They were formed as white protective societies, and while Southern leaders enacted the new Black Codes, they were engaged in "keeping the Negro in his place" and sniping at Northerners who had come south.

Secret societies grew and spread when it became apparent to Southerners that their control was to be broken by Radical Reconstruction. For ten years after 1867 there flourished the Knights of the White Camelia, the Constitutional Union Guards, the Pale Faces, the White Brotherhood, the Council of Safety, the '76 Association, and the Knights of the Ku Klux Klan. Among the numerous local organizations were the White League of Louisiana, the White Line of Mississippi, and the Rifle Clubs of South Carolina. White Southerners expected to do by extralegal or blatantly illegal means what had not been allowed by law: to exercise absolute control over blacks, drive them and their fellows from power, and establish "white supremacy." Radical Reconstruction was to be ended at all costs, and the tactics of terrorist groups were the first step of Southern white leaders toward achieving this goal.

The Camelias and the Klan were the most powerful of the secret orders. Armed with guns, swords, or other weapons, their members patrolled some parts of the South day and night. Scattered Union troops proved wholly ineffectual in coping with them, for the members were sworn to secrecy, disguised themselves and their deeds in many ways, and had the respect and support of the white community. They used intimidation, force, ostracism in business and society, bribery at the polls, arson, and even murder to accomplish their deeds. Depriving blacks of political equality became, to them, a holy crusade in which a noble end justified any means. Blacks were run out of communities if they disobeyed orders to desist from voting, and the more resolute and therefore insubordinate blacks were whipped, maimed, and hanged. In 1871 several black officials in South Carolina were given fifteen days to resign, and they were warned that if they failed to do so, "then retributive justice will as surely be used as night follows day." A similar situation prevailed in Kentucky where the major purpose of violence against blacks was to eliminate their participation in politics. In 1874 a committee of the Colored Convention assembled in Atlanta informed the state legislature that they could not point "to any locality in Georgia where we can in truth say that our lives and our liberties are perfectly secure."

Local efforts to suppress the outlaw organizations were on the whole unsuccessful. In 1868 Alabama, for example, passed a law imposing heavy fines and long jail sentences on anyone caught away from home wearing a mask or committing such acts as destroying property and molesting people, but this law was generally disregarded. Congress undertook to suppress the Klan and similar groups in a series of laws passed in 1870 and 1871. It was a punishable crime for any person to prevent another from voting by bribery, force, or intimidation, and the president was authorized to use land and naval forces to prevent such crimes. In 1871 a second law was passed to strengthen the first. After an extensive investigation, members of Congress were convinced that the Klan was still active, and in April 1871 a law designed to put an end to the movement was enacted. The president was authorized to suspend the writ of habeas corpus in order to suppress "armed combinations." Acts of conspiracy were declared tantamount to rebellion and were to be punished accordingly. As a result, hundreds of arrests were made, and many were found guilty of conspiracy. In South Carolina alone, nearly 100 were sentenced and fined in one year.

The struggle between organized Southern whites on the one hand and the Union League, Freedmen's Bureau, federal troops, and blacks on the other was essentially a struggle for political control of the South. From the Northern point of view it was a question of whether the gains of the war were to be nullified by the rebels who had brought the nation to the brink of disaster in 1861. From the Southern point of view it was a question of home rule—a right that they would defend to the end—and of who should rule at home, which they felt was largely academic since blacks were not qualified. As surely as the struggle between 1861 and 1865 was civil war, so was the conflict from 1865 to 1877, with as much bitterness and hatred but less bloodshed. The peace was being lost because of the vigorous efforts of both parties and sections to recruit their strength from the ruins of war. Peace could not prevail in such a warlike environment.

■ The Overthrow of Reconstruction

Reconstruction did not end abruptly as the result of congressional or presidential action. Rather it came to a gradual end as restraints were relaxed and stringent legislation repealed. Just as Reconstruction had begun long before the war was over, so it drew to a close long before the final withdrawal of troops from Southern soil. As early as 1865 many white Southerners had resumed their places at home as respected citizens of their communities, and they entered affairs on taking the oath of allegiance. Even during Radical Reconstruction they continued to return to the fold and to aid in restoring home rule. In 1869 the ex-Confederates of Tennessee were enfranchised. Within a few months large numbers of white Southerners in other states reclaimed their citizenship through individual acts of amnesty. In 1871 the "ironclad" oath, which Congress had imposed at the beginning of Radical Reconstruction to disqualify many ex-Confederates, was repealed. In the following year a general amnesty restored the franchise to all but about 600 ex-Confederate officials. It then became possible for the South to take up where it left off in 1861 and to govern itself.

The effect of pardoning white Southerners was seen early in the revival of the Democratic party. In 1870 the border states began to go Democratic; North Carolina and Virginia came under the control of Conservatives, who outnumbered the Republican combination of blacks, scalawags, and carpetbaggers. In the following year Georgia Democrats returned to power. In other states controlled by Republicans, Democrats won partial control, especially in the so-called white counties. In 1874 and 1875 they resumed the rule of Texas, Arkansas, and Alabama. All that Republicans could claim in the South by 1876 were South Carolina, Florida, and Louisiana. The cause of the Democrats had gained so much momentum that the overthrow of Republicanism was regarded by many as a crusade.

It looked as though the Civil War would break out anew as the Democrats resorted to every possible device to overthrow the Radicals. In 1875 Mississippi was on the verge of war. The black militia maintained by Governor Adelbert Ames was especially offensive to the resurgent Democrats, and when the governor ordered 100 copies of *Infantry Tactics*, presumably for the blacks, the whites thought it time for a "protective" white militia to step forward. Both sides imported arms, paraded, and actually skirmished. Although Ames promised to disband the black militia, disorder and killings continued until the election, when the Democrats carried the state by more than 30,000. Within two months the Republican party was dissolved. In

John R. Lynch Foresees End of Republican Rule—1874

I was well aware of the fact . . . that it was the result of the state and congressional elections at the North in 1874 that had convinced the Southern Democrats that Republican ascendancy in the national government would soon be a thing of the past—that the Democrats would be successful in the presidential and congressional elections of 1876 and that that party would no doubt remain in power for at least a quarter of a century. It was this, and not the unsuccessful effort to pass a Federal Elections Bill that produced the marked change that was noticeable on every hand. Every indication seemed to point to a confirmation of the impression that Democratic national success was practically an assured fact.

There had been a disastrous financial panic in 1873 which was no doubt largely responsible for the political upheaval in 1874, but that was lost sight of in accounting for that result. In fact, they made no effort to explain it or account for it except in their own way. The Democrats had carried the country, the reasons for which they construed to suit themselves. The construction they placed upon it was that it was a national condemnation and repudiation of the congressional plan of reconstruction and they intended to govern themselves accordingly.

John Roy Lynch, *Reminiscences of an Active Life* (Chicago, 1970), pp. 164–165.

Louisiana, the Conservatives organized "White Leagues" and apparently planned to overthrow the Radical government by violence as early as 1874. The Radicals tried to seize the arms of the White Leagues, an attempt that resulted in a riot in New Orleans, killing 40 and wounding more than a 100 people. Intermittent warfare continued through the election of 1876, and there was no peace until President Hayes withdrew the federal troops the following year. In South Carolina, the "Red Shirts" dominated campaign meetings and openly carried arms as a measure of "protection" against Radical "tyranny." Workingmen's Democratic Associations were organized, and whites were urged to employ only Democrats. Many sections of the state were in constant turmoil, particularly Edgefield County, where Ben Tillman was rapidly becoming a public figure.

The town of Hamburg, South Carolina, was the scene of one of the bloodiest race clashes. When the black militia paraded on July 4, 1876, several blacks were arrested on a charge of blocking traffic. And when their trial was postponed, a large number of armed white men, estimated at several hundred, came into town to see that justice was meted out to the black offenders. An ex-Confederate general ordered the blacks to apologize and to surrender their arms, which they refused to do; heavier arms and more munitions were then imported by the whites. Gunfire followed. The blacks tried to escape, but too late, and several were killed in the attempt, besides five who were killed after being captured. It was not until Wade Hampton succeeded Daniel H. Chamberlain as governor in 1877 that South Carolina had even a semblance of peace.

The overthrow of the Radicals was accomplished not only by Southerners returning to political action and restoring Conservative governments but also by other circumstances favorable to white Southerners. Intimidation of blacks was effective. Even where there were no riots, whites kept blacks from the polls by terrorism and thus ensured Democratic victory. After the official dissolution of the Ku Klux Klan in 1869, other methods of intimidation were employed to render blacks politically inconsequential. Indeed, intimidation was most effective after 1870, although the Ku Klux Klan disclaimed all responsibility because of its increasing violence. The crops of blacks were destroyed, their barns and houses burned, and they were whipped and lynched for voting Republican. Organized whites became bolder as they patrolled polling places to guarantee "fair, peaceful, and Democratic" elections. Blacks more and more remained at home, and political power changed from Republican to Democratic hands.

Disclosures of corruption in Republican governments served to hasten the overthrow of Radical Reconstruction. The case for Democrats was strengthened considerably as they pointed to misgovernment through bribery, embezzlement, misappropriation of funds, and other corrupt practices. The federal government was unable to rush to the defense of Southern Republican governments because it was having difficulty in purging itself of corruption. It did not matter that white Southerners had also been corrupt before the war or that the provisional governments under Johnson were extravagant and corrupt. The Democrats were not in power in 1874 and consequently had all the advantages that the "outs" usually enjoy in such cases. Corruption discredited Radical Reconstruction, and with the loss of conscientious but disillusioned supporters, complete white home rule could be restored in the South.

The North had grown weary of the crusade for blacks. Perhaps Stevens, Sumner, Butler, and old antislavery leaders could have gone on with it, but younger people, with less zeal for blacks, took their places. They were loyal party men, practical politicians who cared more about industrial interests in the North and South than Radical governments in the South. The assumption of Republican leadership by men like Rutherford B. Hayes, James G. Blaine, Roscoe Conkling, and John A. Logan was a signal for the party to turn to more profitable and practical pursuits.

Not even the Supreme Court postponed the overthrow of Radical Reconstruction. As a matter of fact, its decisions had the effect of hastening the end. In 1875, several indictments under the Enforcement Act of 1870 charged defendants with preventing blacks from exercising their right to vote in elections. In *United States v. Reese* the Court declared that the Fifteenth

Amendment did not confer the right of suffrage upon anyone. "It prevents the States or the United States . . . from giving preference . . . to one citizen of the United States over another on account of race, color, or previous condition of servitude," the Court declared. In *United States v. Cruikshank* the Court held that the Enforcement Act of 1870 covered more offenses than were punishable under the terms of the Fifteenth Amendment and was, therefore, unconstitutional. Neither blacks nor Republicans could expect much support from a court that brushed aside the very laws with which they hoped to implement the franchise amendment. As far as the Court was concerned, the South was free to settle its problems as best it could.

The campaign of 1876 was the great test for both parties. The Democrats were committed to a program to end Reconstruction in the South; the Republicans had not openly promised to do so, but there was at least one wing of the party that was willing to withdraw troops and leave the South to its own devices. In the three states that had not been "redeemed," South Carolina, Louisiana, and Florida, the election campaign approached civil war. The result was, in the case of the first two, a hotly disputed election with both sides claiming victory and establishing dual governments. The presidency of the United States hung on the decision regarding their disputed votes. To break the impasse, the Republicans promised not only to withdraw troops but also to assist the South in its long-cherished ambition to obtain federal subsidies for internal improvements and better representation in affairs in Washington. Thus when Hayes became president, the South was soon assuaged in its grief by his prompt withdrawal of troops. At last the South could rule itself without Northern interference or black influence.

With troops out of the South and in a spirit of great conciliation, Congress removed other restrictions. In 1878 the use of armed forces in elections was forbidden. In 1894 appropriations for special federal marshals and supervisors of elections were cut off. In 1898 the last disabilities laid on disloyal and rebellious Southerners were removed in a final amnesty. Before the dawn of a new century there was complete recognition in law of what the South had itself accomplished in fact even before the election of 1876.

■ The Movement for Disfranchisement

After the Democrats returned to power in the South, they confronted the problem of finding ways either to nullify the political strength of blacks or to disfranchise them altogether. Complete disfranchisement by state legislation was viewed with some misgivings as long as the Fourteenth and Fifteenth Amendments remained a part of the fundamental law. Until it was feasible, the Democrats contented themselves with other methods—some extralegal, others incorporated in state codes—of preventing black participation in politics. Intimidation continued on an extensive scale. Earlier it had been justified in order to wrest political control from unworthy Republicans, both white and black, but once control was secured, it appeared irresponsible to the more sensitive white Southerners to depend upon night riders and Red Shirts to maintain them in power. For many white Southerners, however, violence was still the surest means of keeping blacks politically impotent, and in countless communities they were not allowed, under penalties of severe reprisals, to show their faces in town on election day.

Other devices, hardly more legal than violence and intimidation, had a more respectable appearance. Polling places were frequently set up far from black communities, and the more diligent blacks failed to reach them upon finding roads blocked and ferries conveniently out of repair at election time. Polling places were sometimes changed without notifying black voters; or, if they were notified, election officials thought nothing of making a last-minute decision not to change the place after all. Election laws were so imperfect that in many communities uniform ballots were not required, and officials winked at Democrats who made up several extra ballots to cast with the one given them. The practice of stuffing ballot boxes was widespread. Criminal manipulation of the counting gave point to the assertion of an enthusiastic Democrat that "the white and black Republicans may outvote us, but we can outcount them."

For what black votes were cast and counted, the white factions vied with each other. Dances and parties, with plenty of barbecue and whiskey, were held for black voters on election eve as a reminder that they should vote for their benefactors. Some planters brought their black workers to the polls and "voted them like a senseless herd of cattle." At times black candidates were nominated by whites in order to divide the vote of the race, while the whites all voted for one of their own race. A few candidates sought black votes by advocating measures favorable to them. In 1882, when he was running for the Georgia legislature, Tom Watson won many black votes by demanding free black schools and condemning the convict lease system, which was especially burdensome to blacks.

Where possible the legislatures, now controlled by zealous white-supremacy Democrats, helped to disfranchise blacks. Areas with a heavy concentration of blacks were divided by a system of gerrymandering that rendered the black vote ineffective. Poll tax requirements, elaborate and confusing election schemes, complicated balloting processes, and highly centralized election codes were all statutory techniques by which blacks were disfranchised. Some states went the limit in establishing "legal" barriers to black suffrage. Virginia, for example, reapportioned, or gerrymandered, its voting districts five times within seventeen years in order to nullify black ballots. Petty larceny, of which countless blacks were convicted, was added to the long list of suffrage disqualifications, and the poll tax was made a prerequisite for voting. The elaborate election code of 1894 required that registration and poll tax certificates be shown at the polls, that the names of candidates be printed on the ballot not by party but by office (an extremely confusing arrangement for semiliterate and illiterate voters), and that if others were waiting to vote, an elector must not remain in a booth more than two and a half minutes. Such requirements virtually disfranchised Virginia's illiterate voters, whether white or black.

South Carolina was most adroit in making voting difficult. The law of 1882 required that special ballots and boxes be placed at every polling place for each office on the ballot and that voters put their ballots in the correct boxes. No one was allowed to speak to a voter, and if he failed to find the correct box his vote was thrown out. South Carolina and Virginia were not alone in devising ingenious schemes to render the black vote ineffective. All the Southern states used some device or other. The result appeared so satisfactory on the whole that by 1889 Henry W. Grady could say, "The Negro as a political force has dropped out of serious consideration."

Strangely enough, however, the elimination of blacks from the political picture created circumstances that brought them back into the picture. By the 1880s the menace of black Republicanism had disappeared, and with it the great cohesive force among Southern whites. Almost immediately sharp class lines appeared, and irregularity in party voting cropped out. Now that white Southern farmers did not fear "Negro rule," they were more concerned with their own plight and held the dominant white groups responsible for their impending ruin. The coalition of classes that had united only to oppose another race began to disintegrate, as the poor whites came to distrust the Bourbons for substantial economic and political reasons.

An agricultural depression, caused largely by the overexpansion and increased production of cotton, settled down on the South after 1870. The panic of 1873 was especially disastrous because thousands of small farmers lost their land. In their distress they turned upon the money powers that foreclosed their mortgages, the railroads that charged excessive freight rates but received subsidies from state and federal taxes, the corporations that sought higher tariffs and charged higher prices for farm machinery, and the government that steadily raised taxes. In the South, moreover, a significant change had taken place in the leadership of the Democratic party. It no longer followed solely the plantation aristocrats, with whom the small farmers felt that they had something in common; industrialists and merchants, whom the small farmers disliked intensely, had come forward and were assuming important roles in party politics. In some states they were the dominant figures. The radical farmers, who wanted regulation of railroads, state aid for agriculture, and higher taxes on corporations, did not take to these new leaders and consequently wavered in their party regularity. The threat of a black balance of power did not frighten hungry white farmers, whose unconcern about race alarmed loyal Democrats. Small wonder that Henry W. Grady deplored the defections he saw everywhere among whites.

Radical agrarian organizations had flourished all over the United States after the Civil War. The National Grange, or Patrons of Husbandry, was attracting thousands of farmers by 1870, but it was kept within bounds in the South during Reconstruction because of the dangers of "Negro-Radical" rule. Prostrated by depression, however, Southern farmers organized and adopted a radical program. By 1889 the Southern Farmers' Alliance had branches in every Southern state. Although they did not admit black members, they believed that blacks should at least be lined up in a parallel organization. In 1886, therefore, the Colored Farmers' National Alliance and Cooperative Union came into existence. It grew rapidly and by 1891 claimed more than a million members in twelve state organizations. There were local chapters wherever black farmers were sufficiently numerous. After a national organization was perfected in 1888, there was for a time close cooperation between the white and black groups. But when the Colored Farmers' Alliance proposed to call a general strike of black cotton pickers, Leonidas L. Polk, president of the National Farmers' Alliance, opposed it with the argument that blacks were attempting to better their condition at the expense of whites. He insisted that farmers should leave their cotton in the field rather than pay 50 cents per 100 pounds to have it picked.

As the program of radical agrarianism evolved during the last two decades of the century, however, black and white farmers in the South drifted closer together and white solidarity became more difficult to maintain. Radical leaders like Tom Watson of Georgia told poor whites and blacks that they were being deliberately kept apart and fleeced. He called on them to stand together and work for the common good. Along with other leaders, he was at the time opposed to black disfranchisement and looked forward to a coalition of black and white farmers to drive the Bourbons from power. Then it would be possible to adopt progressive laws especially beneficial to the poor man. C. Vann Woodward says that under the tutelage of radical agrarian leaders the white masses of the South were learning to regard blacks as political allies bound to them by economic ties and a common destiny. "Never before or since have the two races in the South come so close together as they did during the Populist struggles."

The Populist, or People's, party was the political agency of these resurgent farmers. In 1892 the Populists sought to win the black vote in most of the Southern states and in many instances resorted to desperate means to secure the franchise for blacks in communities where by custom and practice they had been barred from voting for more than a decade. The Democrats, alarmed to desperation, made overtures to the Populists, but to no avail. They then turned to the blacks. In some communities blacks were forced to vote for Democrats by the very people who had dared them to attempt such an exercise of the "white man's prerogative" only a few years before. Blacks were hauled to towns in wagons and made to vote repeatedly. In Augusta, Georgia, they were even imported from South Carolina to vote for Democrats.

Many blacks, however, stood by the Populists, who advocated political if not social equality. One of the most zealous advocates of Tom Watson in Georgia was a young Negro preacher, H. S. Doyle, who made sixty-three speeches for Watson in the face of numerous threats. Democrats resorted to violence. A black Populist in Dalton, Georgia, was murdered in his home, and it is estimated that fifteen were killed in Georgia during the state elections of 1892. Riots also broke out in Virginia and North Carolina. If black rule meant chaos and disorder to the Democrats, the mere threat of it was enough for them to resort to violence themselves.

In some states there was a successful fusion between the newly organized Populists and the remnants of old Republican organizations. In 1894 such a combination seized control of the North Carolina legislature. The Democratic election machinery was immediately dismantled, and voting was made easier so that more blacks could vote and make their influence felt once more. Black officeholding soon became common in the eastern black belt of the state. The action of the fusion legislature of 1895 led to the election of 300 black magistrates. Many counties had black deputy sheriffs. Wilmington had 14 black police officers, and New Bern had both black policemen and aldermen. One prominent black, James H. Young, was made chief fertilizer inspector and a director of the state asylum for the blind; another, John C. Dancy, was appointed collector for the port of Wilmington.

White Conservatives who witnessed the political resurgence of blacks in North Carolina, Georgia, and other Southern states deeply resented the blacks' exercise of power when they were unable to control them. As blacks returned to prominence, either as electors or as an election issue, sentiment against their participation in politics grew. The Democrats, failing to control the black vote, moaned dismally about the return of black Republicanism. Even when they controlled them, they said that they made for corruption in politics. Although the Populists could on occasion have had the black vote, apparently they preferred not to have it because of the dangers involved. The election laws, as they stood, might actually be turned against poor, ignorant whites if the Democrats became vindictive and sought to disfranchise the Populists as well as their black allies. It was much better, therefore, to have clear-cut constitutional disfranchisement of blacks and to leave white groups to fight elections out among themselves. Where the Populists were unable to control the black vote, as in Georgia in 1894, they believed that the Democrats had never completely disfranchised blacks because their votes were needed if the Democrats were to stay in power. This belief led the defeated and disappointed Tom Watson to support a constitutional amendment excluding blacks from the franchise—a complete reversal of his position in denouncing South Carolina for adopting such an amendment in 1895.

With the collapse of the agrarian revolt in 1896, the movement for complete disfranchisement of blacks helped to reunite the white South. The poor, ignorant white farmers reverted to their old habits of thinking and acting, comforted in their poverty by Conservative assurances that "Negro rule" must be avoided at any cost. They might look back to the time in the 1890s when they were on the verge of joining their darker brothers and sisters to fight for a common cause. The poor whites could say with one of their leaders that the "Negro question" was an everlasting, overshadowing problem that served to hamper the progress of poor whites and prevent them from becoming realistic in social, economic, and political matters.

■ The Triumph of White Supremacy

When it became evident that white factions would compete with one another for the black vote and thus frequently give blacks the balance of power, it was time for complete disfranchisement of blacks, the Fifteenth Amendment notwithstanding. On this, most Southern whites were agreed. They differed only over the method of disfranchising blacks. The view prevailed that none but people of property and intelligence were entitled to suffrage. As one writer put it, white Southerners believed that "no person should enjoy the suffrage unless he gives sufficient evidence of his permanent interest in and attachment to the community." And yet there were many who opposed such stringent disfranchisement because it would disqualify numerous whites. Not surprisingly, poor whites were especially apprehensive. Some of them had been disfranchised by earlier measures, and when competition grew keen between rival white groups, the Conservatives actually barred Radical whites from the polls and at the same time permitted their own black supporters to vote. More poor whites were bound to be disfranchised by any new measures. The sponsors of a stricter suffrage had to be certain that they did not contravene the Fifteenth Amendment. Despite the fact that the Supreme Court had refused to apply it in the Reese and Cruikshank cases, there was no guarantee that the Court would view so favorably any state action obviously designed to disfranchise a group because of its race.

These were the problems that had to be solved by state constitutional conventions when they undertook to write into their fundamental law a guarantee of white supremacy. It was in Mississippi, where a majority of the population was black, that the problem was first faced and solved. As early as 1886 sentiment was strong for constitutional revision; a convention met in 1890 for the primary purpose of disfranchising blacks. A suffrage amendment was written that imposed a poll tax of $2 and excluded voters convicted of bribery, burglary, theft, arson, perjury, murder, or bigamy. It also barred all who could not read any section of the state constitution, or understand it when read, or give a reasonable interpretation of it. Isaiah T. Montgomery, the only black delegate to the convention, said that the poll tax and education requirements would disfranchise 123,000 blacks and only 11,000 whites. He, nevertheless, supported the proposed amendments. Before the convention, black delegates from forty counties had met and protested their impending disfranchisement to President Harrison. Doubtless they would have fought ratification, but the Conservatives would run no risk of having their handiwork rejected; after the convention approved the constitution, it was promulgated and declared to be in effect.

South Carolina followed Mississippi by disfranchising blacks in 1895. Ben

Tillman had worked toward this goal after he was elected governor in 1890, but he was unable to obtain sufficient support for a constitutional convention until 1894. Tillman was then in the United States Senate, but he returned to the convention to serve as chairman of the Committee on Rights of Suffrage and thus to be certain that blacks were effectively disfranchised. The clause, when adopted, called for two years' residence, a poll tax of $1, the ability to read and write any section of the constitution or to understand it when read aloud, or the owning of property worth $300, and the disqualification of convicts.

Black delegates bitterly denounced this sweeping disfranchisement. In answer to Tillman's charge that blacks had done nothing to demonstrate their capacity in government, Thomas E. Miller replied that they were largely responsible for "the laws relative to finance, the building of penal and charitable institutions, and, greatest of all, the establishment of the public school system." He declared that numerous reform laws "touching every department of state, county, municipal and town governments . . . stand as living witnesses [on the statute books of South Carolina] of the Negro's fitness to vote and legislate on the rights of mankind." James Wigg of Beaufort County said,

> The Negro . . . has a right to demand that in accordance with his wealth, his intelligence and his services to the state he be accorded an equal and exact share in its government. . . . You charge that the Negro is too ignorant to be trusted with the suffrage. I answer that you have not, nor dare you, make a purely educational test of the right to vote. You say that he is a figurehead, an encumbrance to the state, that he pays little or no taxes. I answer you, you have not, nor dare you make a purely property test of the right to vote. . . . We submit our cause to the judgment of an enlightened public opinion and to the arbitrament of a Christian civilization.

Only two whites joined the six blacks in voting against the constitution of 1895.

The story was essentially the same in Louisiana in 1898 when a new device, the "grandfather clause," was written into the constitution. This called for an addition to the permanent registration list of the names of all male persons whose fathers and grandfathers were qualified to vote on January 1, 1867. At that time, of course, no blacks were qualified to vote in Louisiana. If any blacks were to vote, they would have to comply with educational and property requirements. Booker Washington attempted to prick the conscience of Louisiana Democrats by writing them that he hoped the law would be so clear that "no one clothed with state authority will be tempted to perjure and degrade himself by putting one interpretation upon it for the white man and another for the black man." Blacks led by T. B. Stamps and D. W. Boatner appeared before the suffrage committee and admitted that a qualified suffrage might remedy demoralized conditions, but they pleaded for an honest test, honestly administered.

By 1898 the pattern for constitutional disfranchisement of blacks had been completely drawn. In subsequent years other states followed the lead of Mississippi, South Carolina, and Louisiana. By 1910 blacks had been effectively disfranchised by constitutional provisions in North Carolina, Alabama, Virginia, Georgia, and Oklahoma. The tension arising from campaigns for white suffrage sometimes flared up into violent race wars. In Wilmington, North Carolina, three white men were wounded and eleven blacks killed and twenty-five wounded in a riot in 1898. In Atlanta, there were four days of rioting after an election in 1906 in which disfranchisement was the main issue. Robbery, murder, and brutality were not uncommon during this period.

For the cause of white supremacy the effect was most salutary. In 1896 there were 130,344 blacks registered in Louisiana, constituting a majority in twenty-six parishes. In 1900, two years after the adoption of the new constitution, only 5,320 blacks were on the registration books, and in no parish did they make up a majority of voters. Of 181,471 black males of voting age in Alabama in 1900, only 3,000 registered after the new constitutional provisions went into effect. On the floor of the Virginia convention Carter Glass had said that the delegates were elected "to discriminate to the very extremity of permissible action under the limitations of the Federal Constitution, with a view to the elimination of every Negro voter who can be gotten rid of, legally, without materially impairing the numerical strength of the white electorate." This was accomplished not only in Virginia, but in every state where whites resorted to such means.

The South universally hailed the disfranchisement of blacks as a constructive act of statesmanship. African Americans were viewed as aliens whose ignorance, poverty, and racial inferiority were incompatible with logical and orderly processes of government. Southern whites said that blacks had done nothing to warrant suffrage. But as blacks made progress in many walks of life, it became increasingly difficult to allege that they were naturally shiftless and incapable of advancement. The framers of the new suffrage laws, however, were committed to the complete and permanent disfranchisement of blacks regardless of their progress. The Southern white view was summed up by J. K. Vardaman of Mississippi: "I am just as opposed to Booker Washington as a voter, with all his Anglo-Saxon re-enforcements, as I am to the coconut-headed, chocolate-colored, typical little coon, Andy Dotson, who blacks my shoes every morning. Neither is fit to perform the supreme function of citizenship." Southerners would have to depend on administration of the suffrage laws to keep blacks disfranchised, for there were many who would gradually meet even the most stringent constitutional qualifications. White supremacy would require an abiding belief in racial inequality, reinforced perhaps by hatred born of bitter memories.

Once blacks were disfranchised, everything else necessary for white supremacy could be done. With the emergence of white Democratic primaries, from which all blacks were excluded by the rules of the party, whites

TABLE 5
Population by Race (White and Black) in the Former
Confederate States of America As Shown in 1880

STATE	WHITE (In Thousands)	BLACK (In Thousands)
Alabama	662	600
Arkansas	592	211
Florida	143	127
Georgia	817	725
Louisiana	455	484
Mississippi	479	650
North Carolina	867	531
South Carolina	391	604
Tennessee	1,139	403
Texas	1,197	393
Virginia	881	632

Source: U.S. Bureau of the Census, *Historical Statistics of the United States, Colonial Times to 1970, Bicentennial Edition* [Part 2]. Washington, D.C., 1975, pp. 24–37.

planned their strategy in caucuses, and the party itself became the government in the South. Whites solemnly resolved to keep the races completely separate, for there could be no normal relationships between them. Laws for racial segregation had made a brief appearance during Reconstruction, only to disappear by 1868. When the Conservatives resumed power, they revived the segregation of the races. Beginning in Tennessee in 1870, white Southerners enacted laws against intermarriage of the races in every Southern state. Five years later, Tennessee adopted the first "Jim Crow" law, and the rest of the South rapidly fell in line. Blacks and whites were separated on trains, in depots, and on wharves. After the Supreme Court in 1883 outlawed the Civil Rights Acts of 1875, blacks were banned from white hotels, barber shops, restaurants, and theaters. By 1885 most Southern states had laws requiring separate schools. With the adoption of new constitutions the states firmly established the color line by the most stringent segregation of the races, and in 1896 the Supreme Court upheld segregation in its "separate but equal" doctrine set forth in *Plessy v. Ferguson.*

It was a dear price that the whites of the South paid for this color line. Since all other issues were subordinated to the issue of "the Negro," it became impossible to have free and open discussion of problems affecting all the people. There could be no two-party system, for the temptation to call upon blacks to decide between opposing factions would be too great. Interest in politics waned to a point where only professionals, who skillfully deflected the interest from issues to races, were concerned with public life. The expense of maintaining a double system of schools and of other public institutions was high, but not too high for advocates of white supremacy, who kept the races apart in order to maintain things as they were.

Peace had not yet come to the South. The new century opened tragically with 214 lynchings in the first two years. Clashes between the races occurred almost daily, and the atmosphere of tension in which people of both races lived was conducive to little more than a struggle for mere survival, with a feeble groping in the direction of progress. The law, the courts, the schools, and almost every institution in the South favored whites. This was white supremacy.

Bibliographical
Notes

We shall make no attempt here to list all of the primary and secondary works that we consulted in writing this book. Instead, we shall cite a selected number of the more important works, primarily those in English that are generally available, with a view to guiding the interested reader to further study. Those available in paperback editions are marked with an asterisk. It is well to mention that in this computer age most libraries can provide bibliographies through an on-line catalog. On-line catalogs also allow researchers to create specialized bibliographies for their research needs. For many years the best general bibliographical aid in the study of African Americans was Monroe R. Work's *A Bibliography of the Negro in Africa and America* (New York, 1928). Although out of date, it continues to have value, but it should be supplemented by other aids. The most exhaustive and excellent bibliographical aid is James M. McPherson and others, *Blacks in America: Bibliographical Essays** (Garden City, N.Y., 1971), now unfortunately out of print. There are several other bibliographies of value. Among them are Dorothy B. Porter, *The Negro in the United States: A Selected Bibliography* (Washington, D.C., 1970); and Elizabeth W. Miller, *The Negro in America, A Bibliography** (Cambridge, Mass., 1966, revised edition, 1970). The lists of materials in the major African-American collections should also be consulted. Among them are those at Fisk University and Hampton University, the Moorland-Spingarn Research Center at Howard University, the Slaughter Collection at Atlanta University, the James Weldon Johnson Collection at Yale University, the Schomburg Center for Research in Black Culture at the New York Public Library, and the Vivian Harsh Collection at the Chicago Public Library. Of special interest and importance is Debra Newman Ham, ed., *The African American Mosaic: A Library of Congress Resource Guide for the Study of Black History and Culture* (Washington, D.C., 1993).

It is widely known that a large and curious assortment of general histories of

265

African Americans has appeared in the past century. While some have only historiographical value, others are important sources of information. Among the former are James W. C. Pennington, *Text Book of the Origin and History of the Colored People* (Hartford, Conn., 1841); William T. Alexander, *History of the Colored Race in America* (Kansas City, 1887); Harold M. Tarver, *The Negro in the History of the United States from the Beginning of the English Settlements in 1607, to the Present Time* (Austin, Tex., 1905); and E. A. Johnson, *School History of the Negro Race* (Raleigh, N.C., 1893). Of much greater value is George W. Williams, *History of the Negro Race in America*, two volumes (New York, 1882, reprinted 1968), which was the first such work to attract the attention of serious students. Two works of a similar nature, but less exhaustive, are Booker T. Washington, *The Story of the Negro: The Rise of the Race from Slavery*, two volumes (New York, 1909) and Willis D. Weatherford, *The Negro from Africa to America* (New York, 1924). Other efforts in the general field include Benjamin Brawley, *A Short History of the American Negro* (New York, 1913); Merle R. Eppse, *The Negro, Too, in American History* (Chicago, 1939); and Edwin R. Embree, *Brown Americans: The Story of a Tenth of the Nation** (New York, 1945).

The pioneer modern work was written in 1922 by Carter G. Woodson. The tenth edition was prepared by Charles H. Wesley under the title *The Negro in Our History* (Washington, D.C., 1962). For certain aspects of the history of African Americans, the work of W. E. B. Du Bois, *Black Folk, Then and Now: An Essay in the History and Sociology of the Negro Race** (New York, 1939), is invaluable. In the last four decades the number of general histories of African Americans has greatly increased. Among them are Roi Ottley, *Black Odyssey* (New York, 1948); Rayford W. Logan, *The Negro in the United States** (New York, 1957); Lerone Bennett, *Before the Mayflower,** revised edition (Chicago, 1987); J. Saunders Redding, *They Came in Chains* (New York, 1952, revised edition, 1973) and *Lonesome Road* (New York, 1958); W. Z. Foster, *The Negro People in American History** (New York, 1970); Benjamin Quarles, *The Negro in the Making of America** (New York, 1964); Eli Ginzberg and Alfred S. Eichner, *The Troublesome Presence: American Democracy and the Negro* (Glencoe, Ill., 1964); August Meier and Elliott Rudwick, *From Plantation to Ghetto: An Interpretive History of American Negroes,** third edition (New York, 1976); C. Eric Lincoln, *The Negro Pilgrimage in America** (New York, 1969); Nathan Huggins, *Black Odyssey: The Afro-American Ordeal in Slavery** (New York, 1977); Philip S. Foner, *History of Black Americans,* three volumes (Westport, Conn., 1975), which brings the story up until the end of the Civil War; Vincent Harding, *There Is a River: The Black Struggle for Freedom in America** (New York, 1981); and Mary Frances Berry and John Blassingame, *Long Memory: The Black Experience in America** (New York, 1982). One should not miss an especially unique and thoroughly fascinating work by John Langston Gwaltney, *Drylongso: A Self-Portrait of Black America** (New York, 1981).

Three works of a special nature that cover most of the period are Vincent P. Franklin, *Black Self-Determination: A Cultural History of the Faith of the Fathers* (Westport, Conn., 1984); Jacqueline Jones, *Labor of Love, Labor of Sorrow: Black Women, Work, and the Family from Slavery to the Present* (New York, 1985); and Darlene Clark Hine, *Black Women in United States History* (New York, 1993).

A different approach to the history of black Americans is undertaken in Earl E. Thorpe, *The Mind of the Negro: An Intellectual History of Afro-Americans* (Baton Rouge, La., 1961). The interest of foreign writers in the subject can be seen in J. W. Schulte Nordholdt, *The People That Walk in Darkness* (London, 1960); Frank K. Schoell, *Histoire de la race noire aux Etats-Unis du XVIIe siècle à nos jours* (Paris, 1959); and Jean Daridan,

De Lincoln à Johnson: noirs et blancs (Paris, 1965). There is much historical material in Gunnar Myrdal, *An American Dilemma: The Negro Problem and Modern Democracy** (New York, 1944 and 1964); E. Franklin Frazier, *The Negro in the United States,* revised edition (New York, 1957); Margaret J. Butcher, *The Negro in American Culture** (New York, 1956, revised edition, 1972); and Mabel M. Smythe, ed., *The Black American Reference Book* (Englewood Cliffs, N.J., 1976).

Volumes documenting the general history of African Americans have not been numerous. Outstanding are Herbert Aptheker, *A Documentary History of the Negro People in the United States,** three volumes (New York, 1951, 1973, 1974); Leslie Fishel and Benjamin Quarles, *The Black American: A Documentary History** (Glenview, Ill., 1976); and William Loren Katz, *Eyewitness, The Negro in American History** (New York, 1967, revised edition, 1974). See also Richard Wade, *The Negro in American Life, Selected Readings** (New York, 1970); Milton Meltzer, *In Their Own Words: A History of the American Negro, 1619–1865,** three volumes (New York, 1967); and Milton Sernett, *Afro-American Religious History: A Documentary Witness* (Durham, N.C., 1985). Richard Bardolph, *The Negro Vanguard* (New York, 1959) contains a wealth of material on individual African Americans. A monumental achievement dealing with individual African Americans is Rayford W. Logan and Michael R. Winston, eds., *Dictionary of American Negro Biography* (New York, 1982). See also, Edgar A. Toppin, *A Biographical History of Blacks in America Since 1528* (New York, 1971). Among pictorial representations are the following: Langston Hughes and Milton Meltzer, *A Pictorial History of the Negro in America* (New York, 1968); Russell L. Adams, *Great Negroes, Past and Present** (Chicago, 1969); Year's *Picture History of the American Negro* (New York, 1965); Lucille A. Chambers, *America's Tenth Man* (New York, 1957); *Ebony Pictorial History of Black America,* three volumes (Chicago, 1971); and John Hope Franklin and the editors of Time-Life Books, *An Illustrated History of Black Americans* (New York, 1970).

With the increased interest in the history of African Americans, a considerable number of anthologies, curriculum guides, and teachers' aids have appeared. Among the better anthologies are August Meier and Elliott Rudwick, eds., *The Making of Black America,** two volumes (New York, 1969); Nathan Huggins and others, eds., *Key Issues in the Afro-American Experience,** two volumes (New York, 1971); Eric Foner, ed., *America's Black Past, A Reader in Afro-American History** (New York, 1970); Melvin Drimmer, ed., *Black History, A Reappraisal** (Garden City, N.Y., 1968); and Talcott Parsons and Kenneth B. Clark, eds., *The Negro American** (Boston, 1966). The following are valuable as curriculum aids and teachers' guides: Philip T. Drotning, *A Guide to Negro History in America** (Garden City, N.Y., 1970); William Loren Katz, *Teachers' Guide to American Negro History** (Chicago, 1971); San Francisco Unified School District, *The Negro in American Life and History** (San Francisco, 1967); and Robert L. Harris, *Teaching Afro-American History** (Washington, D.C., 1985).

There have been many books and articles dealing with the treatment of African Americans in American history. Among them are Earl E. Thorpe, *Negro Historians in the United States* (Baton Rouge, La., 1958), and *Black Historians: A Critique* (New York, 1971); John Hope Franklin, "The New Negro History," *Journal of Negro History,* XLII (April 1957), "The Future of Negro American History," *University of Chicago Magazine,* LXII (January–February 1970), and "Mirror for Americans: A Century of Reconstruction History," *American Historical Review,* LXXXV (February, 1980); and Ernest Kaiser, "Trends in American Negro Historiography," *Journal of Negro Education,* XXXI (Fall 1962). John Hope Franklin, *George Washington Williams: A Biography* (Chicago, 1985), is a full-length study of the first serious historian of African Americans. Recent works on the state of the art are Eugene D. Genovese, *In Red and Black: Marxian Explorations in Southern and Afro-American History* (New York, 1968); Darlene Clark Hine, *The State of Afro-American History* (Baton Rouge, La., 1986); and August Meier and Elliott Rudwick, *Black History and the Historical Profession, 1915–1980* (Urbana, Ill., 1986). See also John Hope Franklin, *Race and History: Selected Essays, 1938–1988** (Baton Rouge, La., 1989).

More and more African Americans have become the subject of serious study, and numerous monographs have appeared that shed considerable light on their condition. While these works are specialized in subject matter, their scope in time or approach is sufficiently broad to warrant their consideration among the studies that are generally useful in works of this nature. The problems of adjustment and integration are extensively discussed in Myrdal, *An American Dilemma;* Melville J. Herskovits, *The American Negro: A Study in Racial Crossing** (New York, 1928); John G. Van Deusen, *Black Man in White America* (Washington, D.C., 1944); E. Franklin Frazier, *The Negro in the United States;* Maurice R. Davie, *Negroes in American Society* (New York, 1949); and Oscar Handlin, *Race and Nationality in American Life** (Boston, 1948). A wide-ranging effort to update the Myrdal study was made by the National Research Council, through the Committee on the Status of Black Americans, in a volume edited by Gerald David Jaynes and Robin M. Williams, Jr., *A Common Destiny: Blacks and American Society* (Washington, D.C., 1989). The pioneer study of the history and sociology of the black family is E. Franklin Frazier, *The Negro Family in the United States* (Chicago, 1939). A new and revisionist approach is Herbert Gutman, *The Black Family in Slavery and Freedom, 1750–1825** (New York, 1976). Sociobiological problems are treated in Samuel J. Holmes, *The Negro's Struggle for Survival: A Study in Human Ecology* (Berkeley, Calif., 1937) and Julian H. Lewis, *The Biology of the Negro* (Chicago, 1942).

The political and legal aspects of African-Americans' history and status have been treated in several books, among which are Paul Lewinson, *Race, Class and Party: A History of Negro Suffrage and White Politics in the South** (London, 1932); and Charles S. Mangum, *The Legal Status of the Negro* (Chapel Hill, N.C., 1940). More recent and more sophisticated are Pauli Murray, *States' Laws on Race and Color* (Cincinnati, 1950); V. O. Key, *Southern Politics in State and Nation** (New York, 1949); and Jack Greenberg, *Race Relations and American Law* (New York, 1959). Three works by Paul Finkelman should be consulted: *An Imperfect Union: Slavery, Federalism, and Comity* (Chapel Hill, N.C., 1981); *Slavery in the Courtroom* (Washington, D.C., 1985); and *The Law of Freedom and Bondage: A Casebook** (New York, 1986). A valuable study is A. Leon Higginbotham, Jr., *In the Matter of Color: Race and the American Legal Process* (New York, 1978). See also Howard Brotz, ed., *Negro Social and Political Thought, 1850–1920** (New York, 1966); Richard Bardolph, ed., *The Civil Rights Record: Black Americans and the Law, 1849–1970** (New York, 1970); Albert Blaustein and Robert Zangrando, eds., *Civil Rights and the American Negro: A Documentary History** (New York, 1968); and Herbert Storing, ed., *What Country Have I? Political Writings by Black Americans** (New York, 1970).

In the field of the economic history of African Americans, Charles H. Wesley, *Negro Labor in the United States, 1850–1925* (New York, 1927, reprinted 1967) is much more comprehensive than the title suggests, while *The Negro Wage Earner* (Washington, D.C., 1930) by Lorenzo J. Greene and Carter G. Woodson confines itself primarily to the history of black labor. A penetrating study of the history of African Americans and organized labor is the work by Sterling D. Spero and Abram L. Harris, *The Black*

Worker: The Negro and the Labor Movement* (New York, 1931); but for a very special aspect of the problem, see Herbert Hill, *Black Labor and the American Legal System** (Washington, D.C., 1977). Another phase of economic life is treated in Abram L. Harris, *The Negro as Capitalist: A Study of Banking and Business among American Negroes* (Philadelphia, 1936).

Among the better general studies on the social and intellectual history of African Americans are the following. For education, Horace M. Bond, *The Education of the Negro in the American Social Order* (New York, 1934, revised edition, 1965); Dwight O. W. Holmes, *The Evolution of the Negro College* (New York, 1934); and Henry Allen Bullock, *A History of Negro Education in the South from 1619 to the Present* (Cambridge, Mass., 1967). In the area of the fine arts, two works by Alain Locke, *Negro Art: Past and Present** (Washington, D.C., 1936) and *The Negro and His Music** (Washington, D.C., 1936) should be consulted, as well as James Porter, *Modern Negro Art* (New York, 1943) and Samella Lewis, *Art: African American* (New York, 1978). These works should be supplemented by use of the periodical *The International Review of African American Art* (formerly *Black Art*) edited by Samella Lewis. Significant recent works in the history of music are LeRoi Jones, *Blues People: Negro Music in White America** (New York, 1963); Eileen Southern, *The Music of Black Americans, A History** (New York, 1971); John Lovell, *Black Song: The Forge and the Flame* (New York, 1972); and Mildred Roach, *Black American Music: Past and Present* (Boston, 1973). The best studies in religion are Carter G. Woodson, *History of the Negro Church* (Washington, D.C., 1921); Benjamin E. Mays and Joseph W. Nicholson, *The Negro's Church* (New York, 1933); E. Franklin Frazier, *The Negro Church in America** (New York, 1963); Joseph R. Washington, *Black Religion** (Boston, 1964); C. Eric Lincoln and Lawrence H. Mamiya, *The Black Church In The African American Experience** (Durham, N.C., 1990); and Cyprian Davis, *The History of Black Catholics in the United States* (New York, 1990). The literary history of the Negro may be traced in Benjamin Brawley, *The Negro in Literature and Art in the United States*, third edition (New York, 1971); Vernon Loggins, *The Negro Author: His Development in America* (New York, 1931); Sterling Brown, *The Negro in American Fiction** (Washington, D.C., 1937); J. Saunders Redding, *To Make a Poet Black* (Chapel Hill, N.C., 1939); Hugh Gloster, *Negro Voices in American Fiction* (Chapel Hill, N.C., 1948); and Robert Bone, *The Negro Novel in America** (New Haven, Conn., 1958, revised edition, 1965). See also Seymour Gross and John E. Hardy, eds., *Images of the Negro in American Literature** (Chicago, 1966); Loften Mitchell, *Black Drama: The Story of the American Negro in the Theatre** (New York, 1967); and Edith J. R. Isaacs, *The Negro in the American Theater* (New York, 1947). Satisfactory collections of Negro writings are Otelia Cromwell and others, *Readings from Negro Authors* (New York, 1931); Sterling Brown and others, *The Negro Caravan* (New York, 1941); Ruth Miller, ed., *Black American Literature: 1760 to the Present** (Encino, Calif., 1971); Charles T. Davis and Daniel Walden, eds., *On Being Black; Writings by Afro-Americans from Frederick Douglass to the Present** (New York, 1970); and Robert Hayden and others, eds., *Afro-American Literature: A Thematic Reader** (New York, 1971). For representative recent writing, do not overlook Herbert Hill, *Soon One Morning: New Writing by American Negroes* (New York, 1963); Francis Kearns, ed., *The Black Experience: An Anthology of American Literature for the 1970s** (New York, 1971); Michael S. Harper and Robert B. Stepto, eds., *Chant of Saints: A Gathering of Afro-American Literature, Art, and Scholarship** (Urbana, Ill., 1979); Blyden Jackson, *A History of Afro-American Literature, Volume I: The Long Beginning, 1746–1895* (Baton Rouge, 1989). The pioneer study on African-American newspapers was done by Irvine Garland Penn in *The*

Afro-American Press and Its Editors (Springfield, 1891, reprinted 1975). Less encyclopedic but more critical is Frederick G. Detweiler, *The Negro Press in the United States* (Chicago, 1922). More recent treatments are Maxwell Brooks, *The Negro Press Re-examined* (Boston, 1959); and Jack Lyle, ed., *The Black American and the Press* (Los Angeles, 1968).

1. Land of Their Ancestors

Maurice Delafosse has made many important contributions to the history of African civilization. Among those that have been translated from the French is *The Negroes of Africa: History and Culture* (Washington, D.C., 1931), which contains a mine of information on the early African states. Carter G. Woodson, *Africa Background Outlined* (Washington, D.C., 1936) is excellent for its bibliographical and other study aids, while his *African Heroes and Heroines* (Washington, D.C., 1939) contains informal human interest accounts of many of the leaders in West Africa. Among the many works that Basil Davidson has written to illuminate the history of West Africa, *The Lost Cities of Africa** (Boston, 1959, revised edition, 1970) is especially valuable. Generally helpful works are Philip Curtin and others, *African History** (Boston, 1978); J. D. Fage, *A History of Africa** (New York, 1978); J. F. A. Ajayi and Michael Crowder, *History of West Africa* (London, 1976); and J. D. Fage and Roland Oliver, *Cambridge History of Africa* (Cambridge, 1975–1984). Du Bois' *Black Folk, Then and Now* has excellent chapters on the early African states. A classical and reliable description of the political and social scene may be found in the writings of a contemporary, Joannes Leo Africanus, *The History and Description of Africa* (London, 1896). A popular but generally reliable account of the early history of the Western Sudan is Flora Louisa Lugard, *A Tropical Dependency* (London, 1905).

In *Black Athena: The Afroasiatic Roots of Classical Civilization*, Volume 2: *The Archaeological and Documentary Evidence* (New Brunswick, N.J., 1991), Martin Bernal offers a complex and controversial argument that the culture and thought of ancient Greece were similar to and in many ways derived from the cultures of the darker peoples of the eastern and southern Mediterranean. For critical and qualifying responses to Bernal, see Molly M. Levine, "The Use and Abuse of *Black Athena*"; Robert L. Pounder, "*Black Athena 2:* History Without Rules"; and Janet J. Ewald, "Slavery in Africa and the Slave Trades in Africa" in "Review Articles," *American Historical Review*, LXXXXVII (April 1992).

2. The African Way of Life

Perhaps the best general accounts of the culture and civilization of West Africa in addition to those previously mentioned are to be found in Delafosse, *The Negroes of Africa;* Du Bois, *Black Folk, Then and Now;* Basil Davidson, *The African Past** (Boston, 1964); E. W. Bovill, *Golden Trade of the Moors** (New York, 1958, reprinted 1970); John K. Thornton, *The Kingdom of Kongo* (Madison, Wisc., 1983); Alia A. Mazrui, ed., *The Warrior Tradition in Modern Africa* (Leiden, 1977); and Woodson, *The African Background Outlined.* The works of Melville J. Herskovits in the field have long been regarded as highly significant. Among them are *Dahomey; An Ancient West African Kingdom,* two volumes (New York, 1938, reprinted 1967), a modern anthropological study that sheds considerable light on the earlier period, and "The Art of the Congo," *Opportunity,* V (May 1927). A provocative work by the same author is *Myth of the Negro Past** (New York, 1941, reprinted 1958), in which Herskovits contends that the blacks of West Africa had developed a complex civilization and that much of it survived in the New World. In this connection one should also read his "On the Provenience of the New World Negroes," *Social Forces,* XII (December 1933). George W. Ellis, *Negro Culture in West Africa* (New York, 1914, reprinted 1971) is valuable largely for its discussion of how an African group developed its own alphabet and written language. An important work dealing with various aspects of African culture, including the complex problem of language, is Robin Hallett, *Africa to 1875* (Ann Arbor, Mich., 1970). See also Basil Davidson, *The African Genius** (Boston, 1969) and John A. Davis, ed., *Africa from the Point of View of American Negro Scholars** (Paris, 1958). Three brief studies that emphasize the importance of the culture of Africans are Franz Boas, *Old African Civilizations* (Atlanta, 1906); James Weldon Johnson, *Native African Races and Culture* (Charlottesville, Va., 1927); and Roland F. Oliver, *Africa in the Iron Age* (Cambridge, 1975).

Special aspects of African culture are treated in *Harvard African Studies,* No. 1 (Cambridge, Mass., 1917) and No. 11 (Cambridge, Mass., 1918), edited by Oric Bates. These studies are especially satisfactory for their treatment of early African art and of implements. A. O. Stafford, "The Tarik E. Soudan," *Journal of Negro History,* II (April 1917) is a valuable study of an early African literary work. In addition to several works already mentioned, two special studies of African art will prove helpful. They are James J. Sweeney, *African Negro Art* (New York, 1935) and Frank Willett, *African Art* (London, 1971).

3. The Slave Trade and the New World

Of the works dealing with the history of the slave trade, there is nothing to compare with the monumental four-volume work of Elizabeth Donnan, *Documents Illustrative of the History of the Slave Trade to America* (Washington, D.C., 1930–1935). The introductions to each volume provide a most satisfactory running account of the traffic, and the notes on the documents themselves illuminate the period considerably. A good general account of the trade is presented in Daniel R. Mannix, *Black Cargoes: A History of the Atlantic Slave Trade, 1518–1865** (New York, 1962). See also Basil Davidson, *Black Mother: The Years of the African Slave Trade** (London, 1961). An exhaustive examination of the slave trade in terms of numbers involved, sources of supply, and distribution in the New World is Philip D. Curtin, *The Atlantic Slave Trade: A Census** (Madison, Wisc., 1969). A vigorous challenge to what he calls Curtin's underestimation is in J. E. Inikori, "Measuring the African Slave Trade: A Rejoinder," *Journal of African History,* XVII (No. 4, 1976). Another valuable work is Peter Duignan and Clarence Clendenen, *The United States and the African Slave Trade, 1619–1862* (Westport, Conn., 1963). The significance of the trade in the growth of capitalistic enterprise is discussed in Wilson E. Williams, *Africa and the Rise of Capitalism** (Washington, D.C., 1938) and Eric Williams, *Capitalism and Slavery** (Chapel Hill, N.C., 1944). Two pioneer works that give some attention to the slave trade are W. E. B. Du Bois, *Suppression of the African Slave Trade to the United States, 1638–1870** (Cambridge, Mass., 1896, reprinted 1969) and U. B. Phillips, *American Negro Slavery** (New York, 1918). Herbert S. Klein, *The Middle Passage: Comparative Studies in the Atlantic Slave Trade* (Princeton, N.J., 1978), is most valuable for perspective and balance. Specific phases of the trade are discussed in several papers published in the *Journal of Negro History:* Jerome Dowd, "The African Slave Trade," II (January 1917); George F. Zook, "The Company of Royal Adventurers Trading in Africa," IV (April 1919); Luther P. Jackson, "Elizabethan Seamen and the African Slave Trade," IX (January 1924); and Eric Williams, "The Golden Age of the Slave System in Britain," XXV (January 1940).

For a discussion of Africans in the New World before Columbus, see Leo Wiener, *Africa and the Discovery of America,* three volumes (Philadelphia, 1922); Harold G. Lawrence, "African Explorers of the New World," *The Crisis,* CLIX (June–July 1962); and Ivan Van Sertima, *They Came Before Columbus* (New York, 1976). The participation of blacks in the exploration of the New World first received attention at the hands of Richard R. Wright in an article published in *The American Anthropologist* in 1902. It is reprinted under the title, "Negro Companions of the Spanish Explorers," *Phylon,* II (Fourth Quarter 1941), to which Rayford W. Logan has appended some valuable notes. Other papers on the subject include J. F. Rippy, "The Negro and Spanish Pioneers in the New World," *Journal of Negro History,* VI (April 1921); James B. Browning, "Negro Companions of the Spanish Pioneers in the New World," *Howard University Studies in History* (Washington, D.C., 1930); and Rayford W. Logan, "Estevanico, Negro Discoverer of the Southwest," *Phylon,* I (Fourth Quarter 1940).

The horrors of the middle passage are described in several of the preceding works, notably in the *Documents* edited by Donnan and in the work by Phillips. See also Du Bois, *Black Folk, Then and Now;* Weatherford, *The Negro from Africa to America;* and Mannix, *Black Cargoes.* H. A. Wyndham, *The Atlantic and Slavery* (London, 1935), deals in a scholarly manner with this and many other aspects of the slave trade. The effect of the slave trade on the future of Africa is treated by a number of scholars in J. E. Inikori, ed., *Forced Migration: The Impact of the Export Slave Trade on African Societies* (New York, 1982).

One of the most important works in the economic history of the Caribbean is Lowell J. Ragatz, *The Fall of the Planter Class in the British Caribbean* (New York, 1928), in which ample attention is given to the institution of slavery. The rivalry of the European countries is treated by Arthur P. Newton, *The European Nations in the West Indies, 1493–1688* (London, 1933). For the treatment of slavery on an important British island, see W. J. Gardner, *A History of Jamaica* (London, 1909). Herbert S. Klein, *Slavery in the Americas* (Chicago, 1967) compares slavery in Cuba with slavery in Virginia. A fresh approach is in David Barry Gaspar, *Bondmen and Rebels: A Study of Master-Slave Relations in Antigua* (Baltimore, 1985). There are several important essays on the West Indies in Laura Foner and Eugene Genovese, eds., *Slavery in the New World: A Reader in Comparative History* (Englewood Cliffs, N.J., 1969).

Among general works on Latin America that give some attention to various aspects of life among Africans in the New World are Charles E. Chapman, *Colonial Hispanic America: A History* (New York, 1933) and Bernard Moses, *South America on the Eve of Emancipation* (New York, 1908). Considerable statistical data as well as provocative interpretations are provided in Frank Tannenbaum, *Slave and Citizen** (New York, 1947). Especially important are Herbert S. Klein, *Slavery in the Americas* (Chicago, 1967); David B. Davis, *The Problem of Slavery in Western Culture* (Ithaca,

N.Y., 1966); and Franklin W. Knight, *The African Dimension in Latin American Societies* (Madison, Wisc., 1970).

The literature on Brazil is abundant. Among the more important pioneer works of scholarship are the following: Gilberto Freyre, *The Masters and the Slaves: A Study in the Development of Brazilian Civilization** (New York, 1946); Donald Pierson, *Negroes in Brazil, A Study of Race Contact at Bahia* (Chicago, 1942); Florestan Fernandes, *The Negro in Brazilian Society* (New York, 1969); Robert B. Toplin, *The Abolition of Slavery in Brazil* (New York, 1972); and Carl N. Degler, *Neither Black Nor White: Slavery and Race Relations in Brazil and the United States** (New York, 1971). C. R. Boxer, *The Golden Age of Brazil, 1695–1750: Growing Pains of a Colonial Society* (Berkeley, Calif., 1969) contains many valuable insights and interpretations.

4. Colonial Slavery

A good way to begin a study of Africans in the English colonies is with David B. Davis, *The Problem of Slavery in Western Culture* (Ithaca, N.Y., 1966) and Winthrop Jordan, *White over Black; American Attitudes toward the Negro, 1550–1812** (Chapel Hill, N.C., 1968). See also Gary B. Nash and Richard Weiss, eds., *The Great Fear: Race in the Mind of America** (New York, 1970). A clear exposition of this period is in Donald R. Wright, *African Americans in the Colonial Era: From African Origins Through the American Revolution* (Arlington Heights, Ill., 1990). The view that the first blacks in Virginia were servants rather than slaves is set forth by John H. Russell in *The Free Negro in Virginia, 1619–1865** (Baltimore, 1913). Details concerning the early years of slavery in Virginia are provided in James C. Ballagh, *A History of Slavery in Virginia* (Baltimore, 1902), while *The Negro in Virginia* (New York, 1940) by the Writers' Program of the Work Projects Administration furnishes valuable additional information. See also Thad W. Tate, Jr., *The Negro in Eighteenth-Century Williamsburg** (Williamsburg, Va., 1965); Gerald W. Mullin, *Flight and Rebellion: Slave Resistance in Eighteenth-Century Virginia** (New York, 1972); and T. H. Breen and Stephen Innes, *"Myne Owne Ground": Race and Freedom on Virginia's Eastern Shore, 1640–1676** (New York, 1980). Jeffrey R. Brackett, *The Negro in Maryland: A Study of the Institution of Slavery* (Baltimore, 1889) gives the essential information concerning slavery in that colony. The problem for North Carolina has been treated by John Spencer Bassett in *Slavery and Servitude in the Colony of North Carolina* (Baltimore, 1896), but Guion G. Johnson, *Antebellum North Carolina* (Chapel Hill, N.C., 1937) deals most satisfactorily with the colonial as well as the later period. Frank J. Klingberg, *An Appraisal of the Negro in Colonial South Carolina* (Washington, D.C., 1941, reprinted 1975) is a pioneer modern treatment, but one must also study carefully Peter Wood's *Black Majority: Negroes in Colonial South Carolina from 1670 through the Stono Rebellion** (New York, 1974) and Daniel F. Littlefield, *Rice and Slaves: Ethnicity and the Slave Trade in Colonial South Carolina* (Baton Rouge, La., 1981). A special problem is treated in Thomas J. Davis, *A Rumor of Revolt: The Great Negro Plot in Colonial New York* (New York, 1985). Beginnings in Georgia are covered in Ralph B. Flanders, *Plantation Slavery in Georgia* (Chapel Hill, N.C., 1933). A more modern and up-to-date version is Betty Wood, *Slavery in Colonial Georgia, 1730–1775* (Athens, Ga., 1984). Marcus W. Jernegan, *Laboring and Dependent Classes in Colonial America, 1607–1783* (Chicago, 1931) illuminates many aspects of the problem.

The social and economic life of Negroes in early New York is treated in Samuel McKee, *Labor in Colonial New York, 1664–1776* (New York, 1935) and Edwin V. Morgan, *Slavery in New York* (Washington, D.C., 1891). William R. Riddell, "The Slave in Early New York," *Journal of Negro History*, XIII (January 1928) is a valuable addition to the literature. Another useful study is Edgar J. McManus, *A History of Negro Slavery in New York* (Syracuse, N.Y. 1966). Henry S. Cooley, *A Study of Slavery in New Jersey* (Baltimore, 1896, reprinted 1973); Marion T. Wright, *Education of Negroes in New Jersey* (New York, 1941) and "New Jersey Laws and the Negro," *Journal of Negro History*, XXVIII (April 1943) by the same author all shed considerable light on blacks in that colony. Standard works on Pennsylvania are Edward R. Turner, *The Negro in Pennsylvania* (Washington, D.C., 1911, reprinted 1969) and Jean R. Soderlund, *Quakers and Slavery: A Divided Spirit* (New York, 1985). For an excellent survey of some works on the early history of African Americans see Peter Wood, "'I Did the Best I Could for My Day': The Study of Early Black History during the Second Reconstruction, 1960 to 1976," *William and Mary Quarterly*, Third Series, XXXV (April 1978).

The most important single volume dealing with slavery in the New England colonies is Lorenzo J. Greene, *The Negro in Colonial New England** (New York, 1942). Valuable studies on individual states are George H. Moore's anti-Puritan *Notes on Slavery in Massachusetts* (New York, 1866); William Johnston, *Slavery in Rhode Island, 1755–1776* (Providence, 1894); Edward Channing, *The Narragansett Planters* (Baltimore, 1886, reprinted 1973); and Bernard C. Steiner, *History of Slavery in Connecticut* (Baltimore, 1893). An interesting sidelight on New England social history is provided in Lorenzo J. Greene, "The New England Negro as Seen in Advertisements for Runaway Slaves," *Journal of Negro History*, XXIX (April 1944). Two general works are valuable: Edmund Morgan, *American Slavery, American Freedom* (New York, 1975) and Jack P. Greene and J. R. Pole, *Colonial British America: Essays in the New History of the Early Modern Era* (New York, 1984).

Two studies that put forth the provocative argument that Christianity in the British North American colonies played a crucial role in the construction of racist thought and practice in the future United States are H. Shelton Smith, *In His Image, But . . . : Racism in Southern Religion, 1780–1910* (Durham, N.C., 1972) and Forrest G. Wood, *The Arrogance of Faith: Christianity and Race in America from the Colonial Era to the Twentieth Century* (New York, 1990).

5. That All May Be Free

The outstanding work covering the period of the American Revolution is Benjamin Quarles, *The Negro in the American Revolution** (Chapel Hill, N.C., 1961). The paradoxes of slavery and the revolutionary philosophy are discussed in George Livermore, *An Historical Research Respecting the Opinions of the Founders of the Republic on Negroes as Slaves, as Citizens, and as Soldiers* (Boston, 1862); George H. Moore, *Historical Notes on the Employment of Negroes in the American Army of the Revolution* (New York, 1862); Walter H. Mazyck, *George Washington and the Negro* (Washington, D.C., 1932); Duncan J. MacLeod, *Slavery, Race and the American Revolution** (Cambridge, 1975); and Ira Berlin and Ronald Hoffman, *Slavery and Freedom in the Age of the American Revolution* (Charlottesville, Va., 1983). In Sylvia Frey's study, *Water From the Rock: Black Resistance In a Revolutionary Age* (Princeton, N.J., 1991), white southerners' fight for independence is secondary to their struggle to retain control of their slave property and to preserve order. Two works that argue that the failure to rid the former British colonies of slavery lay as much with white northerners as with white southerners are Gary B. Nash, *Freedom and Revolution* (Madison, Wisc., 1991) and Gary B. Nash and Jean R. Soderlund, *Freedom by Degrees: Emancipation in Pennsylvania and Its Aftermath* (New York, 1991). A useful study of emancipation in northern cities is Shane White, *Somewhat More Independent: The End of Slavery in New York City, 1770–1810* (Athens, Ga., 1991). Among the studies of African Americans as fighters in the War for Independence, the following are outstanding: William C. Nell, *The Colored Patriots of the American Revolution* (Boston, 1855) and Luther P. Jackson, "Virginia Negro Soldiers and Seamen in the American Revolution," *Journal of Negro History,* XXVII (July 1942). In George W. Williams, *A History of the Negro Troops in the War of the Rebellion* (New York, 1887) and Joseph T. Wilson, *The Black Phalanx* (Hartford, Conn., 1888) there are chapters on black soldiers in the War for Independence. A unique work with numerous authentic illustrations is Sidney Kaplan, *The Black Presence in the Era of the American Revolution, 1770–1800** (Boston, 1973).

The antislavery movement in the Revolutionary period is treated in Quarles, *The Negro in the American Revolution,* as well as in Mary S. Locke, *Antislavery in America* (Boston, 1901). More recent scholarship on the subject is in Arthur Zilversmit, *The First Emancipation: The Abolition of Slavery in the North** (Chicago, 1967) and David Brion Davis, *The Problem of Slavery in the Age of Revolution* (Ithaca, N.Y., 1975). See also William Cohen, "Thomas Jefferson and the Problem of Slavery," *Journal of American History,* LVI (December 1968) and Paul Finkelman, "Jefferson and Slavery" 'Treason against the Hopes of the World'," in Peter S. Onuf, *Jeffersonian Legacies* (Charlottesville, Va., 1993). Important for its interpretation is John Franklin Jameson, *The American Revolution Considered as a Social Movement* (Princeton, N.J., 1926). Charles A. Beard, *An Economic Interpretation of the Constitution of the United States* (New York, 1913) is an excellent interpretation of the problem of slavery at the Constitutional Convention. See also Staughton Lynd, *Class Conflict, Slavery, and the United States Constitution** (Indianapolis, Ind., 1967). One of the best brief accounts of the convention is Max Farrand, *The Framing of the Constitution* (New Haven, Conn., 1913), but there is no substitute for the monumental *Records of the Federal Convention of 1787,* three volumes (New Haven, Conn., 1911), edited by Max Farrand. It contains much discussion on the status of blacks at the time that has not been extensively used in other works.

6. Blacks in the New Republic

The best source of information concerning the numbers and distribution of the black population is the publication by the United States Bureau of the Census, *Negro Population, 1790–1915* (Washington, D.C., 1918), while significant changes of an economic and social nature are dealt with in Charles A. Beard, *Economic Origins of Jeffersonian Democracy* (New York, 1915) and in Ira Berlin, "Time, Space, and the Evolution of Afro-American Society on British Mainland North America," *American Historical Review,* 85, 1 (February, 1980). An excellent general treatment is Donald R. Wright, *African Americans in the Early Republic, 1789–1831* (Arlington Heights, Ill., 1993). One should not overlook Robert McColley, *Slavery and Jeffersonian Virginia,**

second edition (Urbana, Ill., 1974). The impact of the Industrial Revolution on slavery is treated in Lewis C. Gray, *History of Agriculture in the Southern United States to 1860* (Washington, D.C., 1933). The uprising in the Caribbean is vividly described in C. L. R. James, *The Black Jacobins: Toussaint Louverture and the San Domingo Revolution* (New York, 1938). *The Suppression of the African Slave Trade* by W. E. B. Du Bois is an early but still authoritative account of the movement to close the slave trade.

Brief discussions of the works of early black writers are given in Benjamin Brawley, *Early Negro American Writers* (Chapel Hill, N.C., 1935); Brown and others, *The Negro Caravan;* and Dorothy B. Porter, ed., *Early Negro Writings, 1760–1837* (Boston, 1971). The following are satisfactory treatments of individual Negroes: Edward D. Seeber, "Phillis Wheatley," *Journal of Negro History,* XXIV (July 1939); Henry Baker, "Benjamin Banneker, Negro Mathematician and Astronomer," *Journal of Negro History,* III (April 1918); P. L. Phillips, "The Negro, Benjamin Banneker: Astronomer and Mathematician," *Records of the Columbia Historical Society,* XX (Washington, D.C., 1917); H. N. Sherwood, "Paul Cuffe," *Journal of Negro History,* VIII (April 1923); and W. H. Morse, "Lemuel Haynes," *Journal of Negro History,* IV (January 1919). Essays of Phillis Wheatley and George Moses Horton are in M. A. Richmond, *Bid the Vassal Soar* (Washington, D.C., 1974). One treatment of Cuffe is Sheldon H. Harris, *Paul Cuffe, Black America and the African Return** (New York, 1972). The most recent, however, is Lamont D. Thomas, *Rise to Be a People, A Biography of Paul Cuffe* (Champaign, Ill., 1986). For discussions of education, see Carter G. Woodson, *Education of the Negro Prior to 1861* (New York, 1915) and Charles C. Andrews, *History of the New York African Free Schools* (New York, 1830). The best accounts of the origins of black religious constitutions are Woodson, *History of the Negro Church;* Charles H. Wesley, *Richard Allen, Apostle of Freedom* (Washington, D.C., 1935); and Mechal Sobel, *Traveling On: The Slave Journal to an Afro-Baptist Faith* (Westport, Conn., 1979). For information on African-American Masonry, see George W. Crawford, *Prince Hall and His Followers* (New York, 1914) and William Upton, *Negro Masonry* (Cambridge, 1902, reprinted 1975). A useful study of blacks in an urban setting is Gary B. Nash, *Forging Freedom: The Formation of Philadelphia's Black Community, 1720–1840* (New York, 1988).

7. Blacks and Manifest Destiny

Frontier influences are treated in a series of highly significant essays in Frederick J. Turner, *The Frontier in American History* (New York, 1920). William Loren Katz, *The Black West** (New York, 1971) is a documentary and pictorial history of African Americans in the westward movement. Two other works on the subject are Kenneth W. Porter, *The Negro on the American Frontier* (New York, 1971) and W. Sherman Savage, *Blacks in the West* (Westport, Conn., 1976). The movement of African Americans into frontier areas has also been discussed in several essays in the *Journal of Negro History,* among which are the following: Eugene P. Southall, "Negroes in Florida Prior to the Civil War," XIX (January 1934); Harry E. Davis, "John Malvin, A Western Reserve Pioneer," XXIII (October 1938); Alrutheus A. Taylor, "The Movement of Negroes from the East to the Gulf States from 1830 to 1850," VIII (October 1923); and Carter G. Woodson, "Freedom and Slavery in Appalachian America," I (April 1916). The War of 1812 is treated in Laura E. Wilkes, *Missing Pages* *in American History* (Washington, D.C., 1919); George W. Williams, *A History of Negro Troops in the War of the Rebellion* (New York, 1888); Roland McConnell, *Negro Troops in Antebellum Louisiana* (Baton Rouge, La., 1968); and Wilson, *The Black Phalanx.* William C. Nell, *Services of Colored Americans in the Wars of 1776 and 1812* (Boston, 1851) should also be read.

The growth of the cotton kingdom is treated in William E. Dodd, *The Cotton Kingdom* (New Haven, Conn., 1919); Gray, *History of Agriculture in the Southern United States;* Frederick J. Turner, *Rise of the New West* (New York, 1906); and Ulrich B. Phillips, *American Negro Slavery** (New York, 1918). For a critical discussion of the highly questionable conclusions reached by Phillips, see Richard Hofstadter, "U. B. Phillips and the Plantation Legend," *Journal of Negro History,* XXIX (April 1944). The influence of the doctrine of Manifest Destiny on the emergence of the cotton kingdom is handled in Albert K. Weinberg, *Manifest Destiny, A Study of National Expansionism in American History** (Baltimore, 1935). Most of the works on slavery deal with the domestic slave trade, but the best account is in Frederick Bancroft, *Slave Trading in the Old South** (Baltimore, 1931). W. H. Stephenson, *Isaac Franklin, Slave Trader and Planter of the Old South* (University, La., 1938) is an important supplement. See also William T. Laprade, "The Domestic Slave Trade in the District of Columbia," *Journal of Negro History,* XI (January 1926). For discussions of the persistence of the African Trade, see Du Bois, *Suppression of the African Slave Trade;* Charles H. Wesley, "Manifests of Slave Shipments along the Waterways, 1808–1864," *Journal of Negro History,* XXVII (April 1942); and Eric Williams, "The British West Indian Slave Trade after Its Abolition in 1807," *Journal of Negro History,* XXVII (April 1942).

8. That Peculiar Institution

Most of the works on slavery in the United States should be read with critical care because of their tendency to emphasize the large plantation at the expense of the smaller unit, on which most of the slaves were to be found. A convenient and reliable reference is Randall M. Miller and John David Smith, eds., *Dictionary of Afro-American Slavery* (New York, 1968). A monumental work on the subject is the several volumes by David Brion Davis beginning with *The Problem of Slavery in Western Culture* (Ithaca, N.Y., 1960). For a detached view of how United States historians deal with slavery, see the work by British historian Peter J. Parish, *Slavery: History and Historians* (New York, 1989). Ulrich B. Phillips, *Life and Labor in the Old South** (Boston, 1929), like his *American Negro Slavery,* tends to apologize for the institution.

Kenneth M. Stampp, *The Peculiar Institution** (New York, 1956) is a more exhaustive study of slavery that takes sharp issue with Phillips on many points. Eugene D. Genovese, *The Political Economy of Slavery** (New York, 1965) discusses slavery as a part of a total way of life in the South. See also his *The World the Slaveholders Made** (New York, 1971). His *Roll, Jordan, Roll: The World the Slaves Made** (New York, 1974) is an extensive examination of slave life and the relationship of masters to it. The most recent and one of the best general treatments of slavery is Peter Kolchin, *American Slavery, 1619–1877* (New York, 1993). In *Slavery and Freedom: An Interpretation of the Old South* (New York, 1990), James Oakes argues that the Civil War was a conflict rooted in the fundamentals of capitalistic society, a salient feature of the slave system. Discussions of the development of culture and institutions from the slave perspective are found in John Blassingame, *The Slave Community, Plantation Life in the Antebellum South** (New York, 1974); Leslie Howard Owens, *This Species of Property: Slave Life and Culture in the Old South** (New York, 1976); Thomas L. Webber, *Deep Like the Rivers: Education in the Slave Quarter Community, 1831–1865** (New York, 1978); and Charles Joyner, *Down by the Riverside: A South Carolina Slave Community* (Urbana, Ill., 1984). See also Blassingame's *Slave Testimony: Two Centuries of Letters, Speeches, Interviews, and Autobiographies** (Baton Rouge, La., 1977). Stanley Elkins, *Slavery: A Problem in American Institutional and Intellectual Life,** third edition (Chicago, 1976), is concerned primarily with the effect of slavery on personality. For a critical discussion of the Elkins thesis, see Ann J. Lane, ed., *The Debate over Slavery: Stanley Elkins and His Critics** (Urbana, Ill., 1971). Richard C. Wade, *Slavery in the Cities: The South 1820–1860** (New York, 1964) argues that slavery in urban areas was different in virtually every way from slavery in rural areas. A counterargument is advanced in Claudia D. Goldin, *Urban Slavery in the American South, 1820–1860: A Quantitative History* (Chicago, 1976). For a discussion of the problem of determining the profitability of slavery, see Alfred H. Conrad and John R. Meyer, *The Economics of Slavery and Other Econometric Studies* (Chicago, 1964) and Robert W. Fogel and Stanley L. Engerman, eds., *The Reinterpretation of American Economic History* (New York, 1971). See also Thomas P. Govan, "Was Plantation Slavery Profitable," *Journal of Southern History,* VII (November 1942) and Harold D. Woodman, "The Profitability of Slavery: A Historical Perennial," *Journal of Southern History,* XXIX (August 1963). An excellent recent addition to this discussion is Michael Tadman, *Speculators and Slaves: Masters, Traders, and Slaves in the Old South* (Madison, Wisc., 1989). In *Time on the Cross,* two volumes (New York, 1974), Robert Fogel and Stanley Engerman make greater claims for the mitigating factors in slavery than they are able to prove. Among the several critical analyses of their position see Paul David and others, *Reckoning with Slavery: A Critical Study in the Quantitative History of American Negro Slavery* (New York, 1976) and Herbert Gutman, *Slavery and the Numbers Game: A Critique of Time on the Cross* (Urbana, Ill., 1975). Other problems of management are discussed in John S. Bassett, *The Southern Plantation Overseer as Revealed in His Letters* (Northampton, Mass., 1925, reprinted 1968) and in William L. Van Deburg, *The Slave Drivers: Black Agricultural Labor Supervisors in the Ante-Bellum South** (Westport, Conn., 1979). Janet Duitsman Cornelius, *"When I Can Read My Title Clear": Literacy, Slavery, and Religion in the Antebellum South* (Columbia, S.C., 1991) is an important contribution to this subject.

The following are among the more satisfactory discussions of slavery in specific states: Guion Johnson, *Ante-Bellum North Carolina;* Charles S. Sydnor, *Slavery in Mississippi* (New York, 1933); Roger W. Shugg, *Origins of Class Struggle in Louisiana** (University, La., 1939); Chase C. Mooney, *Slavery in Tennessee** (Bloomington, Ind., 1957); J. Winston Coleman, *Slavery Times in Kentucky* (Chapel Hill, N.C., 1940); Harrison A. Trexler, *Slavery in Missouri, 1804–1865* (Baltimore, 1914); James B. Sellers, *Slavery in Alabama* (University, Ala., 1950); Julian Floyd Smith, *Slavery and Plantation Growth in Antebellum Florida, 1821–1860* (Gainesville, Fla., 1973); and Orville W. Taylor, *Negro Slavery in Arkansas* (Durham, N.C., 1958). One of the very best treatments of slavery in one state that goes beyond the borders of the state is Ann Patton Malone, *Sweet Chariot, Slave Family and Household Structure in Nineteenth Century Louisiana* (Chapel Hill, N.C., 1992). The best travel account, more authoritative than many secondary works, is Frederick L. Olmsted, *The Cotton Kingdom: A Traveller's Observations on Cotton and Slavery in the American Slave States,* two volumes (New York, 1861). A special aspect of slavery in treated in Robert S. Starobin, *Industrial Slavery in the Old South** (New York, 1970).

The laws affecting slaves are summarized in John C. Hurd, *Law of Freedom and Bondage in the United States,* two volumes (Boston, 1858), while interpretations of the law may be found in Helen T. Catterall, ed., *Judicial Cases Concerning American Slavery and the Negro,* five volumes (Washington, D.C., 1926). Howell M. Henry, *The Police Control of the Slave in South Carolina* (Emory, Va., 1914) and Wilbert E. Moore, "Slave Law and the Social Structure," *Journal of Negro History,* XXVI (April 1941) discuss the problem of enforcing the Black Codes. Numerous slaves have told of their own experiences, often with the assistance of others. *The Narrative of Frederick Douglass** (Boston, 1845) is the best known; another is *Father Henson's Story of His Own Life* (Boston, 1858). A remarkable document is Harriet A. Jacobs, *Incidents in the Life of a Slave Girl Written by Herself,* edited by Jean F. Yellin (Cambridge, Mass., 1987). The reminiscences of several slaves are recorded in the following works: B. A. Botkin, ed., *Lay My Burden Down: A Folk History of Slavery** (Chicago, 1945); George P. Rawick, *The American Slave: A Composite Autobiography,* nineteen volumes (Westport, Conn., 1971); Arna Bontemps, ed., *Great Slave Narratives** (Boston, 1969); Gilbert Osofsky, ed., *Puttin' on Ole Massa** (New York, 1969); and Charles H. Nichols, *Many Thousand Gone** (Bloomington, Ind., 1969). Evaluations of the importance of the narrative are in Marion W. Starling, *The Slave Narrative: Its Place in American History* (Boston, 1981); John Sekora and Darwin T. Turner, eds., *The Art of Slave Narrative: Original Essays in Criticism and Theory* (Macomb, Ill. 1983); and Charles T. Davis and Henry L. Gates, *The Slave's Narrative* (New York, 1985).

The problems of the slave family are discussed in Frazier, *The Negro Family in the United States,* and Gutman, *The Black Family in Slavery and Freedom.* See also Deborah Gray White, *Ar'nt I a Woman? Female Slaves in the Plantation South* (New York, 1985). See Elizabeth Fox Genovese, *Within the Plantation Household: Black and White Women of the Old South* (Chapel Hill, N.C., 1989) that argues that a special relationship existed between female members of the ownership class and those who were slaves. Melton McLaurin, *Celia, A Slave* (Athens, Ga., 1992) examines a female slave's resistance to sexual exploitation. A special aspect of social relationships is considered in E. Ophelia Settle, "Slave Attitudes during the Slave Regime: Household Servants versus Field Hands," *Publications of the American Sociological Society,* XXVIII (1934). The relationships of slaves with others is discussed in several works, including the following: James H. Johnston, *Race Relations in Virginia and Miscegenation in the South, 1776–1860* (Amherst, Mass., 1970); Carter G. Woodson, "Beginnings of the Miscegenation of the Whites and Blacks," *Journal of Negro History,* III (October 1918); Avery O. Craven, "Poor Whites and Negroes in the Antebellum South," *Journal of Negro History,* XV (January 1930); and Kenneth W. Porter, "Relations between Negroes and Indians within the Present Limits of the United States," *Journal of Negro History,* XVII (July 1932). In addition to Woodson, *History of the Negro Church,* Henry J. Cadbury, "Negro Membership in the Society of Friends," *Journal of Negro History,* XXI (April 1936) and Luther P. Jackson, "Religious Development of the Negro in Virginia from 1760 to 1860," *Journal of Negro History,* XVI (April 1931) may be read with profit. Albert Raboteau, *Slave Religion: The Invisible Institution in the Antebellum South* (New York, 1978), with its careful discussion of African survivals, brings a fresh perspective to this discussion, while Jon Butler, *Awash in a Sea of Faith: Christianizing the American People* (Cambridge, Mass., 1990) focuses on the ways in which Christianity eliminated African religious practices. For a discussion of the origins of spirituals and work songs, see Miles M. Fisher, *Negro Slave Songs in the United States** (Ithaca, N.Y., 1953). An interesting form of slave recreation is handled in Ira DeA. Reid, "The John Canoe Festival," *Phylon,* III (Fourth Quarter 1942). For a stimulating discussion of the influence of Africa on slave culture, see Sterling Stuckey, *Slave Culture: Nationalist Theory and the Foundations of Black America** (New York, 1987). See also Barbara H. Fields, *Slavery and Freedom on the Middle Ground: Maryland during the Nineteenth Century* (New Haven, Conn., 1985).

The best account of resistance to slavery is Herbert Aptheker, *American Negro Slave Revolts** (New York, 1943). His "Maroons within the Present Limits of the United States," *Journal of Negro History*, XXIV (April 1939) is also valuable. Other studies are Joseph C. Carroll, *Slave Insurrections in the United States, 1800–1860* (Boston, 1938); Nicholas Halasz, *Rattling Chains: Slave Unrest and Revolt in the Antebellum South* (New York, 1966); Raymond and Alice Bauer, "Day to Day Resistance to Slavery," *Journal of Negro History*, XXVII (October 1942); Lorenzo J. Greene, "Mutiny on the Slave Ships," *Phylon*, V (Fourth Quarter 1944); Vincent Harding, "Religion and Resistance among Ante-Bellum Negroes, 1800–1860," in August Meier and Elliott Rudwick, eds., *The Making of Black America*, Volume I* (New York, 1969); and Gerald W. Mullin, *Flight and Rebellion: Slave Resistance in Eighteenth Century Virginia* (New York, 1972). An engrossing account of one slave uprising is contained in John Lofton, *Insurrection in South Carolina: The Turbulent World of Denmark Vesey* (Yellow Springs, Ohio, 1964), but see also Richard Wade, "The Vesey Plot: A Reconsideration," *Journal of Southern History*, XXX (May 1964). William Styron's novel, *The Confessions of Nat Turner** (New York, 1966), was bitterly assailed by many, and the principal attacks may be found in John Henrik Clarke, ed., *William Styron's Nat Turner: Ten Black Writers Respond** (Boston, 1968). See also John B. Duff and Peter M. Mitchell, eds., *The Nat Turner Rebellion: The Historical Event and the Modern Controversy** (New York, 1971). Surprisingly little has been written on runaway slaves beyond several volumes of advertisements for fugitives. But see Freddie L. Parker, *Running for Freedom: Slave Runaways in North Carolina, 1775–1840* (New York, 1993) and Michael P. Johnson, "Runaway Slaves and the Slave Community in South Carolina, 1799–1830," *William and Mary Quarterly*, Third Series, XXXVIII (July 1981).

9. Quasi-Free Blacks

The first full-length general treatment of free blacks is Ira Berlin, *Slaves without Masters: The Free Negro in the Antebellum South** (New York, 1975). A detailed study of free blacks in one locale is offered in Michael P. Johnson and James L. Roark's two books, *No Chariot Let Down: Charleston's Free People of Color on the Eve of the Civil War* (Chapel Hill, N.C., 1984) and *Black Masters: A Free Family of Color in the Old South* (New York, 1984). See also Larry Koger, *Black Slaveowners: Free Black Slave Masters in South Carolina* (Jefferson, N.C., 1985) and Loren Schweninger, *Black Property Owners in the South, 1790–1915* (Urbana, Ill., 1990). An excellent summary statement concerning the group is found in Carter G. Woodson, *Free Negro Heads of Families in the United States in 1830* (Washington, D.C., 1925). The problem in the North is treated in Leon Litwack, *North of Slavery, The Negro in the Free States, 1790–1860** (Chicago, 1961); Emma L. Thornbrough, *The Negro in Indiana, A Study of a Minority* (Indianapolis, Ind., 1957); James Oliver Horton and Lois Horton, *Black Bostonians: Family Life and Community Struggle in the Ante-Bellum North** (New York, 1979); James Oliver Horton, *Free People of Color: Inside the African American Community* (Washington, D.C., 1993); Leonard P. Curry, *The Free Black in Urban America, 1800–1850* (Chicago, 1981); and

Robert Cottrol, *The Afro-Yankees: Providence's Black Community in the Ante-Bellum Era* (New York, 1982). Information on Southern free black women is presented in Suzanne Lebsock, *The Free Women of Petersburg: Status and Culture in a Southern Town* (New York, 1984) and Ellen N. Lawson and Marlene D. Merrill, *The Three Sarahs: Documents on Antebellum Black-College Women* (Lewiston, N.Y., 1984). Several monographs deal with the subject in different states. They are James M. Wright, *The Free Negro in Maryland, 1634–1860* (New York, 1921); John Russell, *The Free Negro in Virginia, 1619–1865** (Baltimore, 1913); Luther P. Jackson, *Free Negro Labor and Property Holding in Virginia, 1830–1860** (New York, 1942); H. E. Sterkx, *The Free Negro in Antebellum Louisiana* (Rutherford, N.J., 1972); Edward F. Sweat, *Economics Status of Free Blacks in Antebellum Georgia* (Atlanta, 1974); and John Hope Franklin, *The Free Negro in North Carolina, 1790–1860** (Chapel Hill, N.C., 1943). For a discussion of free blacks in the nation's capital, see Letitia Woods Brown, *Free Negroes in the District of Columbia, 1790–1846* (New York, 1972) and James Borchert, *Alley Life in Washington, D.C.: Family, Community, Religion and Folklife in the City, 1850–1870* (Urbana, Ill., 1980). A rare personal testimony is found in W. R. Hogan and E. A. Davis, eds., *William Johnson's Natchez: The Ante-Bellum Diary of a Free Negro* (Baton Rouge, La., 1951). Briefer works deal with free blacks in other localities: E. Horace Fitchett, "The Origin and Growth of the Free Negro Population of Charleston, South Carolina," *Journal of Negro History*, XXVI (October 1941); Ralph B. Flanders, "The Free Negro in Ante-Bellum Georgia," *North Carolina Historical Review*, IX (July 1932); W. McDowell Rogers, "Free Negro Legislation in Georgia," *Georgia Historical Quarterly*, XVI (March 1932); David Y. Thomas, "The Free Negro in Florida before 1865," *South Atlantic Quarterly*, X (October 1911); J. Merton England, "The Free Negro in Ante-Bellum Tennessee," *Journal of Southern History*, IX (February 1943); William L. Imes, "The Legal Status of Free Negroes and Slaves in Tennessee," *Journal of Negro History*, IV (July 1919); Charles S. Sydnor, "The Free Negro in Mississippi before the Civil War," *American Historical Review*, XXXII (July 1927); Alice D. Nelson, "People of Color in Louisiana," *Journal of Negro History*, I (October 1916) and II (January 1917); and Harold Schoen, "The Free Negro in the Republic of Texas," *Southwestern Historical Quarterly*, XL (April 1926) and succeeding issues. A special phase of the free black's legal status is treated in Roger W. Shugg, "Negro Voting in the Ante-Bellum South," *Journal of Negro History*, XXI (October 1936). For the fortunes and misfortunes of an individual free black, see John Hope Franklin, "James Boon, Free Negro Artisan," *Journal of Negro History*, XXX (April 1945) and Juliet E. K. Walker, *Free Frank: A Black Pioneer on the Ante-Bellum Frontier* (Lexington, Ky., 1984).

The ownership of slaves by free blacks is discussed in John H. Russell, "Colored Freemen as Slave Owners in Virginia," *Journal of Negro History*, I (July 1916); C. D. Wilson, "Negroes Who Owned Slaves," *Popular Science Monthly*, LXXXI (November 1912); Michael P. Johnson and James L. Roark, *Black Masters: A Free Family of Color in the Old South* (New York, 1984); and Loren Schweninger, "John Carruthers Stanly and the Anomaly of Black Slaveholding," *North Carolina Historical Review* LXVII (April 1990). Statistics are provided in Carter G. Woodson, *Free Negro Owners of Slaves in the United States in 1830* (Washington, D.C., 1925).

Some of the peculiar social problems of free blacks are treated in E. Franklin Frazier, *The Free Negro Family* (Nashville, 1932), while economic matters are handled in Martin R. Delany, *The Condition, Elevation, Emigration, and Destiny of the Colored People of the United States* (Philadelphia, 1852) and Wesley, *Negro Labor in the United States.* Other works that deal with the problems that Northern free blacks faced are

Edward R. Turner, *The Negro in Pennsylvania* (Washington, D.C., 1911) and Carter G. Woodson, "The Negroes of Cincinnati Prior to the Civil War," *Journal of Negro History*, I (January 1916). White Southerners viewed the plight of Northern free blacks in John Hope Franklin, *A Southern Odyssey: Travelers in the Antebellum North** (Baton Rouge, La., 1976). Early African-American organizations are considered in John W. Cromwell, *The Early Negro Convention Movement* (Washington, D.C., 1904) and Bella Gross, "The First National Negro Convention," *Journal of Negro History*, XXXI (October 1946). For an important phase of cultural history, see Dorothy B. Porter, "The Organized Educational Activities of Negro Literary Societies, 1828–1846," *Journal of Negro Education*, V (October 1936).

The pioneer work on the major colonization organizations is Early L. Fox, *The American Colonization Society, 1817–1840* (Baltimore, 1919). It has been superseded by Philip J. Staudenraus, *The African Colonization Movement, 1816–1865* (New York, 1961) and by the essays of Frederick Bancroft in Jacob E. Cooke, *Frederick Bancroft, Historian* (Norman, Okla., 1957). H. N. Sherwood, "The Formation of the American Colonization Society," *Journal of Negro History*, II (July 1917) should also be read. Additional works on various phases of the subject are Charles A. Earp, "The Role of Education in the Maryland Colonization Movement," *Journal of Negro History*, XXVI (July 1941); Miles M. Fisher, "Lott Cary, the Colonizing Missionary," *Journal of Negro History*, VII (October 1922); H. N. Sherwood, "Early Negro Deportation Projects," *Mississippi Valley Historical Review*, II (March 1916); N. Andrew Cleven, "Some Plans for Colonizing Liberated Negro Slaves in Hispanic America," *Journal of Negro History*, XI (January 1926); Louis R. Mehlinger, "The Attitude of the Free Negro toward Colonization," *Journal of Negro History*, I (July 1916); and Floyd John Miller, *The Search for a Black Nationality: Black Colonization and Emigration, 1787–1863* (Urbana, Ill., 1975).

10. Slavery and Intersectional Strife

The beginnings of abolition are discussed in Alice D. Adams, *The Neglected Period of Anti-Slavery in America, 1808–1831* (Boston, 1908). For the relationship between abolitionism and the other reform movements, see Alice F. Tyler, *Freedom's Ferment: Phases of American Social History to 1860** (Minneapolis, Minn., 1944). One of the best discussions of the abolition movement is Gilbert H. Barnes, *The Antislavery Impulse, 1830–1844** (New York, 1933). Several works of excellent quality that deal with abolitionism are Louis Filler, *The Crusade against Slavery, 1830–1860** (New York, 1960); Dwight L. Dumond, *Anti-Slavery: The Crusade for Freedom in America** (Ann Arbor, Mich., 1961); Martin L. Duberman, ed., *The Antislavery Vanguard** (Princeton, N.J., 1965); and Hugh Hawkins, ed., *The Abolitionists: Immediatism and the Question of Means** (Boston, 1964). An important reexamination of the movement is in Aileen Kraditor, *Means and Ends in American Abolitionism: Garrison and His Critics on Strategy and Tactics, 1834–1850** (New York, 1969). Biographies of abolitionists that should be consulted include Irving Bartlett, *Wendell Phillips, Brahmin Radical* (Boston, 1961) and John L. Thomas, *The Liberator: William Lloyd Garrison* (Boston, 1963). One excellent work on this subject is Herbert Aptheker's "Militant Abolitionism," *Journal of Negro History*, XXVI (October 1941). The international aspects of abolitionism are treated in Frank J. Klingberg, *The Anti-Slavery Movement in England* (New Haven, 1926). The growth and dissemination of ideas in the abolition movement may be studied in

Lorenzo D. Turner, *Anti-Slavery Sentiment in American Literature* (Washington, D.C., 1929) and W. Sherman Savage, *The Controversy over the Distribution of Abolition Literature* (Washington, D.C., 1938). The *Dictionary of American Biography* and W. J. Simmons, *Men of Mark* (Louisville, Ky., 1887, reprinted 1970) include sketches of the lives of the leading abolitionists.

The major work on black participation in the antislavery movement is Benjamin Quarles's excellent *Black Abolitionists** (New York, 1969). Other noteworthy studies are Herbert Aptheker, *The Negro in the Abolitionist Movement* (New York, 1941); Charles H. Wesley, "The Negroes of New York in the Emancipation Movement," *Journal of Negro History*, XXIV (January 1939); John Bracey and others, eds., *Blacks in the Abolitionist Movement* (Belmont, Calif., 1971); R. J. M. Blackett, *Building an Anti-Slavery Wall: Black Americans in the Atlantic Abolitionist Movement** (Baton Rouge, La., 1983); and Merton L. Dillon, *Slavery Attacked: Southern Slaves and Their Allies, 1619–1865* (Baton Rouge, La., 1990). *Witness for Freedom: African American Voices on Race, Slavery, and Emancipation*, three volumes (Chapel Hill, N.C., 1985–1991), edited by C. Peter Ripley, Roy E. Finkbine, Michael F. Hembree, and Donald Yacovone, is an invaluable source of information on African-American abolitionist thought and activity. The outstanding piece of abolitionist writing by a black person is David Walker's *Appeal in Four Articles* (Boston, 1830), two paperback editions of which appeared in 1965. The narratives mentioned in the text of Chapter 8 provide valuable information concerning blacks in the abolition movement, as does Carter G. Woodson, *The Mind of the Negro as Reflected in Letters during the Crisis, 1800–1860** (Washington, D.C., 1926). There are numerous biographies and sketches of individual blacks. *The Life and Times of Frederick Douglass* (Hartford, Conn., 1881) is a classic of American autobiography. The work by Shirley Graham, *There Was Once a Slave* (New York, 1947) is one of the best biographies. The definitive biography of Douglass is Benjamin Quarles, *Frederick Douglass** (Washington, D.C., 1948). One should also consult Philip S. Foner, *Frederick Douglass* (New York, 1964) and, of course, Foner's *The Life and Writings of Frederick Douglass**, four volumes (New York, 1950–1955). Publications offering additional insights on Douglass include Waldo E. Martin, Jr., *The Mind of Frederick Douglass* (Chapel Hill, N.C., 1984) and the comprehensive new edition of Douglass's *Papers* edited by John Blassingame and others, of which two volumes have been published (New Haven, Conn., 1979, 1982); David W. Blight, *Frederick Douglass' Civil War: Keeping Faith in Jubilee* (Baton Rouge, La., 1989); William S. McFeely, *Frederick Douglass* (New York, 1991); and Shirley J. Yee, *Black Women Abolitionists: A Study in Activism, 1828–1860* (Knoxville, Tenn., 1992). See also Earl Conrad, *Harriet Tubman** (Washington, D.C., 1943); Arthur H. Fauset, *Sojourner Truth, God's Faithful Pilgrim* (Chapel Hill, N.C., 1938); Dorothy B. Porter, "David M. Ruggles, An Apostle of Human Rights," *Journal of Negro History*, XXVIII (January 1943); Monroe N. Work, "The Life of Charles B. Ray," *Journal of Negro History*, IV (October 1919); William E. Farrison, *William Wells Brown: Author and Reformer* (Chicago, 1969); and William Cheek and Aimee Lee Cheek, *John Mercer Langston and the Fight for Black Freedom* (Urbana, Ill., 1989). The conflict between the leading white and black abolitionists is discussed in Benjamin Quarles, "The Breach between Douglass and Garrison," *Journal of Negro History*, XXIII (April 1938).

The works of Wilbur H. Siebert have made him the outstanding authority on the Underground Railroad. His major work is *The Underground Railroad from Slavery to Freedom* (New York, 1898). Others include "The Underground Railroad in Massachusetts," *Proceedings of the American Antiquarian Society*, New Series, XLV (Worcester,

Mass., 1935) and "Light on the Underground Railroad," *American Historical Review*, I (April 1896). An invaluable collection of documents and accounts of incidents by a participant is William Still's *The Underground Railroad* (Philadelphia, 1872). See also Horatio T. Strother, *The Underground Railroad in Connecticut** (Middletown, Conn., 1962) and Henrietta Buckmaster, *Let My People Go** (New York, 1941), a popular account of the railroad. Two articles by E. D. Preston in the *Journal of Negro History* shed considerable light on two aspects of the Underground Railroad: "Genesis of the Underground Railroad," XVIII (April 1933) and "The Underground Railroad in Northwest Ohio," XVII (October 1932). A critical view of the railroad is given in Larry Gara, *The Liberty Line: The Legend of the Underground Railroad** (Lexington, Ky., 1961). The Southern fight against the Underground Railroad is discussed in Stanley W. Campbell, *The Slave Catchers: Enforcement of the Fugitive Slave Law, 1850–1860** (Chapel Hill, N.C., 1970). The definitive work on the Canadian phase is Robin Winks, *Blacks in Canada* (New Haven, 1971), but one should not overlook William H. and Jane Pease, *Black Utopia: Negro Communal Experiments in America** (Madison, Wisc., 1963).

The fate of the antislavery movement in the South is discussed in John S. Bassett, *Anti-Slavery Leaders in North Carolina* (Baltimore, 1931); Ruth Scarborough, *The Opposition to Slavery in Georgia Prior to 1860* (Nashville, 1933); and Kenneth M. Stampp, "The Fate of the Southern Antislavery Movement," *Journal of Negro History*, XXVIII (January 1943). The growth of proslavery sentiment in the South is carefully traced and analyzed in William S. Jenkins, *Pro-Slavery Thought in the Old South* (Chapel Hill, N.C., 1935). An excellent collection of proslavery essays is edited and introduced by Drew Gilpin Faust, *The Ideology of Slavery: Proslavery Thought in the Antebellum South, 1830–1860** (Baton Rouge, La., 1981). See also William R. Stanton, *The Leopard's Spots: Scientific Attitudes toward Race in America, 1815–1859** (Chicago, 1960) and William B. Hesseltine, "Some New Aspects of the Proslavery Argument," *Journal of Negro History*, XXI (January 1936). The disappearance of liberalism is treated in Clement Eaton, *Freedom of Thought in the Old South* (Durham, N.C., 1940), while the psychological effect of proslavery thought is discussed in Jesse Carpenter, *The South as a Conscious Minority, 1789–1861* (New York, 1930). Two works by Dwight L. Dumond discuss the breakdown of intersectional relations: *The Secession Movement* (New York, 1931) and *Antislavery Origins of the Civil War in the United States** (London, 1939). In this connection see also Arthur C. Cole, *The Irrepressible Conflict* (New York, 1938) and John Hope Franklin, *The Militant South 1800–1861** (Cambridge, Mass., 1956) and *Southern Odyssey*.

11. Civil War

For general works on blacks in the Civil War, see the able study by the pioneer black historian, George W. Williams, *A History of the Negro Troops in the War of the Rebellion* (New York, 1888). Another study that may also be consulted with profit is Joseph T. Wilson, *The Black Phalanx: A History of the Negro Soldiers of the United States in the Wars of 1775–1812, 1861–1865* (Hartford, Conn., 1888). Of less importance, but of some value, is William W. Brown, *The Negro in the American Rebellion* (New York, 1888). Easily the outstanding modern treatment is Benjamin Quarles, *The Negro in the Civil War** (Boston, 1953). See also his *Lincoln and the Negro* (New York, 1962) and William O. Douglas, *Mr. Lincoln and the Negroes: The Long Road to Equality* (New York, 1963).

Herbert Aptheker, *The Negro in the Civil War* (New York, 1938) is a brief but valuable work. Bell Irvin Wiley, *Southern Negroes, 1861–1865** (New York, 1953) ably deals with numerous aspects of the Union and the Confederate policies. Emerson D. Fite, *Social and Industrial Conditions in the North during the Civil War* (New York, 1910) discusses the effect of draft laws on blacks. The problem of emancipation is covered in John Hope Franklin, *The Emancipation Proclamation** (New York, 1963). See also Hans L. Trefousse, *Lincoln's Decision for Emancipation* (Philadelphia, 1975) and Charles H. Wesley and Patricia Romero, *Negro Americans in the Civil War: From Slavery to Citizenship* (Washington, D.C., 1969). Works dealing with problems of transition from slavery to freedom during the war are Clarence L. Mohr, *On the Threshold of Freedom: Masters and Slaves in Civil War Georgia* (Athens, Ga., 1985); C. Peter Ripley, *Slaves and Freedmen in Civil War Louisiana* (Baton Rouge, La., 1975); Roger L. Ransom and Richard Sutch, *One Kind of Freedom: The Economic Consequences of Emancipation* (Cambridge, 1977); Louis Gerteis, *From Contraband to Freeman: Federal Policy toward Southern Blacks, 1861–1865* (Westport, Conn., 1973); and LaWanda Cox, *Lincoln and Black Freedom: A Study in Presidential Leadership* (Columbia, 1981) and Samuel L. Horst, *Education for Manhood: The Education of Blacks in Virginia during the Civil War* (Lanham, 1987). See also Herman Belz, *Emancipation and Equal Rights: Politics and Constitutionalism in the Civil War Era* (New York, 1978) and Eric Foner, *Nothing But Freedom* (Baton Rouge, La., 1983). Among the many works on the service of black soldiers, Thomas W. Higginson, *Army Life in a Black Regiment* (Boston, 1870) is outstanding. Also of great merit is Dudley T. Cornish, *The Sable Arm: Negro Troops in the Union Army, 1861–1865** (New York, 1956). The most recent discussion of the subject is in Ira Berlin, Joseph P. Reidy, and Leslie S. Rowland, *The Black Military Experience* (Cambridge, Mass., 1982). Herbert Aptheker, "Negro Casualties in the Civil War," *Journal of Negro History,* XXXII (January 1947) is an invaluable study on the subject. The black's own experience is conveyed in James McPherson, *The Negro's Civil War: How American Negroes Felt and Acted during the War for the Union** (New York, 1965). See also McPherson's *The Struggle for Equality: Abolitionists and the Negro in the Civil War and Reconstruction** (Princeton, N.J., 1964) and Joseph T. Glatthar, *Forged in Battle: The Civil War Alliance of Black Soldiers and White Officers* (New York, 1990).

Several works deal primarily with the condition of blacks under the Confederacy. Robert F. Durden, *The Gray and the Black: The Confederate Debate on Emancipation* (Baton Rouge, La., 1972) and Charles B. Dew, *Ironmaker to the Confederacy: Joseph R. Anderson and the Tredegar Iron Works* (New Haven, Conn., 1966) are important. See also Brainerd Dyer, "The Treatment of Colored Union Troops by the Confederates, 1861–1865," *Journal of Negro History,* XX (July 1935); Charles H. Wesley, "The Employment of Negroes as Soldiers in the Confederate Army," *Journal of Negro History,* IV (July 1919); and Harvey Wish, "Slave Disloyalty under the Confederacy," *Journal of Negro History,* XXIII (October 1938). The role of blacks on the home front and with the Confederate military forces is well treated in James H. Brewer, *The Confederate Negro: Virginia's Craftsmen and Military Laborers, 1861–1865* (Durham, N.C., 1969).

12. The Effort to Attain Peace

For many years a great portion of the literature on Reconstruction, while written in the framework of "scientific" history, contained such strong presuppositions regarding the inherent unfitness of blacks for citizenship and the justification for the Ku Klux Klan to restore "order" in the South that its value was severely limited by its bias. That was especially true of the works written under the supervision of William Archibald Dunning at Columbia University early in the twentieth century. Among the better-known works of this "school" of writing are Walter L. Fleming, *Civil War and Reconstruction in Alabama* (New York, 1905) and Joseph G. DeRoulhac Hamilton, *Reconstruction in North Carolina* (New York, 1914). The problems involved in the writing of Reconstruction history have been ably discussed by several historians: Howard K. Beale, "On Rewriting Reconstruction History," *American Historical Review,* XLV (July 1940); Francis B. Simkins, "New Viewpoints of Southern Reconstruction," *Journal of Southern History,* V (February 1939); A. A. Taylor, "Historians of the Reconstruction," *Journal of Negro History,* XXIII (January 1938); and Bernard Weisberger, "The Dark and Bloody Ground of Reconstruction Historiography," *Journal of Southern History,* XXV (November 1959). See also W. E. B. Du Bois, "Reconstruction and Its Benefits," *American Historical Review,* XV (July 1910). A broader approach to the problems of Reconstruction was made by Francis B. Simkins and R. H. Woody in *South Carolina during Reconstruction* (Chapel Hill, N.C., 1932), while an attempt to redress the balance was made by W. E. B. Du Bois, in *Black Reconstruction** (New York, 1935), which seeks to apply Marxist doctrine to the problem of Reconstruction. See also James Allen, *Reconstruction: The Battle for Democracy** (New York, 1937).

Two works by Horace M. Bond suggest a revision of the history of Reconstruction in terms of the influence exercised by powerful business interests: "Social and Economic Forces in Alabama Reconstruction," *Journal of Negro History,* XXIII (July 1938) and *Negro Education in Alabama** (Washington, D.C., 1939). See also A. B. Moore, "Railroad Building in Alabama during the Reconstruction," *Journal of Southern History,* I (November 1935) and James L. Sellers, "The Economic Incidence of the Civil War in the South," *Mississippi Valley Historical Review,* XIV (September 1927). During the period of initial reexamination of Reconstruction several general studies appeared. E. Merton Coulter, *The South during Reconstruction* (Baton Rouge, La., 1947) reaffirmed the position advanced by the Dunning School. Hodding Carter, *The Angry Scar* (New York, 1959) is a popular account. John Hope Franklin, *Reconstruction after the Civil War** (Chicago, 1961) and Kenneth M. Stampp, *The Era of Reconstruction** (New York, 1965) are revisionist in approach and interpretation. See also Robert Cruden, *The Negro in Reconstruction** (Englewood Cliffs, N.J., 1969); Lerone Bennett, *Black Power, U.S.A.: The Human Side of Reconstruction, 1867–1877** (Chicago, 1967); Peter Kolchin, *First Freedom: The Responses of Alabama's Blacks to Emancipation and Reconstruction* (Westport, Conn., 1972); and Forrest G. Wood, *Black Scare: The Racist Response to Emancipation and Reconstruction** (Berkeley, 1968). In recent years there have been numerous general works and monographs that have provided new perspectives as well as new knowledge about the era of Reconstruction. Among them are Leon F. Litwack, *Been In the Storm So Long: The Aftermath of Slavery* (New York, 1979); Claude F. Oubre, *Forty Acres and a Mule: The Freedmen's Bureau and Black Land Ownership* (Baton Rouge, La., 1978); Lawrence Levine, *Black Culture and Black Consciousness* (New York, 1977); Howard Rabinowitz, ed., *Southern Black Leaders of the Reconstruction Era* (1982); Otto Olsen, ed., *Reconstruction and Redemption in the South* (Baton Rouge, La., 1980); J. Morgan Kousser and James M. McPherson, eds., *Region, Race and Reconstruction* (New York, 1982); and George C. Cable, *But There Was No Peace* (Athens, Ga., 1984). A well-received general work is Eric Foner, *Reconstruction: America's Unfinished Revolution, 1863–1877* (New York, 1988). Two stimulating works by Michael Perman have contributed to the understanding of politics in the Reconstruction South: *Reunion without Compromise: The South and Reconstruction, 1865–1868* (Cambridge, Mass., 1973) and *The Road to Redemption: Southern Politics, 1869–1878* (Chapel Hill, N.C., 1984). Two recent works in this area are Earl M. Maltz, *Civil Rights, The Constitution, and Congress, 1863–1869* (Lawrence, 1990) and Eric Anderson & Alfred A. Moss, Jr., eds., *The Facts of Reconstruction: Essays in Honor of John Hope Franklin* (Baton Rouge, 1991). Important documents of the period, with interpretation, are in Ira Berlin, and others, eds., *Freedom: A Documentary History of Emancipation, 1861–1867: Selected from the Holdings of the National Archives* (Cambridge, Mass., 1985).

Several African Americans who lived through the period have attempted to tell their story. Among them are John R. Lynch, *The Facts of Reconstruction** (New York, 1913); John Hope Franklin, ed., *Reminiscences of an Active Life: The Autobiography of John Roy Lynch* (Chicago, 1970); John Wallace, *Carpetbag Rule in Florida* (Jacksonville, Fla., 1888); and Ray Billington, ed., *The Journal of Charlotte Forten* (New York, 1953). Among the better biographical studies are Loren Schweninger, *James T. Rapier and Reconstruction* (Chicago, 1978); Peter D. Klingman, *Josiah Walls: Florida's Black Congressman of Reconstruction* (Gainesville, Fla., 1976); Okon E. Uya, *From Slavery to Public Service, Robert Smalls, 1839–1915** (New York, 1971); and Edward F. Sweat, "Francis L. Cardoza: Profile of Integrity in Reconstruction Politics," *Journal of Negro History*, XLVI (January 1961). The works of Alrutheus A. Taylor should be consulted. They are *The Negro in the Reconstruction of Virginia* (Washington, D.C., 1926); *The Negro in South Carolina during Reconstruction* (Washington, D.C., 1924); and *The Negro in Tennessee, 1865–1880* (Washington, D.C., 1938). Local studies of Reconstruction in the several states have illuminated the greater picture. One of the most significant is Vernon L. Wharton, *The Negro in Mississippi, 1865–1890** (Chapel Hill, N.C., 1947). Another is Thomas Holt, *Black over White: Negro Political Leadership in South Carolina during Reconstruction* (Urbana, Ill., 1977). Others are Joel Williamson, *After Slavery, The Negro in South Carolina during Reconstruction** (Chapel Hill, N.C., 1965); Joe M. Richardson, *The Negro in the Reconstruction of Florida, 1865–1877* (Tallahassee, Fla., 1966); Alan Conway, *The Reconstruction of Georgia* (Minneapolis, 1966); Joe Gray Taylor, *Louisiana Reconstructed, 1863–1877* (Baton Rouge, La., 1975); Carl H. Moneyhon, *Republicanism in Reconstruction Texas* (Austin, 1980); John Blassingame, *Black New Orleans, 1860–1880* (Chicago, 1973); Roberta Alexander, *North Carolina Faces the Freedmen: Race Relations during Presidential Reconstruction, 1865–1867* (Durham, N.C., 1985); and Barbara J. Fields, *Slavery and Freedom on the Middle Ground: Maryland during the Nineteenth Century* (New Haven, Conn., 1985).

Among the numerous works dealing with the conflict between the president and Congress and the triumph of Radical Reconstruction is Howard K. Beale, *The Critical Year, A Study of Andrew Johnson and Reconstruction* (New York, 1930). It has been superseded, to a great extent, by Eric L. McKitrick, *Andrew Johnson and Reconstruction** (Chicago, 1960), La Wanda and John Cox, *Politics, Principle, and Prejudice** (Glencoe, Ill., 1963); Hans L. Trefousse, *Impeachment of a President: Andrew Johnson, the Blacks, and Reconstruction* (Knoxville, Tenn., 1975); and David Warren Brown, *Andrew Johnson and the Negro* (Knoxville, Tenn., 1989). See also David Donald, *The Politics of Reconstruction** (Baton Rouge, La., 1965). Other important works are Horace E. Flack, *The Adoption of the Fourteenth Amendment* (Baltimore, 1908); Benjamin B. Kendrick, *The Journal of the Joint Committee of Fifteen on Reconstruction* (New York, 1914); Jacobus Ten Broek, *The Anti-Slavery Origins of the Fourteenth Amendment* (Berkeley, Calif.,

1951); and William Gillette, *The Right to Vote: Politics and the Passage of the Fifteenth Amendment** (Baltimore, 1965). The pioneer study of the Freedmen's Bureau was Paul S. Peirce, *The Freedmen's Bureau, A Chapter in the History of Reconstruction* (Iowa City, Iowa, 1904). A more recent work is George R. Bentley, *A History of the Freedmen's Bureau* (Philadelphia, 1955). Excellent state studies are Martin Abbott, *The Freedmen's Bureau in South Carolina, 1865–1872* (Chapel Hill, N.C., 1967) and Howard A. White, *The Freedmen's Bureau in Louisiana* (Baton Rouge, La., 1970). Educational activities are covered in Bullock, *A History of Negro Education in the South** (Cambridge, Mass., 1967); Holmes, *The Evolution of the Negro College;* Luther P. Jackson, "The Educational Efforts of the Freedmen's Bureau and Freedmen's Aid Societies in South Carolina, 1862–1872," *Journal of Negro History,* VIII (January 1923); Henry L. Swint, *The Northern Teacher in the South, 1862–1870* (Nashville, Tenn., 1941); Willie Lee Rose, *Rehearsal for Reconstruction: The Port Royal Experiment** (Indianapolis, Ind., 1964); Robert C. Morris, *Reading, 'Riting and Reconstruction: The Education of Freedmen in the South, 1861–1870* (Chicago, 1981); and Ronald E. Butchart, *Northern Schools, Southern Blacks, and Reconstruction: Freedmen's Education, 1862–1875* (Westport, Conn., 1980). In addition to the works already cited, Carl R. Osthaus, *Freedmen, Philanthropy and Fraud: A History of the Freedmen's Savings Bank* (Urbana, Ill., 1976) and Wesley, *Negro Labor in the United States* shed considerable light on certain economic aspects of Reconstruction.

Political currents are discussed in Luther P. Jackson, *Negro Office-Holders in Virginia** (Norfolk, Va., 1945); Samuel D. Smith, *The Negro in Congress, 1870–1901* (Chapel Hill, N.C., 1940); Peggy Lamson, *Glorious Failure: Black Congressman Robert Brown Elliott and the Reconstruction in South Carolina** (New York, 1973); Alrutheus A. Taylor, "Negro Congressmen a Generation After," *Journal of Negro History,* VII (April 1922); G. David Houston, "A Negro Senator," *Journal of Negro History,* VII (July 1922); William A. Russ, "The Negro and White Disfranchisement during Radical Reconstruction," *Journal of Negro History,* XIX (April 1934); and R. H. Woody, "Jonathan J. Wright, Associate Justice of the Supreme Court of South Carolina, 1870–1877," *Journal of Negro History,* XVIII (April 1933). A convenient source for studying the careers of African Americans in Congress is by a member of Congress in the 1990s, William L. Clay, *Just Permanent Interests: Black Americans in Congress, 1870–1991* (New York, 1992). For other aspects, see Otis A. Singletary, *Negro Militia and Reconstruction* (Austin, Tex., 1957) and McPherson, *The Struggle for Equality.* The major documents may be examined in La Wanda and John N. Cox, eds., *Reconstruction, the Negro and the New South** (New York, 1973).

13. Losing the Peace

Many of the titles listed for the previous chapter provide valuable information on the overthrow of Reconstruction. Michael W. Fitzgerald's *The Union League Movement in the Deep South: Politics and Agricultural Change during Reconstruction* (Baton Rouge, La., 1989) is an excellent resource. A fresh and stimulating discussion of the forces behind the overthrow and the way in which the compromise of 1877 was reached is contained in C. Vann Woodward, *Reunion and Reaction: The Compromise of 1877 and the End of Reconstruction** (Boston, 1951). For a general view of the plight of African Americans, see Rayford W. Logan, *The Negro in American Life and Thought: The Nadir,*

*1877–1901** (New York, 1954). Southern blacks are discussed in C. Vann Woodward, *Origins of the New South, 1877–1913** (Baton Rouge, La., 1951). Two books covering Republican policy are Vincent P. DeSantis, *Republicans Face the Southern Question* (Baltimore, 1959) and Stanley P. Hirshon, *Farewell to the Bloody Shirt** (Bloomington, Ind., 1962). Reconstruction and post-Reconstruction violence is treated in many of the preceding titles. For Klan activities see John C. Lester, *The Ku Klux Klan: Its Origin, Growth, and Disbandment* (New York, 1905); Stanley F. Horn, *Invisible Empire: The Story of the Ku Klux Klan, 1866–1871* (Boston, 1939); Allen W. Trelease, *White Terror: The Ku Klux Klan Conspiracy and Southern Reconstruction* (New York, 1971); and David M. Chalmers, *Hooded Americanism: The First Century of the Ku Klux Klan** (New York, 1965). See also Francis B. Simkins, *The Tillman Movement in South Carolina* (Durham, N.C., 1926) and Alfred B. Williams, *Hampton and His Red Shirts* (Charleston, S.C., 1935).

The deterioration of the status of African Americans has been discussed by many authors. For general treatments of the political situation, see Key, *Southern Politics*; Lewinson, *Race, Class, and Party**; William A. Mabry, *Studies in the Disfranchisement of the Negro in the South* (Durham, N.C., 1933); Michael L. Lanza, *Agrarianism and Reconstruction Politics: The Southern Homestead Act* (Baton Rouge, La., 1990); and Loren Schweninger, *Black Property Owners in the South* (Urbana, Ill., 1990). At the state level consult Wharton, *The Negro in Mississippi**, Albert D. Kirwan, *Revolt of the Rednecks: Mississippi Politics, 1876–1925** (Lexington, Ky., 1951, reprinted 1964); Helen G. Edmonds, *The Negro and Fusion Politics in North Carolina* (Chapel Hill, N.C., 1951); Eric Anderson, *Race and Politics in North Carolina, 1872–1901* (Baton Rouge, La., 1981); H. Leon Prather, *We Have Taken a City: The Wilmington Massacre and Coup of 1898* (Rutherford, N.J., 1984); Frenise A. Logan, *The Negro in North Carolina, 1876–1894* (Chapel Hill, N.C., 1964); George Tindall, *South Carolina Negroes, 1877–1900** (Columbia, S.C., 1952); and Robert E. Martin, *Negro Disenfranchisement in Virginia** (Washington, D.C., 1938). Economic deterioration can be followed in Daniel A. Novak, *The Wheel of Servitude: Black Forced Labor after Slavery* (Lexington, Ky., 1978); Dwight B. Billings, *Planters and the Making of a "New South": Class Politics and Development in North Carolina* (Chapel Hill, N.C., 1980); Peter J. Rachleff, *Black Labor in the South: Richmond, Virginia, 1865–1890* (Philadelphia, 1984); Charles L. Flynn, *White Land, Black Labor: Caste and Class in Late 19th Century Georgia* (Baton Rouge, La., 1983); Stephen J. DeCanio, *Agriculture in the Post-Bellum South: The Economics of Production and Supply* (Cambridge, Mass., 1974); and John William Graves, *Race Relations in an Urban-Rural Context, Arkansas, 1865–1905* (Fayetteville, Ark., 1990). Various aspects of the problem are explored in William Cohen, *At Freedom's Edge: Black Mobility and the Southern White Quest for Racial Control, 1861–1915* (Baton Rouge, La., 1991).

The effect of the decline of the blacks' position on African Americans themselves is ably discussed in August Meier, *Negro Thought in America, 1880–1915** (Ann Arbor, Mich., 1963). Many aspects of life among blacks are explored in Arnold Taylor, *Travail and Triumph: Black Life and Culture in the South Since the Civil War* (Westport, Conn., 1976). For a discussion of the role of women, see Paula Giddings, *"When and Where I Enter . . .": The Impact of Black Women on Race and Sex in America* (New York, 1984). For an articulate African American's reaction, see T. Thomas Fortune, *Black and White: Land, Labor, and Politics in the South* (New York, 1884) and Emma Lou Thornbrough, *T. Thomas Fortune, Militant Journalist* (Chicago, 1972). The views of a Southern white man sympathetic to African Americans are expressed in George Cable, *The Negro Question,** edited by Arlin Turner (New York, 1958).

C. Vann Woodward has discussed the beginnings of segregation in several of his books. See especially the revised edition of *The Strange Career of Jim Crow,** third edition (New York, 1974). An important work is Howard Rabinowitz's *Race Relations in the Urban South, 1865–1890* (New York, 1978). For other aspects of the start of segregation, see Joseph H. Cartwright, *The Triumph of Jim Crow: Tennessee Race Relations in the 1880s* (Knoxville, Tenn., 1976); Charles E. Wynes, *Race Relations in Virginia, 1870–1902* (Charlottesville, Va., 1961); and John Hope Franklin, "Jim Crow Goes to School: The Genesis of Legal Segregation in Southern Schools," *South Atlantic Quarterly*, LVIII (Spring 1959). Phillip Durham and Everett L. Jones, *Negro Cowboys** (New York, 1965) describes a little-known phase of African-American life.

Appendix

The Emancipation Proclamation

By the President of the United States of America. A Proclamation.

Whereas on the 22d day of September, A. D. 1862, a proclamation was issued by the President of the United States, containing, among other things, the following, to wit:

> That on the 1st day of January, A. D. 1863, all persons held as slaves within any State or designated part of a State the people whereof shall then be in rebellion against the United States shall be then, thenceforward, and forever free; and the executive government of the United States, including the military and naval authority thereof, will recognize and maintain the freedom of such persons and will do no act or acts to repress such persons, or any of them, in any efforts they may make for their actual freedom.
>
> That the Executive will on the 1st day of January aforesaid, by proclamation, designate the States and parts of States, if any, in which the people thereof, respectively, shall then be in rebellion against the United States; and the fact that any State or the people thereof shall on that day be in good faith represented in the Congress of the United States by members chosen thereto at elections wherein a majority of the qualified voters of such States shall have participated shall, in the absence of strong countervailing testimony, be deemed conclusive evidence that such State and the people thereof are not then in rebellion against the United States.

Now, therefore, I, Abraham Lincoln, President of the United States, by virtue of the power in me vested as Commander in Chief of the Army and Navy of the United States in time of actual armed rebellion against the authority and Government of the United States, and as a fit and necessary war measure for suppressing said rebellion, do, on this 1st day of January, A. D. 1863, and in accordance with my purpose so to do, publicly proclaimed for the full period of one hundred days from the days first above mentioned, order and designate as the States and parts of States wherein the people thereof, respectively, are this day in rebellion against the United States the following, to wit:

Arkansas, Texas, Louisiana (except the parishes of St. Bernard, Plaquemines, Jefferson, St. John, St. Charles, St. James, Ascension, Assumption, Terrebonne, Lafourche, St. Mary, St. Martin, and Orleans, including the city of New Orleans), Mississippi, Alabama, Florida, Georgia, South Carolina, North Carolina, and Virginia (except the forty-eight counties designated as West Virginia, and also the counties of Berkeley, Accomac, Northampton, Elizabeth City, York, Princess Anne, and Norfolk, including the cities of Norfolk and Portsmouth), and which excepted parts are for the present left precisely as if this proclamation were not issued.

And by virtue of the power and for the purpose aforesaid, I do order and declare that all persons held as slaves within said designated States and parts of States are and henceforward shall be free, and that the executive government of the United States, including the military and naval authorities thereof, will recognize and maintain the freedom of said persons.

And I hereby enjoin upon the people so declared to be free to abstain from all violence, unless in necessary self-defense; and I recommend to them that in all cases when allowed they labor faithfully for reasonable wages.

And I further declare and make known that such persons of suitable condition will be received into the armed service of the United States to garrison forts, positions, stations, and other places and to man vessels of all sorts in said service.

And upon this act, sincerely believed to be an act of justice, warranted by the Constitution upon military necessity, I invoke the considerate judgment and mankind and the gracious favor of Almighty God.

In witness whereof I have hereunto set my hand and caused the seal of the United States to be affixed.

Done at the city of Washington, this 1st day of January, A. D. 1863, and of the Independence of the United States of America the eighty-seventh.

ABRAHAM LINCOLN.

By the President:
WILLIAM H. SEWARD, *Secretary of State.*

Acknowledgments

Pp. 38–39: Adapted from "The African Diaspora Map — I" produced by Clark University Cartographic Service, based on research by Joseph E. Harris. © 1990 Joseph E. Harris. Used by permission.

P. 155: Leonard P. Curry, *The Free Black in Urban America, 1800–1850: The Shadow of the Dream*, p. 267. © 1981 by The University of Chicago. All rights reserved. Reprinted by permission of The University of Chicago Press.

P. 161: *From Tennessee Slave to St. Louis Entrepreneur: The Autobiography of James Thomas*, ed. Loren Schweninger. Columbia, Missouri: University of Missouri Press, 1984, pp. 31–32. Reprinted by permission of Loren Schweninger.

P. 252: *Reminiscences of an Active Life: The Autobiography of John Roy Lynch*, ed. John Hope Franklin, pp. 164–165. Negro American Biographies and Autobiographies Series. © 1970 by The University of Chicago. All rights reserved. Reprinted by permission of The University of Chicago Press.

Index

Note: Page numbers 1–197 are found only in Volume One; page numbers 264–572 are found only in Volume Two.

Notes

Notes

Notes

Notes

Notes